Risk Assessment

Risk Assessment

Etti G. Baranoff, PhD, FLMI
Associate Professor of Insurance and Finance
Virginia Commonwealth University

Scott E. Harrington, PhD
Professor of Health Care Systems and
Insurance and Risk Management
The Wharton School
University of Pennsylvania

Gregory R. Niehaus, PhD
Professor of Insurance and Finance
Moore School of Business
The University of South Carolina

Coordinating Authors

Connor M. Harrison, CPCU, AU, ARe
Director of Curriculum
American Institute for CPCU/Insurance Institute of America

Charles M. Nyce, PhD, CPCU, API
Director of Curriculum
American Institute for CPCU/Insurance Institute of America

First Edition • Third Printing

American Institute for Chartered Property Casualty Underwriters/
Insurance Institute of America
720 Providence Road, Malvern, Pennsylvania 19355

First Edition · Third Printing · March 2007

Library of Congress Control Number: 2005929614

ISBN 978-0-89463-256-3

Foreword

The American Institute for Chartered Property Casualty Underwriters and the Insurance Institute of America (the Institutes) are independent, not-for-profit organizations committed to expanding the knowledge of professionals in risk management, insurance, financial services, and related fields through education and research.

In accordance with our belief that professionalism is grounded in education, experience, and ethical behavior, the Institutes provide a wide range of educational programs designed to meet the needs of individuals working in property-casualty insurance and risk management. The American Institute offers the Chartered Property Casualty Underwriter (CPCU®) professional designation. You select a specialization in the CPCU program with either a commercial or a personal risk management and insurance focus, depending on your professional needs. In addition to this specialization, the CPCU program gives you a broad understanding of the property-casualty insurance industry.

The Insurance Institute of America (IIA) offers designations and certificate programs in a wide range of disciplines, including the following:

- Claims
- Commercial underwriting
- Fidelity and surety bonding
- General insurance
- Insurance accounting and finance
- Insurance information technology
- Insurance production and agency management
- Insurance regulation and compliance
- Management
- Marine insurance
- Personal insurance
- Premium auditing
- Quality insurance services
- Reinsurance
- Risk management
- Surplus lines

No matter which Institute program you choose, you will gain practical knowledge and skills that will help you to grow personally and professionally.

The American Institute for CPCU was founded in 1942 through a collaborative effort between industry professionals and academics, led by the faculty members at The Wharton School of the University of Pennsylvania. In 1953, the American Institute for CPCU merged with the IIA, which was founded in 1909 and which remains the oldest continuously functioning national organization offering educational programs for the property-casualty insurance business. The Institutes continuously strive to maximize the value of your education and qualifications in the expanding insurance market. In 2005, the Institutes extended their global reach by forming the CPCU Institute of Greater China (CPCUIGC). In addition, many CPCU and IIA courses now qualify for credits towards certain associate's, bachelor's, and master's degrees at several prestigious colleges and universities, and all CPCU and IIA courses carry college credit recommendations from the American Council on Education (ACE).

The Insurance Research Council (IRC), founded in 1977, helps the Institutes fulfill the research aspect of their mission. The IRC is a division of the Institutes and is supported by industry members. The IRC is a not-for-profit research organization that examines public policy issues of interest to property-casualty insurers, insurance customers, and the general public. IRC research reports are distributed widely to insurance-related organizations, public policy authorities, and the media.

Our textbooks are an essential component of the education we provide. Each book is specifically designed both to provide you with the practical knowledge and skills you need to enhance your job performance and career and also to deliver that knowledge in a clear manner. The content is developed by the Institutes in collaboration with insurance and risk management professionals and members of the academic community. We welcome comments from our students and course leaders because your feedback helps us to continuously improve the quality of our study materials. Through our combined efforts, we will truly be *succeeding together*.

Peter L. Miller, CPCU
President and CEO
American Institute for CPCU
Insurance Institute of America

Preface

Risk Assessment provides the reader with a comprehensive overview of the loss exposures that organizations face and quantitative foundations needed to gauge their importance and predict their effect. It is written for students working toward the AICPCU/IIA's Associate in Risk Management (ARM) designation.

The contents of Risk Assessment can be summarized as follows:

- Chapters 1 and 2 provide an overview of risk management including a description of what risk management is, how risk management professionals design programs to address their organizations' loss exposures, and what the risk management process involves.

- Chapters 3 through 10 categorize and describe the loss exposures that an organization may face. The loss exposure categories are property, liability, personnel, and net income.

- Chapters 11 through 14 present quantitative tools that risk management professionals can use to assess the significance of a loss exposure to an organization.

Content from *Essentials of Risk Management* is incorporated into this text. We are indebted to the following authors for this content: George L. Head, PhD, CPCU, ARM; and Stephen Horn II, CPCU, ARM, AAI.

For more information about the Institutes' programs, please call our Customer Support Department at (800) 644-2101, e-mail us at customersupport@cpcuiia.org, or visit our Web site at www.aicpcu.org.

Connor M. Harrison, CPCU, AU, ARe

Charles M. Nyce, PhD, CPCU, API

Contributing Authors

The following individuals were instumental in helping to analyze the audience for the Associate in Risk Management (ARM) program and to design the revisions and updates of the study materials for Risk Assessment that took effect in 2005.

Michael M. Barth, PhD, CPCU, AU
Georgia Southern University,
Department of Finance and Quantitative Analysis

Arthur L. Flitner, CPCU, ARM, AIC
AICPCU/IIA

Melissa O. Leuck, ARM
Weather & Commodity Risk Solutions and
Gallagher Financial Products

Jerome Trupin, CPCU, CLU, ChFC
Trupin Insurance Services

Kevin M. Quinley, CPCU, ARM, AIC
MEDMARK Insurance Company and
Hamilton Resources Corporation

Contents

Chapter 1

Direct Your Learning

Understanding Risk Management and Establishing a Risk Management Program

After learning the content of this chapter and completing the corresponding course guide assignment, you should be able to:

- Describe risk management and its broad scope.

- Identify the costs and benefits of risk management for a particular organization and for the entire economy.

- Describe the pre-loss and post-loss goals of a risk management program and the possible trade-offs among these goals.

- Describe the risk management department structure, including:

  - Departments with which the risk management professional should cooperate and the types of information these departments provide

  - Communication of information into and out of the risk management department and organization

  - Information management and risk management information systems used to improve decision making

- Describe the likely responsibilities and reporting relationships of a risk management professional.

- Describe the purpose and content of a written risk management policy statement.

- Explain how to monitor, and when appropriate to take corrective action to improve, the performance of an organization's risk management program through results standards and activity standards.

- Define or describe each of the Key Words and Phrases for this chapter.

Develop Your Perspective

What are the main topics covered in the chapter?

Risk management helps people and organizations to realize the opportunities and avert the threats associated with risk. This chapter describes risk management and how organizations can establish risk management programs to prevent or mitigate accidental losses.

Review your organization's written risk management policy statement to determine its scope.

- What are the general goals in your organization's risk management policy statement?

- Does your organization's risk management policy statement emphasize the importance of risk management's role in achieving organizational objectives?

Why is it important to learn about these topics?

Risk is present in all activities, yet people and organizations are often unaware of risk or of the significance of the financial consequences associated with accidental losses. Risk management is a process that risk management professionals use to assess and manage risk.

Consider some of the pre-loss and post-loss risk management program goals at your organization.

- Which goals strive to reduce the cost of risk?

- Which goals strive to reduce the deterrence effects of uncertainty?

- Do any of the goals serve both purposes?

How can you use what you will learn?

Analyze your organization's risk management program goals from last year against the corresponding results standards and activity standards.

- How well did the risk management program meet the risk management goals?

- What changes might you make to the program for this year?

Chapter 1

Understanding Risk Management and Establishing a Risk Management Program

Risk management helps people and organizations to realize the opportunities and avert the threats associated with risk. In the safety and insurance fields, risk management focuses on risk control, which primarily involves loss prevention and loss reduction. In finance, risk management focuses on the asset and liability risks present on an organization's balance sheet and on issues such as the currency and stock fluctuations that represent an opportunity for gain as well as potential for loss. Although risk intuitively seems to be only negative, risk management is increasingly being recognized as a method for addressing both the positive and negative aspects of risk or uncertainties.

This chapter describes the scope of risk management as well as the costs and benefits associated with risk management both to particular organizations and to the entire economy. The benefits of risk management are usually realized by implementing a risk management program that supports the organization's overall goals. Therefore, the chapter describes what pre-loss and post-loss goals an organization might achieve through its risk management program and how the risk management function might be structured and administered to achieve these goals. To reinforce this structure and administration, an organization may choose to adopt a written risk management policy statement. The chapter concludes with a discussion of how to monitor a risk management program and take corrective action when required.

RISK MANAGEMENT

Traditionally, risk management has been applied to the risks associated with accidental losses. However, risk management is increasingly being used in other contexts. For example, in the context of the banking industry, risk management might be used to refer to minimizing the default rate on a portfolio of loans. Alternatively, the healthcare industry might use risk management as a means to safeguard patient survival. Those other areas of risk management can be distinguished from traditional risk management, which focuses on accidental loss and is the main focus of this text.

Risk and Risk Management Defined

Risk
Uncertainty about outcomes that can be either negative or positive.

Risk has many different meanings within the risk management and insurance communities. In this text, **risk** is defined as uncertainty about outcomes that can be either negative or positive. Exhibit 1-1 sets out some of the other common definitions of risk.

EXHIBIT 1-1

Risk Definitions

What is risk?

Risk can be defined in many ways. However, the definition of risk presented in this text (uncertainty about outcomes that can be either negative or positive) is relatively narrow. Because risk can be used in many contexts, ARM students should know that risk can have many other meanings, including any of the following:

- The subject matter of an insurance policy, for example, a structure, an auto fleet, or the possibility of a liability claim arising from an insured's activities
- The insurance applicant (the insured)
- The possibility of a loss or injury
- A cause of loss (or peril), such as fire, lightning, or explosion
- Variability associated with a future outcome

Traditional risk management deals primarily with the uncertainty about potential accidental losses (outcomes) that may not occur but, if they do, have only negative consequences. In this context, accidental losses are losses that are accidental (unintended) from the affected person's or organization's perspective. For example, although robbery and arson are intentional acts committed by the robber or arsonist, the victims did not intend for these acts to be committed. Consequently, the acts are considered accidental from the affected person's or organization's perspective and are also considered accidental for risk management purposes.

Organizations have a fundamental goal of survival as well as several other goals including profit, growth, public service, or the performance of a governmental function. Beyond ensuring an organization's survival, senior management should also try to prevent any accidental losses that could reduce profits or cash flows, slow growth, or interrupt its operations.

Risk management involves the four management functions of planning, organizing, leading, and controlling the organization's resources and activities to minimize the adverse effects of accidental losses on the organization at a reasonable cost. However, risk management can also refer to a decision-making process related to potential accidental losses. Risk management as a decision-making process involves the following six steps:

1. Identifying loss exposures
2. Analyzing loss exposures

3. Examining the feasibility of risk management techniques
4. Selecting the appropriate risk management techniques
5. Implementing the selected risk management techniques
6. Monitoring results and revising the risk management program

Those two descriptions of risk management—one emphasizing its managerial aspects, the other its decision-making aspects—can be unified into the following definition: **risk management** is the process of making and implementing decisions that will minimize the adverse effects of accidental losses on an organization. Making these decisions involves the six-step risk management process. Implementing these decisions involves performing the four management functions. These four management functions are usually performed as part of an overall risk management program.

Risk management
The process of making and implementing decisions that will minimize the adverse effects of accidental losses on an organization.

The risk management process is ongoing because past choices of risk management techniques must be continually reevaluated in light of changes in the following:

*   An organization's resources and activities and its resulting additional exposures to accidental loss
*   The relative costs of alternative risk management techniques
*   An organization's legal requirements
*   An organization's goals
*   The economic environment

Risk Management Scope

Risk management has a broad scope. Experts in many fields use risk management to cope with a wide range of uncertainties and to make the outcomes of their efforts more foreseeable (less risky).

The following examples illustrate the broad scope of risk management application:

*   Loan officers of banks and other financial institutions want to manage the risk that a borrower may not repay a loan or that a group of loans in a portfolio may develop a high default rate.
*   Corporate and public entity financial managers want to manage the risk associated with the timing and amount of their organizations' aggregate cash inflows and outflows to prevent having insufficient cash.
*   Traders in international currencies want to manage the risk associated with their inability to forecast how interest rates and other factors that exchange rates among currencies will change in the short term.
*   Project managers want to manage the risks that may interfere with the timely completion of their projects within their budgets.
*   Investment managers want to manage the upside risk for profit or the downside risk for loss associated with securities, as well as the predictability of the securities' market price or dividend performance.
*   Meteorologists want to manage the risk of inaccurate weather forecasts.

These examples illustrate how risk management can extend beyond its traditional focus on accidental losses.

The potential scope of risk management has led some organizations to view risk on an enterprise-wide basis so that risk management also includes risk arising from business activities, known as business risk. **Business risk** refers to risk that is inherent in the operation of a particular organization, including the possibility of loss, no loss, or gain. Risk management professionals often refer to business risk as speculative risk. **Hazard risk** (also called pure risk) refers to risk from accidental loss, including the possibility of loss and no loss. Hazard risks affect property, liability, personnel, and net income loss exposures. A **loss exposure** is any condition that presents a possibility of loss, whether or not an actual loss occurs. For example, an organization's introduction of a new product may be met by market acceptance and consequential financial gain, or by rejection and consequential financial loss. **Enterprise risk management**, the term commonly used to describe a broader view of risk management, is an approach to managing all of an organization's key business risks and opportunities with the intent of maximizing shareholder value.

Enterprise risk management differs from traditional risk management in the following ways:

- Enterprise risk management encompasses both hazard risk and business risk; traditional risk management focuses on hazard risk.
- Enterprise risk management seeks to enable an organization to fulfill its greatest productive potential; traditional risk management seeks to restore an organization to its former pre-loss condition.
- Enterprise risk management focuses on the value of the organization; traditional risk management focuses on the value of the accidental loss.
- Enterprise risk management focuses on an organization as a whole; traditional risk management focuses on specific loss exposures.

Traditional risk management can be viewed as part of enterprise risk management. Therefore, traditional risk management is both its own discipline and part of the broader enterprise risk management discipline.

Regardless of whether an organization adopts a traditional risk management or an enterprise risk management approach, risk management can bring benefits both to the organization and to the economy as a whole. However, there may also be significant costs associated with risk management.

RISK MANAGEMENT COSTS AND BENEFITS

The costs imposed by accidental losses—both actual and potential—fall into the following three broad categories:

1. Reduction in property value, income, earning capacity, or quality of life because of damage, destruction, or injury

---

Business risk
Risk that is inherent in the operation of a particular organization, including the possibility of loss, no loss, or gain.

Hazard risk
Risk from accidental loss, including the possibility of loss and no loss.

Loss exposure
Any condition that presents a possibility of loss, whether or not an actual loss occurs.

Enterprise risk management
An approach to managing all of an organization's key business risks and opportunities with the intent of maximizing shareholder value.

Categories of Risk Included in Enterprise Risk Management

In the evolving area of enterprise risk management, various models have been developed that categorize risks. One such model is as follows:

Strategic risks are those uncertainties associated with the organization's overall long-term goals and management, for example:

- Partnerships that could strengthen the organization's brand

- Technology that could position the organization for growth

- Organizational expansion that could maximize shareholder value

Operational risks are those uncertainties associated with the organization's operations, for example:

- Adequacy of the utilities that supply the organization

- Ability of suppliers to meet the organization's demands

Financial risks are those uncertainties associated with the organization's financial activities, for example:

- Currency conversion, that is, converting one country's currency to another, with the possibility of a change in value as a result of the conversion

- Fluctuations in the value of a security because of changes in interest rates

Hazard risks are those uncertainties associated with the organization's reduction in value resulting from the effects of accidental losses, for example:

- Damage to structures owned by the organization caused by a boiler explosion

- Bodily injury that consumers could suffer as a result of using the organization's product

Some enterprise risk management models include more than these four categories of risk, thereby recognizing that additional risk categories may need to be considered separately. Additional risk categories could include reputation risk, regulatory risk, contractual risk, and information risk.

2. Loss of net benefits that could have been gained from deterred activities, that is, those activities not undertaken because they were judged too risky

3. Cost of resources devoted to managing accidental losses, that is, resources that could have been put to alternative uses had there been no exposures to any possible accidental losses

The third category of costs represents the costs of risk management. However, risk management can provide benefits by managing the first two categories of costs. Therefore, an effective risk management program minimizes the total of all three categories of costs. To identify the ways in which these categories of costs can be minimized, it is helpful to consider the costs and benefits of risk management for a particular organization, and then for the entire economy.

For a Particular Organization

All organizations face potential accidental losses and therefore incur a cost of risk simply by operating. In addition, organizations may be deterred from potentially profitable (or otherwise beneficial) activities because they are too risky. Two benefits to a particular organization of risk management are it reduces the cost of risk of the organization's current activities and it reduces deterrence effects; that is, it enables the organization to cost-effectively undertake activities it once considered not worth the cost of risk.

Reduced Cost of Risk

Cost of risk
The total cost incurred by an organization because of the possibility of accidental loss.

In risk management, an organization's **cost of risk** of a given asset or activity is the total cost incurred by the organization because of the possibility of accidental loss. That cost of risk is comprised of the first and third of the three broad categories of costs previously identified—that is, the reduction in values caused by accidents and the cost of the resources devoted to risk management.

More specifically, an organization's cost of risk associated with a particular asset or activity is the total of the following:

*   Costs of accidental losses not reimbursed by insurance or other outside sources
*   Insurance premiums or expenses incurred for noninsurance indemnity
*   Costs of risk control techniques to prevent or reduce the size of accidental losses
*   Costs of administering risk management activities

Risk management aims to reduce the long-term overall cost of risk for the organization without precluding or otherwise interfering with the organization's achieving its goals or engaging in its normal activities. The reduction in the overall cost of risk can increase the organization's profits (or, for a not-for-profit organization, reduce the budget it needs for a particular activity). Risk management also supports safety while minimizing the financial effect of safety measures on the organization's productivity.

Reduced Deterrence Effects

The fear of possible future losses tends to make senior management reluctant to undertake activities they consider too risky. Consequently, the organization is deprived of the benefits that could be achieved if managers were willing to undertake these riskier activities. Risk management reduces the deterrence effects of uncertainty about potential future accidental losses by making these losses either less frequent, less severe, or more foreseeable. The resulting reduction in uncertainty generates the following benefits for an organization:

- Alleviates or reduces management's fears about potential losses, thereby increasing the feasibility of ventures that once appeared too risky

- Increases profit potential as a result of greater participation in investment or production activities

- Makes the organization a safer investment, and, therefore, more attractive to suppliers of investment capital through which the organization can expand

Many new products and manufacturing processes have become attractive only when better ways of preventing and paying for accidental losses have reduced related uncertainty.

Like an organization's senior managers, those who would provide the organization with funds seek assurances: stockholders or other investors seek assurance that their equity is safe and will generate future income; creditors seek assurance that the money they have loaned will be repaid on time with interest. The security sought by these sources of new capital rests, at least partly, on confidence that the organization will prosper despite any accidental losses that might befall it. Consequently, an organization's ability to attract willing investors depends to a significant degree on the effectiveness of its risk management program to protect investors' capital against the cost of accidental losses.

For the Entire Economy

The economy at both local and national levels incurs certain costs associated with risk and its management, as well as uncertainty about future losses. For example, a major hurricane can have widespread effects on the national economy, not just on individual organizations. Beyond a single loss occurrence like a hurricane, the cumulative effect of many smaller losses also adversely affects the national and local economies. For example, many retail stores in a shopping mall would suffer reduced sales if one of the anchor stores were closed because of an accidental loss. Depending on the magnitude of the loss and the length of time required for the anchor store to recover, the local community may sustain lost jobs, reduced tax revenue, and an overall reduction in the quality of life that was enjoyed when the mall was fully operational and thriving.

An economy's cost of risk management includes the resources consumed by or devoted to combating accidental losses. For example, uncertainty throughout the economy causes organizations to be more risk averse. This in turn causes allocation of the economy's resources away from assets or activities that seem to be too risky so that the economy is not as productive as it might otherwise be. Consequently, average living standards can be reduced. Risk management benefits the entire economy by reducing waste of resources and by improving allocation of productive resources.

Reduced Waste of Resources

Any economy possesses a given quantity of resources with which to produce goods and services. If an accidental loss reduces those resources, such as when a fire or an earthquake demolishes a factory or destroys a highway, that economy's overall productive resources are reduced. Risk management prevents or minimizes the waste of these productive resources.

Whenever there is a risk that accidental losses may occur, some portion of the economy's resources must be devoted to risk management. Allocating such resources is a cost because the resources cannot be used for other purposes that could promote growth. However, without such resources the economy would suffer even more in the event of an accidental loss.

Improved Allocation of Productive Resources

Risk management also improves the allocation of productive resources because when economic uncertainty is reduced for individual organizations, allocating productive resources is improved. Risk management makes those who own or run an organization more willing to undertake formerly risky activities because they are better protected against the accidental losses those activities might have produced. That greater willingness makes senior managers, workers, and suppliers of financial capital more free to pursue activities that maximize profits, returns on investments, and ultimately wages. Such a shift increases overall productivity within an economy and, on balance, improves everyone's average standard of living.

The benefits of risk management are usually realized by implementing a risk management program that supports an organization's overall goals.

RISK MANAGEMENT PROGRAM GOALS

Risk management program
A system for planning, organizing, leading, and controlling the resources and activities that an organization needs to protect itself from the adverse effects of accidental losses.

A **risk management program** is a system for planning, organizing, leading, and controlling the resources and activities that an organization needs to protect itself from the adverse effects of accidental losses. A structured, logical program that is appropriate for a particular organization is the foundation on which the entire risk management effort rests. In this text, the term "risk management professional" means any person who has responsibility under an organization's risk management program.

The support of an organization's senior management—or the owners of small private organizations or the elected and appointed officials of public entities—is essential to an effective risk management program. To gain that support, a risk management professional should design a program that fosters the organization's overall goals. With a clear understanding of these overall goals, the risk management professional can formulate specific pre-loss and post-loss goals for the risk management program that support and enable the organization's overall goals.

Pre-loss goals are risk management goals that should be in place even if no significant losses occur. These pre-loss goals should include economy of operations, tolerable uncertainty, legality, and social responsibility. **Post-loss goals** are risk management goals that should be in place in the event of a significant loss. Possible post-loss goals include survival, continuity of operations, profitability, earnings stability, social responsibility, and growth. These goals describe the organization's operating and financial condition that its senior management consider acceptable after the most significant foreseeable loss.

Pre-loss goals
Risk management goals that should be in place even if no significant losses occur.

Post-loss goals
Risk management goals that should be in place in the event of a significant loss.

Pre-Loss Goals

Regardless of its loss experience, every organization has operational goals—pre-loss goals—that its risk management activities should support. Four such pre-loss goals are as follows:

1. Economy of operations
2. Tolerable uncertainty
3. Legality
4. Social responsibility

Economy of Operations

Risk management should operate economically and efficiently; that is, the organization generally should not incur substantial costs for slight benefits gained. Risk management programs themselves should be operated economically and efficiently.

One way to measure the economy of a risk management program is through benchmarking, in which an organization's risk management costs are compared with those of similar organizations. The Risk and Insurance Management Society (RIMS), a global organization of risk management professionals, conducts an annual survey that can be used by organizations to compare their cost of risk with other organizations in their industry. RIMS' cost-of-risk survey combines expenditures for risk assessment, risk control, and risk financing, as well as the administrative costs of risk management programs. These costs are then related to revenue so that comparisons can be made between organizations and industry sectors. Exhibit 1-2 shows how the all-industry cost of risk varied between 1990 and 2003. For example, the all-industry cost of risk per $1,000 of revenue rose from $8.91 in 2002 to $11.96 in 2003. Cost of risk information, specific to the risk management professional's industry, indicates whether the organization is at a competitive advantage or disadvantage in its marketplace as a result of the resources it has committed to managing risk.

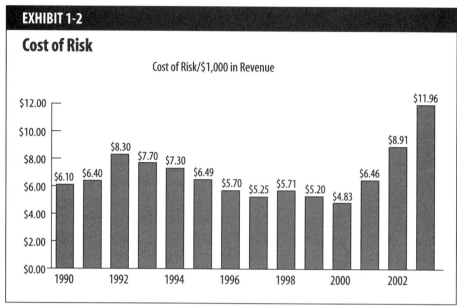

EXHIBIT 1-2

Cost of Risk

Cost of Risk/$1,000 in Revenue

Source: 2003 RIMS Benchmark Survey

Risk and Insurance Management Society, Inc. (RIMS)

The Risk and Insurance Management Society, Inc. (RIMS) is a proactive voice on behalf of risk managers, dedicated to supporting their function and enhancing their profile as vital elements in organizational success. Founded in 1950, RIMS represents nearly 4,800 industrial service, nonprofit, charitable, and governmental entities. The Society serves 8,900 risk management professionals around the world.

Source: www.rims.org/Template.cfm?Section+About_RIMS (accessed February 18, 2005).

Tolerable Uncertainty

Another pre-loss goal is tolerable uncertainty, which means keeping managers' uncertainty about accidental losses at tolerable levels. Managers want to be assured that whatever might happen will be within the bounds of what was anticipated and will be effectively treated by the risk management program. As well as making all personnel aware of potential loss exposures, a risk management program should also provide assurances (through both risk control and risk financing) that loss exposures are being managed well.

Legality

An important pre-loss goal is for the risk management program to help to ensure that the organization's legal obligations are satisfied. These legal obligations will typically be based on the following:

- Standard of care that is owed to others
- Contracts entered into by the organization
- Federal, state, and local laws and regulations

A risk management professional has an essential role in helping the organization avoid tort liability by meeting the standard of care that it owes to others. The risk management professional and the organization's legal counsel manage lawsuits brought by others for monetary damages arising out of the wrongful or negligent acts or omissions of the organization. Some public and charitable entities are immune from negligence claims because of long-standing constitutional and other judicial doctrines that exempt them. However, such immunities have eroded over time, and many entities who might be eligible for such immunity choose to purchase liability insurance rather than to invoke immunity.

The risk management professional should also understand the organization's contractual obligations as well as the contractual obligations that others owe to the organization. If the organization does not fulfill its obligations under a contract, the other party may bring a lawsuit against the organization for breach of contract. If the other party does not fulfill its obligation and the organization does not pursue it, the other party may be relieved of its obligations under the contract.

Risk management professionals need to be aware of the federal, state, and local laws and regulations that apply to their organizations and should work with others to ensure compliance. Examples of laws and regulations of particular concern to the risk management function are occupational health and safety regulations, labeling requirements for consumer products, regulations about hazardous waste disposal, and statutes establishing mandatory insurance requirements.

Social Responsibility

Social responsibility is both a pre-loss and a post-loss goal for many organizations. Social responsibility includes the organization's ethical conduct as well as the philanthropic commitments that the owners of the organization have made to the community and society as a whole. Beyond the altruistic interests of the organization's owners, many organizations justify pursuing the pre- and post-loss goals of social responsibility because such activities enhance the organization's reputation. Risk management professionals should consider the organization's societal commitments when developing its risk management program so that these commitments can be met even if accidental losses affect the organization.

Post-Loss Goals

While pre-loss goals are not dependent on actual loss, post-loss goals are the operating and financial conditions that the organization's senior management considers acceptable after a significant loss has occurred. Six possible post-loss goals include the following:

1. Survival
2. Continuity of operations
3. Profitability

4. Earnings stability

5. Social responsibility

6. Growth

After a severe loss, the most basic goal is survival, while the most ambitious goal is growth. The more ambitious a particular post-loss goal the more difficult and costly it is to achieve. This relationship of post-loss goals and their respective resource requirements is shown in Exhibit 1-3.

EXHIBIT 1-3

Range of Post-Loss Goals of a Risk Management Program

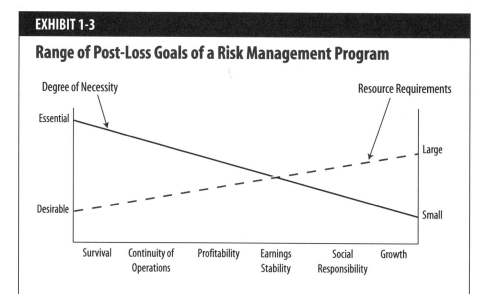

This illustration shows the range of post-loss goals. The solid line indicates the degree of necessity of the post-loss goals, ranging from survival as the most essential to growth as the least essential. The declining importance of those goals is indicated by the line's downward slope. The dashed line indicates the relative cost, commitment, or resources typically needed to reach each of those post-loss goals. Survival is the least expensive goal, and growth is the most expensive, as shown by the upward slope. The location and slope of lines will differ by organization. However, as a guideline, the essential goals of a risk management program generally require smaller commitments of an organization's resources than do the desirable goals.

Survival

After a major accidental loss occurs—for example, fire, flood, tornado, airplane crash, or large embezzlement—an organization's first goal is to survive. Many organizations permanently cease operations in the few months after a major loss.

For risk management purposes, an organization can be viewed as a structured system of resources such as machinery and raw materials, employees, and managerial leadership. The organization generates incomes for its employees and owners by producing goods or services that meet others' needs. Within that context, an organization survives an accidental loss when that loss does not permanently halt the organization's production and the incomes of those who work for or own it.

Survival requires that key functional departments, such as production, marketing, and finance, continue unabated. The organization needs managers to direct these and other functions. Therefore, any accidental loss that is so severe that it prevents production, marketing, or financing to be carried out under effective leadership threatens the organization's survival. Similarly, if an organization's only office or plant is destroyed, the organization is not likely to survive. Even if it can reopen after a long interruption, loss of its customers to competitors could deprive the organization of the minimum market share necessary for viability.

Adverse legal rulings also could force an organization to close. A tort liability judgment or an out-of-court settlement could drain so much of an organization's cash, and therefore its credit resources, that the organization could not continue to operate. Similarly, a regulatory ruling banning an organization's products or requiring it to radically alter its production process could make operations prohibitively expensive.

Finally, the death or disability of a key executive or technician could deprive an organization of essential leadership or of some vital expertise. If no one has been trained to do the work of that key employee, then the organization may have difficulty functioning.

Continuity of Operations

Continuity of operations is a key post-loss goal for many private organizations and an essential goal for all public entities. Although survival requires simply that no loss (no matter how severe) permanently shuts down an organization, the goal of continuity of operations is more demanding. With continuity, no loss can be allowed to interrupt the organization's operations for any appreciable time. Within this context, "appreciable" is a relative term and depends on the goods or service produced. One organization might be unable to tolerate even one day's shutdown, while another's output may continue even though some of its activities halt for a month or two. When an organization's senior management sets continuity of operations as a goal, its risk management professionals must have a clear, detailed understanding of the specific operations whose continuity is essential and the maximum tolerable interruption interval for each operation.

Any organization for which continuous operations are essential must take steps, and probably incur additional expenses, to forestall an intolerable shutdown. The steps such an organization should take are as follows:

- Identify activities whose interruptions cannot be tolerated
- Identify the types of accidents that could interrupt such activities
- Determine the standby resources that must be immediately available to counter the effects of those accidents
- Ensure the availability of the standby resources at even the most unlikely and difficult times

Ensuring the availability of standby resources is likely to add significant expense to an organization. Consequently, continuity of operations tends to be more costly than the more basic goal of survival. However, for organizations that give high priority to continuity of operations, this added cost is preferable to the alternative of interruption.

For public entities—particularly cities, counties, and other governing bodies, as well as schools and public utilities—maintaining public services without interruption is perhaps the most important risk management goal. Any sustained interruption in police or fire protection, supplies of clean water, removal of trash or sewage, or public education is likely to have serious consequences. The essential purpose of most public entities is to provide some sort of service, and therefore any significant interruption interferes with the well-being of individual citizens and the community at large. Consequently, many public entities go to considerable lengths and expense to design and implement contingency plans for their organization's continued operations despite severe accidental losses to facilities or resources.

Profitability

If an organization has survived an accidental loss and continued its operations, then the next post-loss goal is profitability. Beyond the physical effects an accident might have on an organization's operations, management may be concerned with how such a loss would affect the organization's profitability. In a for-profit organization, this is the ability to generate net income. In a not-for-profit organization, this is the ability to operate within its budget. An organization's senior management might have established a minimum amount of profit (or surplus, for not-for-profit organizations) that no accidental loss can be allowed to reduce. To achieve that minimum amount, the risk management program is likely to emphasize insurance and other means of transferring the financial consequences of loss so that actual financial results fall within an acceptable range. Such an organization tends to spend more on risk management, particularly risk financing, than does an organization that tolerates an occasional unprofitable financial result.

Earnings Stability

Earnings stability can also be a post-loss goal. Rather than strive for the highest possible level of current profits (or surpluses, for not-for-profit organizations) in a given period, some organizations emphasize earnings stability over time. Striving for earnings stability requires precision in forecasting risk management costs, which are principally costs for insurance or loss prevention. Other risk financing techniques could be less expensive than insurance, but their costs could fluctuate greatly.

Social Responsibility

As discussed in the context of an organization's pre-loss goals, accidental losses affect an organization's ability to fulfill its real or perceived obligations to the community and to society as a whole. For example, an organization may have planned to sponsor a 5-K foot race for a local charity before one of its production facilities suffered an accidental loss, forcing it to close for repairs. The organization may not be able to justify to its owners and employees the use of resources to sponsor the 5-K instead of to restore the closed production facility. However, failing to sponsor the race could have implications for relationships with customers, suppliers, employees, taxpayers, and members of the public. These relationships, even though they do not involve legal obligations for the organization, often are the force behind the organization' overall mission. Consequently, many not-for-profit organizations and many public entities are unable to distinguish between the post-loss goals of survival and social responsibility because of the community service focus of their activities.

Growth

The ultimate post-loss goal is growth. Emphasizing growth—for example, enlarging an organization's market share, the size and scope of its activities or products, or its assets—might have two distinctly opposing effects on its risk management program. Those effects depend on managers' and owners' tolerance for uncertainty of accidental losses. If striving to expand makes owners and managers more willing to accept greater uncertainty in exchange for minimizing risk management costs, the organization's explicit costs for risk management are likely to be quite low. Such an organization's risk management professionals may find it difficult to obtain a budget adequate to protect against expanding loss exposures. Moreover, if such an organization suffers a severe loss for which it has not adequately prepared, its real cost of risk management—more accurately, its real cost of not adequately managing loss exposures—may be quite high and involve sacrificing much of the growth the organization has attained.

In contrast, the goal of risk management in a growing organization might be to protect its expanding resources so that the organization's path of expansion is not blocked or reversed by a substantial accidental loss. Risk management costs are likely to be high because such an organization is seeking increased earnings, that is growth, rather than survival, or stability of earnings. Consequently, the organization lowers its tolerance for unanticipated retained loss and requires greater emphasis on risk control and risk financing.

Trade-Offs Among Goals

Pre-loss and post-loss goals are interrelated, but sometimes they are not consistent with one another. Therefore, an organization may discover that fully achieving all goals simultaneously is impossible. In particular, the post-loss goals may conflict with pre-loss goals, or the pre-loss goals may compete with each other.

Achieving any post-loss goal costs money, which might conflict with the pre-loss goal of economy of operations. The more ambitious and costly the post-loss goal, the greater the conflict. For example, to obtain tolerable uncertainty, the risk management professional must be confident that certain organizational post-loss goals will be achieved. Gaining that confidence requires allocating some of the organization's limited resources, including money, to risk management efforts. This may involve purchasing insurance, installing safety equipment, and maintaining duplicate copies of records in case originals are destroyed. The cost of such efforts can conflict with the goal of economy of operations.

The legality and social responsibility goals may also conflict with the economy of operations goal. Some externally imposed legal obligations, such as safety standards dictated by building codes, are nonnegotiable. Therefore, costs associated with these obligations are unavoidable. Other nonlegal obligations, such as charitable contributions, may be negotiable. However, while meeting social responsibility may raise costs in the short term, it can have worthwhile long-term benefits that make the costs acceptable.

In working with others regarding the trade-offs among organizational goals, a risk management professional must consider the likely effects of alternative risk management techniques and the costs and benefits of each. The interests and concerns of the various groups affected by an organization's risk management program should also be considered.

The way in which a risk management department is structured, how it cooperates with other departments, and how it handles communication of information are all relevant in enabling risk management professionals to respond to the goals and concerns of the organization and of affected parties.

RISK MANAGEMENT DEPARTMENT STRUCTURE

No one way of structuring a risk management department can accommodate all situations. The head of the risk management department should thoroughly assess the organization's operations, current activities, and the capabilities of the existing risk management staff to determine the proper structure, the level of activity required, and, consequently, the number of staff needed. Only after a proper assessment can the appropriate structure and mode of operation be determined.

Internal Structure

In small organizations, the risk management department typically consists of one person. As organizations grow and have more loss exposures, the department needs to expand. The rate at which staff are added depends on the organization's operations and its management's attitudes about risk management's role in the organization. Even when risk management is integrated into the organization, some organizations pride themselves on having minimal corporate staffing to serve decentralized branches or departments. Others prefer a large staff, centralized to perform many tasks for each branch or department.

For a small risk management department, additions to personnel often begin with a safety and loss prevention manager and a claim manager, as shown in Exhibit 1-4. Any additions to professional staff should bring new, specialized expertise to the department.

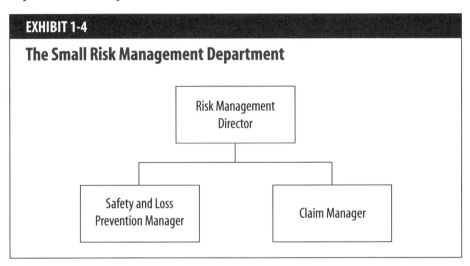

EXHIBIT 1-4

The Small Risk Management Department

As an organization grows, or as the value of the risk management process is increasingly accepted, the risk management department may expand to a medium-sized department. Generally, more assistance is required when insurance is used to finance risk, when more complex aspects of safety and loss prevention emerge, and when volume of claims increases. Exhibit 1-5 shows a departmental expansion that caters to these increased complexities.

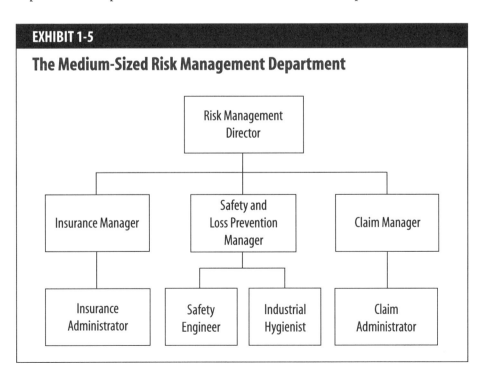

EXHIBIT 1-5

The Medium-Sized Risk Management Department

For a large department, the risk management director becomes less involved in implementing the technical aspects of risk management and more involved in managerial functions. That change of emphasis is reflected in the departmental structure shown in Exhibit 1-6.

The large department may also contain several positions in safety/loss prevention, health, and claim administration. In addition to significant risk control efforts, large organizations usually have more complex risk financing arrangements, including substantial retentions, multi-layered insurance programs, and alternative risk financing techniques. A large risk management department is also likely to have specialized claim personnel—some specializing in property claims, others in liability claims, and some in employee benefits. High frequency of particular types of retained losses, such as workers' compensation claims or products liability claims, increases the need for specifically trained claim personnel.

EXHIBIT 1-6

The Large Risk Management Department

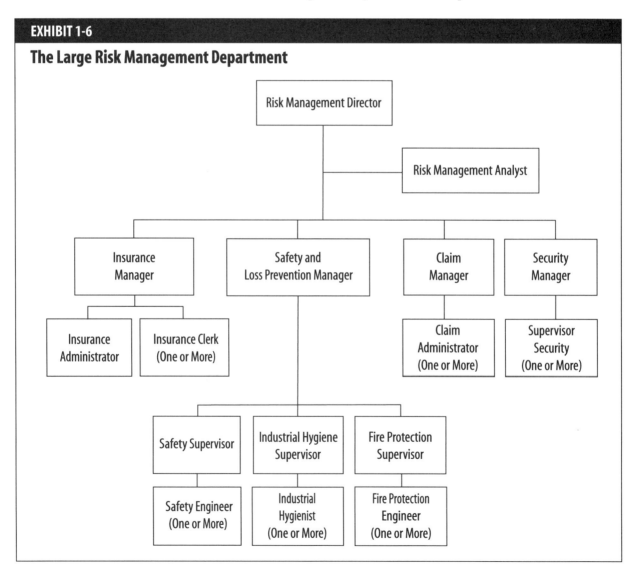

Cooperation With Other Departments

Cooperation with other departments is essential for the risk management program to be successful. Risk management professionals usually have only a support role in most organizations and therefore have neither the direct authority nor the budget needed to implement the many aspects of a risk management program. Consequently, interdepartmental cooperation is required.

Risk management professionals depend on the departments within the organization to communicate exposures to accidental loss that they become aware of and that might not be evident to a risk management professional as part of routine risk assessment activities. Additionally, a risk management professional relies on these other departments for information to implement effective risk control and risk financing programs. The following are examples of departments that provide information to the risk management professional and the type of information they may provide:

- *Accounting.* The organization's accounting department can provide historical cost information that helps a risk management professional to determine the current and replacement cost of the organization's physical assets and properties. Additionally, the accounting department is a key resource in determining continuing expenses and revenue reductions that could be caused by a business interruption.

- *Information Systems.* Risk management professionals typically rely on the organization's information systems department to track the organization's loss exposures. This information enables a risk management professional to perform analytical evaluations that might reveal unexpected opportunities and threats to operations.

- *Legal.* Risk management professionals usually rely on the organization's legal department for advice on matters such as how to handle specific liability claims, the wording that should appear on product labels, and procedures that might be used if a product failure were to occur.

- *Human Resources.* Risk management professionals often depend on the organization's human resources department to help identify those employees who are essential to the organization's survival if a business interruption were to occur. For many organizations, personnel loss exposures are addressed by human resources with little or no intervention from the risk management department.

- *Production.* Risk management professionals often rely on the organization's production department for information about essential processes or equipment. Additionally, production has information about key suppliers and customers that might not be readily available elsewhere in the organization.

- *Marketing.* The first time a risk management professional may hear about a consumer complaint is when he or she is informed about it by the organization's marketing department. Marketing might be the first department in the organization to be aware of product or service deficiencies that create liability loss exposures.

In addition to each of these departments serving as a risk management information resource, they are also sources of the potential accidental losses to which the organization is exposed. Therefore, interdepartmental communication is essential to the risk management effort.

Communication

Communication encompasses all flows of information into and out of the risk management department and organization. Communication can be classified in terms of, but should not be restricted to, each of the following:

- Whether the communication is internal to the organization, sent to external entities, or both

- Whether the communication is incoming to or outgoing from the risk management department

- Which of the steps in the risk management process the communication most directly promotes

For example, information about identifying or analyzing loss exposures that comes into the risk management department from within the organization may include periodic loss exposure reports prepared according to a schedule and format established by the risk management department.

Information going from the risk management department to others within the organization may include bulletins on new or intensified loss exposures (such as newly discovered toxic substances or new court rulings) as well as requests that all departments be especially alert to these new loss exposures.

Information coming into the risk management department from outside the organization may include briefs from trade associations, reports from governmental agencies, and information gathered from seminars on risk management techniques.

Information sent from the risk management department to others outside the organization may include data reported to trade associations or governmental agencies. It may also include facts or procedures that a risk management professional shares at professional meetings or through letters or articles submitted to risk management periodicals.

However, communication is not limited to loss exposure identification and analysis. Monitoring the results of selected risk management techniques is also required and involves an ongoing dialogue among various groups. For example, a risk management professional may direct other departments on how to report and analyze accidents and how to compile data about each department's risk management costs. Government entities may send the risk management department bulletins on setting standards for acceptable levels of safety, fire protection, or industrial hygiene. The risk management department may provide outside regulatory authorities with certifications indicating compliance with government standards.

A particularly important risk management document, frequently including information supporting all six steps in the risk management process, is the risk management annual report. An increasing number of risk management departments are providing such reports, on request or on their own initiative, to their senior management. Most risk management professionals believe that some kind of annual report to management is needed to detail the current risk management program and to propose significant changes. A risk management annual report must be tailored to an organization's situation and to senior management's knowledge and attitudes. However, some information is routinely provided in most risk management annual reports. Exhibit 1-7 provides an outline for information typically contained in such a report.

EXHIBIT 1-7

Sample Risk Management Annual Report

Outline

I.   Insurance and Risk Funding

    A.   Property Insurance

    B.   Fidelity Coverages

    C.   Directors and Officers, Errors and Omissions, and Fiduciary Liability

    D.   Workers' Compensation

    E.   Special Coverage

        1.   Precious Metals Excess

        2.   Blanket Trust Properties

II. Crisis Management

III. Losses and Recoveries

IV. Risk Control Activities

V.   Exhibits

    A.   Organization Chart

    B.   Workers' Compensation

    C.   Losses, Recoveries, and Premiums

With the often extensive flow of information both to and from the risk management function, it is important to have appropriate information management and risk management information systems to enable a risk management professional to assess the quality of the information provided.

Information Management and Risk Management Information Systems

A risk management program is only as sound as its underlying data. As such, a risk management professional needs a framework to assess informational quality. The quality of information can generally be described in one of the following ten ways:

1. *Accessible.* How easily and quickly can the information be accessed? Can data be quickly reviewed via a computer program or in spreadsheet format?
2. *Comprehensive.* Not how voluminous, but how comprehensive is the information in question? Does it convey meaning in its own right or only in relation to some other information?
3. *Accurate.* To what degree is the information free from error?
4. *Appropriate.* Is the information relevant to the user's request or need? Is the information presented in a way that the user can easily apply?
5. *Timely.* How current is the information? Is information readily available when needed for activities and decisions?
6. *Clarity.* How is the information presented? Can an inexperienced or occasional user obtain and understand needed information without aid?
7. *Flexible.* How adaptable is the information? Can it be used for more than one decision or by more than one decision maker?
8. *Verifiable.* Can the validity of information be easily determined?
9. *Free from bias.* Has the information been free from any attempt to alter it in support of a preconceived conclusion?
10. *Quantifiable.* If raw numerical data, to what extent is the information susceptible to mathematical manipulation?

Risk management information systems (RMIS) have become a fundamental part of most risk management programs. Whether simple or complex, an RMIS is a system for gathering, analyzing, and reporting data and information relevant to an organization's risk management program. An RMIS can (1) encompass the entire scope of an organization's risk management program, (2) focus on a particular type of loss exposure (such as products liability), or (3) concentrate on a particular risk management technique (such as prevention of employee injuries). RMIS may be of particular use in developing an organization's risk management policy statement and annual report, in periodically assessing the organization's loss exposures, in managing claims, and in monitoring the results of risk management techniques.

RESPONSIBILITIES AND REPORTING RELATIONSHIPS

The structure of the risk management department will influence the responsibilities and reporting relationships of the risk management professionals. Responsibilities will typically encompass all aspects covered by the risk management program—risk assessment, risk control, and risk financing.

Responsibilities

This section discusses the responsibilities of the person in the most senior risk management position. In large private organizations, these responsibilities may rest with an individual whose title includes "risk management" or "loss control." Alternatively these responsibilities may rest with another manager or executive, such as a vice president, director, treasurer, or controller. In small private organizations, risk management responsibilities may be performed by the chief executive, a senior manager, the organization's insurance producer, or an outside risk management consultant. Large public entities are likely to have a risk management professional on staff or available as a consultant, much like private organizations. In small public entities, particularly towns and school districts, responsibility for risk management is likely to rest with an administrative officer who has many other responsibilities.

Having primary responsibility for risk management requires a senior risk management professional to administer each of the six steps in the risk management process, and to undertake the managerial duties of planning, organizing, leading, and controlling resources and activities.

Except in some small organizations, no risk management professional can personally perform all the tasks these responsibilities entail. Some tasks are assigned to employees within the risk management department. However, many aspects of managing loss exposures must be part of the daily work of managers and other employees throughout the organization. Just as workplace safety is often promoted as being everyone's responsibility, the same is true for risk management, which includes, and goes beyond, safety. Much of a risk management professional's daily efforts must be focused on securing the voluntary cooperation of managers and others at every level of an organization.

The senior risk management professional must decide, or work with other senior managers in jointly deciding, how to handle loss exposures. The specific, nondelegable duties of a risk management professional, although varying somewhat by organization, are essentially similar. These generic duties can be grouped into those involving the following:

- Risk management program
- Risk assessment
- Risk control
- Risk financing

Risk Management Program

An organization's senior risk management professional should know more about its risk management program than any other manager, employee, or outside consultant. Therefore, the senior risk management professional should be directly responsible for designing the program's overall structure and for effectively implementing risk management goals. The senior risk management professional—alone or as a key resource person serving senior management, department heads, or other employees throughout the organization—must do the following:

- Guide senior management in establishing the organization's risk management program

- Plan, organize, lead, and control the resources of the risk management department or function

- Assist senior management in establishing the responsibility for, and channels of communication on, risk management matters throughout the organization

- Work with other managers to define the responsibilities and motivate the actions of those who will implement the risk management program

- Apportion the costs of the risk management program equitably among the organization's departments to reflect differences in loss exposures and to provide incentives for optimum risk management efforts within each area or department

- Adapt the organization's risk management program and use of risk control and financing techniques as loss exposures change and as the cost of using those techniques changes

Risk Assessment

Risk assessment involves identifying and analyzing an organization's loss exposures as well as examining the feasibility of the risk management techniques (risk control and risk financing, discussed next) that might be used to treat them and selecting the appropriate risk management techniques. The balance of this text describes the approaches that risk management professionals use to assess hazard risk so that the most appropriate risk management technique can be implemented.

Risk Control

An organization may use several risk control techniques, including avoidance, loss prevention, loss reduction, separation, duplication, and diversification. The particular tasks a risk management professional performs vary by risk control technique. Overall, however, the senior risk management professional's risk control responsibilities include the following:

- Identifying the benefits as well as measuring and controlling the costs of alternative risk control techniques to develop the most cost-effective risk control program

- Coordinating the efforts of everyone employed by or providing goods or services to the organization in recognizing hazards (conditions that increase the frequency or severity of loss) and implementing appropriate risk control techniques

- Advising senior managers about how to emphasize safety as an integral element of the organization's risk management program, to encourage and reward safe employee performance, and to correct any shortcomings in risk control

- Informing middle managers about how best to fulfill their fundamental responsibilities for preventing accidents in their area of operation

- Helping middle managers implement risk control techniques

A senior risk management professional's direct authority over risk control activities varies among organizations. That authority may include giving directives to personnel other than risk management personnel and, if necessary, invoking sanctions against those not complying. In a few organizations, risk control activities are centralized within a risk management department, giving the senior risk management professional direct authority to require that appropriate risk control techniques be implemented. In many organizations, responsibility for risk control is likely to be dispersed among several departments. For example, production and human resources managers are most directly concerned with employee safety; production personnel focus on quality control; and the legal department is the organization's primary resource on legal matters.

Attention to employee safety and other risk control aspects has predated the coordinated practice of risk management in many organizations. Therefore, a senior risk management professional is likely to find that other managers already have significant risk control authority and responsibility. Instead of centralizing risk control within a risk management department, it may be preferable for the senior risk management professional to simply coordinate the existing risk control efforts.

Risk Financing

Risk financing techniques can be broadly categorized as involving either risk retention or risk transfer. Between the two extremes of total retention and total risk transfer, there are risk financing techniques that consist of both risk retention and risk transfer. For example, commercial property insurance generally provides risk transfer yet requires the insured organization to retain part of each loss that occurs through a deductible. In using risk retention techniques, a risk management professional ensures, to the extent possible, that funds will be available from planned sources within the organization when needed to pay for retained losses. In using risk transfer techniques, the risk management professional relies on external sources of funds to achieve this same assurance. In either case, the same planning, negotiating, recordkeeping, and general administrative skills are required.

When applying risk financing techniques, a senior risk management professional should do the following:

- Work with financial and other senior executives to determine the extent to which the organization should retain losses and the level at which it should transfer the financing of potential losses from specific loss exposures

- Decide, once the appropriate overall balance between retention and transfer has been established, which retention and which transfer techniques should be used to finance losses from specific loss exposures

- Negotiate with appropriate persons and firms either inside or outside the organization to implement the chosen retention or transfer techniques for specific loss exposures
- Activate the appropriate retention or transfer technique when a loss occurs
- Identify the benefits, as well as measure and control the costs, of alternative risk financing techniques to develop the most cost-effective risk financing program

As with all responsibilities, the specific tasks required when applying risk financing techniques differ by organization, by loss exposure, and by risk financing technique.

Reporting Relationships

Risk management reporting relationships within any particular organization vary. The person to whom the senior risk management professional reports, and the title held by the senior risk management professional, depend in large part on how concerned senior management is about its loss exposures and how well the risk management function has been performed in the past.

In part, reporting relationships depend on the nature of the organization. For example, in a hospital, the senior risk management professional probably reports to the hospital's senior administrator; in a bank, to one of the vice presidents. In a medium or large corporation oriented toward production or marketing, risk management is often considered a risk financing function, and the senior risk management professional reports to the treasurer, assistant treasurer, controller, or perhaps the vice president in charge of finance. Similarly, in a public entity like a city or a school district, the senior risk management professional may report to the finance director or perhaps directly to the mayor, city manager, or superintendent.

Another factor influencing reporting relationships is the loss exposure or exposures considered most important by senior management. For example, if much of a particular organization's risk management activity concerns avoiding products liability lawsuits, the senior risk management professional may report to the corporate secretary, assistant secretary, or chief legal counsel. If the organization is more concerned with sound fire protection, the senior risk management professional may report to the vice president of engineering or the chief engineer. In some organizations, the senior risk management professional may report to several key line executives concerned with production, marketing, or financing activities.

RISK MANAGEMENT POLICY STATEMENT

To reinforce the risk management departmental structure and risk management responsibilities and reporting relationships, an organization may produce a risk management policy statement. A **risk management policy statement** is a tool for communicating the goals of the risk management program and the roles that people throughout the organization have in achieving the organization's risk management goals.

Risk management policy statement
A tool for communicating the goals of the risk management program and the roles that people throughout the organization have in achieving the organization's risk management goals.

Purpose

For the organization as a whole, the purpose of a written risk management policy statement is to do the following:

- Establish the general goals of the organization's risk management function
- Define the responsibilities of risk management personnel
- Coordinate the treatment of loss exposures on a reasonably standardized basis among any organizational subdivisions (for example, regions, branches, or departments)
- Establish and improve existing communication channels and information management systems
- Provide for program continuity and facilitate transition during times of risk management personnel changes

In addition, the written risk management policy statement is a continuing guide to risk management personnel and is especially helpful to new departmental employees. For both risk management professionals and staff, this statement can do the following:

- Emphasize the importance of the risk management function
- State risk management's position within the overall organizational structure
- Provide the framework for determining the responsibility for assessing, controlling, and financing loss exposures

Content

Because each organization is different, written risk management policy statements must be individualized. The following discussion suggests some general guidelines for developing such a statement.

A written risk management policy statement should begin with a general description of risk management and its importance to the organization. That description should indicate the position of the risk management personnel or department within the overall organizational structure, describe reporting relationships, and outline the scope of the authority and responsibility of the senior risk management professional. The statement might also describe the risk management department's internal structure, should the organization be large enough to support a large department.

In all organizations, the policy statement should clearly state senior management's risk management goals. Depending on the level of detail the organization typically uses in policy statements for other functions, the risk management policy statement may also specify particular decision rules for selecting various risk management techniques. Exhibit 1-8 shows a hypothetical risk management policy statement.

EXHIBIT 1-8

Hypothetical Risk Management Policy Statement— City Government

The City will adopt risk management principles in order to protect the health, safety, and welfare of its employees and the citizens it serves; to protect its property, assets, and other resources; and to maintain its reputation and good standing in the wider community. Consequently, the City will do the following:

- Establish a risk management committee with representatives from all departments

- Implement the risk management process so that loss exposures may be assessed and monitored

- Support risk control and risk financing initiatives recommended by the risk management committee

The City provides a wide range of services, all of which give rise to some level of risk. The City is fully committed to regularly assessing and treating these risks to minimize their effect on service delivery. In this way the City will better achieve its goals and enhance the value of the services it provides. The underlying objectives of the City's risk management program are to do the following:

- Embed risk management into the culture and operations

- Integrate risk management into service planning and performance management

- Manage risk in accordance with best practices

- Anticipate and respond to changing social, environmental, and legislative requirements

- Make sure that departments have clear accountability for both the ownership and cost of risk and the risk management techniques

These underlying objectives will be achieved by the following:

- Establishing clear roles, responsibilities, and reporting lines within the City for risk management

- Incorporating risk management in the City's decision-making, business planning, and performance management processes

- Monitoring the risk management program on a regular basis

- Reinforcing the importance of effective risk management through training

- Providing suitable insurance or other arrangements to manage the effect of unavoidable risks

RISK MANAGEMENT PROGRAM MONITORING AND REVISING

In order to monitor a risk management program, the senior risk management professional needs to set performance standards, compare actual performance with standards, and take corrective action to improve the program.

Performance Standards

Two major types of standards for controlling any activity are results standards and activity standards. **Results standards** focus on achievements regardless of the efforts they require. **Activity standards** focus on activity undertaken to achieve a particular result regardless of the success of that activity. Risk management professionals can effectively use both types of standards.

Results standards
Standards that focus on achievements regardless of the efforts they require.

Results Standards

Risk management results can be measured in dollars, percentages, ratios, or numbers of losses or claims. Any of those measurements may be expressed in absolute numbers or as percentages of sales, assets, payroll, or some other measure of an organization's activities. For example, if the organization's cost of risk is currently 0.65 percent of sales, the standard set for the next year might be to reduce this cost to 0.64 percent of sales.

Activity standards
Standards that focus on activity undertaken to achieve a particular result regardless of the success of that activity.

Activity Standards

The performance of many risk management departments is measured by their activity. For example, an organization's management may require that a member of its risk management staff make at least one annual visit to each of the organization's facilities. Another organization may require three such visits, perhaps coupled with safety seminars during each visit for all personnel.

Actual Performance Versus Standards

Both results and activity standards should be stated in measurable terms so that actual performance can be meaningfully compared with these standards. Such comparisons can yield any of three results: actual performance can either meet, fall below, or exceed established standards. Any of these three results might require changes in either the performance or the standard by which performance is measured. Whatever changes are needed should be determined by senior management, the senior risk management professional, and any others whose performance is being evaluated.

If performance meets an established standard, it seems natural to assume that both the performance and the standard are appropriate and that no changes need to be made. Although that often is the case, sometimes a standard may not elicit the best attainable risk management performance. A senior risk management professional may therefore still want to review the level at which the standard is set and the performance that may be attainable.

Performance that substantially exceeds a standard suggests that the standard might have been too low. Alternatively, the standard may have been incomplete, focusing on one aspect of performance to which employees devoted a great deal of attention while possibly ignoring equally important (but unmonitored) aspects of their performance. Another possibility may be that the standard is indeed appropriate and that the performance being monitored is exceptional. If that exceptional performance can be expected to continue, recognition or reward is appropriate.

If performance falls below a standard, corrective action may be required. Alternatively, it may indicate that the standard was unrealistic. Realistic standards motivate performance. For example, the goal of zero auto accidents for a sales organization with several hundred people making calls is an unrealistic standard.

Corrective Action

The purpose of corrective action is to improve future performance. Corrective actions must be tailored to each situation. Factors to be considered include the type and importance of the standard that has not been met, the responsibilities and personalities of those who are involved, and the options that are available for reaching acceptable performance levels.

To illustrate, if products liability losses have increased, the increase might be traced to a specific product, a line of products, or a defect in the production process. Here, corrective action should enlist the cooperation of product design and manufacturing personnel. On the other hand, investigation might show that a backlog of claims has developed, which has become more expensive to settle as claims age. If such claims are handled internally, a backlog may indicate that additional personnel are needed in that department. If the claims are handled externally, contracting with a new firm might be considered.

As another example, increasing shoplifting losses may be traced to particular retail stores. Corrective action might require the increased use of electronic article surveillance and stationing a store employee at the store's entrance.

Sometimes performance fails to meet a standard that is determined to have been unrealistically set. A more realistic performance standard may reference the organization's loss history and be set at a modest improvement.

The success of corrective actions will become apparent as the risk management program continues to be monitored. Past experience may help in making future corrective decisions.

SUMMARY

The term "risk" may be used in several ways. This text defines risk as uncertainty about outcomes that can be either negative or positive. Risk management is the process of making and implementing decisions that will minimize the adverse effects of accidental losses on an organization.

Risk management as a decision-making process involves the following six steps:

1. Identifying loss exposures
2. Analyzing loss exposures
3. Examining the feasibility of risk management techniques
4. Selecting the appropriate risk management techniques
5. Implementing the selected risk management techniques
6. Monitoring results and revising the risk management program

For some organizations, risk management has a broad scope that encompasses risk on an enterprise-wide basis. Enterprise risk management is an approach to managing all of an organization's key business risks and opportunities with the intent of maximizing shareholder value. Enterprise risk management is broader than the scope of risk management described in this text, which focuses on hazard risk arising from accidental loss.

The costs imposed by accidental losses—both actual and potential—fall into the following three broad categories:

1. Reduction in property value, income, earning capacity, or quality of life
2. Loss of net benefits that could have been gained from deterred activities
3. Costs of resources devoted to managing accidental losses

For a particular organization, risk management provides two benefits. First, it reduces the cost of risk of an organization's current activities. Second, it reduces the deterrence effects of uncertainty about future accidental losses.

For the entire economy, risk management again provides two benefits. It reduces waste of resources and it improves the allocation of productive resources.

A risk management program is a system for planning, organizing, leading, and controlling the resources and activities that an organization needs to protect itself from the adverse effects of accidental losses. The risk management program reflects the organization's pre- and post-loss goals. Four pre-loss goals include the following:

1. Economy of operations
2. Tolerable uncertainty
3. Legality
4. Social responsibility

Six post-loss goals include the following:

1. Survival
2. Continuity of operations
3. Profitability
4. Earnings stability
5. Social responsibility
6. Growth

Post-loss goals may conflict with pre-loss goals, or the pre-loss goals may compete with each other. Consequently, trade-offs among pre-loss and post-loss goals must be made.

The structure of the risk management department is generally dictated by the size of the organization, as well as the scope of the risk management function in the organization. An effective risk management program requires that other departments cooperate and communicate with the risk management department. A fundamental information resource for the risk management program is a risk management information system (RMIS).

An organization's senior risk management professional may have a variety of responsibilities to fulfill under various reporting relationships. The following duties of risk management professionals may be grouped as those involving the organization's:

- Risk management program
- Risk assessment
- Risk control
- Risk financing

Risk management reporting relationships vary depending in part on how concerned senior management is about its loss exposures and how well the risk management function has been performed in the past.

A written risk management policy statement is an effective tool for communicating the purposes of the risk management program and the roles that people throughout the organization have in achieving the organization's risk management goals.

Risk management program monitoring usually involves the establishment of results standards and activity standards. Results standards focus on achievements regardless of the efforts they require. Activity standards focus on activity undertaken to achieve a particular result regardless of the success of that activity. Comparing actual performance with those standards can highlight when corrective action is required.

Risk management programs use the risk management process to assess and treat loss exposures. This process is key to the operation of the risk management program.

Chapter 2

Direct Your Learning

Understanding the Risk Management Process

After learning the content of this chapter and completing the corresponding course guide assignment, you should be able to:

■ Identify the steps in the risk management process.

■ Describe the four types of loss exposures.

■ Describe the methods of identifying loss exposures.

■ Explain how to analyze loss exposures along the dimensions of loss frequency, loss severity, total dollar losses, timing, and data credibility.

■ Describe the following risk control techniques:

- Avoidance
- Loss prevention
- Loss reduction
- Separation
- Duplication
- Diversification

■ Describe the risk financing techniques of transfer and retention.

■ Explain how to select appropriate risk management techniques.

■ Describe the technical and managerial decisions that must be made to implement the selected risk management techniques.

■ Identify reasons why a risk management program may need to be revised.

■ Define or describe each of the Key Words and Phrases for this chapter.

Develop Your Perspective

What are the main topics covered in the chapter?

This chapter examines the six steps in the risk management process. This process is used by risk management professionals to ensure that loss exposures that the organization faces are being assessed and managed systematically.

Review the six steps in the risk management process.

- Is the risk management process consciously used at your organization when assessing or reassessing loss exposures?

- Is using the risk management process a part of your organization's culture?

Why is it important to learn about these topics?

The risk management process provides organizations and their risk management professionals with a systematic methodology for assessing and managing loss exposures. Risk management professionals should evaluate new loss exposures or significantly changed loss exposures using the risk management process to ensure that the risk management techniques support organizational goals.

Examine the risk management techniques used by your organization to manage loss exposures.

- What are the risk management techniques that are in use?

How can you use what you will learn?

Evaluate the effectiveness of the risk control and risk financing techniques used by your organization.

- How well do the techniques chosen support organizational goals?

- How might you revise the risk management program?

Chapter 2

Understanding the Risk Management Process

The risk management process is comprised of six steps that can be applied to actual or potential accidental losses. It provides organizations and their risk management professionals with a systematic methodology for assessing and treating accidental loss exposures. Applying the risk management process on an ongoing basis enables an organization to meet both its pre-loss and post-loss risk management program goals.

The Six Steps in the Risk Management Process

1. Identifying loss exposures
2. Analyzing loss exposures
3. Examining the feasibility of risk management techniques
4. Selecting the appropriate risk management techniques
5. Implementing the selected risk management techniques
6. Monitoring results and revising the risk management program

---

STEP ONE: IDENTIFYING LOSS EXPOSURES

The loss exposures that are most significant to an organization are those that can interfere with achieving the organization's goals. To identify such loss exposures, the risk management professional must be able to logically classify all possible loss exposures and employ methods of identifying the specific loss exposures that could interfere with the achievement of the organization's primary goals.

Types of Loss Exposures

As defined previously, a loss exposure is any condition that presents a possibility of loss, whether or not an actual loss occurs. Every loss exposure has the following elements:

- Financial value exposed to loss
- Cause of loss (also called a peril)
- Potential financial consequences of that loss

Loss exposures are typically categorized in terms of the first element—the financial value exposed to loss. All loss exposures that concern risk management, excluding loss exposures of purely sentimental value, are one or more of the following four types:

1.   Property loss exposures
2.   Liability loss exposures
3.   Personnel loss exposures
4.   Net income loss exposures

Subsequent chapters examine these four types of loss exposure in detail. The following sections provide an overview.

Property Loss Exposures

A **property loss exposure** is a condition that presents the possibility that a person or organization will sustain a loss resulting from the damage—including the destruction, taking, or loss of use—of property in which that person or organization has a financial interest. The financial interest can be ownership, use, revenue production associated with the property, or other rights associated with the property. Property can be categorized as either tangible or intangible.

Tangible property is property that has a physical form that can be seen or touched. Tangible property can be further categorized as either real or personal property. **Real property** is tangible property consisting of land, all structures permanently attached to the land (such as buildings or sidewalks), and whatever is growing on the land. **Personal property** is tangible or intangible property other than real property (for example, furniture, equipment, and clothing). **Intangible property** is personal property that has no physical form. Examples of intangible property include copyrights, customer goodwill, patents, trade secrets, and trademarks, as well as legal rights (such as the right to own and use property) or privileges (such as the privilege to drive an automobile). Intangible property continues to exist even if the evidence of its existence is destroyed.

Any event that is unintentional from the standpoint of the property owner or user, and that lowers the value of that owner or user's rights or privileges regarding that property, is a property loss.

Tangible property, both real and personal, is subject to both physical damage (including destruction) and wrongful taking. In contrast, intangible property, is not susceptible to physical damage. However, intangible property can be wrongfully taken, such as the theft of trade secrets. Such a theft would diminish the value to the holder of those trade secrets. Furthermore, the value of intangible property can be significantly reduced by a number of events, including physical damage to tangible property. For example, the intangible property right for an organization to conduct business in a municipality loses much of its value if the organization's production facility is destroyed.

Property loss exposure
A condition that presents the possibility that a person or organization will sustain a loss resulting from the damage—including the destruction, taking, or loss of use—of property in which that person or organization has a financial interest.

Tangible property
Property that has a physical form that can be seen or touched.

Real property
Tangible property consisting of land, all structures permanently attached to the land, and whatever is growing on the land.

Personal property
Tangible or intangible property other than real property.

Intangible property
Personal property that has no physical form.

Theft of Trade Secrets from Morabito Baking Company

Mazen Fathi Said, a baker with a business in North Carolina, was found guilty of stealing trade secrets from the Morabito Baking Company of Norristown, Pa. After driving to the Morabito premises in Pennsylvania, Mr. Said took a binder containing recipes valued at $30 million. In addition, Mr. Said was caught on surveillance video trespassing and impersonating an employee. While on the bakery premises, Mr. Said videotaped the bakery's production area and offered bribes to employees for them to teach Mr. Said how to make rolls.

Source: www.bakingbusiness.com/headline_stories.asp?ArticleID=64820#CAAN (accessed September 8, 2004).

Liability Loss Exposures

A **liability loss exposure** is a condition that presents the possibility that a person or an organization will sustain a loss resulting from a claim alleging a person's or an organization's legal responsibility for injury or damage suffered by another party. Because any liability loss exposure can impose a heavy, even bankrupting, burden on an organization, these loss exposures must be carefully managed. A liability loss exposure can cause actual loss in two ways.

First, an organization can incur a liability loss whenever it is sued for having breached a legal duty, allegedly harming another. The organization's loss consists of any money paid to the person claiming harm (bodily injury and/or property damage) as well as any expenses the organization incurs to investigate or defend the claim. An organization need not have committed a legal wrong to incur a liability loss. Merely being sued or being threatened with a lawsuit can result in a liability loss for an organization, if, for example, the organization has to pay for legal or negotiating expertise in its defense.

Second, if found to be in breach of contract, the organization becomes contractually obligated to pay damages for any loss that the other party has suffered. The damages can be money or another remedy of value that the organization must provide to fulfill the contractual obligation or restore the harmed party to pre-loss conditions.

Lawsuits may be brought in civil courts for an organization's civil wrongs or breaches of contract. Alternatively, criminal charges may be brought against an organization for its wrongful conduct that harms society. In these cases it is the government, rather than the individual or entity harmed by the crime, that seeks a remedy from the organization.

Personnel Loss Exposures

A **personnel loss exposure** is a condition that presents the possibility of loss caused by a person's death, disability, retirement, or resignation that deprives an organization of the person's special skill or knowledge that the organization cannot readily replace. The organization also may be obligated to provide

Liability loss exposure
A condition that presents the possibility that a person or an organization will sustain a loss resulting from a claim alleging a person's or an organization's legal responsibility for injury or damage suffered by another party.

Personnel loss exposure
A condition that presents the possibility of loss caused by a person's death, disability, retirement, or resignation that deprives an organization of the person's special skill or knowledge that the organization cannot readily replace.

cannot readily replace. The organization also may be obligated to provide employee benefits to the employee or the employee's dependents under those circumstances.

To avoid an overlap between personnel loss exposures and liability loss exposures, risk management professionals usually classify the diminished value of key employee services as a personnel loss exposure, and the compensation owed to that employee through the employers' liability or workers' compensation statutory benefits as a liability loss exposure.

Net Income Loss Exposures

Net income loss exposure
A condition that presents the possibility of loss caused by a reduction in net income.

A **net income loss exposure** is a condition that presents the possibility of loss caused by a reduction in net income. Net income equals revenues minus expenses in a given accounting period. A net income loss is a reduction in revenue, an increase in expenses, or a combination of both. A net income loss is likely the result of a property, liability, or personnel loss.

Methods of Identifying Loss Exposures

There are several ways in which the four types of loss exposures—property, liability, personnel, and net income—can be identified. Some methods may be more suited to a particular type of loss exposure than others, although they all may be suitable to some extent.

Methods of Identifying Loss Exposures

- Risk assessment questionnaires
- Loss histories
- Financial statements and underlying accounting records
- Other records and documents
- Flowcharts and organizational charts
- Personal inspections
- Expertise within and beyond the organization

Risk Assessment Questionnaires

A risk assessment questionnaire (also called a risk analysis questionnaire) is a document posing general questions that are meaningful for most organizations. The advantage of the standardized makeup of these questionnaires is that the questions may be universally relevant. The disadvantage is that no questionnaire can be expected to uncover all of the exposures characteristic of a given industry, let alone those unique to a given organization. In addition, because these questionnaires often serve insurers' purposes, most of the questions relate only to loss exposures for which commercial insurance is generally available.

Questionnaires are usually comprehensive documents with multiple sections that are completed only when they apply. For example, an organization with several subsidiaries may use a questionnaire that includes sections on owned property, vehicles, mobile equipment, premises liability, products liability, professional liability, and so on. Risk management professionals may use a commercially produced questionnaire, an insurance broker-produced questionnaire, or one that the risk management professional has created that more aptly meets the needs of the organization.

One of the strengths of a risk assessment questionnaire is that, if properly drafted, it can be answered by persons who have minimal expertise in risk management. Risk management professionals in large organizations may find such questionnaires particularly useful in eliciting loss exposure information from the organization's more distant plants, offices, or traveling representatives. In fact, if many locations are to be surveyed, the risk management professional may want to develop a special questionnaire that focuses on the loss exposures that are particularly characteristic or troublesome for that organization.

A potential weakness of a risk assessment questionnaire is that the structure may not stimulate the user to do anything more than fill in the blanks to answer the questions that the questionnaire poses. Most questionnaires do not explain why each particular question is being asked and do not lead the respondent to give additional relevant information that might go beyond the scope of the questions asked and provide the risk management professional with key loss exposure information.

Loss Histories

In addition to eliciting information through questionnaires, a risk management professional can identify an organization's loss exposures using loss histories. Any loss that has happened in the past can theoretically happen again. Conversely, the fact that a loss has not happened in the past does not mean it cannot occur in the future. However, by providing information about the organization's past losses, loss histories can greatly help a risk management professional to both identify and analyze that organization's exposure to accidental losses.

Identifying loss exposures (that is, recognizing what can happen) requires much less historical data on losses than analyzing them (that is, calculating or making informed judgments about how frequent, severe, and predictable these losses are likely to be). Also, analyzing accidental or business losses based on the organizations' historical records relies on the quality of the data that those records contain. Ideally, the data should be relevant, complete, consistent, and organized. For example, data quality is reduced whenever a loss is omitted, whenever any item of information normally collected about losses (such as where or when they occur) is omitted, whenever the conditions under which an organization operates or when those operations themselves change in some fundamental way, or whenever a new cause of losses emerges.

Financial Statements and Underlying Accounting Records

Reviewing financial statements and underlying accounting records is another method of identifying an organization's loss exposures. Financial statements (including the balance sheet, income statement, and statement of cash flows) as well as other accounting records can be used to identify some loss exposures that may not otherwise be apparent using other identification methods. Additionally, financial statements and accounting records can be used to identify future plans of the organization that could lead to new loss exposures.

Balance sheet
A statement of an organization's financial condition as of a particular date.

A **balance sheet** is a statement of an organization's financial condition as of a particular date. The balance sheet lists the organization's assets, the claims against those assets (liabilities), and the organization's resulting net worth. A risk management professional might review the list of assets to identify property values that are exposed to accidental loss. Likewise, the list of liabilities can be used by the risk management professional to identify organizational obligations, such as mortgages or long-term leases, that must be met even if the organization were temporarily closed as a consequence of an accidental loss.

However, there are limitations to using the balance sheet to value loss exposures. Balance sheets list the value of assets and liabilities based on accounting valuation rules, also called historical cost valuation, which may not be the best measure of an asset or liability from a risk management perspective. For example, historical cost may not be a helpful measure when the goal is to replace or repair a damaged asset. Similarly, the risk management professional should recognize that the historical costs of the organization's liabilities may not reflect the organization's future obligations. For example, amounts paid to injured parties to settle product lawsuits in the past may not accurately reflect the organization's future liabilities.

Income statement
A financial report that shows the profit or loss for a specific period.

An **income statement** (also called a profit and loss statement) is a financial report that shows the profit or loss for a specific period. An income statement summarizes revenues and expenses, the difference between them being net income. Risk management professionals often rely on the organization's income statement to identify net income loss exposures. For example, information from the income statement could be used to estimate what the organization would lose if an accidental loss caused a business interruption.

Statement of cash flows
A financial statement that shows an organization's cash receipts and cash payments during a specified period.

A **statement of cash flows** (also called the statement of changes in financial position or the statement of sources and uses of funds) is a financial statement that shows an organization's cash receipts and cash payments during a specified period. It represents the financial capacity an organization has to undertake other activities or meet other obligations within a particular time period. A risk management professional can use this statement to determine the excess resources the organization may have available in order to cover retained accidental losses throughout a time period.

Other Records and Documents

Every record and document that an organization possesses, even correspondence and internal memos, might contain valuable information about its loss exposures. Therefore, a risk management professional should not confine the search for loss exposures only to the organization's financial statements and supporting records. On the other hand, it is not feasible to examine every document produced or received by the organization. Risk management practice requires a systematic approach to identifying and examining those records and documents most likely to reveal changes in loss exposures.

For example, the risk management department should routinely receive and review the minutes of a private organization's board of directors, executive committee, or other senior management group. For a public entity, those documents could include the entity's charter; bylaws; proclamations; orders; and minutes of committee meetings of governing councils, commissions, or boards. Those minutes, or even memoranda exchanged among senior executives or officials, can keep risk management professionals advised of the organization's plans and enable them to recognize potential risk management problems in implementing those plans.

Risk management personnel should also see, and perhaps be given the power of prior approval over, all substantial contracts for sales or purchases involving more than a specified amount. Supervision of these contracts also helps the risk management professional stay abreast of property acquisitions and disposals and of dealings with large suppliers or customers. In addition, any plans or drawings for architectural or engineering changes in the organization's buildings, machinery, work flow, office layouts, and the like should be reviewed for their risk management implications. All of these documents can reveal significant changes in loss exposures.

In short, the risk management department should strive to participate in, or receive the minutes of, as many senior management committees as possible to keep risk management professionals informed on all activities and departments within an organization. The goal is to know the organization as fully as possible in order to remain aware of its loss exposures and to remind operating managers of their continuing responsibilities to help monitor the loss exposures arising from the operations they manage.

In addition to internally generated records and documents, risk management professionals may use relevant information from external sources. For example, many industries are served by associations that gather operational data that can be used for benchmarking, as well as data on the hazard risks that member companies face. An association of heavy equipment operators, for example, may offer operator training, classes on safe excavations, and publications, such as guides to comply with Occupational Safety and Health Administration (OSHA) regulations.

Flowcharts and Organizational Charts

Flowchart
A diagram that graphically and sequentially depicts the activities of a particular organization or process.

Flowcharts and organizational charts are another method of identifying loss exposures. A **flowchart** is a diagram that graphically and sequentially depicts the activities of a particular organization or process. A risk management professional can use a flowchart to identify the consequences of an accidental loss on a particular process. For example, a risk management professional for a winery might construct the flowchart shown in Exhibit 2-1 to help identify key processes. One of the loss exposures illustrated by this flowchart is that the winery may not be able to process grapes if the refrigeration systems for either the fermenting or holding tanks were to fail. System failures such as these may cause the winery to miss an entire season.

EXHIBIT 2-1

Flowchart for Winery

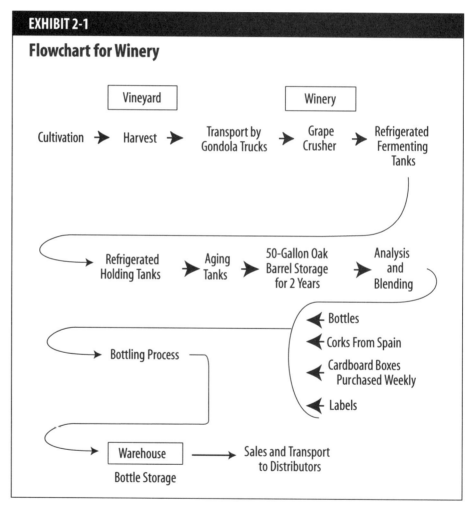

As with all other information sources, flowcharts have their strengths and weaknesses. The major strength of flowcharts is that they add another dimension to loss exposure identification by highlighting interdependencies within an organization and with the organization's suppliers and customers. The weakness of flowcharts is that they are process-oriented and do not typically indicate the loss frequency (how many losses that occur) and loss severity (how bad a loss is when it does occur) in each step of the process. Because of

this weakness, flowcharts should be used in conjunction with other information sources for loss exposure identification and analysis.

A risk management professional can use organizational charts to identify
key decision makers within an organization and the possible effect on the
organization if one or more of these decision makers were incapacitated. An
organizational chart is a graphical depiction of an organization's management
structure. Risk management professionals may also use organizational charts to
identify key employees who are critical to the ongoing success of the organization. For example, a pharmaceutical company's drug development may depend
on only a few, irreplaceable scientists.

Organizational chart
A graphical depiction of an
organization's management
structure.

Personal Inspections

Some loss exposures are apparent only after inspecting the premises involved.
A personal inspection is a method of identifying loss exposures that involves
a first-hand assessment of the organization's critical locations, as well as key
suppliers and customers. During a personal inspection, a risk management professional can become better acquainted with how the organization operates.
Such inspections may reveal loss exposures that were otherwise unidentified,
as well as uncover opportunities to use risk control techniques that were not
previously apparent. In addition, the risk management professional has the
opportunity to talk with employees and managers about untreated loss exposures that they have identified, and to listen to their concerns about safety.
Establishing relationships throughout the organization while conducting
personal inspections improves the likelihood that others in the organization
will support existing and future risk management initiatives aimed at reducing
the risk associated with accidental loss.

Expertise Within and Beyond the Organization

An organization's risk management professional should have a working knowledge
of all of the diverse loss exposures that the organization faces. To complement this
broad knowledge of the organization, the risk management professional should
be able to access the specialized knowledge of experts both inside and outside the
organization on its particular loss exposures.

Organizations usually employ operational experts who are responsible, in
part, for operational success. These experts may be asked to consider the risk
management implications of an activity, process, or product. Risk management
professionals also have access to a variety of risk management experts who
can perform specialized tasks such as conducting claim audits and developing
safety programs. Sometimes the risk management professional needs the professional services of others, such as lawyers and accountants. For example, the
risk management professional might hire a lawyer to conduct an audit review
of the organization's compliance with local, state, and federal statutes.

Finally, if an organization does not have a dedicated risk management department, then as well as relying on expertise within the organization and/or the
professional services of others, the organization may want to periodically hire
risk management consultants.

STEP TWO: ANALYZING LOSS EXPOSURES

Following, and sometimes concurrent with, identifying a loss exposure, the risk management professional analyzes the loss exposure by estimating the likely significance of possible losses. Together, identifying and analyzing loss exposures are probably the most important steps in the risk management process because only a properly identified and analyzed loss exposure can be appropriately managed. Often the best ways to manage a loss exposure become immediately apparent once it has been identified and analyzed. Therefore, the balance of the risk management process flows from identification and analysis.

A risk management professional analyzes loss exposures along the following five dimensions:

1. Loss frequency: the number of losses (such as losses from fires, auto accidents, liability claims) within a specific period
2. Loss severity: the amount, in dollars, of a loss for a specific occurrence
3. Total dollar losses: the total dollar amount of losses for all occurrences during a specific period
4. Timing: when losses occur and when loss payments are made
5. Data credibility: the confidence that can be placed on available data to indicate future losses

Reviewing these dimensions enables a risk management professional to develop loss projections and prioritize loss exposures so that management resources can be properly allocated. The credibility of these projections is critical to the risk evaluation. The greater the credibility (confidence) in the projection, the better the decisions will be about handling loss exposures.

Loss Frequency

Loss frequency
The number of losses that occur within a specified period.

Loss frequency is the number of losses—such as losses from fires, thefts, and floods—that occur within a specified period. The relative frequency is the number of losses that occur within a given time relative to the number of exposure units, for example, the number of buildings or cars. With one exposure unit, loss frequency and relative frequency are the same. For example, for one building (exposure unit) both the loss frequency and the relative frequency of theft losses may be three per year. The loss frequency and relative frequency of the fire losses may be one every ten years (1/10 or 0.10 per year), while the loss frequency and relative frequency of flood losses might be one every hundred years (1/100 or 0.01 per year).

Alternatively, a delivery company may have 50 auto accidents in a given year, but have 5,000 vehicles on the road for the year. The delivery company's loss frequency would be 50 per year, but its relative frequency would be 50/5,000 or 0.01 per year per vehicle. Relative frequency can often be estimated based on past experience (if available).

Loss frequency can be predictable with a high degree of confidence for some loss exposures in large organizations. This degree of confidence can be attained because of the **law of large numbers**, which is a mathematical principle stating that when the number of similar independent exposure units increases, the relative accuracy of predictions about future outcomes (such as losses) based on these exposure units also increases. For example, an Internet-based retailer that ships thousands of packages each day probably can more accurately project the number of annual transit losses, based on past experience and adjusted for any expected changes in future conditions, than can a local retail store that only ships a few hundred packages a year. However, even most large organizations do not have enough exposure units to accurately project low-frequency, high-severity events such as natural catastrophes.

Law of large numbers
A mathematical principle stating that when the number of similar independent exposure units increases, the relative accuracy of predictions about future outcomes based on these exposure units also increases.

Loss Severity

Loss severity is the amount of loss, typically measured in dollars, for a loss that has occurred. Loss severity analysis enables the risk management professional to assess how serious a loss might be. Although typically loss severity is more difficult to predict than loss frequency, loss severity analysis should enable a risk management professional to answer questions such as the following: How much of a building could be damaged in a single fire? How long before operations can resume after a fire? What is the maximum possible loss that may occur?

Loss severity
The amount of loss, typically measured in dollars, for a loss that has occurred.

Maximum Possible Loss (MPL)

Maximum possible loss (MPL) (also called the amount subject) is an estimate of the largest possible loss that might occur. The MPL amount is usually estimated for each location and for a specific cause of loss. For example, an organization may have $10 million in real and personal property at one location. Its MPL for that location would likely be $10 million for most causes of loss.

Maximum possible loss (MPL)
An estimate of the largest possible loss that might occur.

MPL is a loss severity measure that is most often used when analyzing property loss exposures, rather than liability loss exposures. Risk management professionals can make MPL estimates of liability loss exposures, but doing so accurately is problematic. Unlike property loss exposures, which have relatively certain values, liability loss exposures are subject to court determinations of values, which are inherently difficult to predict.

Probable Maximum Loss (PML)

Probable maximum loss (PML) is the value of the largest loss that is likely to occur. PML is typically much less than the value of the MPL. In the case of fire damage to a building or its contents, while the MPL is usually the total value of the building and contents, the PML is significantly less because of the fire reduction effects of sprinkler systems and fire fighting capabilities of the local fire department.

Probable maximum loss (PML)
The value of the largest loss that is likely to occur.

The PML loss can be estimated based on an organization's own experience or on other organizations' experience. If statistical data are available, it may be useful to assume that the PML is close to average past losses. Although risk management professionals need to be cognizant of the MPLs associated with the organization's loss exposures, they often find that PML is a more useful value than MPL when estimating potential loss severity.

Loss Frequency and Loss Severity Interaction

To analyze the significance of a particular loss exposure, a risk management professional must consider the interaction of loss frequency and loss severity. One way to analyze the possible combinations of loss frequency and loss severity is through a method called the Prouty approach, which was developed by Richard Prouty, a corporate risk manager. The **Prouty approach** is a risk exposure analysis method that suggests how to treat loss exposures by classifying loss frequency and loss severity into broad categories. As shown in Exhibit 2-2, there are four broad categories of loss frequency and three broad categories of loss severity. The four categories of loss frequency are as follows:

1. Almost nil: extremely unlikely to happen; virtually no possibility
2. Slight: could happen but is not likely to happen
3. Moderate: happens occasionally
4. Definite: happens regularly

The three categories of loss severity, which include risk treatment alternatives, are as follows:

1. Slight: organization can readily retain each loss
2. Significant: organization cannot retain the entire loss, some part of which must be financed
3. Severe: organization must finance virtually all of the loss or endanger its survival

Although these broad categories of loss frequency and loss severity are subjective, they provide the risk management professional with a means of justifying the priority that they believe should be placed on the various loss exposures confronting the organization and with a means of providing risk treatment suggestions.

Loss frequency and loss severity tend to be inversely related for any given loss exposure. The more severe a loss tends to be, the less frequently it tends to occur and vice versa. Activities with losses that almost definitely will occur but that are of low value tend to be accounted for in the annual budget. Consequently, such activities need not be avoided. At the other extreme, an activity that happens frequently and would generate intolerable loss severity is typically avoided because the activity is too risky to undertake. Therefore, most risk management decisions concern loss exposures for which individual losses, while tolerable, tend to be either significant or severe and have a moderate, slight, or almost nil chance of occurring.

Prouty approach
A risk exposure analysis method that suggests how to treat loss exposures by classifying loss frequency and loss severity into broad categories.

EXHIBIT 2-2

The Prouty Approach

		Loss Frequency			
		Almost Nil	Slight	Moderate	Definite
Loss Severity	Severe	Transfer	Reduce or prevent	Reduce or prevent	Avoid
	Significant	Retain	Transfer	Reduce or prevent	Avoid
	Slight	Retain	Transfer	Prevent	Prevent

A given loss exposure may generate serious negative financial consequences because of either a high-severity individual loss or because of high-frequency, low-severity losses that aggregate to a substantial total. Although it may be tempting to focus on infrequent, high value loss exposures, such as a major fire, it is important not to underestimate the cumulative effect of smaller, more routine loss exposures. For example, many retail organizations suffer greater total losses through shoplifting or pilferage, which occur daily, than through a large fire that might occur every twenty years. Therefore, minor, more frequent losses usually deserve as much risk management attention as do large individual losses.

Total Dollar Losses

When analyzing loss exposures, the risk management professional will typically review losses over a specific time period. However, although loss frequency is measured with reference to a specified period, loss severity is measured according to a particular occurrence. Therefore, the risk management professional will also need to consider total dollar losses. Total dollar losses are the total dollar amount of losses for all occurrences during a specified period. These total dollar losses can be determined either by summing loss amounts for the period or by multiplying loss frequency by average loss severity. Alternatively, future total dollar losses can be estimated by multiplying future loss frequency by future average loss severity. Maximum possible loss can be estimated as well by assuming both high frequency and the worst possible severity. For example, the risk management professional may project total dollar losses for the next period and from that estimate the MPL from an intense earthquake that might happen once every 500 years.

Timing

To effectively analyze loss exposures, the risk management professional must also consider timing; that is, not only when losses are likely to occur, but also when payments for those losses are likely to be made. Some losses, such as earthquake losses, have an equal chance of occurring at any time during the calendar year or business cycle, while others, such as hurricane or flood losses, have a higher chance of occurring during certain seasons.

Funds to pay for property losses are generally disbursed relatively soon after the losses occur. In contrast, payments for liability losses can be delayed depending on when the adverse event occurs, when the occurrence is recognized, how long any litigation lasts, and when loss payment is actually made. Disability claims may be paid over an extended time period. In some cases, especially those involving environmental loss exposures or health risks, the delay can span several decades. The ongoing litigation of asbestos-related claims includes claims for injuries that occurred in the 1940s and 1950s and that remain unsettled.

Data Credibility

The term data credibility is used in risk management to mean the level of confidence that available data are accurate indicators of future losses. After analyzing a loss exposure by examining loss frequency, loss severity, total dollar losses, and timing, a risk management professional then evaluates the credibility of those data.

The pattern shown in Exhibit 2-3 illustrates one organization's expected workers' compensation losses over a ten-year period, assuming steady production and employment. The risk management professional may project that average losses during the coming years would fall along the line labeled "projected" and that the annual probable maximum losses would fall along the line labeled "maximum." Probable minimum loss levels may also be projected as shown on the "minimum" line. If such projections can be made with a high degree of confidence, actual losses would be expected to follow the pattern of the "actual" line on the graph, deviating from the average from one year to the next but in no case exceeding the maximum or falling below the minimum. Because the organization faces little uncertainty, it may choose to retain these losses instead of insuring them.

Another example is outlined in Exhibit 2-4. This exhibit shows products liability claims experienced by an organization for one of its products over a ten-year period. A few losses usually occur each year. In the early part of year 3, almost no losses occurred, while in Year 7 at least one major loss occurred. Risk management professionals must recognize that possibilities exist for substantial losses above the normal loss levels. As such, it may be imprudent for the organization to finance such losses out of its operating budget.

Having identified and analyzed loss exposures, the risk management professional may want to implement risk management measures. It is therefore important to examine the feasibility of risk management techniques.

EXHIBIT 2-3

Projected Losses Versus Actual Losses Within Minimum and Maximum Bounds

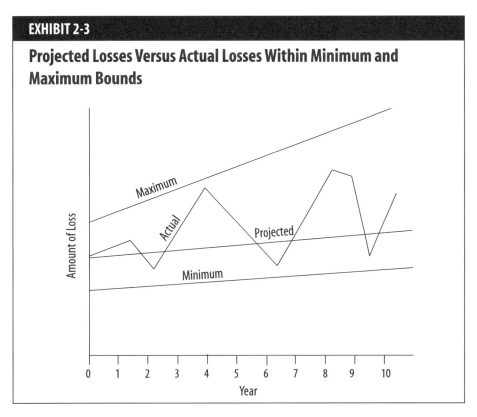

EXHIBIT 2-4

Projected Losses Versus Actual Losses With Minimum and Maximum Bounds Exceeded

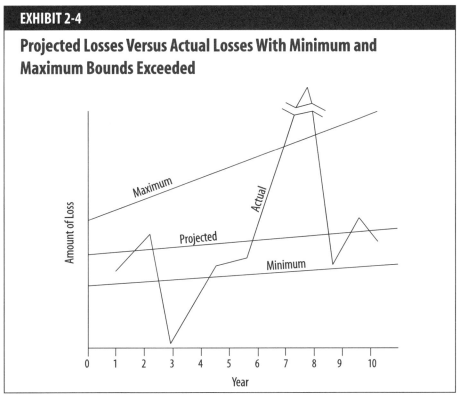

STEP THREE: EXAMINING THE FEASIBILITY OF RISK MANAGEMENT TECHNIQUES

Risk management involves preventing losses before they occur or reducing losses that do occur (risk control) as well as paying for those losses that have occurred (risk financing). This section briefly discusses the fundamental risk control and risk financing techniques for accidental loss exposures. Exhibit 2-5 shows the risk management techniques available for treating accidental loss exposures.

Risk Control Techniques

Risk control
A conscious act or decision not to act that reduces the frequency and severity of losses or makes losses more predictable.

Risk control is a conscious act or decision not to act that reduces the frequency and severity of losses or makes losses more predictable. Risk control techniques include the following:

- Avoidance
- Loss prevention
- Loss reduction
- Separation, duplication, and diversification

Avoidance

Avoidance
A risk control technique that involves ceasing or never undertaking an activity so that the possibility of a future loss occurring from that activity is eliminated.

Avoidance is a risk control technique that involves ceasing or never undertaking an activity so that the possibility of a future loss occurring is eliminated. While avoidance is very effective it is not always practical because the losses in question often arise from activities and circumstances that are fundamental to an organization's goals. For example, the manufacturers of sporting equipment, including bicycle helmets, may determine that the legal liability associated with bicycle helmets is too great relative to the financial rewards available in that marketplace. However, if bicycle helmets are the primary source of revenue for that manufacturer, withdrawing from that market may not be an option.

Avoidance can be called proactive avoidance when the organization decides not to incur a loss exposure in the first place, or it can be called abandonment when the organization decides to eliminate a loss exposure that already exists. An example of proactive avoidance is a medical student choosing not to become an obstetrician because he or she wants to avoid the large professional liability (malpractice) claims associated with that field of the medical profession. An example of abandonment is a manufacturer of child car seats discontinuing this product because of claims for injuries associated with their use.

Avoidance through abandonment is not as effective a risk control technique as proactive avoidance because the liability loss exposure might remain. For example, a child car seat manufacturer continues to be subject to products liability claims arising out of defective seats already sold and in use.

EXHIBIT 2-5

Risk Management Techniques

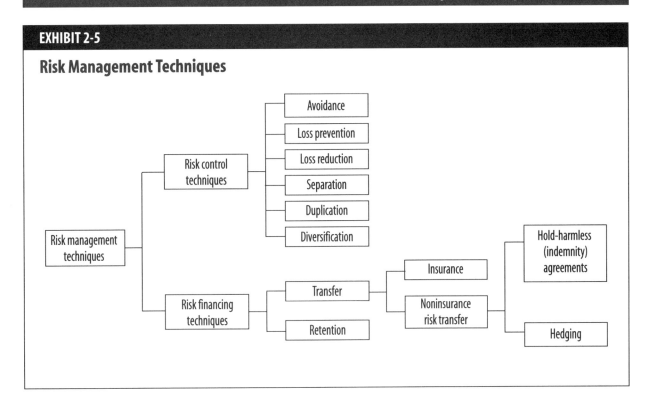

As avoidance is usually not a practical option (because it precludes the organization from enjoying the positive results obtained from avoided activities or products), the risk management professional will want to consider alternative risk control techniques.

Loss Prevention

Loss prevention is a risk control technique that reduces the frequency of a particular loss. For example, an organization could try to prevent employee injury by adding guards to machinery to prevent physical contact with cutting edges, providing eye protection to prevent injury from dust and other foreign particles, or adding air filtration systems to keep the air from becoming contaminated. Unlike avoidance, loss prevention does not completely prevent losses from occurring—it simply reduces the frequency of losses occurring. Therefore, the organization is still exposed to loss and the risk management professional needs to manage these potential loss exposures.

Loss prevention
A risk control technique that reduces the frequency of a particular loss.

Loss Reduction

Loss reduction is a risk control technique that reduces the severity of a particular loss. For example, a shopping mall could reduce its net income loss after a fire by incurring some additional expenses to shorten the amount of time it takes to repair the damage and reopen the mall. The shopping mall can hire a contractor who will have crews work around the clock until repairs are completed. This can reduce the net income loss if the reduction in net

Loss reduction
A risk control technique that reduces the severity of a particular loss.

income losses by reopening the mall sooner outweighs the additional expenses of paying the contractors' work crews additional compensation for working around the clock. The shopping mall owner may also advertise in local newspapers to inform the public of the mall's recovery progress and planned reopening date.

Separation, Duplication, and Diversification

Separation
A risk control technique that disperses a particular asset or activity over several locations and regularly relies on that asset or activity as a part of the organization's working resources.

Separation is a risk control technique that disperses a particular asset or activity over several locations and regularly relies on that asset or activity as a part of the organization's working resources. For example, an organization may store inventory in several warehouses so that a fire in one warehouse would not affect all inventory. Another example of separation is using several suppliers for raw material purchases so that a distribution problem with one supplier will not cut off all supplies of raw materials. Using multiple suppliers may also enable the organization to gain business advantages, such as competitive pricing when purchasing in addition to the risk control benefit derived.

Duplication
A risk control technique that uses backups, spares, or copies of critical property, information, or capabilities and keeps them in reserve.

Duplication is a risk control technique that uses backups, spares, or copies of critical property, information, or capabilities and keeps them in reserve. For example, an organization may make copies of key documents or information, which can be stored at another location. Another example of duplication is an organization maintaining an inventory of spare parts for critical equipment.

The distinction between separation and duplication is how often the organization will be relying on the asset or activity. If the asset or activity is routinely relied upon as a working resource, the risk control technique is separation. If the asset or activity is only to be used in emergency situations, it is duplication. Usually, simultaneously operating several identical warehouses strictly for risk management reasons would not be cost-effective. However, a business may also have other reasons for such an approach. For example, rather than have a single warehouse in Philadelphia, a produce wholesaler may operate matching warehouses in Baltimore and New York, reducing the distance between the warehouses and local stores and restaurants. If it becomes necessary, one of these warehouses could temporarily fill orders in more than one area, despite some extra transportation expense.

Diversification
A risk control technique that spreads loss exposures over numerous projects, products, markets, or regions.

Diversification is a risk control technique that spreads loss exposures over numerous projects, products, markets, or regions. Diversification closely resembles separation but is more commonly applied to managing business risks than risks resulting in accidental losses. As with many other risk control techniques, diversification would not likely be selected as a risk management technique unless there was some other business reason to do so. For example, businesses that are engaged in diversified products or services or that serve a variety of customers may do so for business reasons, but they are also achieving diversification of loss exposures.

Organizations also use diversification when they invest their assets among a mix of stocks and bonds from companies in different industry sectors. For example, an organization may diversify investments by purchasing stock in a bank and a pharmaceutical manufacturer. Because those are unrelated industries, the organization hopes that any losses in one stock will be more than offset by profits in another.

Separation, duplication, and diversification risk control techniques all increase the number of loss exposures for an organization. The increase in loss exposures typically will increase the frequency of loss that the organization will suffer. However, each of these risk control techniques reduces the severity of loss associated with any one of the loss exposures. The net result of the increase in the number of loss exposures and reduction in severity per loss exposure is that losses tend to be more predictable, especially if the number of exposure units is large enough to apply the law of large numbers.

Risk Financing Techniques

In examining the feasibility of risk management alternatives, the risk management professional will consider risk financing as well as risk control. **Risk financing** is a conscious act or decision not to act that generates the funds to pay for losses or offset the variability in cash flows that may occur. Risk financing techniques can be classified into the following two groups:

Risk financing
A conscious act or decision not to act that generates the funds to pay for losses or offset the variability in cash flows that may occur.

1. Transfer, which includes insurance and noninsurance techniques to shift the financial consequences of loss to another party
2. Retention, which involves absorbing the loss by generating funds within the organization to pay for the loss

Risk financing techniques are not necessarily used in isolation. Many techniques involve elements of both retention and transfer. For example, insurance with a deductible comprises retention of the deductible amount and transfer of losses above the deductible.

Transfer

Transfer involves the transfer of risk through insurance and noninsurance techniques to shift the financial consequences of loss to another party. Noninsurance techniques used to transfer risk include hold-harmless agreements and hedging.

Insurance is a risk financing technique that transfers the potential financial consequences of certain specified loss exposures from the insured to the insurer. The insurance buyer substitutes a small certain financial cost, the insurance premium, for the possibility of a large uncertain financial loss, which would be paid by the insurer. Although insurance is only one approach to risk financing, it is a vital component of a risk management program.

Insurance
A risk financing technique that transfers the potential financial consequences of certain specified loss exposures from the insured to the insurer.

Insurance is essentially a funded risk transfer. By accepting a premium, the insurer agrees to pay for all the organization's losses that are covered by the insurance contract. The insurer also agrees to provide necessary services, such as claim handling and defense of liability claims.

Noninsurance risk transfer
A risk financing technique that transfers all or part of the financial consequences of loss to another party, other than an insurer.

Hold-harmless agreement
A contract under which one party (the indemnitor) agrees to assume the liability of a second party (the indemnitee).

Noninsurance risk transfer is a risk financing technique that transfers all or part of the financial consequences of loss to another party, other than an insurer. Contracts that are not insurance contracts but that transfer loss exposures are therefore called noninsurance risk transfers. Some contracts deal solely with the responsibility for losses arising out of a particular relationship or activity. Under these contracts, which are known as **hold-harmless agreements** (also called indemnity agreements), one party (the indemnitor) agrees to assume the liability of a second party (the indemnitee). Exhibit 2-6 shows a hold-harmless agreement that might be included in a lease.

EXHIBIT 2-6

Hold-Harmless Agreement for Use in a Lease

To the fullest extent permitted by law, the lessee shall indemnify, defend and hold harmless the lessor, agents and employees of the lessor, from and against all claims arising out of or resulting from the leased premises.

Hedging
A financial transaction in which one asset is held to offset the risk associated with another asset.

Hedging is also considered a noninsurance risk transfer technique. **Hedging** is a financial transaction in which one asset is held to offset the risk associated with another asset. Hedging often involves business risk rather than hazard risk.

Futures contract
An agreement to buy or sell a commodity or security at a future date at a price that is fixed at the time of the agreement.

Hedging is practical when it is used to offset loss exposures to which one is naturally, voluntarily, or inevitably exposed. For example, a newspaper publisher faces the loss exposure of newsprint price variability. To offset this loss exposure, the publisher might enter into a futures contract with its paper supplier to purchase a fixed quantity of newsprint over the coming year at a pre-agreed price. A **futures contract** is an agreement to buy or sell a commodity or security at a future date at a price that is fixed at the time of the agreement. If the market price of paper increases over the next year, the newspaper publisher will save money by buying paper below the prevailing price. If the market price drops, the newspaper publisher will pay more than the prevailing price for its paper. Either way, the newspaper publisher's loss exposure is reduced because the variability in the newsprint's cost is eliminated from the perspective of the newspaper publisher. The same can be said for the paper supplier. Whether the paper supplier would have made more money or less money depends on what the prevailing market price of paper turns out to be, but the paper supplier was able to reduce the variability by entering into the futures contract.

Retention
A risk financing technique that involves assumption of risk in which losses are retained by generating funds within the organization to pay for the losses.

Retention

Retention is a risk financing technique that involves assumption of risk in which losses are retained by generating funds within the organization to pay for the losses. Because retention can be the most economic risk financing technique available, it is sometimes preferred even when insurance or non-insurance risk transfer is available. Retention can also be the risk financing technique of last resort; the financial burden of any losses that cannot be insured or otherwise transferred *must* be retained.

Retention can be planned or unplanned; complete or partial; or funded or unfunded.

- Planned retention is a deliberate assumption of a loss exposure (and any consequential losses) that has been identified and analyzed. Planned retention may be chosen because it is most cost-effective, because it is most convenient, or because no other alternatives are available.

- Unplanned retention is the inadvertent assumption of a loss exposure (and any consequential losses) because the loss exposure has not been identified or accurately analyzed. For example, many people inadvertently retain flood losses because they do not anticipate that the rains associated with the remnants of hurricanes will endanger their property.

- Complete retention is the assumption of the full cost of any loss that is retained by the organization.

- Partial retention is the assumption of a portion of the cost of a loss by the organization and the transfer of the remaining portion.

- Funded retention is the pre-loss arrangement to ensure that funding is available post-loss to pay for losses that do occur.

- Unfunded retention is the lack of advance funding for losses that do occur.

Three general methods can be used to pay for (fund) retained losses: (1) pre-loss funding, (2) current-loss funding, and (3) post-loss funding.

With **pre-loss funding**, the money to fund retained losses is set aside in advance. The principal advantage of pre-loss funding is that the money needed to fund losses can be saved over several budget periods. The principal disadvantage is that it ties up money that could otherwise be used by the organization and consequently has an opportunity cost for the organization. The reduction of available financial resources keeps pre-loss funding from being widely used except when an organization forms a captive insurer, which is a subsidiary formed to insure the loss exposures of its parents and affiliates.

With **current-loss funding**, money to fund retained losses is provided at the time of the loss or immediately after it. Current-loss funding is the most popular and often the least expensive form of funding. Its main advantage is that it does not tie up funds before they are actually needed. Its principal disadvantage is that there may not be enough money in the current budget to cover the loss and satisfy other cash flow needs.

With **post-loss funding**, the organization pays for its retained losses sometime after losses occur, using borrowing (or some other method of raising additional capital) in the meantime. For example, a building owner may have to take out a mortgage to fund the reconstruction of a damaged uninsured building. The mortgage would be the post-loss funding instrument.

Pre-loss funding
A funded retention arrangement under which money to fund losses is set aside in advance.

Current-loss funding
A funded retention arrangement under which money to fund retained losses is provided at the time of the loss or immediately after it.

Post-loss funding
A funded retention arrangement under which the organization pays for its retained losses sometime after losses occur, using borrowing (or some other method of raising additional capital) in the meantime.

Risk Control and Risk Financing Techniques Applied to Business Risks

As well as being used for hazard risks, both risk control and risk financing techniques have clear applications to business risks—that is, speculative losses that arise from business decisions, changes in technology, customer preferences, or shifting economic conditions. The following examples illustrate these applications:

- Business risk losses can be *avoided* by halting, or by never engaging in, a particular business activity that could lead to such losses.

- Business risk losses can be *prevented* (made less frequent) by using caution in selecting favorable circumstances for engaging in a particular business activity.

- Business risk losses can be *reduced* (made less severe) by limiting an organization's resources committed to a particularly risky project.

- Business risk losses can be *diversified* by participating in numerous projects, products, markets, or regions so that the organization's overall profitability or operating efficiency approaches the average profitability or efficiency of all of these diversified activities.

- Business risk losses can be *transferred* by subcontracting to another organization for a favorable fixed price an activity that an organization may or may not be able to perform profitably. An organization can use noninsurance contractual transfer to limit its potential business losses from that activity.

- Business risk losses can be *retained* by paying for (or absorbing as reduced profits or lowered surpluses) speculative business losses.

- Business risk losses can be *financed* by inserting provisions into business contracts with suppliers, customers, or joint venturers. This is, in effect, a noninsurance transfer for the benefit of the transferring organization that wants to avoid the financial burden of some business risks. The other contracting parties agree to reimburse the transferring organization for specified types of business losses if, for example, an inventory of merchandise does not prove as popular as expected or the price of a particular raw material changes.

Insurance, which is one of the most popular risk financing techniques for exposures to accidental losses, typically is not appropriate for protecting against losses from business risks. By definition, business risks have both a potential for gain as well as a potential for loss. If an organization was able to purchase insurance to remove the potential for loss, all that remains is the potential for gain. In financial terms, this is arbitrage, gaining reward without assuming risk. In properly functioning markets, arbitrage does not exist. That is, it is not possible for an organization to gain reward (profits) without assuming the potential losses associated with the business risk.

In insurance markets, the premium that an insurer would charge to guarantee an insured's profit on a business venture would actually be greater than the insured's expected profit (expected profit plus expenses and the insurer's profit margin), therefore removing any incentive to undertake the business venture.

To make a profit (or generate a surplus) an organization or individual must be willing to tolerate the accompanying potential losses by exposing itself to business risks.

There are advantages to using post-loss funding, including the opportunity to pay the cost of retained losses over several years instead of all at once, and only having to use the amount needed to pay for retained losses. However, post-loss funding also has several disadvantages. The organization using post-loss funding must pay interest on the borrowings. In addition, the loss event that produces the need to borrow may also reduce the organization's credit-worthiness, therefore increasing the loan's cost. Although this disadvantage can be overcome by making pre-loss arrangements for a credit guarantee, that guarantee involves a fee. Also, guaranteeing post-loss credit may reduce the organization's capacity to borrow pre-loss funds that can be used for business operations.

STEP FOUR: SELECTING THE APPROPRIATE RISK MANAGEMENT TECHNIQUES

After a risk management professional systematically considers the feasibility of applying various risk control and risk financing techniques to particular loss exposures, the next step is to establish and apply criteria to select the appropriate risk management techniques that support the organization's goals. The selection is based on both quantitative financial considerations and qualitative nonfinancial considerations.

Selecting the appropriate risk management technique, or combination of techniques as is more often the case, involves two processes. The first is forecasting the effects that the available risk management techniques are likely to have on the organization's ability to fulfill its goals and the costs of those techniques. The second is defining and applying selection criteria that measure how well each alternative risk management technique contributes financially and nonfinancially to organizational goals.

Forecasts as the Basis for Selection

The selection of the appropriate risk management techniques requires an in-depth understanding of the loss exposures to be managed and of the benefits and costs of each alternative technique. Therefore, determining the effects of available risk management techniques on an organization's ability to fulfill its goals involves three different forecasts: (1) a forecast of the frequency and severity of the future losses; (2) a forecast of the effects that various risk control and risk financing techniques are likely to have on the frequency, severity, and predictability of future losses; and (3) a forecast of the costs of these techniques. These forecasts can then be reviewed against available risk management techniques in light of the financial and nonfinancial considerations.

Selection Criteria

Risk management techniques are chosen based on economy and effectiveness, that is, both financial and nonfinancial considerations. A technique is economical if it is the least expensive of the possible effective techniques. For all organizations, risk management costs (potential loss exposures and the cost of possible risk management techniques) must be considered. Every organization must decide the extent to which organizational resources will be used for risk management.

A technique is effective if it enables an organization to achieve desired goals. For example, public entities typically select risk management techniques based on criteria such as the need to maintain certain essential public services and to perform nondelegable governmental functions. Alternatively, an organization may be able to tolerate temporary, partial shutdowns of parts of its facilities but would place high priority on risk management techniques that allow it to comply with all applicable regulations, to prevent regulators from restricting its operations.

The selected technique must be practical for the organization to implement. Some risk management techniques, such as forming a captive insurer, would not be viable for every organization. When selecting techniques, a risk management professional should take account of both financial and nonfinancial considerations.

Financial Considerations

Most private profit-seeking organizations choose risk management techniques by financial criteria; that is, they choose techniques with the greatest positive (or least negative) effect on the organization's value or rate of return.

Also, as with most business decisions about organizational resources, risk management technique selection has cash flow implications. By reducing losses, risk control techniques reduce presumed cash outflows to pay for these losses, but at the same time require cash outflows for implementation. Risk financing techniques often require cash outflows (such as to pay insurance premiums). However, those techniques also reduce other cash outflows (required to pay retained losses) and might even generate cash inflows (for example, investment income from funded reserves). These cash flows must also be considered in evaluating an asset's or activity's rate of return.

Public entities and other not-for-profit organizations, for which profitability is not a directly relevant goal, pursue operating efficiency. Operating efficiency seeks the maximum output for a given resource or attainment of a given target output at minimum cost. Such a goal is as crucial for public and not-for-profit organizations as it is for for-profit ones.

Nonfinancial Considerations

An organization's nonfinancial goals can constrain its financial goals in some respects, leading to the selection of risk management techniques that, while best for that organization in some regards, may be inconsistent with its rate-of-return goal.

For example, a private, family-owned organization may emphasize stability of earnings over time, rather than maximum earnings in any given time period. Consequently, the organization may pay a significant amount for loss prevention devices or safety practices rather than absorb the often minor losses that these devices or practices are designed to prevent. For similar reasons, this private, family-owned organization may be likely to insure against losses that, from a rate-of-return standpoint, it would be better to retain.

Legal and social responsibility goals may impose additional constraints that must be considered in selecting risk management techniques. A risk management program must comply with applicable laws and observe social responsibility concerns. For a private organization, these constraints are likely to compromise the financial goals that a risk management program might otherwise be able to achieve.

Once the appropriate risk management techniques have been selected, the next step in the risk management process is implementing the selected risk management techniques.

STEP FIVE: IMPLEMENTING THE SELECTED RISK MANAGEMENT TECHNIQUES

A risk management program must be planned and implemented so that every risk management technique an organization chooses is one that the organization can successfully implement. Therefore, a risk management professional must determine whether technical and managerial decisions will support a given technique.

Technical Decisions

Once a risk management technique has been selected, risk management professionals must make technical decisions about how to implement it. For example, if an organization decides to insure a particular loss exposure, the risk management professional must select an appropriate insurer, set proper limits and deductibles, and negotiate the purchase of that insurance. These decisions are typically within the direct authority of an organization's senior risk management professional. Nevertheless, the senior risk management professional should be prepared to explain and justify these technical decisions to other managers. Reference to the selection process may be useful in providing explanations.

Managerial Decisions

The persons who are responsible for implementing risk management decisions are not typically subject to the line authority of an organization's senior risk management professional. For example, the senior risk management professional will not have managerial authority over the employees who must integrate risk control techniques into the organization's procedures or production processes. When the senior risk management professional works with others outside his or her direct authority, the ability to influence and persuade becomes critical. Working cooperatively with others requires the senior risk management professional to be alert to the organization's needs and the needs of its separate departments and employees.

STEP SIX: MONITORING RESULTS AND REVISING THE RISK MANAGEMENT PROGRAM

The first five steps of the risk management process create and implement a risk management program. The last of the six steps—monitoring results and revising the risk management program—takes place once the program is in place. The ongoing risk management program requires constant attention to both activities and results. Activity and results standards, discussed previously, serve as a basis for monitoring the risk management program.

Revisions to the risk management program may be required for a variety of reasons, including any of the following:

- New loss exposures have developed. For example, the organization may be manufacturing new products or conducting operations at new locations.

- Existing loss exposures have become significant. For example, a product defect might be uncovered, leading to greater liability exposure.

- Different risk management techniques have become more appropriate. For example, a significant increase in insurance premiums may make a retention program feasible.

If a revision is required, repeating some or all of the risk management process is necessary. Any change in loss exposures must be identified and analyzed. If a change in risk management technique is required, then the feasibility of alternative techniques must be reviewed and alternative techniques must be selected and implemented.

SUMMARY

The six steps in the risk management process are as follows:

1. Identifying loss exposures
2. Analyzing loss exposures
3. Examining the feasibility of risk management techniques
4. Selecting the appropriate risk management techniques
5. Implementing the selected risk management techniques
6. Monitoring results and revising the risk management program

Step one, identifying loss exposures, requires the risk management professional to consider all possible loss exposures that might affect the organization. A loss exposure is any condition that presents a possibility of loss, whether or not an actual loss occurs. Risk management professionals categorize loss exposures as one of the following types:

- *Property loss exposure.* A condition that presents the possibility that a person or organization will sustain a loss resulting from the damage, including the destruction, taking, or loss of use, of property in which that person or organization has a financial interest.

- *Liability loss exposure.* A condition that presents the possibility that a person or organization will sustain a loss resulting from a claim alleging a person's or an organization's legal responsibility for property damage or bodily injury suffered by another party.

- *Personnel loss exposure.* A condition that presents the possibility of loss caused by a person's death, disability, retirement, or resignation that deprives an organization of the person's special skill or knowledge that the organization cannot readily replace.

- *Net income loss exposure.* A condition that presents the possibility of loss caused by a reduction in net income.

Risk management professionals use the following methods of identifying loss exposures:

- Risk assessment questionnaires
- Loss histories
- Financial statements and underlying accounting records
- Other records and documents
- Flowcharts and organizational charts
- Personal inspections
- Expertise within and beyond the organization

Step two, analyzing loss exposures, requires the risk management professional to estimate the likely significance of possible losses. Loss exposures are analyzed along the following five dimensions:

1. Loss frequency: the number of losses
2. Loss severity: the amount, in dollars, of a loss for a specific occurrence
3. Total dollar losses: the total dollar amount of losses for all occurrences during a specified period
4. Timing: when losses occur and when loss payments are made
5. Data credibility: the level of confidence that available data are accurate indicators of future losses

Step three, examining the feasibility of risk management techniques requires the risk management professional to systematically consider risk control and risk financing techniques used to treat loss exposures. Risk control techniques include the following:

- *Avoidance.* A risk control technique that involves ceasing or never undertaking an activity so that the possibility of a future loss occurring from that activity is eliminated.

- *Loss prevention.* A risk control technique that lowers the frequency of a particular loss.

- *Loss reduction.* A risk control technique that lowers the severity of a particular loss.

- *Separation.* A risk control technique that disperses a particular asset or activity over several locations and regularly relies on that asset or activity as part of the organization's working resources.

- *Duplication.* A risk control technique that uses backups, spares, or copies of critical property, information, or capabilities and keeps them in reserve.

- *Diversification.* A risk control technique that spreads loss exposures over numerous projects, products, markets, or regions.

Risk financing techniques include the following:

- *Insurance.* A risk financing technique that transfers the potential financial consequences of certain specified loss exposures from the insured to the insurer.

- *Noninsurance risk transfer.* A risk financing technique that transfers all or part of the financial consequences of loss to another party, other than an insurer.

- *Retention.* A risk financing technique by which losses are retained by generating funds within the organization to pay for the losses.

Step four, selecting the appropriate risk management techniques, requires the risk management professional to establish and apply criteria to select the appropriate risk management techniques that support the organization's goals. Selecting the appropriate risk management technique or combination of techniques involves the following two processes:

- Forecasting the effects that the available risk management techniques are likely to have on the organization's ability to fulfill its goals and the costs of those techniques

- Defining and applying selection criteria that measure how well each alternative risk management technique contributes financially and nonfinancially to organizational goals

Step five, implementing the selected risk management techniques, requires the risk management professional to plan and implement the selected risk management technique as part of the organization's risk management program. A risk management professional must make technical and managerial decisions to implement the selected risk management techniques.

Step six, monitoring results and revising the risk management program, requires the risk management professional to regularly reevaluate the risk management program. Revising the risk management program may be necessary for the program to adequately respond to new loss exposures that have developed, existing loss exposures that have become significant, and consideration of different risk management techniques that have become more appropriate than the ones already implemented.

The organization's risk management professional should apply the risk management process to each loss exposure the organization faces. The four categories of loss exposures are described in detail in subsequent chapters.

Chapter 3

Direct Your Learning

Assessing Property Loss Exposures

After learning the content of this chapter and completing the corresponding course guide assignment, you should be able to:

- Describe property exposed to loss.
- Describe the major causes of loss affecting property.
- Describe the methods of valuing property.
- Describe the legal interests in property.
- Describe the methods of identifying property loss exposures.
- Define or describe each of the Key Words and Phrases for this chapter.

Develop Your Perspective

What are the main topics covered in the chapter?

This chapter examines property loss exposures and the implications of property loss to an organization. Assessment of property loss exposures considers the property exposed to loss, the major causes of loss affecting property, the methods of valuing property, the legal interests in property, and the methods available to risk management professionals for identifying property loss exposures.

Identify the property loss exposures of your organization.

- What methods might you use to identify the loss exposures?
- What causes of loss might these exposures be subject to?

Why is it important to learn about these topics?

Most organizations have significant property assets that are essential to their operation. Property loss exposures to which inappropriate or inadequate risk management techniques have been applied may result in severe financial consequences for an organization.

Analyze the property loss exposures of your organization.

- Is the property exposed to loss real property or personal property?
- Which risk management techniques would you consider implementing to protect this property?

How can you use what you will learn?

Assess your organization's property loss exposures.

- What methods of valuing property would your organization use to assess each exposure?
- Does your organization regularly reevaluate property loss exposures to determine if values, legal interests, or the causes of loss to which they are exposed have changed?

Chapter 3
Assessing Property Loss Exposures

A loss exposure must be assessed, that is, identified and analyzed, before it can be effectively managed. Once a property loss exposure has been assessed, the best techniques to manage it often become apparent. In assessing property loss exposures, a risk management professional needs to follow certain key steps. First is to identify and categorize the property exposed to loss. Next is to consider the major causes of loss that affect property and to determine which of those may apply to the organization's property. The risk management professional then needs to determine the value of the property exposed to loss and the legal interest the organization holds in that property. Having followed these steps, the risk management professional can use a variety of methods to identify the specific property loss exposures faced by the organization.

PROPERTY EXPOSED TO LOSS

The first step in the risk management process is identifying loss exposures. In assessing property loss exposures this involves identifying the property exposed to loss. For legal purposes, property is categorized as either real property or personal property.

Real Property

Real property includes land and all structures permanently attached to the land. Examples of real property include buildings, driveways, sidewalks, underground piping, and radio transmitting towers. Risk management professionals often distinguish between (1) land and (2) buildings and other structures when assessing an organization's property loss exposures because insurance coverages generally treat them separately.

Land

Unimproved land is land in its natural state without any man-made alterations. It can be very challenging for risk management professionals to determine the proper value for unimproved land because each tract has unique attributes.

Unimproved land
Land in its natural state without any man-made alterations.

The following are attributes of unimproved land that might make it difficult to value:

- Water (such as a lake, river, creek, spring, or underground water table)
- Mineral resources (such as coal, iron, oil, copper, bauxite, potash, sand, or stone)
- Natural attractions of commercial value (such as a cave, therapeutic spring or pool, historic site, or artifacts)
- Natural forests
- Resident wild animals

The most important factor affecting the value of unimproved land is its location. For example, wooded acreage that may be developed commercially has much greater value if it is located at the intersection of two major roads than if the land is isolated.

Sometimes an organization overlooks the value that can be lost as a result of damage to unimproved land because unimproved land is perceived to have little intrinsic value. For example, an organization might own a large tract of land that was purchased to address a future need for the organization's facilities. The value of the timber currently on the land that could be destroyed by a forest fire may not have been recognized. Additionally, an organization's unimproved land might be unsupervised for long periods, thereby making it possible for trespassers to occupy the land or for the land to be subject to unauthorized use, such as the dumping of wastes.

Improved land
Land with man-made alterations.

Improved land is land with man-made alterations. Improved land includes buildings and structures that are discussed in the next section, but also includes crops, such as corn, fruit orchards, and planted forests. The presence of these alterations makes it easier to recognize and determine the value of the improved land.

Buildings and Other Structures

Buildings are permanent structures that have walls and a roof, while other structures are anything that is built or under construction. Examples of buildings and other structures that are permanent improvements when added to real property include:

- Buildings: homes (including trailers on cement slabs), churches, schools, stores, factories, and offices
- Outbuildings: sheds, barns, stables, and greenhouses
- Other structures: hookups to sewer and electrical facilities, roads, fences, and retaining walls

Buildings and other structures can be categorized based on physical characteristics that make them either more or less subject to property causes of loss such as fire. Property loss exposures have traditionally been assessed based on four interdependent attributes: construction, occupancy, protection, and external exposure. These attributes are often referred to by the acronym COPE.

Construction refers to how a structure is built. A building's construction has a direct bearing on its ability to withstand damage by causes of loss. Insurance Services Office, Inc. (ISO) divides building construction into the following six types:

1. Frame
2. Joisted masonry
3. Noncombustible
4. Masonry noncombustible
5. Modified fire resistive
6. Fire resistive

These construction types are listed in order from most to least susceptible to loss by fire. Fire is usually considered the most likely cause of loss to affect buildings and other structures. Consequently, risk management professionals usually assess a property loss exposure based on the property's susceptibility to fire before considering other potential causes of loss. Construction is also a factor in a structure's tendency to be damaged from other causes of loss. For example, a wood-frame building might suffer only minor damage during an earthquake because it is somewhat flexible, while a rigid, fire-resistant steel building is more likely to collapse during the same earthquake.

Occupancy refers to how a structure is used. A risk management professional's assessment of a structure's use should include the combustibility of its contents and the contents' susceptibility to other causes of loss. The evaluation of occupancy should also include whether the structure is being used in a manner that is consistent with the use for which it was designed. For example, a structure that was built for an office occupancy is unlikely to be physically suited to the needs of a manufacturer.

Protection refers to those risk control techniques used to prevent or reduce the damage done by fire and other causes of loss. For example, a structure that has an automatic sprinkler system is less likely to suffer extensive fire damage than a structure that is not so equipped.

External exposure refers to causes of loss that originate outside the structure. For example, a structure that is located next to a chemical factory has a higher external exposure to loss than one located next to a grocery store.

Personal Property

Personal property includes all property other than real property, and can be classified as either tangible or intangible. It is relatively straightforward for risk management professionals and others in the organization to recognize the existence and value of tangible personal property. However intangible personal property, because it often has no physical evidence of its existence, is more difficult to recognize and value.

Tangible Personal Property

Tangible personal property is personal property that has a physical form that can be seen or touched. This is a broad category, excluding only property that cannot be seen or touched. For example, the paper on which a contract is written is tangible property; the rights of the contracting parties written on that paper are intangible property.

Tangible property typically falls into one or more of the following eight categories:

1. Money and securities
2. Accounts receivable records
3. Inventory
4. Furniture, equipment, or supplies
5. Computer equipment and media
6. Machinery
7. Valuable papers and records
8. Mobile property

The first category of tangible property is money and securities. This category includes all types of monetary assets, such as cash, bank accounts, certificates of deposit, securities, notes, drafts, and evidence of debt. The magnitude of the money and securities loss exposure varies widely among organizations. For example, a single supermarket typically has large sums of cash on hand that present a significant exposure. In contrast, a large manufacturer may have a small exposure for cash on hand yet face the possibility of large embezzlement losses over time. Organizations that have seasonal patterns of business often have wide variations in monetary assets on hand during the year, and consequently their loss exposures vary considerably. By far the most significant cause of loss for monetary assets is theft by either employees or outsiders.

The second category of tangible personal property is accounts receivable records. Accounts receivable records show the money currently due and previously collected from customer or client accounts. These records are subject to physical damage, destruction, theft, or fraudulent alteration. If accounts receivable records are damaged or destroyed, an organization may have difficulty reconstructing them and therefore may be unable to collect the amounts due. Even if the organization is able to reproduce these records from underlying data, this may be costly, and therefore the loss can be substantial. However, the loss exposure presented by accounts receivable records can be effectively controlled. Organizations often back up financial data daily and store these backup records in other locations, thereby minimizing the potential property loss exposure.

The third category of tangible personal property is inventory. For a wholesaler or retailer, inventory represents goods ready for sale. For a manufacturer, inventory is usually more specifically defined as raw materials, stock in process, and finished goods. Inventory values can fluctuate widely, so valuation can be difficult. For example, value is added to stock in process at each stage of the production process. Additionally, inventory is subject to a wide range of causes of loss, especially as it is moved from one location to another.

The fourth category of tangible personal property is furniture, equipment, or supplies. Examples include much of the contents of office buildings, such as office furniture, typewriters, showcases, counters, office supplies (like stationery and printed forms), manufacturing supplies, and packaging materials. This category of property often consists of many low-value items, but can also include expensive equipment that might not be easily replaced if damaged or destroyed. For example, a direct mail company that handles bulk mailing for others would likely have a substantial investment in sorting equipment. Such equipment is usually customized to meet the organization's specifications as well as being physically adapted to the organization's facility. Therefore, replacing this equipment would be difficult, time-consuming, and expensive.

Even low-value supplies can cumulatively present a significant investment for some organizations. For example, an organization may have a significant investment in forms, stationery, and mailing supplies. However, low-value property is typically a low priority for the risk management professional because tracking it is not cost-effective.

The fifth category of tangible personal property is computer equipment and media. This category includes software and data as well as computer hardware. Computer equipment and media can be subject to damage from excessive heat or moisture. As a result, many computer facilities require a special environmental control system, which itself represents a significant additional property loss exposure. Computers may also be damaged as a result of electrical impulses or power surges.

In addition to the causes of loss that can cause physical damage to the computer facilities, misuse of computer systems can result in other property losses. For example, computer fraud by employees or outsiders sometimes involves theft of property. Alternatively, an employee or outsider may try to sabotage computer equipment. Common forms of sabotage include computer viruses and Trojan horses. A **computer virus** is a software program that is capable of reproducing itself and causing harm to other programs and files. A Trojan horse is a computer program that appears desirable, such as a utility or game, but actually contains harmful programming commands. Finally, although any computer equipment is exposed to theft, this is particularly true for laptop computers because of their portability.

Computer virus
A software program that is capable of reproducing itself and causing harm to other programs and files.

The sixth category of tangible personal property is machinery. Depending on the nature of the organization's business, the organization may be highly dependent on machinery to produce its products. Some machinery is customized, thereby making it difficult to replace. Machinery could also be categorized as equipment or even computer-controlled equipment. For example, a high-speed printer used at a professional print shop may be both machinery and computer equipment. However, machinery is categorized separately because its significant value warrants separate treatment.

The seventh category of tangible personal property is valuable papers and records. Many organizations rely on this category of physical property. For example, physicians maintain medical histories of their patients; businesses maintain customer lists; and photographers, architects, engineers, and journalists maintain files of their previous work to draw on for current projects. Likewise, risk management professionals also have valuable records needed to accomplish their duties. In some instances, these valuable papers and records are the physical manifestation of intangible property, so while they have a value they are easier to replace. For example, stock certificates are evidence of ownership in a publicly traded company but can be replaced for a fee if they are destroyed.

Assigning a value to valuable papers and records is difficult. Usually, the risk management professional values this property based on the cost to reproduce it, which might be incidental in some instances while excessive in other instances. For example, architectural plans, unless there are other copies available, may cost thousands of dollars to replace. Risk management professionals usually find that it is challenging to determine the cost of reproducing these documents.

The eighth category of tangible personal property is mobile property, including autos, aircraft, boats and ships, and heavy mobile equipment used by contractors. Such property can have extremely large values concentrated in a single item. An airplane, a ship, or a piece of earth-moving equipment can be valued in the millions of dollars. In addition to the causes of loss that can strike other property, mobile property is exposed to special hazards, such as slippery roads or speeding vehicles.

Intangible Personal Property

Intangible personal property is property that has no physical form. While this property cannot be touched, it can often have substantial value to an organization. The following are examples of intangible property:

- Copyrights
- Trademarks
- Patents
- Trade secrets
- Goodwill

Copyright
The legal right granted by the United States government to a person or organization for a period of years to exclusively own and control an original written document, piece of music, software, or other form of expression.

A **copyright** is the legal right granted by the United States government to a person or organization for a period of years to exclusively own and control an original written document, piece of music, software, or other form of expression. Copyright is intangible because it pertains to the work itself rather than its physical form. For example, the story contained in a book is copyrighted, not the physical form of the book.

A **trademark** is a distinctive design or set of words that legally identifies a product or service as belonging to a certain organization. Organizations use trademarks to ensure that consumers can recognize their products. Trademarks can be registered federally through the United States Patent and Trademark Office or with individual states. Unlike a copyright, which has a limited life span, a trademark is renewable indefinitely. An example of a well-recognized trademark is the Nike Swoosh.

A **patent** is the right granted by the U.S. government to an inventor or applicant for a limited time period to exclusively own and control a new, useful, and nonobvious invention. A patent covers an invention, which may be an entirely new device or process, or an improvement to an existing invention. A patent holder is granted exclusive rights for a period of twenty years, during which time the patent can be licensed to others or assigned (sold). An example of a product that can be covered by a patent is a pharmaceutical drug. When a drug patent expires, other organizations can begin producing generic versions, which are generally sold at lower cost, thereby reducing the original manufacturer's market share.

A **trade secret** is a practice, method, process, design, or other information used confidentially by an organization to maintain a competitive advantage. For example, recipes, the algorithm used by an Internet search engine, and the quantitative techniques used by a credit scoring company would all be trade secrets. A trade secret provides an organization with a competitive advantage and therefore adds value to that organization. Trade secret holders can ask the courts for an injunction (a court order that restrains a party from carrying on a particular activity) against those possessing a trade secret, such as a former employee who might reveal the secret to others. Trade secrets are not protected through registration as are trademarks and patents. Rather, organizations try to keep their trade secrets from competitors by limiting access to this special knowledge and requiring confidentiality agreements from those who have access to it.

Goodwill is the value an organization has attained beyond the value of its tangible assets because of its favorable reputation. Organizations typically enjoy goodwill as a consequence of successful business relationships. For example, an organization may derive goodwill from its brand name, favorable customer relations, or high employee morale. Sometimes goodwill is quantified for financial statement purposes. For example, if one organization purchased another for more than the acquired organization's fair market value, the acquiring organization shows that excess amount as goodwill on the asset side of the balance sheet. Goodwill shown on the balance sheet must be depreciated over a period of time.

Trademark
A distinctive design or set of words that legally identifies a product or service as belonging to a certain organization.

Patent
The right granted by the United States government to an inventor or applicant for a limited time period to exclusively own and control a new, useful, and nonobvious invention.

Trade secret
A practice, method, process, design, or other information used confidentially by an organization to maintain a competitive advantage.

Goodwill
The value an organization has attained beyond the value of its tangible assets because of its favorable reputation.

MAJOR CAUSES OF LOSS AFFECTING PROPERTY

Having identified property loss exposures, the risk management professional should consider the causes of loss that may affect those loss exposures. A property's susceptibility to a cause of loss should direct the risk management professional's treatment of that loss exposure. Consequently, categorizing causes of loss can help provide a framework for managing the loss exposures. However, no approach to categorizing causes of loss is completely satisfactory. Therefore, some of the causes of loss shown in Exhibit 3-1 could fall into more than one category. The approach to categorizing these causes of loss in Exhibit 3-1—natural, human, and economic—was chosen because it encompasses most causes of loss that might affect property. Because there are relatively few causes of loss that can result in significant loss to an organization, only these select causes of loss are described in this section.

Natural Causes of Loss

Natural causes of loss include acts of nature and acts that do not involve human intervention, for example, windstorm, earthquake, and flood. Although natural causes of loss encompass those causes of loss considered to be natural disasters that affect whole communities, they also include events that affect just one organization, such as a building collapse caused by snow accumulating on the roof. The occurrence of a natural cause of loss is largely beyond human control. Consequently, risk management has little, if any, effect in reducing loss frequency. However, organizations can implement loss reduction measures to control loss severity.

Windstorm

Windstorm
A storm consisting of violent wind capable of causing damage.

Windstorm is a storm consisting of violent wind capable of causing damage. Windstorms need not be hurricanes or tornadoes to cause significant damage. However, hurricanes, tornadoes, and winter storms are significant sources of catastrophic losses.

A hurricane is a severe tropical cyclone, usually accompanied by heavy rains and winds moving at seventy-five miles per hour or more. Tropical storms that form in the Atlantic and Eastern Pacific Oceans are called hurricanes, but tropical storms that form in other parts of the Pacific Ocean are called typhoons or cyclones. Hurricanes are a leading cause of catastrophic loss in the U.S. For example, Florida was subjected to four hurricanes in 2004 that caused an estimated $21.3 billion in insured losses.[1]

A tornado is a localized and violently destructive windstorm occurring over land and characterized by a funnel-shaped cloud extending toward the ground. Tornadoes form in warm, humid, and unsettled weather, and often are the result of thunderstorms and tropical storms. A tornado consists of winds rotating at speeds that can reach up to 300 miles per hour, creating

EXHIBIT 3-1

General Categories of Selected Causes of Loss

Natural Causes of Loss—Acts of nature; no human intervention

Cave-in	Lightning	Temperature extremes
Drought	Meteors	Tidal waves
Earthquake	Mildew	Tides
Erosion	Mold	Uncontrollable vegetation
Evaporation	Perils of the air (such as icing and clear-air turbulence)	Vermin
Fire		Volcanic eruption
Flood	Perils of the sea (such as icebergs, waves, sandbars, and reefs)	Water
Hail		Weeds
Humidity extremes	Rot	Wind (such as tornadoes, hurricanes, typhoons)
Ice	Rust	
Landslide/mudslide		

Human Causes of Loss—Acts of one individual or a small group of individuals

Arson	Human error	Sonic boom
Chemical leakage	Industrial contamination	Terrorism
Collapse	Labor union strikes (direct effects)	Theft, forgery, fraud
Discrimination	Molten materials	Toppling of high-piled objects
Electrical overload	Pollution (smoke, smog, water, noise)	Vandalism, malicious mischief
Embezzlement		
Explosion	Power outage	Vibration
Expropriation (confiscation)	Riot	Water hammer
	Sabotage	
Fire and smoke of human origin	Shrinkage	

Economic Causes of Loss—Acts of large groups of people who respond to particular conditions

Changes in consumer tastes	Inflation	Strikes
	Obsolescence	Technological advances
Currency fluctuations	Stock market declines	War
Depression (recession)		

a partial vacuum at the center. Upward velocity can exceed 200 feet per second. When the tornado makes contact with the ground, it draws debris into the circulating air. The average tornado path is only one-quarter of a mile wide and rarely exceeds 16 miles in length. Tornadoes move forward at an average speed of 40 miles per hour, although some have reached 70 miles per hour.

Tornadoes can occur anywhere in the world; however U.S. weather conditions result in a significant number of tornadoes each year, particularly in certain states. Exhibit 3-2 shows the incidence of tornadoes by state in 2003.

Earthquake

Although earthquakes can occur throughout the U.S., destructive seismic events typically affect only a few areas. More earthquakes strike Alaska than any other state, but the loss exposure is most severe in California, where exposed property values are the highest. However, one of the most severe earthquakes recorded in the U.S. occurred in 1814 along the New Madrid Fault when that area was primarily wilderness. The recurrence of that event today would virtually destroy the city of Memphis, Tennessee. The 1994 earthquake centered in Northridge, California, damaged 114,000 buildings. It caused insured property damage of an estimated $15.5 billion in 2003 dollars, making it the third most costly disaster ever for the insurance industry.[2] Exhibit 3-3 charts seismic potential for the continental U.S.

Seismologists measure earthquakes by either magnitude or intensity. One measure that uses magnitude is the Richter scale, which measures the magnitude of an earthquake by the total amount of energy it releases. The Richter scale measures energy release logarithmically; that is, each unit scale represents the release of ten times the energy of the next lower unit. For example, a magnitude of 6 is ten times as powerful as a magnitude of 5, one hundred times as strong as a magnitude of 4, and so on. There is no upper limit to the Richter scale, as shown in Exhibit 3-4.

The Modified Mercalli scale measures intensity; that is, the damage that an earthquake causes to people, property, and the surface of the earth. Exhibit 3-5 shows the Modified Mercalli Intensity Scale.

Flood

Flood
A rising or overflowing of water onto what is normally dry land.

Flood is a rising or overflowing of water onto what is normally dry land. Flooding is a common event in many areas of the U.S., recurring at regular intervals. Some locations flood every year, but others face unpredictable flood hazards. Floods result from an area's receiving greater precipitation than the land can drain off. For example, the spring of 1997 brought flooding to Grand Forks, North Dakota, when the Red River—swollen by melting snow and a spring snowstorm—overflowed its banks. This flood caught property owners and occupiers by surprise because their area was not known for flooding. Exhibit 3-6 shows the flooding in the downtown area.

EXHIBIT 3-2

Tornadoes by State in 2003

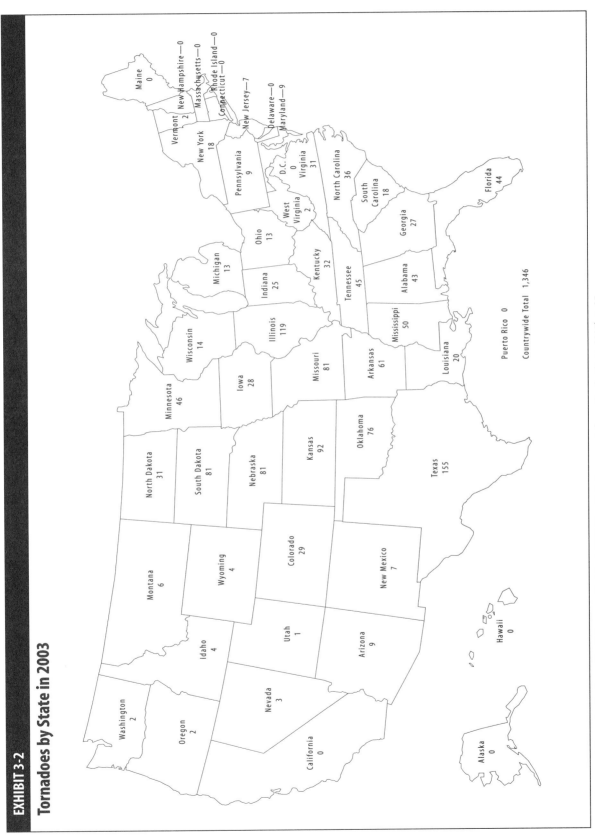

Maine 0
New Hampshire—0
Massachusetts—0
Rhode Island—0
Connecticut—0
Vermont 2
New Jersey—7
New York 18
Delaware—0
Maryland—9
Pennsylvania 9
D.C. 0
Virginia 31
North Carolina 36
West Virginia 2
Ohio 13
South Carolina 18
Florida 44
Michigan 13
Kentucky 32
Georgia 27
Indiana 25
Tennessee 45
Alabama 43
Illinois 119
Mississippi 50
Wisconsin 14
Arkansas 61
Louisiana 20
Iowa 28
Missouri 81
Puerto Rico 0
Minnesota 46
Oklahoma 76
Countrywide Total 1,346
North Dakota 31
South Dakota 81
Nebraska 81
Kansas 92
Texas 155
Montana 6
Wyoming 4
Colorado 29
New Mexico 7
Idaho 4
Utah 1
Arizona 9
Hawaii 0
Washington 2
Oregon 2
Nevada 3
California 0
Alaska 0

Source: Insurance Information Institute, *The III Insurance Fact Book 2005* (New York: Insurance Information Institute, 2005), p. 95.

EXHIBIT 3-3

Seismic Potential for the Continental United States

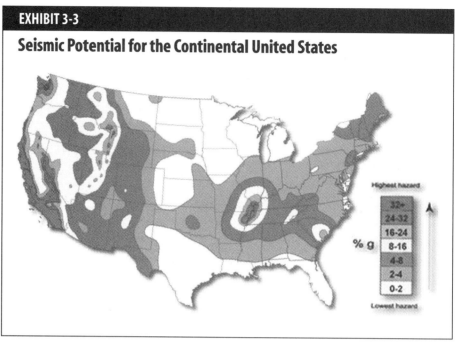

Source: United States Geological Survey (USGS) Earthquake Hazards Program, National Seismic Hazard Map, 2002, http://eqhazmaps.usgs.gov/images/2002US_scale.pdf (accessed June 23, 2005).

EXHIBIT 3-4

Earthquake Severity Measurement—Richter Scale

Richter Magnitude	Earthquake Effects	Average Annually
8 and higher	Great	1[1]
7–7.9	Major	17[2]
6–6.9	Strong	134[2]
5–5.9	Moderate	1,319[2]
4–4.9	Light	13,000[3]
3–3.9	MInor	130,000[3]
2–2.9	Very minor	1,300,000[3]

[1] Based on observations since 1900
[2] Based on observations since 1990
[3] Estimated

Source: United States Geological Survey (USGS), http://earthquake.usgs.gov (accessed December 11, 2004).

EXHIBIT 3-5

The Modified Mercalli Intensity Scale

Level	Description
I.	Not felt except by a very few under especially favorable circumstances.
II.	Felt only by a few persons at rest, especially on upper floors of buildings. Delicately suspended objects may swing.
III.	Felt quite noticeably indoors, especially on upper floors of buildings, but many people do not recognize it as an earthquake. Standing automobiles may rock slightly. Vibration like a passing truck.
IV.	During the day felt indoors by many, outdoors by few. At night, some awakened. Dishes, windows, and doors rattle; walls may make cracking sound. Hanging objects swing noticeably. Sensation like a heavy truck striking a building. Standing automobiles rock noticeably.
V.	Felt by nearly everyone; many awakened. Pictures knock against wall or swing out of place. Small objects move; furnishings move to slight extent. Some dishes, windows, and so forth broken; a few instances of cracked plaster; unstable objects overturned. Disturbance of trees, poles, and other tall objects sometimes noticed. Pendulum clocks may stop.
VI.	Felt by everyone; many awakened; a direction can be estimated. Some dishes and glassware broken; knickknacks and books knocked off shelves; pictures knocked off walls. Church bells may ring. Some heavy furniture moved; a few instances of fallen plaster or damaged chimneys. Damage slight.
VII.	Difficult to stand. Hanging objects quiver. Waves on ponds; water turbid with mud. Small landslides. Damage negligible in buildings of good design and construction; slight to moderate in well-built ordinary structures; considerable in poorly built or badly designed structures; some chimneys broken at roof line. Noticed by persons driving cars.
VIII.	Damage slight in specially designed structures; considerable in ordinary, substantial buildings with partial collapse; great in poorly built structures. Frame houses moved on foundations if not bolted down. Panel walls thrown out of frame structures. Fall of chimneys, factory stacks, columns, monuments, walls, towers and elevated tanks. Heavy furniture overturned. Sand and mud ejected in small amounts. Changes in well water. Steering of cars affected.
IX.	General panic. Damage considerable in specially designed structures; well-designed frame structures thrown out of plumb; great in substantial buildings, with partial collapse. Buildings shifted off foundations. Ground cracked conspicuously. Underground pipes broken. Serious damage to reservoirs.
X.	Some well-built wooden structures destroyed; most masonry and frame structures destroyed with foundations; ground badly cracked. Rails bent. Landslides considerable from river banks and steep slopes. Shifted sand and mud. Water splashed, slopped over banks.
XI.	Few, if any, (masonry) structures remain standing. Bridges destroyed. Broad fissures in ground. Underground pipelines completely out of service. Earth slumps and land slips in soft ground. Rails bent greatly.
XII.	Damage total. Large rock masses displaced. Waves seen on ground surfaces. Lines of sight and level distorted. Objects thrown upward into the air.

EXHIBIT 3-6

Flood—Grand Forks, North Dakota

Photo: Richard Larsen (UND), www.draves.com/gf/fsb/fslo0100.htm (accessed January 19, 2005).

The following seven types of flood are common:

1. Riverine floods occur when rivers, streams, and other watercourses rise and overflow their banks. They result from either heavy rainfall or snow melt upstream in their drainage basins.

2. Tidal floods result from high tides, frequently driven by high winds offshore, and from tropical storms making landfall or passing close offshore. They affect bays and the portions of rivers along the coast.

3. Wind floods can happen whenever a strong wind holds back part of a large body of water from its normal drainage course and raises the water level. Back bays behind barrier islands are especially susceptible to wind floods. Water that cannot escape through normal channels can flow out of these bays across the barrier islands.

4. Rising water levels downstream might prevent drainage upstream, causing a backwater flood. Backwater floods can extend for a substantial distance upstream.

5. Ice jams sometimes develop as ice thaws and begins to move downstream. They block the flow of water, causing it to back up and flood the upstream area. If the ice jam breaks suddenly, it can cause flooding downstream.

6. Accidental floods are caused by the failure of flood control systems. A dam, levee, wall, or dike might break and cause flooding downstream. Blocked floodgates and spillways cause upstream flooding.

7. Man-made topographic changes can also cause floods. For example, instead of being absorbed into the soil, rain water can accumulate on concrete and asphalt parking lots. If storm sewer drains have inadequate capacity or are blocked, water can build up and flood adjacent properties.

As part of National Flood Insurance Program, the U.S. Army Corps of Engineers has mapped areas throughout the country that are known to be subject to flooding. A sample flood map appears in Exhibit 3-7. These maps divide the area into the following three zones, according to their susceptibility to flooding:

1. Zone A includes all land within the boundary of a 100-year flood, that is, areas that could possibly have a flood once every 100 years. Within Zone A, the maps mark the boundaries of the annual, 5-, 10-, and 50-year floods. In some cases, the boundaries are precise enough to identify individual properties protected by elevation.
2. Zone B falls outside the 100-year flood boundary but within the boundary of the 500-year flood.
3. Zone C designates the area exposed to minimum flood potential. Zone C is sometimes referred to as an area with no known flood hazard.

Fire and Lightning

Fire is the rapid oxidation of combustible material, releasing heat and flame. Slower types of oxidation and other chemical reactions might release heat or cause heat buildup. For insurance purposes, damage to a structure caused by fire includes the damage caused by flame, heat, smoke, and the water used to extinguish the fire. However, damage caused by smoke can be considered a separate cause of loss and it is discussed later in this section. In 2003, fire losses in the U.S. totaled an estimated $19.5 billion.[3] In the same year, there were 519,500 structural fires.[4]

Lightning is a natural electric discharge in the atmosphere. In its flow to the ground, lightning can cause damage to property either by a direct hit, by a near miss, or by a ground surge. Lightning damage to a building following a direct hit usually consists of shatter or blast-like damage or resulting fire damage. The likelihood of fire damage depends on the combustibility of materials used in the building and the extent of grounding afforded by lightning rods and metal roofs.

Some engineers have suggested that although all lighting is high-voltage electricity, some bolts are of high amperage (large flow of electricity), but others are of low amperage (small flow of electricity), and that the high amperage electricity causes ignition. Those bolts are called "hot" and "cold," respectively. This distinction also explains why lightning can come into a building on a power line without blowing a fuse. Metal roofs offer protection only if the metal is 3/16 of an inch or more, and only if installed so that they are electrically continuous and adequately grounded. Otherwise, they can attract lightning and provide little protection. Near misses do not usually cause physical damage but can disturb electrical equipment's functioning.

EXHIBIT 3-7

Flood Insurance Rate Map—Township of Willistown, Chester County, Pennsylvania

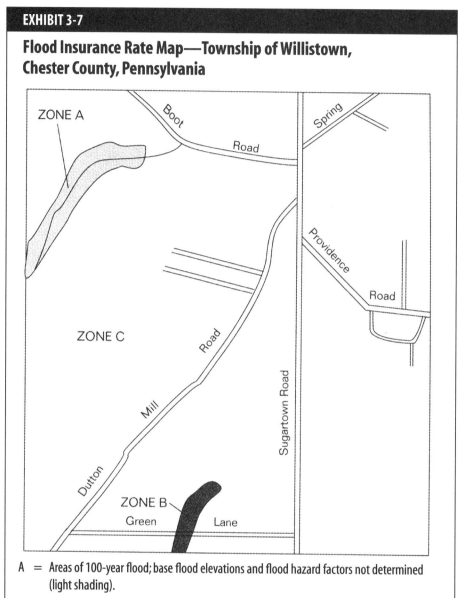

A = Areas of 100-year flood; base flood elevations and flood hazard factors not determined (light shading).

B = Areas between limits of the 100-year flood and 500-year flood; or certain areas subject to 100-year flooding with average depths less than one foot or where the contributing drainage area is less than one square mile; or areas protected by levees from the base flood (medium shading).

C = Areas of minimal flooding (no shading).

Adapted from Federal Emergency Management Agency, Federal Insurance Administration.

Ground surge travels through the ground creating a burrow, usually only for a few hundred feet, before entering a building. The only evidence of a lightning strike might be nonfunctioning electrical equipment. The risk management professional might use weather records to determine that the damage to electrical equipment was caused by lightning.

Smoke

Smoke is hot vapor containing fine particles resulting from combustion. Most fires produce smoke, and in many fires the damage caused by the smoke is significant relative to the size of the fire. For example, a small fire in a supermarket could result in a major loss if the supermarket had to destroy its inventory because of health department restrictions on selling smoke-damaged foods. Alternately, a furrier may have to sell its inventory of furs at steep discount to a salvager because the smoke odor would likely be impossible to completely eliminate even with commercial cleaning of the goods. In addition to smoke produced by an unplanned (hostile) fire at the property, smoke damage may be caused by other sources of smoke, such as burning debris, industrial operations, brush fires, and agricultural smudging.

Hail

Hail is precipitation in the form of small, hard ice pellets. These pellets can cause significant damage on impact. In some parts of the U.S., hail can be the size of a golf ball and it has been known to cause serious damage to roofs, vehicles, crops, and other property left in the open.

Weight of Snow, Sleet, and Ice

Buildings and other structures can be damaged by an accumulation of snow, sleet, and ice. The accumulation can exert great force on a building, causing roof collapse or other structural damage. Flat roofs are especially susceptible. This cause of loss has resulted in severe building and personal property losses. For example, the Hartford Civic Center Arena roof collapsed under the weight of accumulated snow in 1978.

Water

Water that damages a structure can come from several different sources. For example, water damage can occur when a pipe bursts; when a fracture develops in an appliance, thereby allowing water seepage; and when sewer systems back up through toilets, sinks, and drains. Many commercial structures are protected by sprinkler systems, which can leak if not properly maintained or if damaged. For insurance purposes, damage done by water from sprinkler systems is usually considered a consequence of fire if the sprinklers are activated in response to a fire. However, sprinkler leakage can be a form of water damage.

Volcanic Action

The consequences of a volcanic action include airborne volcanic blast or airborne shock waves; ash, dust, or particulate matter; and lava flow. For example, the 1980 eruption of Mount St. Helens in Washington state scattered one cubic mile of volcanic material over 232 square miles. The eruption buried 150 miles of fishing rivers and 26 lakes and killed an estimated one million animals. In addition, volcanic material started landslides and mudflows. A large mudflow traveled 28 miles and blocked shipping channels in the Columbia River.[5]

Sinkhole Collapse

A sinkhole is a depression in the ground usually caused by the collapse of a subterranean limestone cave. This collapse may occur when the roof of a limestone cave becomes weak and no longer can support the weight of the ground above. Often, the weight of the roof is supported by the underground water that created the limestone cave. This underground water may be reduced by water usage to the point that the water no longer helps support the ground above the limestone cave.

Sinkholes can cause extensive and irreparable damage, as evidenced by destruction of the Corporate Plaza building in Allentown, Pennsylvania in 1994. The initial evidence that the area had a sinkhole problem arose when two city reservoirs abruptly dropped several feet and the water mains broke in the vicinity of the building.[6] Sinkholes can also open around a broken water main. For example, a thirty-foot-deep sinkhole that opened in Easton, Pennsylvania, on December 8, 2004, caused the condemnation of an apartment building and disruption of traffic.

Human Causes of Loss

Human causes of loss encompass deliberate acts of individuals or groups, as well as events that are not deliberate acts but that involve some element of human intervention. Examples include terrorism, vandalism, and explosion. The frequency and severity of human causes of loss can be managed to some extent by the application of risk control techniques. As with natural causes of loss, the following discussion does not represent an exhaustive list of human causes of loss. However, it includes those that would be of primary interest to a risk management professional because they can be treated using risk management techniques.

Riot and Civil Commotion

Generally, riot is a violent breach of the peace by three or more persons assembled together and acting with a common intent. A riot need not result from conspiracy; it can be spontaneous. Some states' criminal codes require only two people in order to define the action as a riot, and others require that there be as many as five. The rioters' act or acts must be of an unlawful nature. Riot damage includes fire, breakage, theft, looting, and vandalism.

Civil commotion can be described as an uprising among a mass of people that causes a serious and prolonged disturbance of civil order. Civil commotion and riot are similar, and the two terms include most incidents of civil unrest. Examples of riot and civil commotion are the violent protests at the World Trade Organization meeting in downtown Seattle in 1999 and the demonstrations in Miami during the Elian Gonzales custody dispute in 2000.

Looting frequently accompanies riots and can cause significant financial loss. For example, the civil disorders in Los Angeles in 1992 resulted in $1 billion in insured losses valued in 2003 dollars.[7]

Explosion

The most common types of explosion are combustion explosions (ignition of flammable clouds) and pressure explosions (rupture of confined spaces).

A dust explosion is an example of a combustion explosion. Airborne dust, such as found in a grain elevators, can ignite and result in a significant explosion. For example, the DeBruce grain complex located near Wichita, Kansas exploded in 1998, killing four people and causing extensive damage.

A boiler explosion is an example of a pressure explosion. For example, a boiler at the Ford Motor Company River Rouge complex located in Dearborn, Michigan exploded in 1999, killing six people and seriously injuring fourteen others.

Vandalism

Vandalism is the willful or malicious destruction or defacement of public or private property. For example, a brick thrown through a storefront window out of spite would be considered vandalism. However, damage done to landscaping by deer would not be considered vandalism because animals are unable to form malicious intent.

Vehicles

One type of vehicle damage results from physical contact between a vehicle and property; for example, when a delivery truck hits and damages a building's loading dock. Examples of vehicle-related losses in which physical contact does not occur include the following:

- A building is damaged by the vibrations from heavily loaded logging trucks running on an adjacent road.
- A vehicle collides with a pole owned by a telephone company, and the pole falls on a building, caving in the roof.
- A chain is attached to a loading dock and to a vehicle, and the vehicle drives away, pulling on the chain, which causes damage to the loading dock.

Collapse

Collapse is an abrupt falling down or caving in of a building with the result that the building or any part of the building cannot be occupied for its intended use. Collapse of a structure can be caused by lack of proper maintenance that may result in hidden decay; hidden insect or vermin damage; weight of people or personal property; improper design that allows rain or snow to collect on the roof, which may add more weight than the structure can hold; and the use of defective materials or methods of construction, remodeling, or renovation.

Collapse
An abrupt falling down or caving in of a building with the result that the building or any part of the building cannot be occupied for its intended use.

Aircraft

Aircraft includes airplanes and helicopters. Aircraft damage can be caused as a result of a crash, or from objects falling from aircraft. Property located in the vicinity of airports is more susceptible to aircraft damage. For example, a corporate jet failed to take off from the Teterboro, New Jersey, airport on February 2, 2005, and crashed into a warehouse.

Crime

Property crimes include burglary, larceny-theft, and arson. Burglary and larceny-theft involve taking property without the owner's consent. Property crimes in the U.S. in 2003 totaled an estimated $17 billion. This amount includes $8.6 billion from motor vehicle thefts, $4.9 billion from larceny-thefts, and $3.5 billion from burglaries.[8]

Falling Objects

Falling objects can cause damage to property. For example, a tree branch, or an entire tree, can fall on a structure. The sources of falling objects are almost unlimited, but they could include rocks that roll down a mountainside, tiles falling from a roof, or objects falling from the back of a truck.

Economic Causes of Loss

As well as natural and human causes of loss, a risk management professional should consider economic causes of loss. Economic causes of loss are caused by acts of large groups of people responding to particular conditions. These losses are therefore dynamic in nature and typically involve large segments of the population. Economic causes of loss stem from actions such as strikes or boycotts, war, significant technological changes, or changes in consumer preferences. These causes of loss can generate prosperity for those whom they favor but threaten unemployment and recession for others. Because economic causes of loss are generally beyond the effective range of any risk management program, such causes of loss are often ignored by risk management professionals. However, losses, such as those from unemployment, damage caused by rioting strikers, deterioration of machinery long left idle during a recession, or war damage to an organization's overseas properties, are events that risk management professionals must address under disaster management procedures. The majority of economic causes of loss are beyond the scope of this text.

METHODS OF VALUING PROPERTY

Once the risk management professional has identified the property exposed to loss, he or she needs to determine the value of that property. This will indicate the potential cost of the causes of loss that have also been identified. Organizations value their property in various ways depending on the purpose of the valuation. For example, the market value of a item of property may be different to the value recorded in the organization's financial statements. The following are some of the typical approaches to valuing property:

- Historical cost
- Tax-appraised value
- Book value
- Replacement cost
- Reproduction cost
- Functional replacement cost
- Market value
- Actual cash value
- Economic value

Organizations normally own a considerable amount of property, making it difficult to track the values of all but the most significant items. Additionally, valuing property is a time-consuming task and the values determined usually are relevant for only a limited time because the value of property changes.

Historical Cost

Historical cost is the original cost of a property. Financial statements use the historical cost method for most assets. However, this does not mean that the financial statements simply show the original cost of those assets. For example, for a piece of real estate, the historical cost includes the building's total original purchase price, including the value of the land it occupies, plus real estate commissions, closing costs, and any other legitimate business expenses attributable to that purchase. Any capital improvements to the building are added to the original purchase price as funds are expended. For example, if an organization originally purchased its building ten years ago for $250,000 (including closing costs) and spends $5,000 to reroof the building, the historical cost would be $255,000.

Historical cost
The original cost of a property.

Real property tends to appreciate in value, while personal property may appreciate, remain the same, or depreciate. In the previous example, the building with a $255,000 historical cost might be sold for $350,000. Historical cost accounting does not recognize this value. The problem with valuing any property by its historical cost is that it does not reflect changes in value that may have occurred over time. All that historical cost can really provide is the building's value at one point in time, a value that may not be particularly useful in determining its value for risk management purposes.

Similar problems arise when historical costs are used to value inventory. Historical cost accounting values inventory based on what it cost to acquire the inventory. However, if the inventory was destroyed and needed to be replaced, the value represented by the historical cost might be insufficient.

Tax-Appraised Value

Tax-appraised value
The value assigned to a property for the purpose of tax assessment.

Tax appraised value is the value assigned to a property for the purpose of tax assessment. Property's tax-appraised value has limited usefulness to a risk management professional's assessment of property loss exposures because valuations are often conducted infrequently and therefore a significant disparity often exists between the tax-appraised value and the value for risk management purposes. However, risk management professionals can use the tax-appraised value to determine what the change in property taxes might be if the property were destroyed and then rebuilt. For example, the pre-loss tax-appraised value of a structure might be $500,000. After the structure is rebuilt and reassessed, the tax-appraised value of the structure might be $1 million, thereby doubling the organization's property taxes.

Book Value

Book value
An asset's historical cost minus accumulated depreciation.

Book value is an asset's historical cost minus accumulated depreciation. Therefore, book value is calculated on the accounting assumption that a portion of that asset's useful life has expired. Generally, a long-term asset's book value is lower than its market value because inflation increases the market value while depreciation decreases the book value. Consequently, risk management professionals do not rely on book value for valuing property. However, a property's book value may serve as a starting point in determining an accurate value.

Replacement Cost

Replacement cost
The amount required to replace lost, damaged, or destroyed property with comparable property.

Replacement cost is the amount required to replace lost, damaged, or destroyed property with comparable property. Replacement cost is discussed here as it relates to buildings and personal property.

Buildings

A building's replacement cost is the cost of constructing a new building to replace an existing building that has been damaged or destroyed. Construction costs to replace a building can be estimated with a high degree of accuracy. Appraisers may use a simplified method, often called the unit-cost method of appraisal, in which average local costs are applied on a square or cubic-footage basis to estimate replacement costs. A more detailed method uses the segregated costs, which adds average local costs for each major building element to obtain a more precise estimate of the building's replacement cost.

The most accurate way to determine a building's replacement cost is to ascertain the cost to construct the building from scratch. This involves recognizing costs such as those for architect services, site preparation, and building permits (although it may not be necessary to obtain building permits because the building is being replaced, not built new).

Generally, a risk management professional depends on qualified property appraisers to estimate replacement cost. Expert appraisers often review building plans and specifications, city hall records of actual construction, and original construction costs. A valuation work sheet that an appraiser may complete is shown in Exhibit 3-8.

Exhibit 3-8 does not address all aspects of property appraisals. Unanswered questions might include the following:

- How would the appraiser handle the improvements that tenants have made to the building?

- Are tenants' improvements part of the buildings or part of the interior furnishings?

- How are obsolete building materials valued?

- Would the appraiser estimate costs using identical materials to replace those lost, or should the estimate be based on new types of building materials?

- What building code requirements have to be met if the building is to be constructed?

These and similar questions make a precise determination of replacement cost value almost impossible. Most appraisers state the assumptions underlying their calculations in their reports.

Some buildings might have little economic value but very high replacement costs. That is particularly true of construction styles featuring large and ornate structures as well as structures specifically designed for uses that are obsolete because of technological advances. For example, Airbus's introduction of the A380 with the seven-story tail has made it too large for most hangars. Therefore, replacement hangars would need to be built to larger specifications.

Because of the difficulties in replacing obsolete materials or buildings, an organization must decide whether to try to reconstruct an exact duplicate of the former building or to replace it with a more modern structure that can perform the same function. When choosing between those alternatives, organizations should consider the reproduction cost and the functional replacement cost, both of which are discussed in subsequent sections.

Personal Property

The risk management professional often finds replacement cost the appropriate basis for valuing personal property because, in the event of damage or destruction, the property may have to be replaced for operations to resume. Although estimating the replacement cost of personal property is usually not as difficult as for buildings, it can be more time consuming and require more specialized knowledge because many separate items of property can be involved in one loss exposure.

EXHIBIT 3-8

Valuation Work Sheet

INSURED _____

LOCATION _____

DATE _____   _____ , Engineer

A. UNIT COST METHOD: SQUARE FOOT ☐   CUBIC FOOT ☐

Building Name or Number				
Occupancy				
Class & Quality				
Number of Stories & Ht/Story				
Average Floor Area				
Avg Perimeter or Number of Corners				
Manual Section Used				
Base Cost				
Adjustments				
Heating, Cooling, etc.				
Elevators				
Miscellaneous				
....				
....				
....				
Adjusted Base Cost..........................				
Refinements				
Number of Stories Multiplier				
Ht./Story Multiplier				
Area-Perimeter Multiplier				
Current Cost Multiplier				
Local Cost Multiplier				
Combined Multiplier				
Final Unit Cost				
Area or Volume				
Intermediate Cost				
Lump Sums				
Replacement Cost				
Insurance Exclusions				
%				
Amount				
Insurable Replacement Cost				
Depreciation: Age _____ Cond _____				
%				
Amount				
Insurable Sound Value				

B. SEGREGATED COSTS METHOD: Section _____

Floor Area Costs

	Basement	Other Floors
Excavation		
Foundations...		
Frame		
Floors..		
Floor Cover		
Ceilings		
Interior Const.		
Plumbing		
Sprinklers...		
Heating, Cooling, Ventilation		
Electrical		
....		
Total Cost/Sq. Ft.		
Area		
Total Floor Area Cost		

Wall Area Costs

Exterior Walls.. Area _____ × Cost _____ = _____

Basement Walls .... Area _____ × Cost _____ = _____

Ornamentation .... Area _____ × Cost _____ = _____

    Total Wall Area Costs   ===========

Roof Costs

Roof Cover... Area _____ × Cost _____ = _____

Roof Structure... Area _____ × Cost _____ = _____

Trusses, etc. .... Area _____ × Cost _____ = _____

    Total Roof Area Cost   ===========

Insurance Exclusions	%		Final Calculations	
Basement Excavation	_____		Floor Areas	_____
Foundation Below Ground..	_____		Basement	_____
Piping Below Ground..	_____		Other Floors	_____
Architects Plans & Specifications	_____		Wall Areas	_____
	_____		Roof Areas	_____
	_____		Lump Sums	_____
			Total	_____
	===========		Modifiers	_____
			Architect Fees	_____
			Current Cost	_____
			Local	_____
			Final Modifiers	
			Replacement Cost	_____

LUMP SUMS

Item	Unit Cost	Quantity	Cost B	Architects	Current	Local	Cost A
Total		Section B			Section A		

Valuing an organization's personal property begins by tracking an inventory of all furniture, fixtures, equipment, vehicles, supplies, and other tangible property that the organization owns or uses at each of its facilities. This inventory may be developed from several sources, including purchase records, values reported on insurance policies, personal inspections, and discussions with the organization's personnel.

The next step in the valuation process is to determine how to establish property replacement cost. Replacement cost differs depending on the type of business: manufacturer, wholesaler, or retailer. Every damaged or destroyed piece of inventory could be valued at its production cost (for the manufacturer), its purchase price from the manufacturer (for the wholesaler), or its purchase price from the wholesaler (for the retailer). The production costs or purchase prices that are relevant for the manufacturer, wholesaler, or retailer are the current costs or prices that are required to replace the inventory. The time of replacement could be some time after the inventory suffered the loss. For example, if the event that damaged the inventory also severely damaged the premises and forced temporary closure, lost inventory may not be replaced until the facilities are reopened. At that time, the cost of replacing the inventory could be quite different from the costs or prices at the time the loss occurred.

Reproduction Cost

Reproduction cost
The cost of duplicating property exactly by using materials, artistry, and other expertise comparable to those used for the original property.

The **reproduction cost** of property is the cost of duplicating it exactly by using materials, artistry, and other expertise comparable to those used for the original property. That cost is likely to exceed the costs estimated using any of the other valuation standards.

Reproduction cost is primarily useful in risk management when a need exists to historically or artistically restore properties such as buildings, monuments, or works of art. Organizational goals should guide the risk management professional in determining whether particular property, if damaged or destroyed, should be exactly duplicated or replaced using more modern components. This determines whether reproduction or replacement cost should be used to estimate the financial effect of a property loss exposure.

Reproduction cost has two different applications in risk management. The first deals with recreating property exactly as it originally was. The second deals with the value of records, documents, and the information they contain. Examples of such kinds of property values include the work in process in an architect's or engineer's office, paperwork related to litigation in law firm's offices, the client files of insurance producers, and medical and dental charts. If lost, such documents would have to be reproduced exactly. However, this is not always possible. Therefore, keeping backup copies is often essential for risk management purposes. If these backup facilities are used, then reproduction costs are incurred pre-loss. Otherwise, the reproduction cost can be measured by the cost of recreating the record(s), including the labor required to reconstruct and reenter the information, post-loss.

Functional Replacement Cost

The **functional replacement cost** of property is the cost of acquiring a replacement that, while not identical to the property being replaced, performs the same function with equal efficiency. Often, risk management professionals use functional replacement cost when valuing property that is easily affected by technological changes. For example, an organization may network all of its computers through a server that it purchased several years ago. When purchased, the server was the latest model, but now it is technically obsolete (although it continues to perform its essential functions). Consequently, that model is no longer produced. The risk management professional therefore has to consider the cost of a server that is available in the current market and that can perform the necessary functions. This need not be the latest model.

Functional replacement cost
The cost of acquiring a replacement that, while not identical to the property being replaced, performs the same function with equal efficiency.

Market Value

The **market value** of property is the price that would have to be paid to purchase that property today. Unlike some of the valuation standards previously discussed, market value may be more appropriate in risk management because property that must be replaced will usually be replaced at the going price in today's marketplace.

Market value
The price that would have to be paid to purchase property today.

Perhaps the most appropriate use of market value is for valuing products that are relatively indistinguishable from one another, such as agricultural products, oil, or precious metals. These nonspecialized products are considered to be commodities and are traded as such on organized exchanges. Consequently, these products have a determinable daily market value. For the risk management professional, market value at the date of loss usually is the most appropriate valuation standard for such property. For example, if the grain in a warehouse is lost in a fire, the measure of that loss is the market value of the grain on the date of the fire.

Risk management professionals tend to use market value for other assets as well. For example, the valuation of automobiles is typically at "Blue Book." This refers to the *Kelley Blue Book*, available online,[9] which lists various makes and models of automobiles and all the accessories that affect price, stating a wholesale and retail value for each kind of car based on market conditions. Other online services also offer vehicle values by type, mileage, condition, and ZIP code.

For example, the Blue Book may list the market value of a fully-equipped four-door Ford Explorer that cost $29,000 when new at $10,000. A newer model with similar features might sell for $32,000. The car's market value is not the historical cost ($29,000), and it is not the cost to buy a new one ($32,000); it is the current price that a buyer is ready to pay a seller ($10,000) for the specific make and model of the car in question. Blue Book value and other typical market valuations ignore transaction costs, such as sales commissions and taxes.

The Blue Book, or any other market valuation reference, does not preclude the possibility that a particular vehicle may differ in value from that indicated in the Blue Book. In fact, market research in a particular geographic area may indicate that the car is worth more (or less) than the Blue Book figure. The Blue Book, by its very nature, can report only average values, and the market conditions in a particular area may result in prices different from the average.

Actual Cash Value

Actual cash value
The replacement cost of a property minus its physical depreciation.

Actual cash value is the replacement cost of a property minus its physical depreciation. Physical depreciation refers to the actual deterioration of property over time, resulting from use as well as obsolescence. Accounting depreciation, discussed previously, affects a property's book value. Physical depreciation is generally determined by an appraisal.

Economic Value

Economic value
The amount that property is worth based on the ability of the property to produce income.

Economic value is the amount that property is worth based on the ability of the property to produce income. Unlike other valuation methods, economic value is not affected by the cost of the property or the expense that would be incurred to repair or replace it.

For risk management purposes, economic value can be relevant in measuring property loss exposures for real or personal property that the organization would not replace if it became damaged or destroyed. This is true because economic value focuses on the effect that the loss of the property would have on the organization's future income and, therefore, the property's contribution to the organization's overall value and net worth.

Assume, for example, that a particular metal stamping machine generates annual output with an income value of $10,000 per year after deducting all expenses. If this machine has an expected remaining life of ten years, its economic value is the present value of $10,000 to be received annually over each of the next ten years. As explained in a subsequent chapter, this present value is likely to be significantly less than $100,000 ($10,000 × 10 years) because of the effect of the time value of money.

Another common example of economic value at risk of loss is leasehold value of rental property. A portion of this property's value to the landlord consists of its economic value—that is, the present value of the future rental income for which it could be rented in the existing rental market. To secure the economic value, the owner/landlord must relinquish occupancy (or possession) of the rented property during the period for which the tenant has rented it. Relinquishing this right of present occupancy to secure a rental income tends to reduce the value of the landlord's ownership but also tends to increase the landlord's economic value interest. For the landlord, the total value of property therefore becomes the total of the values of the ownership interest and the economic value interest.

The economic value of property to a landlord/lessor is the present value of the net rental income that the landlord/lessor could generate by renting the property under current rental market conditions for the remainder of the property's expected useful life. Here, net rental income in any given period equals the periodic rent that the landlord could collect from the tenant/lessee, minus the landlord's expenses incurred during that period in making the property available for rent.

Then, as a lease is renewed, periodic rental payments—and therefore the property's economic value—could change with shifting supply and demand factors in the rental market for that particular property. If demand decreases or supply substantially increases, the periodic rental payments that a particular property can command are likely to decrease, lowering its economic value. Opposite changes in supply and demand factors tend to increase rental value, particularly under a long-term lease. As such, the property's economic value might be either more or less than the rental payments. If the current rent that the landlord is charging is more than the current economic value, the landlord is said to have a positive leasehold interest in the property. Conversely, if the landlord is currently charging less for the property than could be charged in the present rental market, perhaps under a lease that the landlord cannot easily break, the landlord is said to have a negative leasehold interest or a leasehold with a negative value.

The effect of a property loss on an organization does not solely depend on the value attached to the property in question. Also relevant is the nature of the legal interest that the organization holds in the property.

LEGAL INTERESTS IN PROPERTY

The type of legal interest an organization holds in property determines the extent to which the organization is harmed if the property is damaged or destroyed. Therefore, in order to select the appropriate risk management technique, a risk management professional needs to understand the legal interests that the organization holds in the property in question. Legal interests in property can be categorized as follows:

- Ownership interest
- Secured creditor's interest
- Seller's and buyer's interest
- Bailee's interest
- Landlord's interest
- Tenant's interest

Ownership Interest

An ownership interest refers to how much of a property someone owns. A property owner suffers a loss to the extent of that ownership interest when that property is damaged or destroyed. Property can be owned by an individual or an organization in its entirety, or it can be owned jointly with others.

Secured Creditor's Interest

Secured creditor

A creditor who has a right to reclaim property for which a loan was extended.

A **secured creditor** is a creditor who has a right to reclaim property for which a loan was extended. For example, an organization may have borrowed money from a bank to purchase its fleet of trucks. If the organization defaults on its repayments to the bank, the bank can take possession of the trucks. A secured creditor's rights are superior to those of nonsecured creditors who must make a general claim against the individual or organization that defaulted. A secured creditor usually retains the property's title and stands to lose the outstanding loan balance if the property is stolen, damaged, or destroyed.

Seller's and Buyer's Interest

When someone buys property, the terms of sale stipulate when the property's title is transferred from the seller to the buyer. When transferred, the seller relinquishes, and the buyer acquires, an interest in the property rights that are the subject of the sales contract. Particularly for personal property, the time of title transfer must be specified so that the seller's and buyer's interests can be adequately protected, usually through insurance.

If the property being bought and sold needs to be shipped from seller to buyer, the risk management professionals for both the seller and the buyer must understand which party has the loss exposure for the property while it is in transit. If, as is often the case, the property has been paid for before it is shipped, the buyer has the loss exposure during transit because the title shifted to the buyer when the purchase price was paid, unless otherwise stipulated. If, however, the buyer makes less than full payment, both parties must be concerned with the consequences of a loss while the property is in transit. Sometimes the entity transporting the property assumes responsibility for safekeeping the property while it is in transit. In this case, neither the buyer nor the seller are responsible for the loss exposure during transit; they can rely on the transporting entity for loss indemnification.

Bailee

A person or entity who receives property from another (the bailor) under a bailment contract.

Bailor

A person or entity who delivers property to another (the bailee) under a bailment contract.

Bailment contract

A contract that requires the bailee to keep the property in safekeeping for a specific purpose and then to return the property to the bailor when the purpose has been fulfilled.

Bailee's Interest

A **bailee** is a person or entity who receives property from another (the **bailor**) under a bailment contract. A **bailment contract** requires the bailee to keep the property in safekeeping for a specific purpose and then to return the property to the bailor when the purpose has been fulfilled. Bailments frequently arise in business transactions involving repair, storage, or transport of personal property. For example, an organization may regularly rotate its fleet of delivery vans through an auto repair shop for routine maintenance thereby creating a bailment.

A bailee assumes responsibility for the reasonable care of the property in its care, custody, or control. If the property is damaged or destroyed, the bailee is responsible for its replacement. Although a bailee's obligation is a liability loss exposure, the extent of that exposure is limited to the property's value. Consequently, risk management professionals who address bailee interests often treat them more as property loss exposures rather than liability loss exposures.

Warehouses and common carriers (those that are available to the general public as carriers for hire) have specific statutory and other legal duties as bailees of the property entrusted to them. Therefore, the risk management professionals for common carriers and warehouses should determine the degree of care legally imposed on them and the financial extent of their obligations to replace property damaged while in their custody. Unless otherwise provided by statute or the common carrier's bill of lading (the contract between the parties that also limits the common carrier's liability), the carrier is responsible for the full value of property transported. However, under a limited bill of lading, a common carrier may limit its liability for property damage to a lower specified dollar amount. State laws might also limit the liability of other bailees. For example, hotels and motels in most states benefit from innkeepers' statutes that limit their liability for their guests' property to a specified amount per person or per family.

Landlord's Interest

The owner of real or personal property (the landlord) may choose to rent or lease it to another (the tenant) for specific periods in exchange for rent that the tenant pays to the landlord. The terms of the rental contract should determine responsibility if the rented property is damaged or destroyed. The risk management professional needs to be aware of the retention or transfer of any legal liabilities. Similarly to bailment, although a landlord's obligations are a liability loss exposure, the risk management professional will also consider the property loss exposures.

Tenant's Interest

Tenants do not own the property they use, but they can have legally protected interests in the occupancy of that property for the length of the lease. They also have an obligation to return that property when their right to use it has expired. A tenant's rights and obligations depend on the terms of the lease (or rental) agreement. If there is no lease agreement, a tenant is usually not liable under common law for damage to a lessor's property. If there is a lease agreement, the agreement defines the rights and obligations of the tenant and the lessor. (The obligations assumed under the terms of a lease contract are legal liability exposures, which will be discussed in a subsequent chapter.)

Apart from this liability exposure, a tenant can have a property interest (known as a tenant's leasehold interest) in rented property when the fair market value of the tenant's rights under a lease is greater than the rent that the tenant is paying. That leasehold interest can be lost if the rented property becomes unusable or if the lessor has the right to terminate the lease.

Improvements and betterments
Alterations to premises made by a tenant that make it more useful for the tenant's purposes, increase the value of the property, and become part of the leased structure.

Tenants occupying leased premises also have a property interest in improvements and betterments that they make. **Improvements and betterments** are alterations to premises made by a tenant that make it more useful for the tenant's purposes, increase the value of the property, and become part of the leased structure. For example, if a restaurateur constructs an internal wall to separate the kitchen from the dining area, this would be considered an improvement. A distinguishing feature of improvements and betterments is that they are intended to remain permanently attached to the portion of the building that the tenant occupies.

Trade fixtures
Fixtures and equipment that may be attached to a building during a tenant's occupancy, with the intention that they be removed when the tenant leaves.

Fixtures and equipment that may be attached to the building during the tenant's occupancy, with the intention that they be removed when the tenant leaves, are known as **trade fixtures**. Trade fixtures are usually treated as personal property. If, for example, a toy store was located in a leased building, all of the shelving and other fixtures it had installed in the building would be considered personal property. Typically, if a building having any of these trade fixtures is damaged, the landlord is obligated to restore only the structure, not the trade fixtures. Unless the lease specifies otherwise, the trade fixtures are considered the property of the tenant. Most leases state that the landlord is not responsible for any damage to the property of the tenant.

METHODS OF IDENTIFYING PROPERTY LOSS EXPOSURES

Having identified the types of, and legal interests in, property exposed to loss, and the causes of loss that typically affect this property, the risk management professional can use the following methods to identify the property loss exposures:

- Risk assessment questionnaires
- Loss histories
- Financial statements and underlying accounting records
- Other records and documents
- Flowcharts
- Personal inspections
- Expertise within and beyond the organization

Risk Assessment Questionnaires

Risk assessment questionnaires are typically lists of questions designed to prompt the risk management professional to consider all of the organization's loss exposures. These questions do not relate the property identified to a potential cause of loss or to the value of the exposed property. Consequently, a risk management professional's knowledge of causes of loss affecting property and various methods of valuing property are essential. However, risk assessment questionnaires can be particularly useful in identifying property loss exposures because they usually include extensive lists of property that an organization might own or lease.

Loss Histories

Loss histories are listings of prior losses. Risk management professionals often review loss histories to determine the types of losses that have happened in the past, the magnitude of these losses, and the frequency of these losses. Past property losses often help to direct the focus of the risk management professional's risk control and risk financing efforts. For example, the organization's loss history might show a pattern of broken windows and other vandalism at one of the warehouses. The risk management professional may choose to implement loss control measures such as fences, exterior lighting, and night watchmen patrols to control this loss exposure. Also, the risk management professional may choose to retain those loss exposures rather than jeopardize its relationship with its property insurer over relatively small losses.

Although useful to risk management professionals, loss histories have the following limitations:

- The organization may have disposed of the items or types of property that suffered loss in the past, or it may have acquired new items or types of property for which it has no loss records.

- The physical, managerial, and economic environment in which the organization operates (especially its loss control management and technology) may have changed so substantially since it began keeping property loss records that the earliest records have little risk management significance.

- Industry averages, which may be available for some organizations, may not be relevant to the organization for which losses are being forecast.

- Because few organizations maintain detailed records of intangible property losses, the historical data often understate the frequency and severity of this type of property loss.

- Historical losses to tangible property (real or personal) may not give reliable indications of property values currently exposed to loss because of changes in the prices of the property concerned.

With these reservations aside, risk management professionals often find past losses to be one of the best indicators of future losses.

Financial Statements and Underlying Accounting Records

An organization's balance sheet, its income statement, and its statement of cash flows can help to identify property loss exposures. Within the balance sheet, each asset category represents a variety of exposed property values that are described in greater detail in the underlying accounting records. For each asset or group of assets, the risk management professional should inquire as to (1) the specific items of property represented by the value entered on the balance sheet, (2) the causes of loss that threaten that property, and (3) the value of that property for risk management purposes—that is, what the organization would have to pay to repair or replace it.

In the organization's income statement, the risk management professional usually focuses on the revenues section of the statement. Key questions include the following:

- From what operations or products does the organization derive its income in whole or in part?
- What items of property are used in the production of this income?

Property assets that are directly involved in producing the largest segments of an organization's revenues are, operationally, the organization's most important assets. Without these assets, major portions of revenues could not be generated. In that sense, an asset's value stems not only from its initial cost or current replacement cost but also from the contribution it makes to the organization's revenues. In identifying property loss exposures, an organization's risk management professional should make special efforts to recognize those assets that contribute greatly to revenues, regardless of their cost. For example, a computer that runs an automated factory may deserve more risk management attention than would an artistic statue on the factory's front lawn, even though the statue would cost $50,000 to replace while the computer could be replaced for only $5,000.

Within an organization's statement of cash flows, key property loss exposures are likely to appear in the cash from investing section. That section shows where the organization is acquiring new assets or increasing its commitments within an existing asset category (such as machinery or inventory). Risk management professionals should be alert to the increased loss potential arising from these new assets. Conversely, if the organization is disposing of particular assets, then they no longer present a property loss exposure. Loss exposures are not static. The statement of cash flows for a particular accounting period can show risk management professionals how an organization's property loss exposures have changed during that time.

Other Records and Documents

An organization has many other records and documents, including its corporate charter; copyrights, trademarks, and patents; architectural drawings of its facilities; minutes from the board meetings or important operating committees; and records of its dealings with customers, such as client lists or medical records.

At one level, these records are important items of property that merit physical protection. For example, patents are easier to protect against infringement if the patent holder has the patent certificate. Having records of dealings with past clients helps maintain client patronage.

Beyond the value of the documents themselves, records are important for the information they can provide about other property exposures. Board minutes and other committee meetings could reveal plans to acquire or dispose of important assets. Records, memoranda, or correspondence involving particular departments within an organization may also reveal property loss exposures. For example, the purchasing department may have documentation that describes the difficulty the organization had in obtaining replacement parts for key machinery. Alternatively, the organization's maintenance department may have records showing the expense involved in maintaining each item of property.

Flowcharts

The physical production process depicted in a flowchart portrays or suggests many items of property arranged in a productive sequence. Almost every step of the process that a flowchart describes—and certainly every location in a multi-facility flowchart—can reveal important property loss exposures. For example, buildings, machinery, inventories of raw materials and finished goods, storerooms of maintenance equipment and spare parts, and materials-handling conveyors connecting buildings are items of property whose existence and importance a flowchart will disclose.

Personal Inspections

What the risk management professional may only visualize in a flowchart can be seen first-hand during a personal inspection of an organization's premises and facilities and those of its suppliers and customers. During such visits, the risk management professional may discover important assets that were never clearly identified on the balance sheet or flowchart. Alternatively he or she may find that reported assets no longer exist. Furthermore, like flowcharts but with more accuracy, a personal inspection can reveal where the specific arrangement of a production process (perhaps a propane tank situated unnecessarily close to a grain storage elevator) might pose an unacceptable property hazard. Through personal inspections, the risk management professional may identify items of property that were not previously considered a possible loss exposure: such as underground storage tanks, artwork and other valuable interior decorations, or even employees' property stored in the on-premises lockers that the organization may feel morally obligated to replace if damaged. Visiting a premises also enables the risk management professional to more accurately interpret future written reports, flowcharts, or other materials that he or she might receive about the facility. A personal visit also allows for potentially informative conversations with employees.

Expertise Within and Beyond the Organization

Discussion with employees can yield valuable ideas on alternative machinery or other assets that might better serve the organization as replacements if the current ones were ever damaged. These employees may also be aware of alternative sources for replacing particular assets or for contracting for prompt repairs.

Among experts outside the organization, professional property appraisers can be vital in determining the replacement costs of particular kinds of assets; preferably before they are damaged or destroyed, when valuation is easier and less subject to dispute. Technology experts may be able to suggest alternative assets or sources of replacement. They may also be aware of impending changes in technology, which could render obsolete some of an organization's current machinery or other assets.

SUMMARY

This chapter examined property loss exposures in terms of (1) the property exposed to loss, (2) the major causes of loss affecting property, (3) the methods of valuing property, (4) the legal interests in property, and (5) the methods available to risk management professionals to identify property loss exposures.

Property values exposed to loss fall into two broad categories: real property and personal property. Real property includes land and all structures permanently attached to the land. Risk management professionals often distinguish between land, both unimproved and improved, and buildings and other structures when assessing an organization's property loss exposures. Personal property includes all property other than real property, and can be classified as either tangible or intangible. Tangible property has a physical form that can be seen or touched, such as inventory or furniture. Intangible personal property is property that has no physical form, such as copyrights.

Property is exposed to virtually an infinite number of causes of loss. The major natural causes of property loss are as follows:

- Windstorm
- Earthquake
- Flood
- Fire and lightning
- Smoke

- Hail
- Weight of snow, sleet, and ice
- Water
- Volcanic action
- Sinkhole collapse

The major human causes of property loss are as follows:

- Riot and civil commotion
- Explosion
- Vandalism
- Vehicles
- Collapse
- Aircraft
- Crime
- Falling objects

The major economic causes of property loss are as follows:

- Strikes or boycotts
- War
- Significant technological changes
- Changes in consumer preferences

Risk management professionals need to value the organization's property so that the magnitude of a property loss can be considered in the risk assessment. Organizations normally own a significant amount of property, making it difficult to track the values of all but the most significant items. Additionally, valuing property is a time-consuming task and the values determined usually are relevant for only a limited time because the value of property changes. The following are the approaches to valuing property discussed in this chapter:

- *Historical cost.* The original cost of the property.
- *Tax-appraised value.* The value assigned to a property for the purpose of tax assessment.
- *Book value.* An asset's historical cost minus accumulated depreciation.
- *Replacement cost.* The amount required to replace lost, damaged, or destroyed property with comparable property.
- *Reproduction cost.* The cost of duplicating property exactly by using materials, artistry, and other expertise comparable to those used for the original property.
- *Functional replacement cost.* The cost of acquiring a replacement that, while not identical to the property being replaced, performs the same function with equal efficiency.

- *Market value.* The price that would have to be paid to purchase property today.
- *Actual cash value.* The replacement cost of property minus its physical depreciation.
- *Economic value.* The amount property is worth based on the ability of property to produce income.

Risk management professionals must identify the organization's legal interest in property. This means to what extent, if at all, the organization is harmed if property is damaged or destroyed. The following are legal interests in property loss exposures that an organization may have:

- Ownership interest
- Secured creditor's interest
- Seller's and buyer's interest
- Bailee's interest
- Landlord's interest
- Tenant's interest

To select the appropriate risk management technique, the risk management professional has to identify the specific property loss exposures. The following are the methods of identifying property loss exposures described in this chapter:

- Risk assessment questionnaires
- Loss histories
- Financial statements and underlying accounting records
- Other records and documents
- Flowcharts
- Personal inspections
- Expertise within and beyond the organization

In addition to the property loss exposures of an organization, the risk management professional must be as concerned with the liability loss exposures. Because liability loss exposures manifest themselves as lawsuits, risk management professionals need to be knowledgeable of both the basic legal concepts and the sources of liability. The next chapter describes legal foundations essential to fully appreciating the sources of liability described in the subsequent three chapters.

CHAPTER NOTES

1. Insurance Information Institute, *The III Insurance Fact Book 2005* (New York: Insurance Information Institute, 2005), p. 92.

2. *The III Insurance Fact Book 2005*, p. 90.

3. *The III Insurance Fact Book 2005*, p. 97.

4. *The III Insurance Fact Book 2005*, p. 97.

5. Roger Smith, *Catastrophes and Disasters* (New York: Chambers, 1992), p. 211.

6. Michael E. Ruane, "For Allentown, a Blast of a Time," *The Philadelphia Inquirer*, March 20, 1994, p. A1.

7. *The III Insurance Fact Book 2005*, p. 102.

8. Federal Bureau of Investigation, www.fbi.gov/ucr/03cius.htm, *Crime in the United States—2003, Section II*, p. 43 (accessed April 26, 2005).

9. *Kelley Blue Book*, www.kbb.com (accessed April 4, 2005).

Chapter 4

Direct Your Learning

Understanding the Legal Foundations of Liability Loss Exposures

After learning the content of this chapter and completing the corresponding course guide assignment, you should be able to:

- Describe liability loss exposures arising out of torts.
- Describe liability loss exposures arising out of contracts.
- Describe liability loss exposures arising out of statutes.
- Define or describe each of the Key Words and Phrases for this chapter.

Develop Your Perspective

What are the main topics covered in the chapter?

This chapter examines the concept of legal liability and how it can be based on torts, contracts, or statutes. Negligence, one type of tort, is examined in depth because it is the basis on which many lawsuits are brought against organizations.

List some of the possible liability claims that could be brought against your organization.

- For a given claim, would the claimant be able to prove all the elements of negligence?
- What type of damages would result from this type of negligence claim, assuming the elements of negligence were met?

Why is it important to learn about these topics?

To effectively apply risk management techniques to commercial liability loss exposures, a risk management professional must understand the various ways in which an organization can become legally liable to others.

Consider the loss exposures you noted previously.

- What actions might your organization take to avoid committing, and being held liable for, libel and nuisance?
- What actions might your organization take to reduce its liability loss exposure?

How can you use what you will learn?

Evaluate your organization's activities for instances in which it could become legally liable to others.

- How well do the organizational procedures currently in place ensure that the standard of care owed to others is being met?
- Are the consequences of contractual breach being given adequate consideration by those binding the organization to those commitments?

Chapter 4

Understanding the Legal Foundations of Liability Loss Exposures

All organizations face liability loss exposures. A liability loss exposure is a condition that presents the possibility of a legal claim or lawsuit being made against an organization. Liability loss exposures can range from frivolous demands to multimillion-dollar judgments. If improperly managed, liability loss exposures can prevent an organization from reaching its goals or can even result in bankruptcy. Therefore, most organizations try to prevent liability loss exposures from occurring and arrange the most efficient way to finance those that cannot be prevented. Risk management professionals need an understanding of legal foundations in order to anticipate the possible liability loss exposures an organization faces. Such a foundation includes liability arising out of torts, contracts, and statutes.

Legal liability is the responsibility imposed by law for an act or the failure to act. If the claimant cannot establish that the alleged wrongdoer is legally liable, the alleged wrongdoer is not required to compensate the claimant. Therefore, anyone who wishes to evaluate an organization's liability loss exposures must be able to understand the various ways in which the organization could become legally liable.

Legal liability
The responsibility imposed by law for an act or the failure to act.

The three main bases of legal liability are torts, contracts, or statutes.

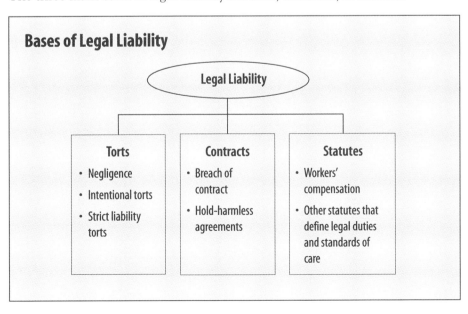

Bases of Legal Liability

Legal Liability

Torts	Contracts	Statutes
• Negligence • Intentional torts • Strict liability torts	• Breach of contract • Hold-harmless agreements	• Workers' compensation • Other statutes that define legal duties and standards of care

---

Civil Law and Criminal Law

The discussion of legal liability in this chapter describes matters of civil law rather than criminal law. Criminal law applies to acts that society deems so harmful to the public welfare that government takes the responsibility for prosecuting and punishing the perpetrators. Civil law applies to legal matters not governed by criminal law. Civil law basically provides remedies for breaches of duties owed to others.

Risk management is concerned with both criminal and civil liability because either type of liability can present a liability loss exposure and prevent an organization from reaching its goals. Therefore, it is essential for an organization to stay informed of all applicable laws and to comply with those laws. This awareness can be viewed as using risk control to reduce the organization's exposure to legal liability. The organization may also have noninsurance risk financing measures in place, such as a funded reserve or a borrowing agreement, to defend itself against allegations of criminal conduct or a civil wrong and pay fines if found guilty.

LEGAL LIABILITY BASED ON TORTS

Tort
A wrongful act or omission, other than a crime or a breach of contract, for which the remedy is usually monetary damages.

A **tort** is a wrongful act or omission, other than a crime or a breach of contract, for which the remedy is usually monetary damages. The person or organization committing a tort is called a wrongdoer or tortfeasor. When two or more persons unite in committing a tort, they are called joint tortfeasors.

Torts can be classified into three broad types: (1) negligence, (2) intentional torts, and (3) strict liability torts. In practice, the lines between these three categories are often blurred. As long as that is kept in mind, the three broad categories provide a useful framework for conveying the general nature of more specific types of torts.

Negligence

Negligence
The failure to exercise the degree of care that a reasonably prudent person would have exercised under similar circumstances to avoid harming another person or legal entity.

The tort of **negligence** is the failure to exercise the degree of care that a reasonably prudent person would have exercised under similar circumstances to avoid harming another person or legal entity. If a person does something that a reasonably prudent person would not have done under similar circumstances, the person's conduct is referred to as a negligent act (or an act of commission). If a person fails to do something that a reasonably prudent person would have done under similar circumstances, the person's conduct is referred to as a negligent omission (or act of omission).

When a claimant (the plaintiff) brings a lawsuit against an allegedly negligent person (the defendant), legal liability will be imposed on the defendant only if the four essential elements of negligence are established to the satisfaction of the court hearing the lawsuit.

Elements of Negligence

A defendant can be held liable for negligence only if the plaintiff can prove all four of the following elements:

1. The defendant owed a legal duty of care to the plaintiff.
2. The defendant breached the legal duty of care owed to the plaintiff.
3. The defendant's breach of duty was the proximate cause of the plaintiff's injury or damage.
4. The plaintiff suffered actual injury or damage.

The first element of negligence is a legal duty of care owed. In the context of negligence law, the legal duty is the obligation to exercise reasonable care for the safety of others. For example, the driver of a car has a legal duty to stay in his or her lane of travel and not cross over the center line into oncoming traffic. These legal duties are created by (1) the common law and (2) statutes or ordinances.

1. The **common law** consists of a body of principles and rules derived from court decisions over time. In the United States, these principles and rules can be found by referring to court decisions and formal published compilations called "restatements."

2. A **statute** is a written law passed by a legislative body. In the U.S., statutes are passed at either the federal or the state level. Written laws at the local level are usually referred to as ordinances. Statutes and ordinances can alter or amend common-law duties, or they can create duties that never existed at common law. Statutes can also create liabilities that can be imposed in the absence of negligence or any other tort. An example is the workers' compensation system.

Common law
A body of principles and rules derived from court decisions over time.

Statute
A written law passed by a legislative body.

Restatement of the Law

The American Law Institute (ALI) was established in 1923 to address the uncertainty and complexity of American law. To this end the ALI introduced the *Restatement of the Law*, which synthesized court rulings into statements of what the law is. Between 1923 and 1944, *Restatement of the Law* was adopted for the law of agency, conflict of laws, contracts, judgments, property, restitution, security, torts, and trusts. Subsequent revisions of the *Restatement of the Law* have revised these topics and expanded into others, such as unfair competition. Although the *Restatement of the Law* does not have binding legal authority, the courts frequently cite it. Moreover, *Restatement of the Law* is a good source for finding other cases that have a bearing on or connection with the lawsuit at hand.

Because statutes and ordinances can modify and define the extent of the duties to be undertaken in connection with certain activities, a violation of a statute can constitute a negligent breach of duty (called negligence per se, described in a subsequent section). For example, a local ordinance may apply to the use and storage of dangerous or flammable material. A violation of the requirements of that ordinance would constitute a breach of the duty of care.

The second element of negligence is breach of the legal duty owed. A person who owes a legal duty to another must exercise reasonable care to observe that duty. The failure to observe the standard of care required under the circumstances is considered a breach of duty. An example is an auto mechanic who fails to bleed a car's brake lines of air, thereby enabling the brakes to fail.

Whether the defendant has breached the duty of care is determined by the trier of fact (usually a jury in a civil suit). Courts have adopted the reasonably prudent person test to evaluate the conduct of a defendant. If the trier of fact believes that a reasonably prudent person would not have made the act or omission committed by the defendant, because of the foreseeable consequences to others of that act or omission, the trier of fact can conclude that the defendant failed to observe the standard of care that was required by the particular circumstances involved. Courts will hold defendants to a higher degree of care if the defendant has specialized knowledge or training. For example, a physician is held to a higher degree of care than a nonphysician in providing medical treatment.

The third element of negligence is proximate cause. A court cannot hold a person liable for negligence merely for proof of a wrongful act and an injury. The wrongful act must also have been the proximate, or direct, cause of the injury. **Proximate cause** is a cause that, in a natural and continuous sequence unbroken by any new and independent cause, produces an event and without which the event would not have happened.

Proximate cause
A cause that, in a natural and continuous sequence unbroken by any new and independent cause, produces an event and without which the event would not have happened.

Proximate cause becomes an issue when there is not an obvious causal connection between the actions (or omissions) of the defendant and the loss or injury suffered by the defendant. The plaintiff must prove that a causal connection exists. The defendant, however, may be able to prove that an independent, intervening event was the actual cause of the loss or injury and that therefore he or she was not negligent.

The fourth element of negligence is actual injury or damage. The plaintiff must establish actual damage of a type recognized by law. This can include mental as well as physical injury. In tort law, the plaintiff can recover the following types of damages:

- Compensatory damages, which compensate the plaintiff
- Punitive damages, which punish the defendant

Damage Versus Damages

In the legal community, a distinction is made between damage and damages. *Damage* is used within the context of a physical loss, bodily injury, or deterioration of value. *Damages*, on the other hand, means monetary compensation for the loss or injury.

Compensatory damages are payment for the losses actually sustained by the plaintiff. Compensatory damages are customarily divided into two categories: special damages and general damages.

Special damages are compensatory damages for actual losses that the plaintiff claims are the result of the defendant's wrongful act or omission. Special damages cover specific out-of-pocket expenses and could include any of the following:

- The cost to repair or replace damaged property
- Costs resulting from the loss of use of damaged property, such as loss of earnings
- Loss of earnings if the plaintiff is physically disabled by the negligence of the defendant
- Reasonable medical expenses incurred by the plaintiff as a result of the wrongful act

General damages are compensatory damages that do not have an economic value and that are presumed to follow from the type of wrong claimed by the plaintiff. Examples of general damages are damages for pain and suffering, mental anguish, bereavement from the death of a loved one, or the loss of the consortium of a deceased or disabled spouse. (Loss of consortium refers to loss of the benefits that one spouse receives from the other, including companionship, affection, and sexual relations.) Any general damages awarded are intended to compensate the plaintiff with the monetary equivalent of such intangibles. The total amount of general damages is determined by the jury deciding the case or, if the claim is settled out of court, by negotiation between the two sides.

In addition to compensatory damages, the defendant may have to pay **punitive damages**, which are damages that are imposed if the defendant acted recklessly or maliciously to punish the defendant, to teach the defendant a lesson, or to deter others from engaging in the same kind of conduct. Because of their role in deterring others by example, punitive damages are also called exemplary damages.

Historically, punitive damages were seldom awarded in ordinary negligence lawsuits. They were imposed on defendants only in gross negligence or intentional

Compensatory damages
Payment for the losses actually sustained by the plaintiff.

Special damages
Compensatory damages for actual losses that the plaintiff claims are the result of the defendant's wrongful act or omission.

General damages
Compensatory damages that do not have an economic value and that are presumed to follow from the type of wrong claimed by the plaintiff.

Punitive damages
Damages that are imposed if the defendant acted recklessly or maliciously to punish the defendant, to teach the defendant a lesson, or to deter others from engaging in the same kind of conduct.

interference lawsuits when the defendant's conduct was wanton and willful, malicious, or outrageous. Although that is still the general rule, the frequency and severity of punitive damages awards have increased noticeably in recent years.

In some legal actions, plaintiffs seek to obtain an injunction instead of, or in addition to, monetary damages. An **injunction** is a court order that requires the defendant to stop doing something (such as unfair employment discrimination) or to do something (such as clean up a toxic landfill).

Injunction
A court order that requires the defendant to stop doing something or to do something.

Although there is ordinarily no upper dollar limit on the amount a court may award in a tort claim, some statutes impose limits on the amount of damages that plaintiffs can collect in certain types of lawsuits. For example, a state legislature might pass a tort reform statute limiting recovery for general damages in a medical malpractice suit to $500,000.

Defenses to Negligence

In a negligence action, the plaintiff cannot recover damages from the defendant unless the plaintiff can prove all of the necessary elements of negligence. Therefore, anything that the defendant can assert in court to preclude the plaintiff from establishing any of the elements of negligence can be considered a defense against the negligence action. For example, the defendant may try to do any of the following:

- Demonstrate that the defendant did not breach the duty of care owed to the plaintiff
- Refute the plaintiff's allegation that the defendant's act or omission was the proximate cause of the plaintiff's injury
- Demonstrate that the plaintiff did not suffer any actual harm (injury or damage), even though the defendant may have breached a duty owed to the plaintiff

Apart from rebutting the plaintiff's allegation of negligence, the defendant can also assert other defenses. These defenses can eliminate or lessen the defendant's liability even though the plaintiff may have proven all of the elements of negligence. The burden is on the defendant to prove any such defense asserted.

Defenses to Negligence

- Contributory negligence
- Comparative negligence
- Assumption of risk
- Statute of limitations
- Immunities

Contributory negligence
The plaintiff's own negligence that in part caused the plaintiff's harm and that prevents the plaintiff from recovering damages.

One defense to negligence actions is contributory negligence. The term **contributory negligence** refers to the plaintiff's negligence that in part caused the plaintiff's harm and that prevents the plaintiff from recovering damages. At one time, contributory negligence was a complete defense against a negligence claim or suit. Therefore, if the plaintiff's own negligence was even a slight contributing cause of the plaintiff's bodily injury or property damage, the plaintiff was not entitled to recover any damages from the defendant. The contributory negligence defense often produced such harsh results that juries gradually began to interpret slight negligence as though it were no negligence. Eventually, a majority of states abolished the contributory negligence defense and replaced it, either by statute or case law, with various comparative negligence rules.

Comparative negligence is the plaintiff's negligence that in part caused the plaintiff's harm and that proportionally reduces the damages that the plaintiff recovers. In a jurisdiction that has adopted comparative negligence, the court apportions damages between the plaintiff and the defendant when both are at fault. Both the contributory and comparative negligence theories recognize that, when a plaintiff's negligence helps cause the plaintiff's own injuries, the damages recoverable by the plaintiff should diminish. Contributory negligence completely prevents a plaintiff from winning a lawsuit, whereas comparative negligence merely reduces the amount of the plaintiff's recovery.

Comparative negligence
The plaintiff's negligence that in part caused the plaintiff's harm and that proportionally reduces the damages that the plaintiff recovers.

The specific rules for comparative negligence differ by state. Some states have pure comparative negligence statutes in which damages are apportioned between the plaintiff and the defendant based on the party's relative fault. However, some states have enacted a modified form of comparative negligence. The modified form excludes recovery by the plaintiff in circumstances in which the plaintiff's negligence was the major cause of the accident.

Two thresholds of modified comparative negligence exist: 50 percent and 51 percent. Under the "50 percent rule," recovery is permitted only if the plaintiff's negligence is less than 50 percent. Under the "51 percent rule," recovery is permitted only if the plaintiff's negligence is no more than that of the defendant (50 percent or less). The challenge for courts in modified comparative negligence states is assessing the relative responsibility of the parties and assigning a percentage of fault to each.

Comparison of Contributory Negligence, Pure Comparative Negligence, and Modified Comparative Negligence

Pam and Tom are involved in an auto accident in which Pam is 50 percent at fault. Pam, who was not hurt in the accident but who sustained $5,000 of damage to her car, brings a negligence claim against Tom.

Contributory Negligence	Pam collects nothing from Tom.
Pure Comparative Negligence	Pam recovers 50% of her loss from Tom.
Modified Comparative Negligence: 50% rule	Pam collects nothing from Tom.
Modified Comparative Negligence: 51% rule	Pam recovers 50% of her loss from Tom.

Assumption of risk
The plaintiff's act of knowingly and voluntarily accepting the possibility of harm.

Under the common law, **assumption of risk** is the plaintiff's act of knowingly and voluntarily accepting the possibility of harm. A plaintiff who has assumed the risks involved in a particular activity cannot later recover damages from a negligent defendant. For example, a participant in a paint-ball battle assumes the risk associated with being fired upon by other participants. However, the assumption-of-risk defense is available only if it has not been abolished by statute or case law. All fifty states have abolished the assumption-of-risk defense to the extent that workers' compensation statutes are applicable to job-related injuries and diseases. Some states have abolished the assumption-of-risk defense under comparative negligence and no-fault auto statutes.

Statute of limitations
A statute that sets forth the periods of time within which various types of legal actions must be brought.

States have enacted **statutes of limitations**, which are statutes that set forth the periods of time within which various types of legal actions must be brought. Failure to sue within the time set forth in the statute terminates the plaintiff's right to enforce a claim. The intention behind this legislation is that there should be some point at which the threat of litigation must cease.

The time periods in statutes of limitations differ by state and within a given state vary by type of legal action. The statutes also provide that the time limitation is automatically extended for certain classes of persons, such as minors and insane persons.

Finally, a potential defense to negligence actions is immunities. Historically, tort liability immunities have been granted to various types of entities under certain circumstances. These entities include governmental entities, public officials, and charitable institutions. A person or an organization that has tort immunity cannot be held liable for torts that are committed within the scope of the immunity granted. These immunities have been gradually restricted or eliminated either by case law or statute. However, in jurisdictions that continue to recognize them, tort immunities remain legal defenses against tort actions.

Governmental immunity (also called sovereign immunity) can apply to the acts of federal, state, or local governments, or to the acts of public officials such as judges or legislators. Because this exemption from tort liability could result in injustices, statutes have been enacted by federal and state governments under which the government can be sued. For example, the Federal Tort Claims Act (FTCA) waives immunity under certain circumstances. Local municipalities, including police and fire departments, school districts, and public hospitals, have also enjoyed at least partial immunity.

Charitable immunity is a common-law exemption from tort liability with the purpose of encouraging charitable work. Most states have abolished charitable immunity. Some states have denied immunity when liability insurance is available but have allowed immunity when payments must be made from the charities' trust funds, reasoning that the funds were donated for charitable purposes and should not be diverted to pay judgments from tort claims.

Family member immunity is a common-law exemption from tort liability with the purpose of preserving family harmony by preventing interfamilial lawsuits, such as spouses suing one another. However, family member immunity has largely been discontinued.

Additional Factors in Proving Negligence

There are additional factors that may affect the proof of negligence. These include the following:

- Negligent entrustment
- Negligence per se
- Joint and several liability
- *Res ipsa loquitur*
- Vicarious liability

Courts have allowed plaintiffs to use negligent entrustment as a proof of breach of duty in actions against defendants who allowed persons who are incompetent, unfit, or reckless to use dangerous objects. For example, a court may allow a plaintiff to bring suit against the owner of a gun if the owner loaned the gun to someone who subsequently shot the plaintiff. Most lawsuits involving negligent entrustment involve auto owners who loaned their auto to someone who was subsequently involved in an accident. Courts sometimes award punitive damages to the plaintiff in lawsuits in which negligent entrustment is proven.

Negligence per se (Latin for "by itself") is an act that is considered inherently negligent because of a violation of a law or ordinance. To constitute negligence per se, the law or ordinance must have been written to protect a class of victims and the plaintiff must be a member of that class. For example if the plaintiff is a school child, and the defendant exceeded the regulated speed limit in a school zone, that violation of speeding laws could be negligence per se. If the defendant is guilty of negligence per se, this constitutes breach of duty of care.

Negligence per se
An act that is considered inherently negligent because of a violation of a law or ordinance.

Negligence per se is limited to use in those circumstances in which the violated law is relevant to harm sustained by the plaintiff, and not in situations in which the violated law is unrelated. For example, a plaintiff injured by an auto with an out-of-date license plate is unlikely to succeed in a lawsuit based on the concept of negligence per se because the violated law did not contribute to the accident.

Joint and several liability is the liability of multiple defendants either collectively or individually for the entire amount of damages sought by the plaintiff regardless of their relative degree of responsibility. For example, during a difficult surgery, a supporting surgeon might be brought in to assist the primary surgeon. If a lawsuit arises out of the surgical procedure, both surgeons would be responsible for the entire amount of damages even if the supporting surgeon's involvement was minimal.

Joint and several liability
The liability of multiple defendants either collectively or individually for the entire amount of damages sought by the plaintiff regardless of their relative degree of responsibility.

Joint and several liability is often called the "deep pocket" rule because it allows plaintiffs to pursue the defendant with the most money, regardless of who has the greatest responsibility for the harm caused. Some states have abolished joint and several liability and have replaced it with several liability in which liability, and consequently damages, are apportioned among defendants based on their relative share of responsibility.

Res ipsa loquitur
A legal doctrine that provides that, in some circumstances, negligence is inferred simply by an accident occurring.

Res ipsa loquitur (Latin for "the thing speaks for itself") is a legal doctrine that provides that, in some circumstances, negligence is inferred simply by an accident occurring. For example, a plaintiff may have medical problems that are found to be caused by a surgical sponge in the plaintiff's abdomen. In this case, the plaintiff may bring a lawsuit against the surgeon who previously removed the plaintiff's gall bladder and left the sponge. To use the *res ipsa loquitur* doctrine in a lawsuit, the plaintiff's case must satisfy the following three conditions:

1. The cause of the accident was within the defendant's exclusive control.
2. The accident was one that would not happen in the ordinary course of events.
3. The accident was not the result of the plaintiff's own negligence.

Res ipsa loquitur is often used in the context of medical malpractice, as in the previous example. However, it has been applied in numerous other situations, such as legal actions against the operators of autos or aircraft that collide with fixed objects, against tenants in fire losses, against beauty shop operators for patrons' hair loss, against building owners for falling elevators, and against manufacturers of defective products. For example, consider a roofing contractor who was performing work on the roof of a two-story building when a large bundle of roofing material fell from the roof of the building and hit a pedestrian on the sidewalk below. In a legal action for negligence, the pedestrian could invoke the doctrine of *res ipsa loquitur*. The pedestrian would need to establish that the roofing contractor had control of the roofing material, that roofing material does not normally fall off a roof unless there is negligence, and that the pedestrian did not contribute to the accident through his or her own negligence.

Vicarious liability
A legal responsibility that occurs when one party is held liable for the actions of a subordinate or associate because of the relationship between the two parties.

In some situations, a person or organization that has not behaved wrongfully can be held legally liable for torts committed by others. This indirect liability is known as vicarious liability. **Vicarious liability** is the legal responsibility that occurs when one party is held liable for the actions of a subordinate or associate because of the relationship between the two parties. Typically vicarious liability arises out of the relationship between an employer and its employees. The main factor that determines whether someone qualifies as an employee (as opposed to being considered an independent contractor, for example) is whether the person is subject to the employer's right or power of control with respect to the physical aspects of service.

The basis for an employer's vicarious liability is the legal doctrine of *respondeat superior* (Latin for "let the superior answer"), also known as the master-servant rule. The *respondeat superior* doctrine holds an employer liable for its employee's torts only if they are committed within the scope of the employment. Any third person injured by the employee's tort can take legal action against both the employee (because each person is responsible for his or her own wrongdoing) and the employer (because of *respondeat superior*).

The employer of an independent contractor is commonly referred to as a principal. An independent contractor is one with whom the principal has contracted for a result that the independent contractor is to bring about. An independent contractor, unlike an employee, has the right to direct or control how the result will be achieved. At one time, the common law followed a rule that a principal was not vicariously liable for torts committed by its independent contractor. Over time, however, U.S. courts have created many exceptions to this rule, including the following:

- *Nondelegable duties.* A principal cannot escape liability for breaching any of a variety of nondelegable duties (duties that cannot be entrusted to another's care). For example, a landlord has a nondelegable duty to keep common areas of rented property safe. This duty cannot be shifted to anyone else, including an independent contractor. If a visitor is injured because of a defect in the common area, the landlord can still be held liable even though the defect resulted from the acts of an independent contractor who was working in the apartment building.

- *Inherently dangerous activities.* Principals that employ independent contractors to carry out inherently dangerous activities are strictly liable for ensuing harm. For example, a principal is strictly liable for harm caused by blasting operations performed by an independent contractor on behalf of the principal.

A principal can also be held legally liable for injury resulting from either negligent selection or negligent supervision of its independent contractors. However, those causes of action (alleging negligence by the principal) would impose direct, not vicarious, liability on the principal.

Intentional Torts

In contrast with negligence, which is an unintentional tort, many torts are classified as intentional torts. An **intentional tort** is a tort committed with general or specific intent to perform the act that is held to be a tort. Intentional torts typically involve the intent to cause harm. However, no actual intent to harm is necessary, simply the intent to perform the act.

Intentional tort
A tort committed with general or specific intent to perform the act that is held to be a tort.

Several examples of intentional torts are described under the following categories:

- Torts against the person
- Torts involving property
- Torts involving business

Torts Against the Person

Intentional torts committed against the person include the following:

- Assault
- Battery
- False imprisonment
- False arrest

- Defamation
- Invasion of privacy
- Malicious prosecution
- Malicious abuse of process

Assault
The threat of force against another person that creates a well-founded fear of imminent harmful or offensive contact.

Battery
Harmful or offensive contact with another person.

False imprisonment
The restraint or confinement of a person without consent or legal authority.

False arrest
The seizure or forcible restraint of a person without legal authority.

Defamation
A false written or oral statement that damages another's reputation.

Libel
A defamatory statement expressed in a written or fixed form.

Slander
A defamatory statement expressed by speech.

Assault and battery often happen together at approximately the same time, but either offense can occur without the other. **Assault** consists of the threat of force against another person that creates a well-founded fear of imminent harmful or offensive contact. A threat such as "Give me your money or I will shoot you!" is an assault. **Battery** consists of harmful or offensive contact with another person. Both assault and battery can also be crimes as well as torts.

False imprisonment and false arrest are the same in most respects. **False imprisonment** is the restraint or confinement of a person without consent or legal authority. **False arrest** is the seizure or forcible restraint of a person without legal authority. Either a police officer or a private individual can commit false imprisonment or false arrest. For example, if a store keeps a suspected shoplifter confined, this may be deemed an act of false arrest or false imprisonment.

A person or organization whose reputation has been harmed by the publication of an untrue statement has a right of action against the person who published the false statement. (To "publish," in this sense, means to make public in any medium, including spoken words.) The general name given to this intentional tort is **defamation**, which covers any false written or oral statement that damages another's reputation.

Defamation may take one of two forms: libel or slander. **Libel** is a defamatory statement expressed in a written or fixed form, whereas **slander** is a defamatory statement expressed by speech. Libel includes defamation through the use of pictures, cartoons, moving pictures, signs, and statues.

The tort of invasion of the right of privacy, or invasion of privacy, includes several different common-law situations, as well as invasion of rights created by state and federal statutes. Some of the common-law torts are listed below.

- *Intrusion on solitude or seclusion.* Examples include using a hidden microphone, eavesdropping, tapping telephone lines, and using telephoto lenses.
- *Physical invasion.* Examples include searching a shopping bag in a store or the unauthorized taking of a blood sample.
- *Public disclosure of private facts.* The right to sue for this tort depends on the plaintiff's public prominence. An entertainer, for example, is not entitled to privacy to the same extent as an ordinary citizen.
- *Unauthorized release of confidential information.* Examples include medical or financial records.

As well as being a tort, invasion of privacy may sometimes be the basis of a lawsuit brought under constitutional law or a statute.

Using the legal process for an improper purpose can result in a tort claim for misuse of legal process, which takes two forms: malicious prosecution and malicious abuse of process.

Malicious prosecution is the improper institution of legal proceedings against another. This tort began as a remedy for the improper institution of criminal proceedings without probable cause. To illustrate the elements of malicious prosecution in criminal proceedings, assume that Arlene filed a criminal complaint against Bob but actually had no valid claim and just wished to harass him. After being acquitted of the criminal charges, Bob may bring civil suit against Arlene for malicious prosecution. Today, a number of jurisdictions also apply malicious prosecution to certain civil proceedings, such as actions to have a person declared bankrupt or incompetent.

Malicious prosecution
The improper institution of legal proceedings against another.

Malicious abuse of process is use of the civil or criminal procedures for a purpose for which they were not designed. The improper act is frequently coercion, such as a creditor's commencing a criminal case to compel a person to pay a debt.

Malicious abuse of process
The use of civil or criminal procedures for a purpose for which they were not designed.

Torts Involving Property

Some intentional torts involve interference with others' property rights. These torts include the following:

- Trespass
- Conversion
- Nuisance
- Interference with a copyright, patent, or trademark

Trespass is unauthorized entry to another person's real property or forcible interference with another person's personal property. The owner or occupier (renter) of land has the right to the exclusive possession and use of the land. Any unauthorized entry onto that land is a trespass to real property. A trespass to real property may occur on the surface of the land, beneath it, or over it within the airspace required by the owner for the peaceful enjoyment of the property.

Trespass
Unauthorized entry to another person's real property or forcible interference with another person's personal property.

Trespass to personal property is the forcible interference with another person's possession of personal property. For example, if a person takes someone's bicycle, rides it, and then returns it, that would be trespass to personal property.

The tort of **conversion** is the unlawful exercise of control over another person's personal property to the detriment of the owner. This tort applies to tangible, movable personal property and not to land. The party must be deprived of possession of the property by a wrongful taking, a wrongful disposal, a wrongful detention, or severe damage or destruction.

Conversion
The unlawful exercise of control over another person's personal property to the detriment of the owner.

Conversion is similar to trespass to real property. An example illustrates how to distinguish the two. An auto owner entrusted her auto to a dealer for the purpose of sale, and the dealer used the car for a ten-mile trip on his own business without the owner's permission. This was trespass to personal property. The use was minimal and did not cause any harm to the auto. If, instead, the dealer had used the car on his own business for a 2,000-mile trip, or had damaged the car, the use would have been conversion. The owner would have been deprived of the use of the car, and driving 2,000 miles or damaging the car would have reduced its value.

Copyright, patent, and trademark rights are rights in intellectual property. Although intellectual property law is a separate body of law, interference with any of these intellectual property rights, called "infringement," has historically been a tort. Today federal legislation preempts the common law and governs most matters concerning these property rights.

Nuisance
Anything interfering with another person's use or enjoyment of property.

The tort of **nuisance** is anything interfering with another person's use or enjoyment of property. Nuisance can be classified as either private or public. A private nuisance is an interference with another person's use or enjoyment of his or her property that does not involve trespass. An example of private nuisance is undue noise from an adjacent apartment. A public nuisance is a nuisance that affects the public at large, or at least a substantial segment of the public. For example, a person who operates a plant that pollutes a river with poisonous waste commits a public nuisance. This pollution may also result in criminal prosecution. Typically, a public nuisance claim must be brought by a governmental entity rather than an individual.

Torts Involving Business

Many intentional torts involve unlawful interference with either personal or business relationships of other parties. This category includes several torts, some of which include the following:

- Fraud
- Bad faith
- Trade disparagement
- Interference with employment relationship

Fraud
A deliberate misrepresentation or concealment of fact in order to make a person act to his or her detriment.

Fraud is a deliberate misrepresentation or concealment of fact in order to make a person act to his or her detriment. Fraud can be both a tort and a crime. Tort liability for fraud involves the following elements:

- A false representation—a true representation made maliciously is not fraud.
- Of a material fact—the misrepresentation must be material (important) and concern a past or existing fact.
- Knowingly made—the defendant must know that the representation is false, or have reckless disregard as to whether the misrepresentation is false.

- With intent to deceive—the defendant must intend for the plaintiff to rely on the misrepresentation.
- On which the other party has placed justifiable reliance—the plaintiff must actually and reasonably rely on the misrepresentation.
- To his or her detriment—the plaintiff must suffer actual damage.

Bad faith can arise out of either tort or breach of contract, depending on the state. Bad faith is based on the theory that, in certain cases, the plaintiff is entitled to additional damages above those typically awarded for breach of contract because the defendant never intended to fulfill the contractual obligation. These cases involve alleged outrageous or extreme conduct, or the defendant's breach of an implied duty of good faith and fair dealings. Bad faith has principally been a separate cause of action in lawsuits for breach of insurance contracts. An example of bad faith by an insurer is a liability insurer's refusal to defend its insured or offer a settlement to a third-party claimant when the insurer is clearly obligated to pay the loss. Bad faith may also apply in cases of breach of employment contracts involving wrongful discharge or discrimination.

The intentional tort of **trade disparagement** is a form of commercial defamation that involves a false or misleading statement about another's business, products, or services. The essence of the tort is a malicious interference with an economically advantageous relationship, resulting in monetary loss.

Trade disparagement
A false or misleading statement about another's business, products, or services.

The tort of interference with employment relationship can take many forms and, in certain instances, overlaps with other torts. Situations in which a person may bring an action for interference with employment relationship include the following:

- A discharged employee may have a right of action against a person who used unlawful means to bring about the employee's discharge.
- A person may have a right of action against another person who prevented him or her from obtaining employment through some unfair means such as false statements or threats. (Slander would be an additional cause of action for this plaintiff. Plaintiffs frequently allege several causes of action.)

Strict Liability

In some situations, **strict liability** is imposed, which is liability that is not based on negligence or intent to cause harm. As well as being imposed in tort, strict liability (also called **absolute liability**) can be imposed by statutes, such as the workers' compensation laws. Strict liability imposed by statute is described subsequently in this chapter. Situations in which strict liability is imposed by tort law include the following:

Strict liability, or
absolute liability
Liability that is not based on negligence or intent to cause harm.

- Abnormally dangerous activities
- The sale of dangerously defective products

Abnormally dangerous activities can include using dynamite, gasoline, noxious chemicals, or explosives; keeping wild animals in captivity; or keeping domesticated animals known to be abnormally dangerous.

Strict liability generally applies to the sale of products that are defective and unreasonably dangerous to the person or property of users or consumers. Mere proof of the defect and the resulting damage are sufficient to support a cause of action against the seller. Liability can be imposed even though the seller has exercised all possible care in the preparation of the product.

LEGAL LIABILITY BASED ON CONTRACTS

In addition to torts, contracts are another basis for imposing legal liability. A contract is a legally enforceable agreement between two or more people that creates an obligation to do, or not do, something. The agreement creates a legal relationship, rights, and duties. Legal liability based on contracts can arise out of either a breach of contract or an agreement to assume the liability of another party (hold-harmless agreement).

Elements of a Contract

The four elements that must be present to create a legally enforceable contract are: (1) agreement, (2) consideration, (3) capacity to contract, and (4) legal purpose.

Elements of a Contract

1. Agreement (includes offer and acceptance)
2. Consideration
3. Capacity to contract
4. Legal purpose

Offer
A promise that requires some action by the intended recipient to make an agreement.

Acceptance
The assent to an offer that occurs when the party to whom an offer has been made either agrees to the proposal or does what has been proposed.

Agreement

The first element of any contract is an agreement between the parties. An agreement consists of an offer and an acceptance of that offer. An **offer** is a promise that requires some action by the intended recipient to make the agreement. The party making the offer is the offeror. An **acceptance** is the assent to an offer that occurs when the party to whom an offer has been made either agrees to the proposal or does what has been proposed. The party to whom the offer is made is the offeree. The act of doing what has been proposed is called performance.

The following are the requirements of an offer:

- Intent to contract
- Definite terms
- Communication to offeree

Duration and Termination of an Offer

Offers do not remain open indefinitely. The length of time during which an offer is binding depends on the following:

- *Lapse of time.* An offer might contain language that specifies its duration. If no duration is specified, the offer lapses after a reasonable period of time.

- *Operation of law.* Operation of law means that rules of law apply automatically to a situation without any act by the parties. For instance, operation of law automatically terminates the offer if the subject matter of the offer is destroyed. Similarly, if performance of a contract becomes illegal after the offer has been made, the offer ends. For example, if a statute makes it unlawful to deal in certain goods, then a preexisting offer to sell those goods automatically terminates.

- *Offeree's rejection.* The offeree's rejection of the offer terminates that offer. A rejection occurs when the offeree notifies the offeror of an intention not to accept.

- *Counteroffers.* If the offeree makes a proposal to the offeror that varies in some material respect from the original offer, the proposal is a counteroffer. A counteroffer rejects the original offer and constitutes a new offer by the offeree. A request for additional information or clarification of terms is not a counteroffer. A counteroffer substantially changes the offer, but a request for additional information or clarification of terms leaves the original offer intact.

- *Offeror's revocation.* A revocation is the offeror's withdrawal of the offer. Generally, an offeror can revoke an offer at any time before an offeree's acceptance.

The party making the offer must intend for the offer to create a legal obligation if it is accepted. If no promise is made, courts will not find intent to contract. A general statement or invitation is not considered an offer to form a contract.

An offer must be sufficiently definite in its terms so that both parties understand the performance expectations if the contract is created. Definite terms make a contract enforceable and make it possible to calculate damages if the contract is broken.

The offer and response can be communicated directly between the two parties, through their agents, or by public announcement.

To create an enforceable agreement, an acceptance has the following requirements:

- The offeree must make the acceptance.
- The acceptance must be unconditional and unequivocal.
- The offeree must communicate the acceptance to the offeror by appropriate word or act.

Only the person or persons to whom an offer is made can accept the offer because the person making the offer has the right to choose with whom to contract. An acceptance expresses the offeree's consent to the offer's terms as binding.

An acceptance must be unconditional and unequivocal. If the acceptance deviates from the offer's terms, it is a counteroffer not an acceptance. An offeree must comply strictly with provisions in an offer relating to time, place, or manner of acceptance.

Unilateral contract
A contract in which only one party makes a promise or undertakes the requested performance.

Bilateral contract
A contract in which each party promises a performance.

The offeree must communicate the acceptance to the offeror by appropriate word or act. What the offeree must communicate depends on the nature of the contract. A **unilateral contract** is one in which only one party makes a promise or undertakes the requested performance. In a unilateral contract offer, acceptance occurs upon completion of the act the offeror requested. A **bilateral contract** is one in which each party promises a performance. In a bilateral contract offer, acceptance occurs upon the offeree's notification of acceptance to the offeror.

Once an offer has been accepted, the offeror is known as the promisor and the offeree is known as the promisee.

Consideration

The second element of a contract is consideration. Consideration is the price paid by each party to the other, or what each party receives and gives in the agreement.

Consideration
Something of value from the promisee that the promisor requested or bargained for in a contract.

A common misconception is that consideration is limited to one party paying money in exchange for the promise of another party. **Consideration** simply means something of value from the promisee that the promisor requested or bargained for in a contract. The consideration necessary to make a contract enforceable might consist of one of the following:

- A return promise
- An act performed
- A promise not to act

Commonly, both parties to a contract are both promisor and promisee and therefore create a bilateral agreement. For example, Jim promises to cut Arthur's grass; in return, Arthur promises to fix Jim's car. In this case, both parties have provided consideration because of the exchange of promises.

Consideration can also mean a promise not to act. For example, Martin has the legal right to sue Louise for damages as a result of a car accident. Louise promises to buy Martin a new auto if Martin will agree not to sue Louise. If Martin and Louise enter into this agreement, it is an enforceable contract as long as all the other necessary contractual elements are present. However, a promise not to perform an act that a person is not legally entitled to do is not consideration. For example, Louise promises not to drive her car over Martin's lawn if Martin will paint Louise's house. Louise does not have the legal right to drive her car over Martin's lawn, so she cannot give up that right as consideration. Similarly, the promise to do something that a person is legally obliged to do anyway is not consideration.

Another requisite for consideration is that it be present or future consideration. Past consideration is not valid consideration. For example, Fred offers Bernie $500 to paint his house, and Bernie agrees to do it. After Bernie has painted Fred's house, Fred says he will give Bernie the $500 for painting his house if Bernie will also paint the garage. Bernie already has a legal right to the $500, and Fred already has the legal obligation to pay Bernie the $500. This past consideration cannot be used as the consideration for a subsequent contract to paint the garage.

Capacity to Contract

Competence is the basic or minimal ability to do something and the mental ability to understand problems and make decisions. **Capacity to contract** is a legal qualification that determines one's ability to enter into an enforceable contract. A party who lacks legal capacity to contract is incompetent under the law. Minors, the mentally incompetent (such as insane persons), and those who are either permanently or temporarily incapacitated (such as those under the influence of drugs or alcohol) are included in this category. An incompetent person who forms a contract can challenge its validity. The term that describes a successful challenge of a contract is "avoiding" the contract.

Legal Purpose

The fourth element of an enforceable contract is that it must have a legal purpose. A legal purpose is one that does not result in a crime or a tort. A performance or promise not to act that is illegal cannot be the basis for an enforceable contract.

Statute of Frauds

Although oral contracts are legally enforceable, all states have enacted statutes that require certain agreements to be in writing to be enforceable. These **statutes of frauds** prevent fraud and perjury by requiring that certain contracts be in writing and contain the signature of the party responsible for

Competence
The basic or minimal ability to do something and the mental ability to understand problems and make decisions.

Capacity to contract
A legal qualification that determines one's ability to enter into an enforceable contract.

Statute of frauds
A law to prevent fraud and perjury by requiring that certain contracts be in writing and contain the signature of the party responsible for performing that contract.

performing that contract. Risk management professionals are usually only interested in the following two situations:

1. *Agreements that cannot be performed within one year.* The statute of frauds usually requires contracts that cannot be performed within a year to be in writing because long-term oral contracts often end up in disputes. Courts generally hold the provision inapplicable if it was possible to perform the contract within one year. Courts have also typically held that this provision is not applicable to insurance contracts. An oral contract of property insurance for a three-year term would be enforceable because the contractual performance can occur at any time an insured suffers a loss. Courts interpret this provision of the statute of frauds strictly, and the possibility of performance within one year takes such policies outside the statute of frauds.

2. *Promises to answer for another's debt.* The statute of frauds requires agreements for one party to answer for the debt of another to be in writing. Again, this provision does not apply to insurance contracts. Insurers are often contractually obligated to pay on behalf of their policyholder to an injured third party.

Breach of Contract

A contract is a legally enforceable promise or set of promises between two or more parties. Each party to the contract has a legal duty to perform as promised. If a party fails to perform as promised under a contract, that party has committed a **breach of contract**. The injured party can sue for monetary damages or may be able to seek the remedy of specific performance, by which the court orders the defendant to do what he or she promised to do in the contract (such as complete a sale of property).

Breach of contract
The failure to perform as promised under a contract.

Damages recoverable for breach of contract can be categorized as follows:

- Compensatory damages—money that will offset the loss sustained. The injured party must have made a reasonable effort to avoid or minimize damages. Plaintiffs are rarely awarded punitive damages in lawsuits based on contract.

- Consequential damages—money awarded when the professional, at the time of the contracting, was aware of some special or unusual circumstance that might occur as a result of the breach. Consequential damages can include loss of profits.

- Liquidated damages—a specified dollar amount stipulated in the contract as the amount to be recovered if a breach occurs. Generally, the amount must be reasonable in light of the actual or anticipated damages.

- Nominal damages—small amounts, such as one dollar, awarded to a plaintiff in a lawsuit in which a wrong occurred but there is no compensable injury.

Moreover, to recover damages, the injured party must prove the amount of loss that he or she suffered as a direct result of the breach of contract.

Hold-Harmless Agreements

Under a hold-harmless (or indemnity) agreement, one party to the contract (A) promises to pay another party (B) for certain losses sustained by B. In some cases, A may agree to pay for damage to B's own property. For example, a tenant in a building may agree in its lease with the building owner to pay for any fire damage to the building that occurs during the term of the lease.

In other cases, A may agree to indemnify B for defense costs and damages resulting from third-party tort claims against B. For example, a building contractor may agree in its construction contract with a landowner to pay the costs of any claim arising from injuries occurring at the building site. The hold-harmless agreement does not change the fact that B may be held legally liable to pay damages to an injured third party. Despite the hold-harmless agreement, the injured third party will still have a legally enforceable claim against B. However, A will be legally obligated to reimburse B for the damages paid to the third party. If A is unable to pay as required, B will still be liable to the third-party claimant.

In hold-harmless agreements, A (as described above) is called the *indemnitor*, and B is called the *indemnitee*. In a risk management context, hold-harmless agreements are noninsurance transfers, comparable in function to insurance policies except that the indemnitor is not an insurer.

Hold-harmless agreements are not always enforceable. Some states have statutes that forbid one party from assuming another party's liability in certain situations. Even if the relevant state law does not prohibit hold-harmless agreements, courts in some instances have held them to be unenforceable because of disparities in the relative bargaining powers of the parties involved in the contract.

When hold-harmless agreements are enforceable, indemnitors often use insurance to finance their obligations to indemnitees. Generally speaking, liability arising out of agreements to indemnify another party for third-party claims can be covered under liability insurance. In contrast, the usual method of insuring an indemnitor against liability arising out of agreements to pay the indemnitee for damage to the indemnitee's own property is the purchase of property insurance on the property in question.

LEGAL LIABILITY BASED ON STATUTES

In addition to torts and contracts, statutes are a third major basis for imposing legal liability. Statutes can be passed by both federal and state governments and can impose both civil and criminal liability.

Some statutes can give certain persons or organizations an absolute legal obligation to compensate other persons if certain events occur. This type of obligation is a form of strict liability, like that discussed previously, except that it is based entirely on requirements imposed by statute rather than on tort law principles. One area governed by strict liability statutes that is of key importance to a risk management professional is workers' compensation.

Workers' Compensation Statutes

A common example of liability imposed by statute in the U.S. is the workers' compensation system, which consists of separate, but similar, laws in all fifty states, the District of Columbia, American Samoa, Guam, Puerto Rico, and the U.S. Virgin Islands. Federal workers' compensation acts have also been enacted with regard to maritime employees, federal employees, and various other categories of employees. Each of the Canadian provinces and territories has a workers' compensation statute, as do some other nations. The basic purpose of all of these laws is to provide prompt compensation to injured employees without the need for a lawsuit.

A typical workers' compensation law requires every employer in the state to pay prescribed benefits for occupational injury or illness of any employee (subject in some states to certain exceptions, such as farm workers). The injury or illness must arise out of and in the course of employment. The prescribed benefits are intended to compensate an injured or ill employee for medical expenses, lost income because of partial or total disability, and rehabilitation services. If an employee dies because of a covered injury or illness, the employer must also pay a burial allowance and survivor benefits to the employee's spouse and dependent children.

To collect workers' compensation benefits, an injured employee does not have to prove or even allege that his or her injury was proximately caused by a tortious act or omission of the employer. Basically, the employee only needs to establish that he or she is covered by the relevant workers' compensation law and that the injury arose out of and in the course of employment. The employer is then legally obligated to pay the required benefits for that injury.

Other Statutes Imposing Strict Liability

In addition to workers' compensation laws, various other statutes impose liability on certain parties regardless of whether the parties were negligent or committed a tort.

For example, some states have statutes that make every auto owner legally liable for negligent operation of the auto by anyone who operates the auto with the owner's permission. Under the common law, an auto owner usually cannot be held liable for the negligence of a permitted user unless (1) the user is an agent or employee of the owner or (2) the owner negligently entrusted the auto to the user. The type of statute under discussion makes the owner liable for the user's negligent acts regardless of whether (1) the user was acting on behalf of the owner or (2) the owner was negligent in entrusting the auto to the user.

SUMMARY

This chapter examined the legal concepts underlying liability loss exposures. A liability loss exposure is a condition that presents the possibility of a legal claim or lawsuit being made against an organization. Risk management professionals must assess an organization's liability loss exposures before they can be effectively addressed through a risk management technique.

Legal liability is ordinarily based on torts, contracts, or statutes. A tort is a wrongful act or omission, other than a crime or a breach of contract, for which the remedy is usually monetary damages. Torts are distinguished from crimes, which are acts that society deems to be so harmful to the public welfare that government takes the responsibility for prosecuting and punishing the perpetrators. There are three broad classifications of torts: negligence, intentional torts, and strict liability torts.

Negligence is an unintentional tort involving the failure to exercise the degree of care that a reasonably prudent person would have exercised under similar circumstances to avoid harming another person or legal entity. The four elements required to prove negligence are as follows:

1. The defendant owed a legal duty to the plaintiff.
2. The defendant breached the legal duty owed to the plaintiff.
3. The defendant's breach of duty was the proximate cause of the plaintiff's injury or damage.
4. The plaintiff suffered actual injury or damage.

Defendants may assert that the elements of negligence are not present or offer any of the following affirmative defenses:

*   Contributory negligence—the plaintiff's own negligence that in part caused the plaintiff's harm and that prevents the plaintiff from recovering damages.
*   Comparative negligence—the plaintiff's negligence that in part caused the plaintiff's harm and that proportionally reduces the damages that the plaintiff recovers.
*   Assumption of risk—the plaintiff's act of knowingly and voluntarily accepting the possibility of harm.
*   Statute of limitations—a statute that sets forth the periods of time within which various types of legal actions must be brought.
*   Immunities—an exemption historically granted by statute to governmental entities, public officials, and charitable institutions.

Additional factors in proving negligence include the following:

- Negligent entrustment—a type of negligent breach of duty involving defendants who allowed persons who are incompetent, unfit, or reckless to use dangerous objects.
- Negligence per se—an act that is considered inherently negligent because of a violation of a law or an ordinance.
- Joint and several liability—the liability of multiple defendants either collectively or individually for the entire amount of damages sought by the plaintiff regardless of their relative degree of responsibility.
- *Res ipsa loquitur*—a legal doctrine that provides that, in some circumstances, negligence is inferred simply by the accident occurring.
- Vicarious liability—a legal responsibility that occurs when one party is held liable for the actions of a subordinate or associate because of the relationship between the two parties.

Tort liability can be imposed both on the person who acted wrongfully (the tortfeasor) and on any person or organization responsible for the tortfeasor's actions. The responsible person or organization is said to have vicarious liability. The most common example of vicarious liability is the liability of an employer for the wrongful acts of its employee. Subject to some exceptions, an employer of an independent contractor is not vicariously liable for the wrongful acts of its independent contractor.

Intentional torts include, but are not limited to, libel, slander, invasion of privacy, fraud, bad faith, trade disparagement, interference with employment relationship, malicious prosecution, trespass, conversion, and nuisance. Although many intentional torts involve an intent to cause harm, that is not an essential element.

Strict liability includes situations in which liability is imposed regardless of whether the defendant acted negligently or with intent to cause harm. Common examples of strict liability imposed under tort principles include abnormally dangerous activities and the sale of dangerously defective products.

In addition to torts, contracts are a second basis for legal liability. Breach of contract (failure to perform as promised in a contract) can give the wronged party a cause of action against the party who breached the contract. The four elements that must be present to create a legally enforceable contract are as follows:

1. Agreement
2. Consideration
3. Capacity to contract
4. Legal purpose

More relevant to risk management purposes (because breach of contract is often not insurable), one party can assume by contract another party's tort liabilities to third parties. Such assumptions of liability are known as hold-harmless agreements.

The third general basis for legal liability is statutes. Some statutes impose strict liability for certain types of claims. The most significant example is workers' compensation laws. These laws, which exist at both the state level and the federal level, obligate an employer to pay defined benefits for occupational injuries and illnesses suffered by covered employees.

Chapter 5

Direct Your Learning

Assessing Liability Loss Exposures, Part I

After learning the content of this chapter and completing the corresponding course guide assignment, you should be able to:

■ Explain how liability loss exposures arise out of premises and operations.

- Describe the basis for liability arising out of premises and operations, including the duty owed to the following:

- Business invitees

- Licensees

- Trespassers

- Describe the liability loss exposures arising out of slip-and-fall in ice and snow.

- Describe the liability loss exposures arising out of premises security.

- Describe the liability loss exposures arising out of mobile equipment.

- Describe the liability loss exposures arising out of liquor liability.

- Describe the liability loss exposures arising out of bailment.

■ Explain how products liability arises out of the following:

- Breach of warranty

- Negligence

- Strict liability in tort

■ Describe the defenses to products liability.

■ Describe the liability loss exposures arising out of completed operations.

■ Describe the liability loss exposures arising out of the ownership, maintenance, or use of automobiles.

■ Identify the liability loss exposures faced by watercraft owners and operators.

■ Define or describe each of the Key Words and Phrases for this chapter.

Develop Your Perspective

What are the main topics covered in the chapter?

Building on the concept of legal liability, this chapter examines liability loss exposures arising out of premises and operations, products, completed operations, automobiles, and watercraft.

Review the types of liability loss exposures.

- Which of these liability loss exposures needs to be addressed by your organization?
- Are some of these liability loss exposures more of a priority than others because of the loss frequency and severity they present?

Why is it important to learn about these topics?

Risk management professionals must be able to assess their organization's likely sources of liability. Once identified and evaluated, these sources of liability can be managed using one or more risk management techniques.

Consider a commercial swim club.

- How does the presence of an attractive nuisance (the pool) affect the care owed by the property owner to trespassing children?
- What degree of care does the swim club owe pool patrons?

How can you use what you will learn?

Evaluate your organization's risk management activities for potential liability loss exposures.

- Does your organization have liability loss exposures that are only an infrequent problem and consequently do not get the attention they deserve despite their possible severity?
- As a risk manager, how might you begin to address these liability loss exposures?

Chapter 5

Assessing Liability Loss Exposures, Part I

Liability loss exposures arise out of the activities in which the organization is engaged. These liability loss exposures can be categorized in many ways, depending in part on the purpose of the categorization. A broad categorization that reflects the approach used by insurers in providing insurance coverage is shown in the box. This approach will be particularly useful to risk management professionals who choose to treat some or all of these liability loss exposures through insurance. This chapter describes the first five categories listed in the box.

Major Categories of Liability Loss Exposures

- Premises and operations
- Products liability
- Completed operations
- Automobile
- Watercraft
- Workers' compensation

- Environmental
- Professional
- Directors and officers
- Employment practices
- Fiduciary responsibility from benefit plans

PREMISES AND OPERATIONS LIABILITY LOSS EXPOSURES

The premises and operations liability loss exposure is the possibility that an organization will be held liable because of bodily injury or property damage caused by either of the following:

- An accident occurring on premises (land, buildings, or other structures) owned or rented by the organization
- An accident occurring away from such premises, but only if it arises out of the organization's ongoing (as opposed to completed) operations

Examples of accidents that could lead to a premises and operations liability claim against the organization include the following:

- A customer or other visitor to the organization's premises is injured because of icy walkways, uneven stairs, sharp objects, unguarded machinery, insufficient security, or a fire.
- A neighbor is injured by falling construction materials while watching a contractor replace the siding on a home.
- A customer's truck is damaged while the operator of a forklift at a nursery is loading the customer's purchase in the truck's flatbed.

An organization's liability for such accidents is usually based on negligence; that is, the organization failed to exercise the appropriate degree of care owed under the circumstances, and the person suffered injury as the direct result of the organization's failure to exercise that degree of care.

This section begins with a description of the legal foundations applicable as a basis for premises and operations liability loss exposure and then discusses the following liability loss exposures that are of particular concern to risk management professionals:

- Slip-and-fall in ice and snow liability
- Premises security liability
- Mobile equipment liability
- Liquor liability
- Bailment liability

Basis for Premises and Operations Liability

Although premises and operations liability can arise out of strict liability in tort or from statutes, the basis for premises and operations liability usually stems from negligence. Under common law, property owners and occupiers owe different duties of care to other persons on the premises, depending on the persons' reasons for being on the premises. For example, the degree of care a property owner or occupier owes to a business guest or to a customer is higher than the degree of care owed to an adult trespasser. This section explains the common law duties that property owners and occupiers owe to others in the context of the elements of negligence.

Legal Duty Owed

The degree of care a property owner or occupier owes to others depends on their reason for being on the property. Individuals who may enter onto the property of others fall into one of the following three categories:

1. Business invitees
2. Licensees
3. Trespassers

The first category of individual who may enter onto the property of others is a business invitee. A **business invitee** is an individual who has express or implied permission to be on the property of another for the purpose of doing business. Examples of business invitees include customers, vendors, and the guests staying at a hotel.

Owners or occupiers owe the highest degree of care to business invitees. The courts expect property owners or occupiers to take reasonable care to make the premises safe for business invitees. It is not sufficient simply to warn the invitee of unsafe conditions. The law requires a reasonable effort to discover and correct hazardous conditions before they cause injury. It is this additional duty that gives business invitees a more protected legal status than others. However, this does not mean that property owners or occupiers are liable for *any* injury caused by an unsafe condition on the premises. The law imposes no liability for conditions that are not known to the owners or occupiers and that a reasonably prudent person would not have discovered on inspection.

Notice is an important consideration in lawsuits involving business invitees. In legal terms, notice signifies knowledge, and it may be actual or constructive. **Actual notice** means information that has been directly given to someone. In the context of premises liability, actual notice means that the property owner or occupier knows about a hazard on the premises. Knowledge may be established through evidence that the property owner or occupier caused, created, or knew of a hazardous condition. It is not necessary for the owner or management to have knowledge for actual notice to occur. For example, if a customer reports a spill to a stock clerk at a grocery store, then the grocery store owner is said to have actual notice of the spill. Actual notice occurs when any store employee learns of a problem. When an accident occurs after actual notice is given, liability usually exists unless the property owner or occupier had no reasonable time to remedy the problem.

Constructive notice is knowledge that a person is assumed by law to have because that knowledge could be gained by reasonable observation or inspection. In the context of premises liability, constructive knowledge is established through evidence that a hazardous condition existed for a sufficient length of time that the property owner or occupier should have known about it. The most controversial liability issues in a premises liability lawsuit usually pertain to whether the property owner or occupier had constructive notice of a hazard, because no law specifies exactly what constitutes a "sufficient length of time." The length of time that a hazard can exist before the property owner or occupier should have known about it depends on the nature and location of the hazard. The proximity of any employees to a hazard may also be relevant in determining the amount of time necessary to establish constructive notice.

For some organizations, the length of time is not as important in establishing constructive notice as is the store's method of merchandising. For example, warehouse stores are essentially self-service. It is therefore foreseeable that these stores might have more items left in aisles by customers than do stores that have clerks to assist customers. Therefore, constructive notice would be more prevalent in warehouse stores.

Business invitee
An individual who has express or implied permission to be on the property of another for the purpose of doing business.

Actual notice
Information that has been directly given to someone.

Constructive notice
Knowledge that a person is assumed by law to have because that knowledge could be gained by reasonable observation or inspection.

If a business invitee enters into part of a premises not open to the public, then that person may lose his or her business invitee status and become a trespasser. If, for example, a customer cannot find what is wanted on the shelf and decides to go to the back storage area marked "Employees Only," then the customer becomes a trespasser. Consequently, the duty of care the store then owes to this customer changes while the customer is trespassing. A business invitee who engages in criminal activities on the premises, such as shoplifting, would also lose the business invitee protection.

The second category of individual who may enter onto the property of others is a licensee. A **licensee** is an individual who has permission to go onto the property of another for his or her own purposes. Although licensees have permission to be on the property they do not necessarily have a specific invitation. Examples of licensees include social guests, meter readers, and people making deliveries.

Licensee
An individual who has permission to go onto the property of another for his or her own purposes.

The duty owed by the property owner or occupier to a licensee is the same duty imposed by ordinary negligence. Licensees generally must accept the condition of the property as it exists, and are owed a degree of ordinary care, such as warnings of known dangers. For example, the owner or occupier of land should post signs to warn licensees of a dog on the premises.

The third category of individual who can enter onto the property of others is a trespasser. A **trespasser** is an individual who intentionally goes onto the property of another without permission or any legal right to do so. Under common law, the only duties that an owner or occupier of land owes to a trespasser are to not intentionally harm them and to not deliberately set traps for them.

Trespasser
An individual who intentionally goes onto the property of another without permission or any legal right to do so.

Generally, a trespasser assumes the risks inherent in entering the land, except under the following circumstances:

- When young children are lured onto the land by an attractive nuisance
- When the land possessor knows and tolerates trespassers

The owner or occupier of land owes a greater duty of care to trespassing children who are enticed onto the property by an attractive nuisance. An **attractive nuisance** is a dangerous object or condition so captivating to young children that it entices them onto another's property. Examples of attractive nuisances include swimming pools, playground equipment, heavy equipment, and water tanks. Attractive nuisances must be artificially created, not natural conditions, such as a hill or a tree.

Attractive nuisance
A dangerous object or condition so captivating to young children that it entices them onto another's property.

The attractive nuisance doctrine applies only when the plaintiff can prove that increased liability on the property owner or occupier is warranted. To establish liability, the plaintiff must offer evidence of each element of the attractive nuisance doctrine:

- The property owner or occupier knows or has reason to know that the attractive object is in an area where children are likely to trespass.
- The property owner or occupier knows or has reason to know that the attractive object poses a serious risk to children.

- The children who trespass are too young to understand the danger posed by the attractive object.
- The benefit that the object has to the property owner or occupier is slight compared to the risk it poses to the children.
- The property owner or occupier fails to use reasonable care to eliminate the danger or protect the children.

The property owner or occupier owes a greater duty of care to trespassers when they are aware of and tolerate the trespassing. For example, the property owner or occupier may know that hunters trespass on the property in pursuit of game during hunting season, or that children take a shortcut across the property to school. In such instances the property owner or occupier owes the same greater degree of care that is afforded to licensees.

The majority of states still use the three categories of trespasser, licensee, and business invitee in determining the duty owed by the property owner or occupier. However, a significant number of states have blurred or eliminated the distinctions among these categories. In states that make no category distinctions, the courts judge the standard of care in terms of reasonable care and the foreseeability of the injury. Even in these states, what constitutes reasonable care varies according to the purpose that the individual has for being on the premises.

Breach of the Legal Duty Owed

Once it has been established that the property owner or occupier owed a duty to the injured party, the injured party must prove that a breach of that duty occurred. Proving breach of duty is usually the most difficult element of negligence to satisfy. To do so, the injured party must prove that the property owner or occupier exercised a lesser degree of care than would be expected of a reasonably prudent person. In other words, the injured party must prove that the property owner's or occupier's conduct was not reasonable under the circumstances.

Property owners and occupiers are *not* responsible for every accident that occurs on their premises. Just because someone to whom a duty of care is owed is injured on the owner's or occupier's property does not necessarily mean that the property owner or occupier is legally liable. For example, a customer who trips over his own shoe laces while walking through a store cannot recover damages from the store owner because the store owner did not breach the duty it owed this business invitee.

The conduct of property owners or occupiers must be evaluated at the time the accident occurred. The issue of foreseeability of harm is essential to assessing premises liability. Although almost every accident would be preventable with perfect knowledge of what was going to happen, courts cannot hold property owners and occupiers to such a high standard. Instead, foreseeability is based on what the property owner or occupier could have reasonably known before an accident and what the property owner or occupier could reasonably have done. The following four factors relate to the issue of foreseeability and are used by judges and juries in evaluating liability:

1. What is the probability that harm would occur from the property owner's or occupier's actions (or failure to take action)?
2. How serious would the harm likely be?
3. What precautions could the property owner or occupier have taken to prevent harm?
4. How burdensome would these precautions have been to the property owner or occupier?

Consider an accident scenario in which a teenager slipped and fell on some pieces of discarded ice from a soft drink spilled on the pavement of a restaurant's large parking lot. With reference to the first foreseeability factor, the probability that anyone would step on the ice before it melts is somewhat small because of the size of the parking lot, and in most cases the spill would not cause someone to fall. But if one assumes that the discarded ice caused the teenager to slip and fall, the likelihood of *serious* harm is also low (factor 2). In most cases, a scraped knee or elbow would be the likely extent of the injury. Regarding what precautions the owner could take (factor 3) to prevent such occurrences, the restaurant owner could hire a number of workers to constantly patrol the parking lot looking for spilled drinks and similar hazards. However, the cost of such efforts would pose an unreasonable financial burden on the restaurant owner, given the potential risks of injuries arising from spilled drinks (factor 4). In examining the four factors as they apply to this situation, a court would likely not assess liability against the restaurant owner. The failure to find and clean up the ice from the spilled soft drink would not be a breach of duty to the customer.

Consider a second accident scenario involving an elderly woman who tripped over a crack in a retirement community's patio. The crack had existed for several weeks. Retirement-community residents and friends frequently gather at the patio. In this accident scenario, the likelihood of harm is much greater than in the soft drink spill in the parking lot. Uneven pavement on a patio is likely to cause people to trip—especially elderly people who might have poor eyesight or difficulty walking. The potential for harm is also much greater for elderly people who might be susceptible to fractures (like broken hips) from a fall. If this accident could have been prevented by a daily, five-minute inspection of the patio, then courts would probably not consider such a daily inspection to have been burdensome. Consequently, courts would likely rule that the retirement community's owner and/or management had breached its duty.

Uneven pavement is a common complaint, but uneven pavement does not always constitute a defect or breach of duty if the unevenness is very slight. Courts also consider the condition of the overall premises and whether the uneven pavement is in an area frequented by pedestrians.

Warnings of known hazards can help reduce the likelihood of injury (which addresses factor 3). If, for example, an area of a store has just been mopped, and bright orange cones are placed around the mopped areas, then the hazard is more visible and less likely to result in an accident. Furthermore, such actions may be the only reasonable precautions that the store can take, as stationing employees around mopped areas would be cost prohibitive. These are important defenses that courts consider.

Warnings might not always be sufficient to preclude liability. Posting warning signs may help reduce, but not necessarily eliminate, liability to business invitees. For instance, an owner of a greenhouse nursery may display a whimsical warning, as shown as Exhibit 5-1, and still be held liable.

EXHIBIT 5-1

Greenhouse Nursery Slip and Fall Warning

To Our Patrons

Take care as you walk among our flowers,

Our floors are wet during store hours,

Plants and flowers are growing thick,

Fallen petals and leaves are slick,

We carefully water and prune and hope for success,

But we are not responsible for injuries on our premises.

Proximate Cause

Having established a breach of duty, the next step in proving negligence is demonstrating that the breach of duty was the proximate cause of the harm. Establishing proximate cause (causation) is a contentious element in proving negligence. The injured party must prove that the property owner's or occupier's act or omission was the direct cause of the subsequent injury or damage, and that the subsequent injury or damage was foreseeable. For example, an organization may face a liability claim for the death of a pedestrian hit by one of the organization's delivery vans even though the pedestrian actually died of a staph infection. The estate of the deceased pedestrian would argue that the pedestrian would not have been exposed to the staph infection but for the auto accident. The defendant organization would argue that the staph infection was an intervening event.

Fault on the part of the injured party may preclude or limit recovery. For example, consider a customer who was injured exiting a convenience store parking lot late at night. The customer was intoxicated and had difficulty walking. The customer tripped over a doormat that had a slight kink in it. Surveillance camera footage showed that hundreds of customers had successfully maneuvered over the mat during the day despite the mat's slight problem. The substantial factor contributing to this injured party's fall was not the mat but the injured party's own intoxication.

Damages and Other Remedies

The final step in proving negligence is showing that the plaintiff suffered some form of damage, such as injury or financial loss. Then the court considers what would be the appropriate remedy. Injured parties usually seek special and general damages in lawsuits arising out of premises liability loss exposures. The damages demanded by the injured party must be related to the injuries sustained and these injuries must be compensable.

Sometimes injured parties seek damages for preexisting injuries that are not related to the accident. Injuries sustained in an accident that aggravate a preexisting condition are compensable. However, natural occurrences related to a preexisting condition would not be. For example, a person with arthritic knees who falls in a store would not be able to recover damages sufficient to pay for knee replacement surgery. Lawsuits involving preexisting conditions are common and require a review of the injured party's past medical records and sometimes an independent medical examination to determine the extent of the damages that are related to the accident.

Not all injuries are compensable. Purely emotional injuries are not recognized in every state. For example, a store customer may slip and fall due to a foreseen hazardous condition, but be unable to recover damages because the only injury they have sustained is embarrassment for falling. Likewise, a customer in a restaurant may experience trauma after seeing a rat run across the floor, but such a pure emotional injury, even though attributable to the restaurant owner's negligence, may not be compensable.

Slip-and-Fall in Ice and Snow Liability

Falling episodes cause a significant number of medically attended injuries and consequently are a common premises liability loss exposure. This exposure worsens when conditions involve ice and snow. Many areas in the United States experience weather that leads to slippery conditions as a result of accumulations of ice and snow. These weather conditions often lead to slip-and-fall lawsuits. There are several legal issues that must be considered in evaluating this premises liability loss exposure.

First, property owners and occupiers have no duty to clear off snow while it is falling. They have a reasonable amount of time after the precipitation stops to remove ice or snow. In several states, sidewalks are considered parts of the street, and the responsibility for removing snow from sidewalks rests with the municipality. If an accident occurs on the sidewalk, the municipality should be notified as soon as possible because some states or municipalities will accept liability only if a claim is brought to their attention within a specified number of days (commonly ninety days) from the date of the accident. Other municipalities require the property owners or occupiers to remove ice and snow from sidewalks, but courts disagree as to whether violations of these snow-removal ordinances constitute negligence per se.

One viable defense is that the snow or ice was a general condition of the community and that the hazards on the owner's or occupier's premises were no worse than those in any other area in the community at the time. Another defense is that the owner or occupier made every reasonable effort to remove the snow or ice. Quite often, some residual snow or ice remains even after removal. Ice melts and then refreezes. Pedestrians have a duty to anticipate this and watch where they are walking. Property owners or occupiers may choose to document the efforts that were taken to remove the ice or snow. Comparative negligence is the most common defense. If a hazard was "open and obvious," then an injured party's own negligence would reduce or eliminate any damages payable by the property owner or occupier.

Timeliness is important in investigating slip-and-fall lawsuits because the alleged hazards will soon melt. Consequently, an initial scene investigation should be conducted as soon as it is safe to do so. Photographs showing the snow or ice that caused the fall and photographs showing the general condition of the community would have to be taken shortly after the accident. Weather reports that describe the dates, times, and accumulation of snow or ice are also useful. Those reports can help in determining whether the property owner or occupier had reasonable time to remedy the condition.

Premises Security Liability

Premises security liability is the civil liability of property owners and occupiers for the foreseeable criminal acts of third parties. It arises when a property owner or occupier fails to provide a reasonably safe environment and, as a result, someone is victimized by a criminal.

Premises security liability loss exposures fall into two broad categories: crimes committed by employees and crimes committed by third parties. In both categories, the foreseeability of the criminal attack is a key liability issue.

Liability for Crimes Committed by Employees

If a business negligently hires or retains an employee who is known to be violent, and the employee then harms one of the business's customers or tenants, the business could be liable.

Negligent hiring occurs when an employer fails to use due diligence in checking employees' backgrounds. With such relevant information easily available to them for a small fee, employers are expected to conduct a reasonable investigation into a person's background before hiring. This inquiry may take the form of an extensive employment application, a job interview, pre-employment testing, a criminal records check, and a reference check. The type and quality of the background investigation to be done are largely dependent on the nature of the job that the prospective employee is to perform. For example, someone applying for a job as a child daycare worker would require a more extensive background investigation than would someone applying for a job as an assembly line worker.

The background check provides the foreseeability of a criminal attack. For example, a store owner hires an employee without doing a background check. The background check would have revealed that this employee had a history of armed robbery. The employee attacks a customer at knife point and steals his wallet. The employer would be liable because this crime would have been foreseeable had the background check been done. Alternatively, if the employer had done the background check and hired the employee anyway, then the attack would still have been foreseeable and the employer would still be liable.

Negligent retention occurs when an employer fails to discharge an employee who is known to pose a danger to others. Once it has been determined that an employee may be dangerous to others, employers may be liable for subsequent attacks committed by these employees because such attacks are foreseeable. For example, if a school discovers that one of its coaches has a history of violence against children, then the school could be liable for any attacks against children that occur after the decision to retain the coach.

Liability for Criminal Attacks Committed by Third Parties

This second category of premises security liability is typically more common and controversial than the liability for crimes committed by employees. It also poses many more legal challenges than lawsuits involving employees. Liability for criminal attacks by third parties is based on one of the following four legal principles:

1. The property owner or occupier had a special relationship with the claimant that required offering a higher level of security.
2. The property owner or occupier voluntarily assumed liability for the claimant's safety.
3. The property owner or occupier violated a statute requiring certain security measures.
4. Special circumstances existed that would make criminal attacks more likely so that the property owner or occupier should have foreseen and tried to prevent a particular attack.

In general, the injured party must prove that the property owner or occupier provided inadequate security for the given circumstances. Inadequate security may be alleged based on such factors as an inadequate number of security personnel, poor lighting in parking lots, faulty locks, inadequate maintenance of security records, or failure to maintain or repair security equipment.

The duties owed to certain individuals may be higher because of the special relationship between the parties. For example, schools have a duty to protect students from violence because the schools have a special relationship with their students. Hotel and motel operators, nursing home and apartment building owners, and common carriers (train, plane, and bus owners) have a high duty of care to protect their patrons. Students, patients, tenants, and people staying overnight at hotels or traveling on trains, planes, or buses entrust their safety to others. Consequently, organizations catering to such people owe a high duty to protect these kinds of customers.

Statutes or ordinances may create specific duties of care. Examples include ordinances requiring abandoned buildings to be boarded up, statutes requiring proper lighting in dark parking lots, and ordinances requiring locks and deadbolts on hotels, motels, or apartments. If an attack occurs as a result of a violation of a statute or an ordinance, then liability for that violation exists as negligence per se. If a motel fails to repair a broken deadbolt on one of its doors and an intruder breaks in and attacks a customer because the door did not have the deadbolt, then the motel owner would be liable as matter of law.

Special circumstances exist when the property owner or occupier knows of previous security problems on the insured's premises that make future criminal attacks foreseeable. In this situation, the property owner or occupier has a duty to provide appropriate security based on these special circumstances.

Mobile Equipment Liability

Many organizations own movable equipment that as far as insurers are concerned is neither considered an auto nor part of business personal property. Because of its mobility and the nature of its use, mobile equipment presents a liability loss exposure. Examples of mobile equipment found in many organizations include forklifts, snow removal equipment, and equipment used in building cleaning, such as large vacuum cleaners, carpet cleaners, and buffers. Some organizations use heavy equipment, such as bulldozers, backhoes, and cherry pickers. With all these types of mobile equipment, people can suffer harm as a result of their use. For example, a warehouse store employee using a forklift may accidentally push product into an adjacent aisle while restocking high rack shelves, negligently injuring customers. In another example, an employee operating a snow blower may cause property damage to vehicles in the parking lot when debris is accidentally blown through the equipment.

Liquor Liability

When an intoxicated person injuries someone, a lawsuit may be filed by the injured party against the establishment that served the alcohol that caused the intoxication. Many jurisdictions now permit recovery based on dram shop statutes, liquor control statutes, or common-law negligence governing employer hosts and social hosts.

Dram Shop and Liquor Control Statutes

All states have liquor control laws, and most have some form of dram shop act. Dram shop acts are statutes holding establishments that serve alcoholic beverages responsible for harm resulting from serving patrons alcohol in violation of those statutes. The statutes apply to owners or lessees of the property, bar, restaurant, or liquor store.

Most of the dram shop acts make establishments liable for serving liquor to minors or to persons who are visibly intoxicated. The definition of "intoxicated" varies by state. One court defined it as follows:

> An abnormal mental or physical condition due to the influence of imbibing intoxicating liquors; a visible excitation of the passions and impairment of judgment, or a derangement or impairment of physical functions and energies. This may be reflected in the intoxicated person's walk or conversation, his common sense actions, or his lack of willpower.[1]

Note that this law does not impose absolute liability against drinking establishments for any person drinking, only for those who are visibly intoxicated.

The majority of these statutes do not protect the intoxicated person but are instead designed to protect innocent parties from the actions of intoxicated persons. Even states that do not have dram shop acts have ordinances or regulations under their liquor control statutes. Such liquor control laws impose criminal liability, but violating them has also been construed in courts as negligence per se.

To help protect innocent parties, many states require, as a prerequisite to obtaining a license to sell liquor, that an applicant furnish a bond or an insurance policy to pay for injuries or damage resulting from a violation of the liquor control statutes.

Employer Hosts

Most of the state dram shop acts do not apply to employers serving alcohol to employees, but employers can still become liable because of the employer-employee relationship. In determining liability, courts often make a distinction between social hosts (friends and family members) and employer hosts because the employer-employee relationship implies some benefit to the employer—even though the employer does not sell drinks for profit. Although it may be true that an employer gets no immediate short-term profit from serving liquor made available to employees without charge, there might be a benefit in establishing or keeping good employer-employee relationships. The same argument is used when an employee entertains a customer or manager in his or her home. These situations benefit the employer and form a principal-agency relationship that makes the employer liable for the acts of an employee who is acting on behalf of the employer at a social event.

Social Hosts

Liquor law liability can provide grounds for bringing co-defendants such as social hosts into a legal action. When liquor is served by a host at a social gathering, the law is more lenient to the host than it is to a commercial seller of alcoholic drinks. As a general rule, social hosts are not held to the same degree of responsibility for acts of their guests as are those serving liquor for a profit. However, a social host who serves alcoholic drinks to an obviously intoxicated guest and who knew that the person would soon be driving may be held liable for the resulting injury caused by the guest's drunken driving. Courts are usually more strict with social hosts who serve liquor to minors A minority of jurisdictions hold that dram shop statutes' liability is broad enough to include social hosts. However, most lawsuits are brought based on violations of statutes specifically addressing liquor liability of those who sell alcoholic beverages.

Common-Law Defenses to Liquor Liability

In some states dram shop acts have replaced tort law regarding liquor liability, and consequentially the common-law defenses of contributory negligence and assumption of risk are no longer valid. However, some states have recognized the noninnocent-party doctrine that prevents an injured party from successfully suing a seller of alcoholic beverages if the injured party contributed to the purchase of the intoxicated driver's drinks.

Bailment Liability

A bailment exists when one person delivers property to another to be held for some special purpose. The purpose may be the safekeeping of the property or performing work on the property, such as cleaning, repairing, or restoring. The parties to the bailment are the bailor, who owns or lawfully possesses the property before the bailment, and the bailee, who receives the property to perform a service.

Types of Bailments

A bailee becomes liable to a bailor when the bailee is negligent. What constitutes negligence depends on the circumstances of the bailment. Bailments are usually divided into three types. The duty owed by the bailee to the bailor varies according to the type of bailment. The three types of bailments are as follows:

1. *Bailments for the sole benefit of the bailor.* These bailments are known as gratuitous bailments. An example of this type of bailment is a person asking a neighbor to keep meat in the neighbor's freezer compartment. In a bailment of this type, the only duty that the bailee owes to the bailor is one of slight care.

2. *Bailments for the sole benefit of the bailee.* An example of this type of bailment is borrowing a lawn mower from a neighbor without compensation of any kind. Because the bailment is for the sole benefit of the bailee, the bailee must exercise a high degree of care to avoid liability for any damage to the bailor's property.

3. *Bailments for the mutual benefit of both parties.* An example of this type of bailment is when an object of any kind is rented or hired for a fee. The bailee must exercise an ordinary degree of care.

What constitutes a slight, ordinary, or high degree of care depends on the circumstances of the claim.

Consider the following examples. Linda asks to leave her car in front of Karen's house instead of in Linda's apartment-complex parking lot while Linda is on vacation. Linda gives Karen the keys to her car. This is a bailment for the bailor's (Linda's) benefit, and Karen would owe only a slight degree of care. Karen could not be held liable for damage to Linda's car from theft or collision caused by another party. Karen would not be expected to check that the car was locked. However, Karen could be liable if she did something to damage Linda's car, such as allowing her children to play on it or scratching the paint with her lawn mower.

On the other hand, if Karen asked Linda whether she could borrow Linda's car for her own use, this would be a bailment for the bailee's (Karen's) benefit. Karen would owe a high degree of care and would be expected to lock the car and park it in a safe place. She may be liable for having parked it on the street rather than in her driveway if a third party collided with it. Some courts might even hold her responsible for damage caused by a tree limb that fell on the car during a windstorm if Karen failed to move the car into the garage once she learned of the impending storm. When a high degree of care is owed, the bailee can be liable for both action and failure to take action.

A distinction should be made between a license and a bailment. A license, in this context, means the right to use a space. For example, purchasing a pass in a commercial parking lot entitles the purchaser to the right to use a parking space. However, with bailment, the control of an object is vested in the bailee, and this requires greater responsibility.

Distinguishing between a bailment and a license depends on the degree of control exercised by the bailee. If an object has been placed in the possession of another person with the intent that that person have complete control over it while it is in his or her possession, then the situation can be considered a bailment. Most courts have declared garage owners to be bailees, and, in some instances, parking lot owners are considered bailees, depending on the extent of their control of the parking lot. If the parking lot attendant is given keys to the automobiles with the understanding that the automobiles can be moved at will, then the situation would likely be considered a bailment (even though the cars could be moved only within a restricted area). On the other hand, if the car's owner parks the car in a parking lot space and then walks away, the situation is more likely to be considered a license. In situations involving a license, the owner may issue a printed ticket exempting himself from liability or at least limiting liability.

Typically, when an employee acts within the scope of employment, the employer is directly responsible for the employee's acts. Even when a bailee's employee acts outside the scope of authority, most jurisdictions still hold the bailee (employer) liable. Some courts will not hold the bailee liable unless the bailee was guilty of negligently hiring the employee or knew of the employee's previous carelessness or history of theft.

Defenses and Limitations on Bailment Liability

Bailees are not strictly liable for everything that happens to bailed property while it is in their care. The same negligence defenses are available to bailees as to any other individual accused of negligence. In addition, written disclaimers and specific laws addressing unique bailment situations provide some defenses and limitations to liability.

An example of when a contributory negligence defense may be used is if a bailor or bailor's agent leaves an automobile with the keys in it on the parking lot of a garage without informing the garage (bailee). Many jurisdictions have enacted legislation to this effect for particular types of bailments. Examples of other bailees covered by this legislation include innkeepers, storekeepers, restaurateurs, and common carriers.

Innkeepers (hotels and motels) have been held strictly liable for guests' property. If items are stolen from a hotel or motel room, the business would be liable for them. However, most states now have laws that limit the amount of liability for which innkeepers are responsible. Innkeepers usually offer safes for storing valuable items, and guests' failure to use these safes can also limit guests' recovery. Innkeepers are also relieved of liability for acts of God, acts of war, or losses due to the negligence of guests.

Storekeepers are sometimes bailees of customers' property. For example, a clothing store is ordinarily responsible for the clothes a customer takes off and puts down temporarily while trying on new clothes.

Restaurateurs, in most jurisdictions, are not liable for the loss of a customer's coat or hat when hooks or clothes racks have been provided close to a customer's seat, particularly when a notice is posted disclaiming responsibility. However, when a checkroom is available the restaurateur accepts responsibility, even when no fee has been paid.

Common carriers offer to transport goods and passengers for the general public. They may operate by truck, rail, or aircraft. Common carriers are usually liable for the loss of or damage to goods in their custody except for losses resulting from acts of God, acts of war, acts of public authorities, inherent vice, or neglect by the person or organization that ships the goods. Contract carriers, on the other hand, operate under a specific contract with a shipper. Liability depends on the terms of the contract.

When bailment exists, courts have typically declared that the bailee may not exempt itself from all liability with a disclaimer. However, courts commonly permit bailees to limit their liability with disclaimers, especially if they were not negligent in causing a loss. For a disclaimer to be valid, the bailee must typically prove that the bailor knew about the disclaimer. For example, if a dry cleaner has a barely visible sign that reads: "Not responsible for stolen articles," the sign may not be considered sufficient to disclaim liability by the bailee (dry cleaner). Notices printed on the back of receipts are a common source of controversy. Normally the bailee must prove that the bailor was aware of the notice in order to be able to rely on it. A clearly written, unambiguous notice would normally be valid.

PRODUCTS LIABILITY LOSS EXPOSURES

Products liability loss exposures arise out of injuries or damage that result from a defective product. Consumer demand for safer products has expanded the loss exposures in this area and led to increased litigation, and large judgments against negligent manufacturers, distributors, and sellers. Concern over litigation and rising insurance costs as well as problems with insurance availability have motivated businesses to make products safer. Additionally, increased litigation has led industry groups to lobby actively for legislative relief from tort liability claims stemming from unsafe products. Tort reform proposals have included capping damages, limiting standards to which products are held, and discouraging frivolous lawsuits.

The liability loss exposures face by product manufacturers, distributors, and sellers arise from the following three sources:

1. Breach of warranty
2. Negligence
3. Strict liability in tort

Breach of Warranty

Breach of warranty

The failure to adhere to an express or implied warranty regarding the title, quality, content, or condition of the goods sold.

The first source of liability for a manufacturer or seller of a defective product is **breach of warranty**, which is the failure to adhere to an express or implied warranty regarding the title, quality, content, or condition of the goods sold. A warranty can be an explicit guarantee, for example, a guarantee of safety, or it can be an assurance that the product has a particular feature or characteristic. Every sale involves a contract, and warranties expressed or implied in that sale are part of the contract. If the manufacturer or seller produces a product that fails to meet the standards expressed in the contract terms or warranties, and if the customer suffers loss as a result, the law holds the manufacturer or seller liable to pay damages or make restitution. This liability is not based on tort but on contract law.

Implied warranty

An obligation that the courts impose on a seller to warrant certain facts about a product even though not expressly stated by the seller.

In all states, common law and the Uniform Commercial Code (UCC) recognize two implied warranties in any contract of sale. An **implied warranty** is an obligation that the courts impose on a seller to warrant certain facts about a product even though not expressly stated by the seller. This obligation arises out of the transaction between the buyer and the seller and is implied without any specific agreement between the parties. The two implied warranties are a warranty that goods are merchantable and a warranty of fitness for a particular purpose.

Uniform Commercial Code

State law, not federal law, governs most commercial transactions. To minimize confusion for businesses operating in several states, the American Law Institute and the National Conference of Commissioners on Uniform State Laws created the Uniform Commercial Code (UCC). The UCC, adopted in all states except Louisiana, governs the sale of goods and other commercial transactions. The UCC covers such areas as sales, leases, negotiable instruments, bank deposits and collections, fund transfers, letters of credit, bulk transfers and bulk sales, warehouse receipts, bills of lading, documents of title, investment securities, and secured transactions.

The **implied warranty of merchantability** is an implied warranty that a product is fit for the ordinary purpose for which it is used. This warranty applies only to merchants, that is, those in the business of buying and selling goods. It does not apply to individuals who occasionally sell goods. The law expects a higher degree of knowledge from those who are in business to buy and sell goods than from others. For example, a person who buys a used lawn mower from a homeowner takes it "as is." No implied warranties of any kind bind the seller. Someone who buys a new lawn mower from a garden supply store, on the other hand, has a right to rely on the implied warranty that the mower is reasonably fit for mowing lawns. If the mower blade becomes loose and injury or damage results, the injured person may sue the merchant on the basis of a breach of the implied warranty of merchantability. Most breach of warranty cases are based on a breach of the implied warranty of merchantability.

> **Implied warranty of merchantability**
> An implied warranty that a product is fit for the ordinary purpose for which it is used.

The **implied warranty of fitness for purpose** is an implied warranty that a product is fit for a particular purpose. It applies if the seller knows about the buyer's purpose for the product. For example, a customer asks the salesperson in a garden shop for a poison to kill the bugs in his vegetable garden, and the salesperson hands the customer a certain poison. The seller's act becomes an implied warranty that the poison selected will be fit for that particular purpose and will not harm the customer when used as directed. This implied warranty would be applicable regardless of whether the seller knew, but failed to mention, that the product should not be used on any plant bearing an edible fruit or vegetable. If the customer's family members became ill after eating the vegetables containing the poison, the customer could sue the garden shop based on the implied warranty of fitness for a particular purpose. Unlike the merchantability warranty, this warranty is not restricted to merchants. In practice, however, usually only a merchant has the skill and knowledge that would invoke the implied warranty. The occasional seller would not be viewed as being so skilled and knowledgeable that the buyer should rely on the seller in determining whether a product is fit for a particular purpose.

> **Implied warranty of fitness for purpose**
> An implied warranty that a product is fit for a particular purpose; applies if the seller knows about the buyer's purpose for the product.

An **express warranty** is a statement or representation about a product's quality or suitability for its intended use. It is most often a representation that the product is suitable for a specific use. Express warranties are part of contracts of sale. Any statement made by the seller creates an express warranty if the buyer relies on it in making a purchase. Although an express warranty can have the same legal effect as an expressed guarantee of safety or adequacy,

> **Express warranty**
> A statement or representation about a product's quality or suitability for its intended use.

the warranty need not be that explicit. It may be something the seller says or something printed on the product or its container. It may even be a statement in the seller's advertising. Whenever a manufacturer has made a statement about a product, the buyer is entitled to rely on that statement. Express warranties are important to wholesale and retail businesses. They may establish liability in certain cases and can also prevent passing that liability along to the manufacturer.

The express warranty need not be in writing or in any specific form. For example, the seller does not have to state, "I warrant..." It is only necessary that a fact be stated and that the fact become a part of the transaction. The seller's own opinion of the value of the product does not create a warranty. An express warranty can be made before or after the sale. For example, a warranty can be contained within packaging that is not opened until after the sale.

Negligence

Negligence is the second basis for products liability claims. Many different steps in the production process provide opportunities for negligence, from the product's design, manufacture, or inspection to the instructions or warnings that accompany it. Regardless of the source of negligence, the result is a defect in the product.

A defective product is one that operates improperly or does not operate at all as a result of improper manufacture or handling. For example, a tire with a defective sidewall could blow out and cause serious injury. A person could bring a lawsuit based on the fact that the manufacturer was negligent in the manufacturing of that particular tire, the tire was defective, and the defect caused harm.

Mass Tort Litigation

Mass tort litigation refers to torts involving numerous people. People who have been subjected to similar products, drugs, pollutants, and conditions can institute mass tort litigation. Examples of this type of litigation are lawsuits involving asbestos, tobacco, latex gloves, silicone breast implants, lead paint, and contaminated water. When several individual lawsuits involve common issues of fact and law, the court may certify a class action to reduce the burden of multiple lawsuits.

Negligence involving improper inspection can also be the basis of a products liability suit. Many manufacturing firms do not inspect every product produced. Instead, a sample (10 or 20 percent, for example) is inspected on the assumption that the quality of the sample will correspond to the quality of all products produced. This procedure may be adequate for a product like a paper clip that is not very likely to cause harm. However, manufacturers of more dangerous products may need to inspect a higher percentage. For example, a company that sells furnaces, aware of the potential for loss of life and property from a defective furnace, may want to inspect each one. Failure to do so might be grounds for a negligence action. Sellers can also be sued for negligence for failing to inspect or for improperly inspecting products with suspected defects if those products cause damage. Auto dealers might face this loss exposure.

The design of a product directly affects its effectiveness and its safety. Manufacturers can be found liable for negligence when products are improperly engineered or designed. Even properly designed products may be updated when additional safety features become available. For example, power lawn mower manufacturers added a safety shield at the rear of the blade housing to prevent the user from pulling the mower back over his or her feet.

Some products are dangerous if used improperly, no matter how well they were manufactured, inspected, or designed. For example, machinery can cause bodily injury, electrical appliances can electrocute their users, and cleaning solvents can poison anyone ingesting them. If the nature of the product prevents making it completely safe, appropriate warning labels are necessary. If the product is difficult or confusing to operate, the manufacturer must give instructions that are adequate and easy to understand. Containers of dangerous liquids or medicine must be clearly identified as such, and the label should warn buyers to keep them out of the reach of children. They should also include instructions on what to do if the product is swallowed. Electrical appliances often carry warnings that only qualified persons should attempt to repair them. Printed warnings must be clear, and if foreign markets are involved, the warnings should be in a language the consumer can understand. In some cases, failure to give proper warnings or instructions may be a violation of a statute and therefore also negligence per se.

Strict Liability in Tort

Strict liability in tort is liability imposed without regard to the defendant's negligence or intent to cause harm. Strict liability in tort is most often imposed in products liability cases to establish liability without having to prove fault. Strict liability in tort can be distinguished from a legal action based on negligence. In a legal action based on negligence, the plaintiff must prove that the defect in the product that caused the injury was due to the negligence of the defendant. This element is not required in legal actions based on strict liability in tort. Almost every state has adopted strict liability in tort in some form.

Strict liability in tort makes the seller liable even if the seller has exercised all possible care in the preparation and sale of the product. Taking due care will usually absolve a seller of any liability in a negligence case. Strict liability in tort makes such defenses irrelevant as long as the elements of strict liability in tort are present. Strict liability in tort also eliminates the defense derived from privity of contract. **Privity of contract**, the relationship that exist between the parties to a contract, was once an effective means of barring a lawsuit.

Privity of contract
The relationship that exists between the parties to a contract.

Separating the purchaser of the product from the person injured by the product enables any injured party to bring suit against anyone in the chain of distribution: manufacturers, distributors, or retail sellers.

Who May Bring an Action?

In determining who may bring an action, either in negligence or in strict liability in tort, most courts use the traditional foreseeability test. Eligible plaintiffs are those that the defendant reasonably could have foreseen as possibly suffering injury from the product.

Some courts have expanded the meaning of "sales" to include bailors and lessors. Therefore, the lessor of an auto with defective brakes can be held strictly liable. Most jurisdictions that accept this expanded definition recognize a distinction between a company engaged in a regular leasing business, such as a rental car agency, and one that leases only occasionally. At least one state has extended the doctrine to persons using products in a service business, such as a beauty parlor.

One significant extension of strict liability in tort in many jurisdictions has been to builders and contractors. Courts have reasoned that the rationale underlying the application of the strict tort liability rule to defective product manufacturers is equally applicable to builders and contractors. Contractors have been held strictly liable for installing a faulty hot-water heater that caused a fire, for installing a defective heating system that had to be replaced, and for failing to properly compact dirt in a filled lot on which a house was later built.

Market Share Liability

Sindell v. Abbot Labs created the market share liability theory. The case involved the drug diethylstilbestrol (DES), which was given to pregnant women to prevent miscarriages. It was later determined that DES had the side effect of potentially causing cancerous vaginal and cervical growths in the daughters of the pregnant women who took the drug. Many of the daughters developed that rare form of cancer linked to the drug but were unable to identify which company manufactured the drug that injured them. In this case, the California Supreme Court decided that each company that manufactured DES would be responsible for a percentage of the damages equal to its market share at this time. Some, but not all, states have adopted this theory of recovery that makes it easier for an injured party to establish a case. [2]

Elements of Strict Liability in Tort

Most products liability lawsuits are brought on the basis of both negligence and strict liability in tort. Understanding the difference between the two is important. For negligence, the buyer (or user) must prove that the manufacturer (or supplier) was not reasonably prudent in the design or manufacture of

Highly Publicized Products Liability Cases

Expanded theories of liability in products liability have made it easier for an injured person to recover for injuries. Additionally, some products liability cases have gained public awareness because of their coverage in the media. The following cases are often cited as examples.

McDonald's Coffee

Many of the facts concerning the McDonald's coffee case were distorted when reported to the public. Many people read or heard that a woman was awarded $2.9 million because a cup of coffee that she held between her legs spilled and gave her third-degree burns. The facts are that the judge reduced the jury award to $640,000 ($160,000 compensatory and $480,000 punitive). Also, the injured party was a passenger, not the driver. Evidence was presented that McDonald's served its coffee at 180 degrees Fahrenheit and that McDonald's had already received hundreds of complaints about the temperature at which its coffee was served.[3]

BMW Paint Job

Dr. Gore, a physician from Alabama, sued BMW for fraud when he discovered his $40,000 car had been extensively repainted to repair acid rain damage that occurred while the vehicle was in transit from Germany to the United States. BMW never disclosed the repair. Lawyers for Dr. Gore proved that the damage, even repaired, diminished the value of the car by 10 percent, or $4,000. In determining damages, the jury multiplied the $4,000 amount Dr. Gore was defrauded by the 1,000 documented cases of similar, undisclosed repairs by BMW, a total of $4 million. The Alabama Supreme Court reduced the punitive award to $2 million because the jury had included all repainted BMWs, not just those in Alabama. The U.S. Supreme Court reversed and remanded the case, holding that even the $2 million punitive damage award was grossly excessive.[4]

the product that caused the injury. A negligence case focuses on the manufacturer's conduct and places the burden of proof on the buyer. Strict liability in tort concerns the product itself and whether the product was unreasonably dangerous. The manufacturer may have exercised the utmost care in making the product, but if the product is unreasonably dangerous, the courts will impose liability under this doctrine. A strict liability in tort action generally requires that the buyer prove the following:

- The product left the manufacturer's custody or control in a defective condition.
- The defective condition made the product unreasonably dangerous. "Unreasonably dangerous" means that the product is dangerous to an extent beyond that which would be contemplated by the ordinary user who has common knowledge about the product. (This element is not required by all courts.)
- The defective product was the proximate cause of the buyer's injury.

"Defective" is a key word in this form of liability. That is, both negligence and defects must arise at the same point in the production process, and the defect is deemed to result from some negligent act. In fact, determining that a product is defective as part of a strict liability in tort claim depends on the manufacturer's past decisions leading to the creation of an unsafe product. A product may be defective in the following three ways that parallel closely the basis for negligence:

1. *Defective because of faulty manufacture or assembly.* In this case, the product is not in the condition that the manufacturer intended. Manufacturing defects usually involve errors in the product's assembly or in the use of faulty materials. This is the easiest element of strict liability in tort to prove because improper manufacture or assembly of the product proves the defect. The question of whether the defect renders the product unreasonably dangerous is not an issue because its causing an injury also demonstrates that it was dangerous. The buyer must prove that the product was defective when it left the manufacturer's possession. If a product was in a safe condition when it left the manufacturer's possession, but subsequent events made it unsafe at the time of use, then the manufacturer is not liable on the basis of a defect in manufacturing. Such might be the case if the product distributor makes alterations to the product before sale. This problem of a superseding or intervening cause is a major area of products liability law.

2. *Defective in design.* In this case, the product is built exactly as the manufacturer intended, but the design is faulty, thereby producing injury. The manufacturer is charged with liability because of a design fault incorporated into all products of the same kind and not just one particular item that caused injury or damage. Lawsuits alleging design errors or defects introduce a different set of problems. A strict liability in tort case based on defective design asserts that the product was properly manufactured or assembled but that the design made it unreasonably dangerous.

   The requirement that the product be unreasonably dangerous is particularly important in cases alleging a design defect. Common interpretation of this requirement is that if the condition is open and obvious, the product cannot be unreasonably dangerous and strict liability in tort does not apply.

   Many design defect cases arise from defective devices or an alleged failure to install safety devices. In such cases, courts will hold the manufacturer liable only if the alleged failure made the product unreasonably dangerous to use. Common situations include lack of guards, or the installation of defective guards, on machines. Litigation in auto design has become focused on components that have caused injury during or following a collision, such as the steering wheel, acceleration pedal, and air bags.

   Many products are designed and built to last. People who are injured by these products claim that their design does not contain the safety devices or construction methods that would have prevented the injury. Manufacturers and sellers are permitted by most courts to introduce evidence that the design of their product was the safest in use at the time the product was made. This "state of the art" evidence is not permitted in every state.

Government agencies and industry organizations often set standards applicable to product design and labeling. Evidence that the manufacturer failed to comply with these standards serves as compelling proof of the existence of a defect. Violation of mandatory standards will lead to an automatic finding of negligence in some states.

The Ford Pinto—Defective in Design

For several years Ford Motor Company manufactured the Pinto, a small car, which was later proven to have a propensity to burst into flames when struck from the rear, even at relatively low speeds. This automobile had the fuel tank under the trunk behind the rear axle. When the car was struck from the rear, the force of the impact drove the Pinto's fuel tank forward into a sharp projection on the rear of the transmission casing. The ruptured tank sprayed gasoline onto the hot transmission casing, causing the car to burst into flames. Ford was aware of the problem and determined that changing the design to eliminate it would have cost $11 per vehicle. Because of the highly competitive market for economy cars, Ford resisted modifications that would have raised the price of the vehicles. This design flaw was linked to several injuries and deaths.

---

3. *Failure to give warning.* The product is not defective in manufacture or in design but has some inherent danger about which the manufacturer has failed to give proper warning.

    The product manufacturer or seller must provide adequate instructions and warnings with its products. A warning is required when a product has a potential for danger that is not generally known by the public. The manufacturer or seller must either know of the condition or should have known of it. Failure to give adequate warning under such conditions renders the product defective for the purpose of strict liability in tort. When a manufacturer or seller provides an adequate warning on its products, courts generally rule in the manufacturer's or seller's favor. In response, manufacturers and sellers today typically provide extensive warnings on their products and comprehensive instructions on precautions that consumers should take when using the product. In court, however, plaintiffs will present their case that had the warnings been adequate, the injury or damage would not have occurred.

Defenses to Products Liability

Several defenses are available for both negligence and strict liability in tort actions. Some are complete defenses, meaning that they totally defeat plaintiffs' claims, while others may only reduce damages.

State of the Art

A defendant may claim that its product was safe according to the state of the art at the time the product was made. State of the art does not mean merely that the product conforms to industry customs and practices, it also refers to the technological feasibility of producing a safer product based on scientific knowledge at the time. If there is neither indication of danger nor any technique for obtaining such knowledge, the manufacturer has no reason to conclude that the product should not be marketed in its existing condition.

Compliance With Product Specifications

It is not unusual for a manufacturer to make a product conform to specifications established by the buyer or another person or entity. In negligence actions, a manufacturer is generally not liable for products built to others' specifications unless the defect is sufficiently obvious to alert the manufacturer to the potential for harm. The reasoning is that the third party should sue the one who prepared the specifications.

Open and Obvious Danger

A manufacturer has no duty to warn about or take other precautions against a common, open, and obvious dangerous propensity of the product. Hazards connected with barbed wire on fences or speed bumps in the road, for example, are well known, and warnings would be superfluous.

Plaintiff's Knowledge

Frequently a product is used by a person whose knowledge of the product is equal to the manufacturer's knowledge. In these cases, the manufacturer has no duty to warn of a danger associated with the product. For example, someone who purchases and consumes high calorie food, such as meals sold at fast-food restaurants, cannot bring a successful lawsuit against the restaurant.[5] However, the court may find in the plaintiff's favor if the defendant used undisclosed ingredients.

Contributory or Comparative Negligence and Assumption of Risk

Assumption of risk can be used as a defense in a strict liability in tort action involving circumstances in which the plaintiff contributed to the injury by knowingly using a defective product. In considering this defense, most courts distinguish between contributory or comparative negligence and assumption of the risk by the user.

The user's failure to discover a defect in the product or to guard against a possible defect may be contributory or comparative negligence. For example, a worker who knows the caustic properties of a certain substance yet puts their bare hands into it anyway would likely have difficulty bringing a successful lawsuit. The defendant has the burden of proving that the plaintiff had knowledge of the defect or danger. Some states allow a comparative negligence defense in strict liability in tort actions.

"Junk" Science

In products liability cases, the lawyers for both the plaintiff and defendant rely extensively on the testimony of expert witnesses. In the *Daubert v. Merrell Dow Pharmaceuticals* case (1993),[6] the U. S. Supreme Court developed a four-factor test to set standards for the admissibility of scientific testimony. The test, sometimes referred to as the Daubert factors, is as follows:

- Has the knowledge offered in the testimony been tested empirically?

- Has the theory or technique presented as fact been subjected to peer review?

- If a theory or technique is presented in testimony, does the theory or technique have a known error rate?

- Is the theory or technique presented generally accepted in the scientific community?

The Supreme Court directed federal judges to serve as gatekeepers for expert witnesses to ensure that the testimony presented is relevant and reliable, thereby eliminating "junk" science. This ruling prompted judges to dismiss expert witnesses who did not have proper credentials.

The Supreme Court extended the applicability of the Daubert factors from scientific evidence to technical and other specialized testimony in March 1999 in deciding the *Carmichael v. Kumho Tire*[7] case. Application of the Daubert factors should increase the reliability of expert testimony.

Product Misuse

Injury or damage may occur because persons other than the manufacturer or plaintiff misuse a product. Misuse or abnormal use of a product is similar to active negligence. For example, if a person tried to open a glass jar by tapping the rim of the lid against another object, and the jar broke and caused an injury, the defendant could assert misuse of the product as a defense. To negate this defense, the plaintiff must prove that the product was defective despite the product misuse and that the defendant should have foreseen how the product would be used.

Product Alteration

The manufacturer is usually not liable for post-sale modifications. One of the elements necessary to prove strict liability in tort is that the product was defective when it left the manufacturer's or supplier's custody or control. Another necessary element is that the defective product was the proximate cause of the plaintiff's injury. Product alterations are an intervening act that breaks the chain of causation. Therefore, most courts hold that third-party alterations, no matter how foreseeable they are from the manufacturer's perspective, do not create liability.

Written Disclaimers

Manufacturers sometimes attempt to use written disclaimers accompanying products in defense of strict liability actions. These can be used in breach of warranty suits under the UCC. However, in strict liability in tort actions the courts, almost without exception, have rejected them.

Although most frequently done with used goods or factory seconds, selling goods on an "as is" basis is possible. The seller may disclaim any responsibility for defects in the goods and injuries or damage resulting from them. Some courts have held such disclaimers to be invalid for bodily injuries but have supported them for property damage losses. Some courts also refuse to uphold any disclaimer of liability for negligence or for a statutory duty unless the facts show that the buyer was aware of the disclaimer and purchased the product with full knowledge of its consequences. Therefore, these courts have not upheld disclaimers in which the buyer was unaware of or later discovered the disclaimer in the package. The rationale behind these decisions is that because the buyer never agreed to such terms, he or she is not bound by them. Disclaimers are usually applicable only to warranty liability and not to strict liability in tort, fraud, or negligence cases. Disclaimers usually apply only to liability to the buyer and not to third parties.

Post-Accident Product Changes

A plaintiff may attempt to present evidence that the manufacturer made subsequent product design or warning changes because of the plaintiff's injuries. The inference the plaintiff would like the jury to make is that such changes were needed because the original design or warning was deficient.

Most courts do not allow post-accident product changes as evidence because doing so would discourage manufacturers from making changes that would improve the safety of their products while lawsuits are pending. Some courts allow post-accident product changes in strict liability in tort cases but not in cases alleging negligence. Such evidence has also been admitted for other purposes, such as to show that the defect occurred while the item was still in the manufacturers' possession. Post-remedial measures include product recalls, warning letters, design changes, and changes in warnings.

Existence of an Intermediary

Products liability cases often raise the issue of the actions of an intermediary who distributes or sells a manufacturer's products. The central question in this issue is whether those actions (or omissions) relieve the manufacturer of liability. If the intermediary's acts or omissions are the cause of the product defect, and if such acts or omissions were not foreseeable, the manufacturer will generally not be held liable. Similarly, if the manufacturer has reason to believe that the intermediary has taken steps to remove a defect or prevent danger, the manufacturer will not be held liable. However, if the manufacturer is held liable for a defect, the liability of the manufacturer would not be relieved by the existence of an intermediary even if the intermediary has conducted a final inspection of the product.

Allergy and Susceptibility

Many products, such as drugs and cosmetics, can potentially cause an allergic reaction. Generally, a manufacturer is not responsible for rare and unforeseeable allergies and susceptibilities that might exist in a particular person. However, should the manufacturer know that a product could adversely affect a large number of people, the manufacturer has a duty to provide an adequate warning. Court decisions have varied, but the trend is for courts to decide that warnings are necessary even when the number of people allergic to the product is small.

COMPLETED OPERATIONS LIABILITY LOSS EXPOSURES

Liability for products and liability for completed operations are so similar to each other that they are usually treated as components of one loss exposure. However, products liability and completed operations liability each have distinguishing characteristics.

Completed operations liability is the legal responsibility of a contractor, repairer, or other entity for bodily injury or property damage arising out of the entity's completed work, including defective parts or materials furnished with the work. The property on which operations have been completed may be real property (a building or some other structure) or personal property (such as a vehicle or machine). Examples of completed operations liability claims include the following:

- Several months after a heating contractor installed a new boiler in an apartment building, the boiler exploded because the contractor had installed it negligently. The boiler explosion damaged the apartment building and injured a tenant. Both the building owner and the tenant successfully sued the contractor for damages.

- Homeowners were hosting a picnic in their backyard. At one point, several guests were dancing on a wooden deck that a contractor had built for the homeowners a few weeks earlier. The deck suddenly collapsed, injuring some of the guests. The injured guests successfully sued the decking contractor for damages.

- A repair shop overhauled a production machine belonging to a manufacturer. After the overhaul was completed and the machine was returned to service, the machine malfunctioned and injured an employee of the manufacturer. The injured employee successfully sued the repair shop for damages.

Some courts have even applied the strict liability in tort rule to completed operations cases in much the same way as in holding the product manufacturer liable to the ultimate consumer or user.

AUTOMOBILE LIABILITY LOSS EXPOSURES

Automobile liability consists of legal responsibility for bodily injury or property damage arising out of the ownership, maintenance, or use of autos. In this chapter, autos means cars, trucks, and trailers. Liability arising out of the ownership, maintenance, or use of mobile equipment—such as forklifts, bulldozers, cranes, and similar equipment—is considered to be part of the premises and operations liability exposure.

Under the common law, mere legal ownership of an auto is generally not enough to create liability on the part of the owner for the negligent operation of that vehicle. When the owner of an auto lends it to another person to be used for that person's own purposes and the owner does not retain control of the vehicle's operation, the owner is generally not responsible under the common law for any negligent operation. However, the owner or any other party having control of a motor vehicle may be held directly liable for injuries resulting from his or her negligent entrustment of the motor vehicle to one who is unskilled in its operation or otherwise incompetent to operate it. For example, loaning a car to a minor or someone who is intoxicated may be considered negligent entrustment.

In order to establish liability for negligent entrustment, the plaintiff must show that the party entrusting the vehicle to the incompetent driver had knowledge of the driver's incompetence, inexperience, or reckless tendency as an operator—or at least that the entrusting party should, in exercising ordinary care, have known of the driver's deficiencies. In fact, liability of a leasing agency might be established by the mere failure to inquire as to the qualifications, competency, or sobriety of the lessee.

Although the owner of an auto can be held responsible for operation of the auto by another, such liability is not based on legal title or ownership, at least under the common law. Several states, however, have modified this rule by statute so that the auto owner is liable for the auto's operation by any person using the auto with the owner's express or implied permission. Therefore, in those states, ownership alone can be the basis for establishing auto liability.

Negligent maintenance of a commercial auto is sometimes the basis of a liability claim. For example, negligent servicing of brakes, tires, or steering apparatus may be the proximate cause of a truck's running into another vehicle. Alternatively, negligent maintenance of a rental car by the rental company may be the cause of an accident. The person responsible for the faulty maintenance, as well as those responsible for that person's conduct, may be held liable to the injured party.

As well as ownership and maintenance, use can create auto liability loss exposures. A person who is injured or whose property is damaged as the proximate result of the negligent use or operation of an auto has a right of action against the negligent operator. The operator's legal duties, for purposes of determining negligence, may be determined by common-law principles, federal and state statutes, local ordinances, contracts, or even the customs of particular trades.

The parties liable are the negligent operator and all others who may be legally responsible for the operator's conduct. For example, an employer is ordinarily held jointly liable for its employee's negligent operation of an auto during the course of employment. The employer, although not actually *operating* the vehicle, was nevertheless *using* it while it was being operated by the employee during the course of the employee's employment.

Use of a commercial auto includes more than its operation on public streets or highways. For example, trucking companies might position trailers to be loaded or unloaded by employees of the customer on the premises of the customer, creating potential liability. Moreover, an auto or auto trailer can be used as a portable office, warehouse, store, library, museum, or clinic, or as a cage for animals or livestock. It can serve any purpose for which a movable building is suitable. It can have mounted equipment such as lifts, hoists, or booms for unloading property from the auto. Liability may arise out of any of these uses.

Liability for Operation by Others

As well as the fact that individuals may become liable for damage caused by their own operation of autos, other relationships may also give rise to auto liability. Among such relationships, the following are especially noteworthy:

- Employer-employee
- Volunteers
- Loaned employees

Employer-Employee

The employer of an independent contractor is generally not responsible for the contractor's negligent operation of autos. However, an employer may be held vicariously liable for injuries and damage that result from the negligence of its employees while using or maintaining autos within the scope of their employment. Under such circumstances, the negligence of the employee is attributed to the employer. The autos may be owned, hired, or borrowed by the employer, or they may be autos that belong to the employees or their family members.

When an employee deviates from the scope of employment, the employer will not normally be liable. Therefore, if a truck driver deviates from a prescribed route in order to drive home for lunch, the employer will not be responsible for an accident that occurs while the driver is on the way home. The employer, however, might be held liable after the employee has finished lunch and is heading back on the ordinary route.

If an employer consents to an employee's use of the employer's auto, that fact does not necessarily render the employer responsible for the employee's negligence. A salesperson may be permitted to take an auto home overnight and use it for personal errands, but the employer is normally not responsible for the negligence of the employee during such personal use.

In some cases an employee may take the vehicle home to serve the purposes of the employer. For example, the employer may not have sufficient garage facilities or parking space. In such cases, the employer may be held liable for an accident that occurs while the employee is driving either home or back to work.

Volunteers

Volunteer (unpaid) workers, such as those who work for a charitable or cultural institution, are not normally considered to be "employees" in the common sense of the word. However, their negligence while operating autos in the scope of their volunteer activities can be imputed to the organizations that direct and control their activities.

Loaned Employees

Commercial auto owners may furnish drivers for autos leased to others. If complete control over the conduct of the driver is relinquished by the driver's general employer—the owner, in this case—then the lessee, rather than the owner, will be liable for the negligence of the driver. If complete control is not relinquished, responsibility for a loaned employee will vary, depending on the particular arrangement. The greater the lessee's control, the greater the likelihood that the lessee will be held liable.

Auto No-Fault Statutes

Provisions in the auto no-fault laws vary widely. Some preserve the tort system intact and merely add compulsory or optional first-party benefits. Others partially abolish the right to sue for torts in motor vehicle cases. Some states in this latter category preserve the right to sue either when injuries exceed a verbal threshold or when medical expenses exceed a monetary threshold. Verbal thresholds typically refer to injury that results in whole or partial loss of a body member or function, permanent disability or disfigurement, or death. In some states, motorists are given the choice of electing either to fully retain the right to sue or to accept some limitations on their right to sue. In the states that offer a choice, the main incentive to motorists to accept limitations on their right to sue for auto accidents is a lower auto liability insurance premium.

WATERCRAFT LIABILITY LOSS EXPOSURES

Organizations engaged as watercraft owners or operators have a liability loss exposure arising from their maritime activities. Risk management professionals need to know the liabilities faced by those organizations in order to implement appropriate risk management techniques.

Vessel owners or operators (vessel owners for simplicity) have the following major loss exposures:

- Bodily injury, illness, or death of:
  - Members of the vessel's crew
  - Shore workers, passengers, or other persons on board
  - Persons not on board the vessel
- Property damage to (and resulting loss of use of):
  - Other vessels, resulting from collision with the owner's vessel
  - Cargo or other property on board other vessels
  - Bridges, piers, docks, navigational locks, and other structures
  - Cargo or other property of others on board the owner's vessel
- Liability for pollution

Vessel owners can also incur "general average losses." General average losses occur when cargo is jettisoned to save the ship from sinking. Because the sacrificed cargo saved the ship and the balance of the cargo, the owner of the ship and the owners of the cargo must contribute proportionately. General average losses can be viewed as a liability loss exposure because a vessel owner (or a cargo owner) can become legally obligated to pay others' losses or expenditures.

Liability Loss Exposures for Bodily Injury

For most vessels (other than those that carry large numbers of passengers), the injury or death of crew members is the most significant liability loss exposure. However, in addition to crew members, other persons may come on board a vessel. These persons include (1) longshore workers, who may be on board for purposes of loading or discharging cargo; (2) passengers on ferries, cruise ships, casino vessels, day excursion vessels, sport fishing vessels, or any other vessel that carries passengers; and (3) various other visitors on board the vessel, such as harbor pilots, employees of ship repairers, cargo surveyors, or social guests. A vessel owner can become liable for the bodily injury or death of any of these persons.

When a vessel owner invites a passenger on board, the owner has the duties of a common carrier and as such must exercise extraordinary vigilance and the highest skill for the passenger's safety. Passenger injury or death can be a catastrophic loss exposure, because some vessels can carry 2,000 or more passengers. A passenger's injury gives rise to causes of action based on breach of contract and negligence.

Visitors may be classified by their purpose for being aboard. A visitor may be a social guest or may be aboard for purely business reasons. Generally speaking, the same duty of care is owed by a vessel owner to all who are aboard. That duty is to exercise appropriate care under the circumstances.

In various situations, a vessel owner may be held liable for injury to persons who are not aboard the owner's vessel. A significant loss exposure in this category is injury to others on board another vessel as the result of a collision with the owner's vessel. The vessel that is at fault in a collision can bear a tremendous liability for bodily injury or death of persons on board the other vessel. Another significant liability loss exposure can arise out of bodily injury caused by the release of pollutants, such as oil.

Liability Loss Exposures for Property Damage

If an owner's vessel collides with another vessel, the vessel owner can be held liable for damage to the other vessel, wreck removal expenses, loss of the vessel's use, loss of freight (the money earned for transporting cargo), and damage to the other vessel's cargo or other property on board. Property not considered cargo could include baggage belonging to passengers.

In addition to cargo loss exposures, vessel owners have other liability loss exposures for property. Vessels sometimes run into bridges, piers, docks, navigational locks, or other structures located on or near the water. If damage results from the negligence of the owner or the vessel's crew, the vessel owner can be held liable.

A carrier (an entity that transports property of others) can become liable for damage to customers' cargo on board the carrier's vessel. This potential liability for cargo loss depends on whether the carrier is a common carrier or a contract carrier. For common carriers transporting ocean cargo to or from the U.S. in foreign trade, a vessel is liable for cargo damage only if the carrier failed to make the vessel seaworthy and suitable for carrying the cargo when the voyage began, and the loss resulted from the unseaworthy condition. A contract carrier's liability for cargo damage is determined by whatever terms the carrier and the party who has chartered the vessel have agreed to.

Liability for Pollution

The owners and operators of tankers and tank barges also have a significant exposure to liability for environmental damage, and cleanup costs, arising from oil spills or the release of other pollutants. Even a vessel that is not a tanker is exposed to pollution liability that might result from (1) negligently colliding with a tanker, (2) spillage of the vessel's own fuel supply, or (3) discharge of any cargo (such as dry chemicals) that could pollute the environment. A vessel owner's liability for environmental damage and cleanup costs depends largely on the law of the nation or state where the pollution occurs.

Following the 11 million gallon Exxon Valdez spill in 1989, Congress enacted the Oil Pollution Act of 1990 (OPA), which greatly increased the potential liability of vessel owners beyond that established in previous federal statutes. OPA prohibits the discharge of oil into the navigable waters of the U.S. and adjoining shorelines, and it imposes liability on any "responsible party" (which includes a vessel owner, operator, or bareboat charterer) for cleanup costs and damages, including damage to property, damage to natural resources, and loss of earnings.

SUMMARY

This is the second of four chapters that address the liability loss exposures to which an organization may be subject. In addition to the foundations of legal liability described previously, risk management professionals need to know the sources of liability loss exposures. The following categories of liability loss exposures were addressed in this chapter: premises and operations, products, completed operations, automobile, and watercraft.

The premises and operations liability loss exposure arises from the possibility that an organization will be held liable because of bodily injury or property damage occurring on or away from an organization's premises but arising out of the organization's ongoing operations. The basis for premises and operations liability stems from negligence. Property owners and occupiers owe different degrees of care to persons on their property depending on each person's reason for being on the property. The three categories of people who may enter onto the property of others are as follows:

1. *Business invitee.* An individual who has express or implied permission to be on the property of another for the purpose of doing business.
2. *Licensee.* An individual who has permission to go onto the property of another for his or her own purposes.
3. *Trespasser.* An individual who intentionally goes onto the property of another without permission or any legal right to do so.

Not all states use these three categories, but have instead adopted a standard of care in terms of reasonable care and the foreseeability of injury.

Once it has been established that the property owner or occupier owed a duty to the injured party, the injured party must prove that a breach of that duty occurred. Proving breach of duty is usually the most difficult element of negligence to satisfy.

The proximate cause (causation) element of negligence requires the injured party prove that the act of omission of the property owner or occupier was the direct cause of the injury or damage, not some intervening event. Lastly, the injured party must sustain actual damage.

A slip and fall is a common occurrence and is often significant enough to require medical attention. Consequently falls are a common premises liability loss exposure. Ice and snow create an additional hazard and typically increase the number of falls that occur. Property owners and occupiers have a duty to clear off ice and snow from sidewalks after it has fallen.

Premises security is another common source of premises liability. Property owners and occupiers have a duty to provide a reasonably safe environment. Premises security liability loss exposures fall into two categories: crimes committed by employees and crimes committed by third parties.

Mobile equipment can cause bodily injury and property damage. Consequentially, it is another source of premises liability with which risk management professionals need to be concerned.

Organizations that serve liquor have a significant liquor liability loss exposure. Additionally, most organizations have a limited liquor liability loss exposure arising out of organization-hosted events.

Bailment liability loss exposures arise out of bailments, that is, when property is in the custody of another. The three types of bailment are as follows:

1. Bailments for the sole benefit of the bailor.
2. Bailments for the sole benefit of the bailee.
3. Bailments for the mutual benefit of both parties.

Bailees are not strictly liable for everything that happens to bailed property while it is in their care. Bailees may rely on negligence defenses and may be able to present written disclaimers to negate or limit liability.

Organizations that manufacturer, distribute, or sell products have a products liability loss exposure. Products liability loss exposures can arise out of breach of warranty, negligence, or strict liability in tort.

Breach of warranty is the failure to adhere to an express or implied warranty regarding the title, quality, content, or condition of the goods sold.

A valid negligence lawsuit may arise out of a defect arising from a product's design, manufacture, inspection, or from the product's accompanying instructions or warnings.

Strict liability in tort makes the product's seller liable even if the seller has exercised all reasonable care. A strict liability in tort action generally requires that the buyer prove the following:

- The product left the manufacturer's custody or control in a defective condition.
- The defective condition made the product unreasonably dangerous.
- The defective product was the proximate cause of the buyer's injury.

"Defective" is a key word in this doctrine. A product may be defective in the following three ways that parallel closely the basis for negligence:

1. Defective because of faulty manufacture or assembly
2. Defective in design
3. Failure to give warning

Several defenses are available for both negligence and strict liability in tort actions. These defenses include the following:

- State of the art
- Compliance with product specifications
- Open and obvious danger
- Plaintiff's knowledge
- Contributory and comparative negligence and assumption of risk
- Product misuse
- Product alteration
- Written disclaimers
- Post-accident product changes
- Existence of an intermediary
- Allergy and susceptibility

Completed operations liability arises out of an organization's completed work, including defective parts or materials furnished with the work.

Automobile liability consists of legal responsibility for bodily injury or property damage arising out of the ownership, maintenance, or use of autos. Organizations may also be liable for the operation of autos by others who are related to the organization. Such relationships include the following:

- Employer-employee
- Volunteers
- Loaned employees

Owners and operators of watercraft have a liability loss exposure arising out of this activity. Vessel owners or operators (vessel owners for simplicity) have the following major loss exposures:

- Bodily injury, illness, or death of:
  - Members of the vessel's crew
  - Shore workers, passengers, or other persons on board
  - Persons not on board the vessel
- Property damage to (and resulting loss of use of):
  - Other vessels, resulting from collision with the owner's vessel
  - Cargo or other property on board other vessels
  - Bridges, piers, docks, navigational locks, and other structures
  - Cargo or other property of others on board the owner's vessel
- Liability for pollution

Risk management professionals are particularly concerned about liability loss exposures because of their severity and unpredictability. Additional liability loss exposures are described in the next chapter.

CHAPTER NOTES

1. *Sanders v. Officers Club of Connecticut, Inc.*, 196 Conn. 341, 493 A.2d 184 (1985).

2. *Sindell v. Abbot Laboratories*, 607 P.2d 924 (California Supreme Court, 1980).

3. *Liebeck v. McDonald's*, 1995 WL 360309 (N.M. Dist.).

4. *BMW of North America v. Gore*, 517 U.S. 559, 116 S. Ct. 1589 (1996).

5. *Perlman v. McDonald's Corp.*, 237 F. Supp. 2d 512 (S.D.N.Y. 2003).

6. *Daubert v. Merrell Dow Pharmaceuticals, Inc.*, 509 U.S. 579 (1993).

7. *Kumho Tire Co., Ltd. v. Carmichael*, 119 S. Ct. 1167 (1999).

Chapter 6

Direct Your Learning

Assessing Liability Loss Exposures, Part II

After learning the content of this chapter and completing the corresponding course guide assignment, you should be able to:

■ Describe the liability loss exposures arising out of workers' compensation.

■ Describe the liability loss exposures arising out of environmental pollution.

■ Describe the liability loss exposures arising out of professional activities, including physicians, accountants, insurance agents and brokers, and architects and engineers.

■ Define or describe each of the Key Words and Phrases for this chapter.

Develop Your Perspective

What are the main topics covered in the chapter?

This chapter continues the discussion of liability loss exposures by examining liability loss exposures arising out of workers' compensation, environmental pollution, and professional activities.

Select a local utility company, or a local organization that has environmental liability loss exposures.

- What actual or alleged pollutants could be released from this utility or organization?

- How might this utility violate a law designed to protect human health or the environment from those pollutants?

Why is it important to know about these topics?

Risk management professionals must be able to assess their organization's likely sources of liability. Once identified and evaluated, these sources of liability can be managed using a variety of risk management techniques.

Contrast the professional liability loss exposures faced by the various types of professionals.

- What liability loss exposures might an accountant face?

- How might these exposures be similar or different than those facing an architect?

How can you use this information?

Assess the liability loss exposures facing your organization.

- Which liability loss exposures are not currently being adequately managed? Why?

- Is your employer actively taking steps to mitigate these liability loss exposures?

Assessing Liability Loss Exposures, Part II

Organizations are subject to legal liability arising from various sources. This chapter continues the discussion of sources of liability loss exposures and addresses liability arising out of the following:

- Workers' compensation
- Environmental pollution
- Professional activities

Most organizations have a workers' compensation liability loss exposure. Environmental pollution liability loss exposures are not limited to those organizations typically thought of as polluters. In addition, most if not all organizations face some environmental loss exposures. Professional liability loss exposures arise out of professional activities and are consequently only a concern for professionals undertaking those activities.

WORKERS' COMPENSATION LIABILITY LOSS EXPOSURES

Workers' compensation is a comprehensive term used to refer to the statutes that provide financial awards for workers' compensation benefits. These benefits include disability income, medical expense reimbursement, rehabilitation services, and death benefits that are paid to employees or their dependents in cases of employment-related injuries and diseases. As workers' compensation statutes impose strict liability, those awards are granted regardless of the employer's negligence or fault. However, workers' compensation laws are intended to benefit the employer as well as the employee. These statutes have created a "no-fault" system in which the employee loses the right to sue for common-law damages in return for the employer's strict liability for work-related accidents.

Risk management professionals must understand the basis for workers' compensation liability and the loss exposures created by that liability in order to implement effective risk management techniques. However, they must also understand that despite the existence of workers' compensation laws, employers can in some instances be sued under common law as a result of employee injury or disease.

Employers' Liability Under Common Law

Before workers' compensation statutes were enacted, courts applied common-law concepts to the disposition of occupational injury and disease claims by an employee against an employer. Workers' compensation laws made an extraordinary departure from the way in which the common law established responsibility for an injury on fault. This departure resulted from the inadequacies in the common law that prevented it from dealing appropriately with work-related injuries. However, understanding the common-law concepts applicable to employers' liability is important because the various workers' compensation laws have exceptions for certain employments or circumstances. When a worker is outside the scope of workers' compensation laws, he or she retains the right to sue the employer under the common law. In some cases, even an employee who is covered by workers' compensation may be able to bring a common-law suit.

Employers' Duty of Care

Under the common law, an employer is obligated to exercise a reasonable degree of care for an employee's safety. The following specific duties have been derived from this reasonable duty of care:

- Providing a safe place to work
- Providing competent fellow employees
- Providing safe tools and equipment
- Warning employees of inherent dangers
- Making and enforcing rules for the safety of all employees

If the employer's failure to exercise such care as the circumstances require is the proximate cause of an employee's injury, the employer can be held legally liable to pay damages for negligence, in the absence of a valid legal defense. In all cases, it is up to the employee to establish the employer's negligence.

Common-Law Defenses

One of the primary factors that drove the reform of how injured workers were compensated in the United States, and that led to the enactment of workers' compensation statutes, was employers' successful reliance on certain defenses to negligence. However, there are circumstances in which an employer is subject to common-law negligence claims but is barred from relying on these defenses; for example, if the employer fails to provide workers' compensation through insurance or other means.

Where the employer is not barred from relying on common-law defenses, the available defenses are as follows:

- Contributory negligence
- Comparative negligence
- Negligence of a fellow employee
- Statute of limitations

Under the common law, everyone is required to exercise care for his or her own safety. If an employee fails to exercise such care, he or she will be deemed to be contributorily negligent even though the negligence of the employer was also a contributing cause of the injury. The common-law rule is that if the employee's contributory negligence is responsible *to any degree* in causing the accident, the employee is barred from recovery. Therefore, even if the employer's negligence was the primary cause of the injury, the employee will not be entitled to damages.

The contributory negligence defense has been largely replaced by the comparative negligence defense under which the employee's negligence is taken into account in reducing the amount of recovery. Comparative negligence laws enable employees to recover a portion of their damages even when they are partially at fault.

Employers can avoid liability if the employee's injury resulted from the negligent act or omission of a fellow employee. As mentioned previously, these employer defenses—contributory negligence, comparative negligence, and negligence of a fellow employee—successfully defeated most employees' lawsuits. Workers' compensation statutes were enacted to prevent employers from relying on these common-law defenses to defeat employee claims.

The operation of statutes of limitations may also preclude an injured worker from bringing suit against the employer. The period of time in which an action can be brought varies by state. However, the period is generally two years.

Employers' Liability Under Statutes

All fifty states, the District of Columbia, Puerto Rico, Guam, the U.S. Virgin Islands, and all the Canadian provinces have workers' compensation laws, which balance the interests of both employer and employee. Workers give up their existing legal remedy, the right of a tort action for negligent injury against the employer. In so doing, workers also give up the right to recover damages for pain and suffering or inconvenience. The employer gives up various common-law defenses and becomes obligated to respond to the employee's injury according to the law's terms. In return, the workers' compensation laws provide relative certainty about the amount of benefits to be paid for specified injuries. The following are principles of the workers' compensation system:[1]

1. Provide sure, prompt, and reasonable income and medical benefits to work-accident victims or income benefits to their dependents, regardless of fault;
2. Provide a single remedy and reduce court delays, costs, and workloads arising out of personal injury litigation;
3. Relieve public and private charities of financially draining incidents associated with uncompensated industrial accidents;
4. Eliminate payment of fees to lawyers and witnesses as well as time-consuming trials and appeals;

5. Encourage maximum employer interest in safety and rehabilitation through appropriate experience rating mechanisms; and

6. Promote frank study of causes of accidents (rather than concealment of fault), thereby reducing the number of preventable accidents and consequent human suffering.

The following features are particularly important in the U.S. workers' compensation laws. Risk management professionals should understand these common features because they affect the scope of workers' compensation loss exposures.

-   Choice of law
-· Persons and employments covered
-   Injuries and diseases covered
-   Benefits provided
-   Procedures for obtaining benefits

Choice of Law

In any given case of an employment-related injury, the laws of numerous states may apply if the employment and injury occur in different states. Factors that might be considered when determining which state's workers' compensation benefits apply include the place of injury, the place of hire, the place of employment, the location of the employer, the residence of the employee, and any state whose compensation laws are adopted by contract. In general, the laws of the states where the injury occurred, where the employment usually occurs, and where the employee was hired *all* apply to a loss. The employee cannot receive duplicate benefits but can select the state with the most generous benefits.

Persons and Employments Covered

Workers' compensation statutes cover most public and private employments. Some of the earlier workers' compensation statutes covered only employments carried on for pecuniary gain. Such a provision would eliminate all public employees such as police officers, firefighters, and sanitation workers, as well as those employed by a charity, because none of these workers are employed by profit-making enterprises. A few laws still retain this provision. In addition, the workers' compensation laws of some states exclude domestic and farm workers, who therefore retain their common-law rights of action against their employers.

As a general rule, an employer's legal obligations for occupational injury or disease extend to employees only, not to independent contractors. The distinction between an employee and an independent contractor is therefore an important one. It is best expressed in terms of the extent of the employer's right to direct and control the work-related activities of each as follows:

-   An employee is one for whom the employer typically fixes the hours of employment, provides the tools with which to do the work, and defines and supervises the results of the work, as well as the methods and means of doing the work.

- An independent contractor is one for whom the employer does not typically fix the hours of employment and may or may not provide the tools with which to do the work. The employer defines the results of the work but, perhaps most important, does not define and supervise the methods and means of doing the work.

Many states' workers' compensation statutes contain an important exception to the general rule that an employer's workers' compensation obligations do not extend to independent contractors. This exception provides workers' compensation coverage for statutory employees. A **statutory employee** is an independent contractor's employee who, because the independent contractor has not maintained workers' compensation insurance, is considered to be an employee of the principal employing the independent contractor. Therefore, if an employee of the uninsured independent contractor sustains a compensable injury, the principal can be held liable to provide workers' compensation benefits to the injured employee. However, after paying benefits to a statutory employee, the principal ordinarily has the right to seek recovery from the independent contractor.

Statutory employee
An independent contractor's employee who, because the independent contractor has not maintained workers' compensation insurance, is considered to be an employee of the principal employing the independent contractor.

A principal's obligation to provide workers' compensation benefits to statutory employees also applies to a general contractor that has hired a subcontractor. That is, the employees of an uninsured subcontractor can be deemed statutory employees of the general contractor.

Because of the provisions regarding statutory employees, a principal that hires independent contractors should obtain certificates of insurance from those independent contractors before they begin their operations for the principal. Moreover, because a certificate of insurance does not guarantee that the insurance will be in effect beyond the date that the certificate was issued, the principal should also maintain valid workers' compensation insurance in case the contractor does not have insurance at the time a loss actually occurs.

Many employers make use of temporary employees and/or leased employees in addition to their regular employees. Temporary and leased employees differ from one another. Temporary employees are hired for short-term assignments to cope with peak loads or to replace an employee who is out ill, on vacation, and so on. The organization supplying temporary employees provides workers' compensation insurance for these employees; the temporary employee is an employee of the providing organization, not of the organization that is using the temporary employee's services.

Leased employees, on the other hand, have all the outward appearance of regular employees. They work continuously for the same organization and are subject to control by the organization just as they would be if they were direct employees of the organization. Technically, however, they are co-employees of the leasing contractor, sometimes referred to as a professional employer organization (PEO), and the client organization. Sometimes an organization will transfer all of its employees to the PEO and then lease them back. The PEO is responsible for all payroll taxes, employee benefits, and workers' compensation coverage. Generally, a separate workers' compensation policy is purchased in the names of the PEO and the client organization, although the requirements imposed by law vary by state.

Injuries and Diseases Covered

Workers' compensation provides benefits only for occupational injury—injury arising from the worker's employment. The most obvious work-related losses are caused by industrial accidents. Therefore, early workers' compensation laws often referred only to "accidents" occurring within the scope of employment; they contained no provision with regard to occupational disease. Now statutes define occupational disease and the proof required to qualify both injuries and occupational diseases for coverage. Not all occupational diseases are covered, and the requirements to prove compensability for injury and disease differ by statute.

With regard to occupational injuries, an employee seeking workers' compensation benefits typically must show that (1) he or she suffered an injury caused by an accident, (2) the injury arose out of employment, and (3) the injury occurred in the course of employment. For an occupational disease (as opposed to an injury) to be compensable, (1) the disease must be covered by the statute as one that normally results from the nature of the employment, and (2) the exposure to the disease must arise from employment.

The laws of the great majority of the states define an occupational injury as one that "arises out of and in the course of employment." Therefore, there has to be a causal connection between employment and occupational injury. To be compensable, the injury must not only occur while the employee is at work, but it must also be related to that work. Most jurisdictions also require that the injury be an accident. The courts have defined "accident" as an undesigned, sudden, and unexpected event. Therefore, persons who willfully injure themselves are not entitled to workers' compensation. The compensation statute will often further define accidental injury by stating that injuries arising from certain causes are not covered, such as injuries caused by intoxication, willful failure to use a safety appliance or observe safety regulations, or failure to perform a duty required by statute.

These requirements can entail many gray areas. For example, lunchtime injuries are generally considered to occur outside the scope of employment except when the employer continues to exercise authority over the employee during the lunch break.[2] However, when an employee is required to attend a company function, injuries sustained at that function are generally covered by the applicable workers' compensation statute.

Positional risk doctrine
A legal doctrine stating that an injury arises out of the claimant's employment if it would not have occurred but for the fact that the conditions and obligations of the employment placed the claimant in the position where he or she was injured.

Some states have adopted a **positional risk doctrine**, which states that an injury arises out of the claimant's employment if it would not have occurred but for the fact that the conditions and obligations of the employment placed the claimant in the position where he or she was injured. For example, in a state that has adopted the positional risk doctrine, the injury an employee receives when an out-of-control car crashes through the employer's storefront would be covered by the workers' compensation statute. States that do not observe the positional risk doctrine would rule that the injury did not arise out of employment and therefore is not covered by the workers' compensation statute.[3]

Benefits Provided

Workers' compensation statutes provide the following four types of benefits:

1. Medical benefits
2. Disability benefits
3. Rehabilitation services
4. Death benefits

The first type of workers' compensation benefit is medical benefits. Almost all states cover all necessary medical expenses. However, in some states, the statute sets payment amounts according to a fee schedule, and approved medical providers must accept the amounts specified in the fee schedule as full compensation.

The scope of covered medical care is broad and includes items such as physician fees, emergency room fees, hospital care, diagnostic testing, nursing care, medications, and prosthetic devices. Care by chiropractors is also covered in some states. Coverage for medical expenses begins immediately after the injury, even if disability benefits are subject to a waiting period.

In most states, employees with compensable injuries can choose their own medical practitioners. In other states, the choice may be limited to medical practitioners shown on a list provided by the employer. Alternatively, employees may be restricted to practitioners within a managed care organization for treatment of their work-related injuries.

The employer (and therefore its workers' compensation insurer) generally has the right to have the injured employee examined by an independent medical examiner (IME) of its choice. The IME is a healthcare provider, such as a physician or a dentist, who has agreed to evaluate an injured employee for a fee and who is not involved in the injured employee's treatment.

The second type of workers' compensation benefit is disability benefits. Disability benefits are cash payments to injured workers to replace income lost because of the worker's inability to return to work or inability return to work in the position he or she held before the occurrence of the occupational injury or disease.

Disability benefits are not payable to disabled workers immediately after the injury. Rather, workers' compensation statutes require that disabled workers wait a specified number of days (waiting period) before becoming eligible for benefits. This waiting period serves the same purpose as a deductible; that is, reducing the cost of benefits and encouraging slightly injured workers to recover quickly. Workers' compensation statutes usually provide disability benefits from the first day of disability once the disabled worker has been unable to return to work beyond a specified period. For example, some states have a seven-day waiting period and fourteen-day retroactive period, so that injured workers who are unable return to work for fifteen or more days are provided disability income for the entire period.

For those injured workers who are unable to return to work, the workers' compensation statutes provide benefits based on the permanency and the duration of the injury. The following disability classifications are used by workers' compensation statutes:

- Temporary total disability
- Permanent total disability
- Temporary partial disability
- Permanent partial disability

Most workers' compensation disabilities are temporary total disability; that is, the injured worker is expected to recover fully, but until recovery is achieved, the injured worker is unable to work at all. Permanent total disability means that the injured worker will never be able to return to gainful employment. Temporary partial disability means the injured worker can return to work in some capacity and eventually will be able to perform the job held prior to the occurrence of the injury or disease. Permanent partial disability means that the worker is permanently limited in some respect.

Cash payments to a disabled worker are usually expressed as a percentage of the worker's wage prior to the injury (most states use 66⅔ percent) while providing a minimum and maximum weekly payment. Cash payments for permanent total disability generally last the injured worker's lifetime. Injured workers with permanent partial disabilities usually receive a reduced benefit that is based on the difference between the injured worker's wages prior to and after the injury. Some states provide a specified cash benefit for certain injuries, such as the loss of a hand. Temporary disability benefits end with the injured worker's return to work.

The disability benefits available vary by state. The U.S. Chamber of Commerce summarizes state workers' compensation laws, including disability benefits, in its annual publication, *Analysis of Workers' Compensation Laws.*

The third type of workers' compensation benefit is rehabilitation services. Rehabilitation services are a means to reduce the seriousness and, therefore, the cost of disabling injuries. They do so, in part, by providing vocational or physical assistance to injured employees so that they can return to employment. Although considered an integral part of complete medical treatment, rehabilitation may go much further and include such services as vocational training or training to drive a specially equipped car.

Even if a state does not include specific rehabilitation provisions in its workers' compensation laws, rehabilitation services are available. Rehabilitation services often reduce the ultimate loss costs because the rehabilitated workers are able to seek employment earlier.

The fourth type of workers' compensation benefit is death benefits. Like disability benefits, death benefits to surviving spouses and dependents vary by state. In a majority of states these income replacement benefits are limited in time. Both the amount and the duration of the weekly benefit typically depend on whether the deceased employee has minor children. Benefits may also be limited or terminated if the surviving spouse remarries. As is true for permanent total disability benefits, about one-fourth of the states adjust death benefits annually to match all or part of the increase in prices or wages. In addition to income replacement benefits, all states pay a burial allowance.

Procedures for Obtaining Benefits

The workers' compensation laws require the employee to notify the employer of an injury within a certain period of time (often thirty days) in order to obtain benefits. Notice must be given to the employer, supervisor, or someone in a managerial position. Failure to give notice is generally excused when the employer witnessed or heard about the occurrence of the accident, or when the failure to give notice did not prejudice the employer's right to investigate and verify the details of the accident.

The employee or the employee's survivor is required to file a claim for compensation within a designated time, usually one year. Failure to file a claim within the statutory period renders the claim unenforceable, even if it has merit. The statute of limitations, together with the notice requirement, recognizes that the employer should not be required to respond to claims that cannot be investigated and defended and that might result in an accrued liability for which the employer had not planned.

Federal Compensation Laws

A large percentage of the work force is eligible for state workers' compensation benefits. Nevertheless, these state workers' compensation laws do not apply to all employees. Many employees are covered by the federal laws discussed below and summarized in Exhibit 6-1. These laws include the following:

* Longshore and Harbor Workers' Compensation Act (LHWCA)
* Extensions of the LHWCA
* Federal Employers' Liability Act
* Migrant and Seasonal Agricultural Worker Protection Act
* Federal Employees' Compensation Act

Longshore and Harbor Workers' Compensation Act

The Longshore and Harbor Workers' Compensation Act (LHWCA), administered by the U.S. Department of Labor, provides medical benefits, compensation for lost wages, and rehabilitation services to longshoremen, harbor workers, and other maritime workers who are injured during the course of employment or who suffer from diseases caused or worsened by conditions of employment. The courts have interpreted maritime employment broadly

EXHIBIT 6-1

Remedies for Occupational Injuries Other Than State Workers' Compensation

Employees Subject to Remedy	Source of Remedy	Nature of Remedy
Maritime workers, with some exceptions (such as the master or crew of a vessel)	Longshore and Harbor Workers' Compensation Act (LHWCA)	No-fault benefits as defined by the statute
1. Civilian employees at U.S. military bases acquired from foreign governments 2. Civilian employees working overseas under contracts with agencies of the U.S. government	Defense Base Act	No-fault benefits as defined by the statute
Workers on fixed offshore drilling and production platforms on the Outer Continental Shelf of the U.S.	Outer Continental Shelf Lands Act (OCSLA)	No-fault benefits as defined by the statute
Civilian employees of "nonappropriated fund instrumentalities" on U.S. military bases, such as stores and theaters	Nonappropriated Fund Instrumentalities Act	No-fault benefits as defined by the statute
Members of a vessel's crew	Jones Act	Negligence suit against employer
	Death on the High Seas Act	Survivors may sue employer for death occurring beyond a marine league from the shore of any state
	Admiralty case law: maintenance and cure	Vessel owner must pay food, lodging, and medical care, irrespective of fault, until maximum medical cure achieved
	Admiralty case law: vessel owner's breach of warranty of vessel's seaworthiness	Negligence suit against vessel owner
	Admiralty case law: Moragne remedy	Wrongful death action against vessel owner
Employees of interstate railroads	Federal Employers' Liability Act (FELA)	Negligence suit against employer
Migrant and seasonal farm workers	Migrant and Seasonal Agricultural Worker Protection Act (MSPA)	Suit against employer if employee is not covered by WC insurance
Nonmilitary employees of the U.S. government	Federal Employees' Compensation Act (FECA)	No-fault benefits as defined by the statute

so that a wide range of workers are covered by LHWCA if they are injured while working on navigable waters. Navigable waters include rivers, canals, harbors, and the high seas. The LHWCA has extended applicability of the LHWCA to persons working on piers, wharfs, dry docks, terminals, marine railroads, or other adjoining areas customarily used by an employer in loading and unloading, repairing, dismantling, or building vessels.

Amendments to the LHWCA have defined classes of workers who are not eligible for benefits under the act. Some of these worker classes are precluded from the LHWCA if they are subject to state workers' compensation benefits. These amendments have reduced the number of injured workers who were able to choose between the usually more generous benefits of the LHWCA and state workers' compensation benefits.

Extensions of the LHWCA

Some federal statutes extend the benefits of the LHWCA to additional classes of employees. These federal statutes include the following:

- Defense Base Act
- Outer Continental Shelf Lands Act
- Nonappropriated Fund Instrumentalities Act

The Defense Base Act applies the benefits of the LHWCA to (1) civilian employees at any military, air, or naval bases acquired by the U.S. (after January 1, 1940) from foreign governments and (2) civilian employees working at overseas locations under contracts being performed for agencies of the U.S. government.

The Outer Continental Shelf Lands Act (OCSLA) extends the benefits of the LHWCA to workers, other than members of a vessel's crew, engaged in the exploration for or production of natural resources on the outer continental shelf of the U.S. Typically, employees subject to OCSLA are workers situated on offshore drilling and production platforms. OCSLA defines the outer continental shelf as the submerged lands of the U.S. adjacent to the coast but outside the area of the particular state's territorial boundaries. The territorial boundaries of Florida and Texas extend to ten nautical miles from their coastlines, and those of all other coastal states extend to three nautical miles from their coastlines.[4]

The Nonappropriated Fund Instrumentalities Act extends the benefits of the LHWCA to civilian employees of "nonappropriated fund instrumentalities," which include various facilities on military bases such as stores, daycare centers, and movie theaters.

Federal Employers' Liability Act

The Federal Employers' Liability Act (FELA) enables injured railroad employees to sue their employer for occupational injuries resulting from the employer's negligence while preventing the employer from asserting the common-law defenses. Injured workers can recover damages for lost wages, medical expenses, and pain and suffering. Survivors of killed employees are also entitled to benefits.

Migrant and Seasonal Agricultural Worker Protection Act

The Migrant and Seasonal Agricultural Worker Protection Act (MSPA) provides various protections to migrant and seasonal agricultural workers. Among the protections provided to such workers is the right to sue their employers for occupational injury or illness if the workers are not covered by workers' compensation insurance.

The Federal Employees' Compensation Act

The Federal Employees' Compensation Act (FECA), administered by the U.S. Department of Labor, provides workers' compensation benefits to federal civilian employees for work-related injuries or illnesses, and to their surviving dependents if a work-related injury or illness results in the employee's death. The federal government self-insures this liability loss exposure.

ENVIRONMENTAL LIABILITY LOSS EXPOSURES

Many organizations have significant environmental liability loss exposures because of the nature of the business they are in. For example, waste haulers, asbestos remediators, and landfill operators all conduct businesses in which environmental liability is a major concern. However, all organizations potentially have some environmental liability exposures. For example, an office has a slight environmental loss exposure from photocopy machine printer cartridges and cleaning chemicals. Environmental loss exposures are sometimes overlooked. Some of those loss exposures are insignificant, or they seem to be. Other loss exposures are overlooked because they were incurred many years earlier or were considered to be insignificant at the time.

Managing environmental loss exposures is an important consideration for a wide range of organizations because of the far-reaching cost recovery provisions of environmental statutes. Risk management professionals need to be aware of how an organization can incur environmental liability in order to implement appropriate risk management techniques.

Environmental Liability Causes of Loss

An organization can incur environmental liability under tort, contract, or statute. Environmental losses are most frequently caused by the actual or alleged release of pollutants, the violation of a law designed to protect human health and the environment from those pollutants, or the enforcement of environmental protection laws that require remediation expense payment.

Tort

Tort liability for pollution can be based on negligence, intentional torts, or strict liability. The following are examples of negligent acts that have resulted in actual environmental liability:

- A contractor working at a manufacturing facility left a valve open on a process line overnight. The next day it was discovered that the contents of a storage tank connected to the process line had been released into an adjacent stream. The pollutant caused bodily injury and property damage, including natural resource damage.

- A hazardous waste hauler transporting toxic waste to a disposal facility was at fault in causing an auto accident in the downtown section of a city. The hazardous waste being transported was released, creating a hazardous waste spill on the street. Passersby inhaled the fumes, and the business district of the city was evacuated for two days as cleanup contractors responded to the spill. Lawsuits were filed against the transporter alleging bodily injury, property damage, and loss of business income.

Other possible sources of liability for the negligent release of pollutants include hazardous product manufacturing, testing, and transporting; hazardous waste disposal; product failures; inadequate emergency response procedures; and incompetent environmental consulting. When hazardous materials are involved, the organization may face a strict liability tort claim.

The intentional torts most commonly alleged in environmental lawsuits are nuisance and trespass. If a neighbor or another third party engages in an activity that interferes with the owner's right of enjoyment of the property, the owner may bring an action alleging nuisance against the party causing the interference. Potential environmental liability loss exposures alleging nuisance can involve loud noises, noxious odors, bright lights, fog generation, electrical waves, and electromagnetic fields.

Unlike nuisance, which requires no transmission of pollutants from one property to another, environmental trespass involves physically depositing pollutants onto the property of the party alleging injury. The pollutants that are deposited may be toxic substances, but they do not have to be. For example, lawsuits have also resulted from releases or deposits of water, sand, and clean soil. As long as the deposits are objectionable to the property owner, an environmental trespass lawsuit can be brought against the party responsible for the release or deposit. Environmental trespass could result from the release of dust or particulate into the air, the discharge of chemicals into a stream, the runoff of pesticides onto a neighbor's property, or thermal emissions into a river.

Strict liability can be a basis for environmental liability when manufacturing operations use ultrahazardous activities or materials. If strict liability applies, it eliminates the common-law defenses normally available to the defendant in a negligence suit. No degree of care is considered to be adequate for ultrahazardous activities or materials. For example, a remediation contractor working on a job to incinerate nerve gas could face strict liability if a release of the nerve gas injures a third party, even if the contractor exercised a very high degree of care in performing the work. Some examples of materials that could create strict liability for environmental injury include nuclear materials, explosives, polychlorinated biphenyl (PCB) materials, pesticides, highly toxic chemicals, and hazardous waste.

Contract

In addition to torts, environmental liability can be created by contract. An organization can assume liability for environmental losses under a hold-harmless agreement. For example, a general contractor that agrees to indemnify a project owner for all claims made against the owner during the course of the project may incur an environmental loss under the contract if the project owner is the subject of a lawsuit. For example, a worker who is employed by a subcontractor at the project and is injured as a result of breathing ammonia may sue the project owner. The general contractor would have to reimburse the project owner for any legal costs and any damages paid to the subcontractor.

Statute

Environmental liability can also be created by statute. The majority of environmental statutes regulate materials that are reactive, corrosive, toxic, or flammable. These statutes contain provisions that can lead to injunctions, fines, and other penalties for noncompliance, such as revocation of permits. The statutes also contain provisions for the criminal prosecution of individuals, including corporate officers.

One of the first pieces of environmental legislation was the National Environmental Policy Act (NEPA) of 1969. NEPA resulted from the efforts of conservationists to compel the federal government to consider the environmental ramifications of proposals for new highways, dams, and other public projects capable of affecting wildlife or scenic areas. Since the passage of NEPA, many environmental laws have been passed to protect human health and the environment.

Many environmental laws do not require fault or negligence on the part of the party charged with responsibility, in effect creating strict liability by statute. One of the common principles that runs through most of these laws is the theory that the person who caused the pollution should be responsible to pay for the cleanup of that pollution in the event of a spill or release. This principle is commonly called a "let the polluter pay" funding scheme.

Federal statutes provide the baseline standards for state and local environmental laws. The major federal environmental laws are summarized in Exhibit 6-2 and discussed in more detail in the sections that follow. Most states actually administer these laws under state statutes that have different names from those shown in the exhibit but virtually the same content as the federal laws.

EXHIBIT 6-2

Summary of the Major Federal Environmental Laws

Name of Law	Basic Purpose of Law
The National Environmental Policy Act (NEPA) (1969)	To establish a national policy for the environment and to provide for the establishment of a Council on Environmental Quality
Clean Air Act (1969)	To improve the quality of ambient air by regulating emissions from both mobile and stationary sources of air pollution
Clean Water Act (1970)	To improve the quality of surface waters by prohibiting or regulating the discharge of pollutants into navigable waters and restoring them to "fishable" or "swimmable" quality
Toxic Substance Control Act (1979)	To regulate the chemical manufacturing industry and prevent the importation or manufacture of dangerous chemical substances without adequate safeguards
Resource Conservation and Recovery Act (RCRA) (1979)	To provide "cradle-to-grave" regulation of hazardous waste; impose strict waste management requirements on generators and transporters of hazardous wastes and on hazardous waste treatment, storage, and disposal facilities; to regulate underground storage tanks, medical wastes, and nonhazardous solid wastes; and to impose proof of financial responsibility requirements on permit holders
Motor Carrier Act (1980)	To protect the environment from releases of harmful materials during transportation of such materials by motor carriers in interstate or intrastate commerce
Comprehensive Environmental Response, Compensation, and Liability Act (CERCLA) (1980)	To facilitate the cleanup of any abandoned or uncontrolled sites containing hazardous substances and to impose strict liability for cleanup costs on potentially responsible parties
Oil Pollution Act (OPA) (1990)	To reduce the risk of spills of petroleum or hazardous materials into U.S. coastal or navigable waters by mandating technical standards and requiring proof of financial responsibility for facilities and vessels operating in or near such waters

In addition, local governments are able to establish standards that are more restrictive than the federal standard. This legislative freedom and the public interest in laws protecting the environment lead to a profusion of environmental regulations that vary by state.

The Clean Air Act of 1969 seeks to improve the quality of ambient air by regulating emissions from both mobile and stationary sources of air pollution. Permits are required for parties that intend to construct or operate sources of air emissions. The terms of the permit vary from one emission source to another and from one pollutant to another. Similarly, restrictions are tighter in areas of poor air quality (such as urban areas) than elsewhere. The zones around cities where ambient air quality fails to meet Clean Air Act requirements are classified as nonattainment areas. In these areas, regulators can curtail new industrial or commercial development by denying the required air permits.

The Clean Water Act of 1970 seeks to improve the quality of surface waters by prohibiting or regulating the discharge of pollutants into navigable waters and restoring them to a condition in which they are safe for fishing and swimming. A number of activities are regulated under this legislation, including active pollutant discharge into waterways as well as storm water runoff. The Clean Water Act also mandates a Spill Prevention, Control, and Countermeasure Plan for certain regulated facilities, such as oil-handling facilities.

The Toxic Substance Control Act of 1979 regulates the chemical manufacturing industry and prevents the importation or manufacture of dangerous chemical substances without adequate safeguards to ensure that their use does not harm human health or the environment. The act also facilitates extensive regulation of individual hazardous substances on a case-by-case basis. Consequently, the act has been used to regulate polychlorinated biphenyls (PCBs) and, to a more limited extent, asbestos and radon. The Environmental Protection Agency (EPA) has also contemplated using the Toxic Substance Control Act to impose extensive regulations on the use of lead. Under this act, manufacturers of chemical substances must provide extensive information to the EPA regarding the formulation, use, and risks of each substance they manufacture or import, including any information on known or suspected adverse health or environmental effects.

The Resource Conservation and Recovery Act of 1979 (RCRA) provides "cradle-to-grave" regulation of hazardous waste. RCRA imposes strict waste management requirements on generators and transporters of hazardous wastes and on hazardous waste treatment, storage, and disposal facilities. In addition, RCRA regulates underground storage tanks, medical wastes, and nonhazardous solid wastes, although the requirements for some of these waste categories are considerably less stringent than those for hazardous wastes.

RCRA was one of the first environmental statutes to adopt proof of financial responsibility requirements for permit holders. Under these requirements, the owners of hazardous waste treatment, storage or treatment facilities, landfills, and underground storage tanks are required to provide evidence that they have the financial resources to clean up any material from the facility that causes environmental damage and to compensate victims for bodily injury and property damage. Permit holders have a number of options available to evidence this proof, including specially endorsed insurance policies, performance bonds, letters of credit, cash in escrow, or self-insurer status. The amounts of required proof vary by the type of facility and by state regulations. Risk management professionals in need of advice on compliance with these regulations should consult with the state environmental regulators for the current requirements and acceptable methods of providing the proof of financial responsibility.

RCRA includes a wide variety of wastes within the scope of its regulatory program. The most notable exceptions are waste oil and certain high-volume, low-toxicity wastes (such as certain mine wastes and incinerator ash). Under this regulatory program, waste generators must manage hazardous wastes in accordance with detailed requirements governing containers, labels, record-keeping, storage, spill prevention and control, and employee training. On-site storage is limited both with respect to time and quantity. Shipments of hazardous waste require completing a shipping manifest that tracks the journey from "cradle to grave," thereby ensuring final disposal only at proper facilities.

The Motor Carrier Act of 1980 seeks to protect the environment from releases of harmful materials during the transportation of such materials by motor carriers in interstate or intrastate commerce. It established minimum levels of financial responsibility sufficient to cover third-party liability, including property damage and environmental restoration for both private and for-hire carriers of hazardous materials.

The Comprehensive Environmental Response, Compensation, and Liability Act (CERCLA or Superfund) was passed in 1980 to facilitate the cleanup of any abandoned or uncontrolled sites containing hazardous substances, including numerous old dump sites. CERCLA was passed because RCRA regulations only cover active, not abandoned, waste disposal sites.

The EPA has established a list of sites where known releases or threatened releases of hazardous substances, pollutants, or contaminates are located. This list, known as the National Priorities List, is used by the EPA to prioritize site investigation and cleanup. The average cost of a Superfund cleanup of a site on the National Priorities List, is approximately $30 million, exclusive of substantial transaction costs. Approximately 1,300 Superfund sites appear on the National Priority List, and more than 3,500 sites are targeted for cleanup under state programs similar to CERCLA. These sites can take more than twenty-five years to remediate if groundwater is involved. The EPA estimates that as many as 350,000 contaminated sites will need cleanup by 2035 and that the estimated cleanup costs could be as much as $250 billion.[5]

Potentially responsible parties (PRPs) are the persons or entities that are potentially legally responsible for the costs of remediating a Superfund site. Parties involved with a Superfund site are referred to as PRPs until liability under CERCLA is established. At that point they become responsible parties (RPs). RPs are responsible for all costs associated with cleaning up the site, including the costs of identifying and evaluating contaminants and developing a plan for remediation.

Following the "let the polluter pay" principle, the drafters of the original legislation included as PRPs all parties who enjoyed an economic benefit from the waste disposal activities or in the ownership of the site. PRPs can therefore include any of the following:

* The current owners and operators of a site (even if they had no involvement with the original waste disposal activities)
* Prior owners and operators who may or may not have been involved with the site during the disposal of hazardous materials
* The generators of the waste materials disposed of at the site
* The transporters who hauled waste to the site
* Anyone who arranged for the disposal of materials at the site

Parent corporations may be liable for subsidiaries that are PRPs, depending on the extent of control over their subsidiaries and the subsidiaries' involvement in waste disposal practices or decisions. Similarly, if a corporation buys a corporation that is a PRP, the purchasing corporation may become a PRP. Lessees may be liable as operators of the site, as may corporate officers or shareholders of closely held corporations (corporations with a small number of shareholders). Even bankrupt parties may incur liability under CERCLA.

Superfund liability is strict liability and retroactive. Many of the disposal sites that ultimately became Superfund sites were permitted, legal operations at the time the sites were actively accepting waste. However, because liability is retroactive, these organizations may be liable for these previously legal operations.

Superfund liability is also joint and several liability, meaning any liable party may be responsible for the entire amount, regardless of its fair share of responsibility. In allocating liability for the cleanup costs of a particular site, a PRP's assessment can be based on the volume of waste contributed to the site, not the toxicity of the waste. Therefore, the contributor of large volumes of nonhazardous materials to a Superfund site could be responsible for a large part of the cleanup cost even though it contributed only nonhazardous waste to the site. However, CERCLA allows one or a group of PRPs to bring an action that seeks recovery of costs from another PRP.

Although the EPA has investigated thousands of potential Superfund sites, only a small percentage of them have actually been cleaned up under CERCLA. The EPA is authorized under CERCLA to clean up sites where there is a release or threatened release of a hazardous substance into the environment. The EPA can either have its own contractors clean up the site or force liable parties to conduct the cleanup. If the EPA conducts the work, it can seek cost recovery from the RPs for up to three times the amount of the actual cleanup expenses.

As an alternative to EPA-contracted cleanups, private parties may conduct a cleanup voluntarily and, under appropriate circumstances, recover their costs from other RPs. A private CERCLA recovery action may be brought against any RP regardless of whether the federal government has initiated either cleanup or a cost recovery action of its own. However, parties that settle with the government are not liable for contribution to a private party.

Only three defenses to liability exist under CERCLA: (1) acts of God, (2) acts of war, and (3) acts of an unrelated third party. The third-party defense is narrowly defined and rarely applies. It is largely intended to be limited to such occurrences as the unanticipated acts of vandals. The third-party defense includes a provision known as the "innocent landowner defense," an important provision for lenders and those who lease or acquire real property. CERCLA excludes liability for persons who acquire contaminated property, did not know and had no reason to know that it was contaminated, and did not contribute to the contamination. The purchaser must, at the time of acquisition (which may have occurred many years earlier), have undertaken all appropriate inquiry into previous ownership and used the property consistently with good commercial and customary practices in an effort to minimize liability.

Loss Exposure Under CERCLA

Atwell Manufacturing Company, a hypothetical organization, disposed of its off-specification chemical materials in Danford's Dump between 1960 and 1970. Danford's Dump was licensed for this entire period by the state in which it was located, under a law applicable to municipal solid waste disposal facilities. Atwell hired Spring's Sanitary Service to transport the hazardous waste material from Atwell to Danford's Dump. In 1972, Partridge Products Incorporated bought Danford's Dump. Partridge still owns the land but discontinued use of the landfill in 1980.

In 1984, the drinking water supply of a nearby municipality was found to be contaminated. Groundwater investigations determined that Danford's Dump was the source of the contamination. The cost to clean up, remediate, and reconstruct Danford's Dump was expected to be $30 million. Under CERCLA, the following are potentially responsible parties (PRPs) and are subject to strict liability for the cleanup expenses:

- Danford's Dump as an owner/operator
- Atwell Manufacturing Company as a waste generator
- Spring's Sanitary Service as a transporter to the site
- Partridge Products Incorporated as the current owner and a past operator of the site

All PRPs face joint and several liability for the cleanup expenses. In this case, if Danford's Dump, Atwell Manufacturing, Spring's Sanitary Service, and other PRPs were out of business at the time of the EPA Superfund cleanup action, Partridge Products Incorporated could be assessed the entire cleanup expense.

The Oil Pollution Act of 1990 (OPA) seeks to reduce the risk of spills of petroleum or hazardous materials into U.S. coastal or navigable waters by mandating technical standards for facilities and vessels operating in or near such waters. OPA also imposes requirements on owners of facilities and vessels to prevent releases and to pay for the costs of releases that are not prevented. Similar in concept to the proof of financial responsibility requirements under RCRA, OPA mandates that each party responsible for a vessel or facility from which oil is discharged (or is threatening to be discharged) into or upon navigable waters, adjoining shorelines, or the exclusive economic zone of the U.S., is liable for removal costs and damages.

The amounts of required financial responsibility for a single vessel can be in the millions of dollars. Similar to RCRA, the methods that may be used to meet this responsibility include specially-endorsed insurance, a surety bond, a letter of credit, or qualification as a self-insurer.

PROFESSIONAL LIABILITY LOSS EXPOSURES

Organizations employing professionals face professional liability loss exposures. Risk management professionals for these organizations must be conscious of the potential legal consequences of the errors and omissions of these employed professionals. It is important to understand the sources of professional liability and how tort liability in particular places a greater burden of conduct on those that hold themselves out to be professionals. This section describes the professional liability causes of loss as well as the liability loss exposures that may be faced by the following four representative types of professions:

1. Physicians
2. Accountants
3. Insurance agents and brokers
4. Architects and engineers

Professional Liability Causes of Loss

Professional liability arises out of the practice of a profession, which was traditionally associated with law, medicine, education, and the clergy. However, as the number of occupations requiring extensive technical training has increased, the number of occupations that are considered to be professions has also increased. Therefore, professional liability now includes occupations such as accountants, insurance agents and brokers, architects, engineers, computer programmers, and management consultants.

Professionals are bound by law to perform the services for which they were hired and perform those services in accordance with standards of reasonable care and skill. The first duty is contractual; the second duty arises from tort. Additionally, professionals may be bound by responsibilities imposed by statute.

Tort

Members of a skilled profession are liable for any damage to another person caused by the professional's failure to perform with reasonable professional care and skill. The most common tort to which professionals are exposed is negligence.

In nonprofessional negligence cases, jurors can usually evaluate the defendant's conduct in light of their own experience and background. For example, no special knowledge is required to judge whether a driver who failed to stop at a stop sign was negligent. Professional cases are different. Without special knowledge, jurors would often have difficulty in determining whether the professional used the required level of skill and care. Therefore, the jury needs to be informed of the standards that pertain to that particular profession. For example, consider an accountant who prepared a tax return that contained errors a reasonably competent accountant would not have made. An accounting expert would be required to explain to the jury what could be expected from a reasonably competent accountant.

Contract

Whereas tort liability is based on the allegation that the professional failed to exercise reasonable professional care and skill, contractual liability is based on the allegation that the professional failed to do something that was required by contract. For example, an insurance agent failed to place the insurance that the agent contractually agreed to obtain for the plaintiff.

Statute

In addition to contractual and tort-based liability, many professionals are subject to potential liability based on statutes governing the practice of their professions. Statutes range from generalized ones to those governing specific professions. For example, attorneys, accountants, and stockholders have been charged under the provisions of the Racketeer Influenced and Corrupt Organizations (RICO) Act, which was enacted to prosecute organized crime but which has been broadly applied in civil lawsuits.

In the area of more specific regulation, state and federal securities laws and the Securities and Exchange Commission (SEC) all impose standards on stockbrokers, as well as on attorneys and accountants whose practices includes securities law or accounting.

Physicians' Professional Liability Loss Exposures

Physicians' professional liability loss exposures arise from the legal duties and requirements imposed on them under common law and statute. The healthcare profession is one that is subject to numerous laws and regulations. While many of these laws and regulations increase potential legal liability (for example, laws and regulations governing the operation of hospitals), others, such as those that place financial limits on noneconomic damages, lessen the effect of common-law liability rules.

Physicians can be held liable under negligence for injuries to their patients. The law generally requires the plaintiff to prove that the proper standard of care applicable to the medical treatment was not received, as well as proving the causal connection between the failure to observe the proper standard of care and the resulting injury. Most courts require that expert testimony be produced to establish the appropriate standard of care. Courts usually restrict experts to those persons who have specialized knowledge in the same field as that of the defendant.

Specialists are required to possess and apply that extra degree of skill and care used by prudent specialists practicing in the same field. If a patient's condition requires consultation with or care by a specialist, the attending physician has a duty either to tell the patient about the seriousness of the condition or to refer the patient to a specialist. Physicians are ordinarily not held liable for a specialist's negligence unless they exercise control over the specialist's course of treatment. Likewise, physicians are generally not held liable for the acts of surgeons when the physicians do not assist in the surgical procedures. Nor would attending physicians be liable for the acts of substitute physicians, unless an attending physician failed to use reasonable care in the selection of a substitute.

Physicians, like other employers, can be held vicariously liable for the negligence of their employees. For example, a physician might employ an office nurse to administer medications. If the nurse commits an error while administering medicine and an injury results, the physician could be held responsible. Likewise, physicians can be held legally liable for the negligence of other physicians with whom they have entered into a partnership or a professional corporation for the practice of medicine.

Less clear are cases in which a doctor delegates a task to an employee of a hospital, particularly during surgery. It has previously been the case that courts held that a physician could not be charged with the negligence of a hospital employee if delegating the particular task to a hospital employee was customary, unless the physician directly supervised the performance of the work. However, some courts have imposed liability on a physician in such a situation. Physicians have a duty to treat a patient throughout the patient's illness. A physician's failure to do so is considered to be abandonment, and the physician is liable for any damages proximately caused. What exactly constitutes abandonment is an evolving issue and is being applied to other healthcare providers.

In order to perform an operation, a physician must obtain the informed consent of the patient (or someone legally authorized to give consent), except under emergency conditions or in unanticipated situations. Failure to do so would constitute criminal assault and battery. In addition, the surgeon or attending physician must reasonably disclose to the patient or the patient's qualified representative the potential problems associated with the surgery or treatment so that the patient or representative can make an informed decision.

To obtain such informed consent, a physician is generally required to disclose information to the patient on the following topics:

- The nature of the patient's condition or problem
- The nature or purpose of the procedure or treatment that the physician is proposing
- The risks associated with the proposed procedure or treatment
- The anticipated benefits (results) of the proposed procedure or treatment
- Alternative procedures or treatments and the risks associated with them

Most common professional liability loss exposures of physicians include the duties required of them with regard to surgery, diagnosis, diagnostic tests, and consent. All these loss exposures can result in a physician being held liable for injuries to the patient.

A physician who performs surgery has the duty to exercise the reasonable care and skill that surgeons in similar situations usually exercise. For example, failure to remove instruments, surgical sponges, or other foreign substances from the patient's body before the incision has been closed has been held to be negligence on the part of the operating surgeon.

One of the fundamental duties of a physician is to make a proper diagnosis of ailments. If a physician fails to apply reasonable care and skill in developing the diagnosis, the physician may be held liable to the patient for any resulting damage. However, a misdiagnosis caused by an error in judgment does not necessarily create liability if the physician used reasonable care and skill.

Physicians have a duty to use the proper diagnostic tests to determine the condition of a patient. Whether the failure to conduct such tests constitutes a lack of reasonable care and skill depends on whether the standards of skill and care require such a test or an examination in a particular case.

Failure to disclose in advance the known, significant risks of a particular procedure or treatment may render the physician or surgeon liable. Such disclosures form the basis of informed consent.

Accountants' Professional Liability Loss Exposures

Certified public accountants (CPAs) are accountants who have met experience and education requirements and are bound by a code of professional ethics. Only CPAs can perform the external audits that the SEC requires to be performed on all publicly traded U.S. companies.

Accountants have professional loss exposures for their accounting errors and omissions. Risk management professionals for accounting organizations and organizations that employ accountants need to be aware of these professional liability loss exposures. Professional liability loss exposures for accountants may arise from the duties and requirements imposed by either tort, contract, or statute.

As members of a profession, accountants are liable for their failure to perform with the degree of professional care and skill that is appropriate given their specialist expertise. The skills expected of accountants will vary depending on the nature of the work they have been hired to do. For example, courts tend to measure an external auditor's potential liability in light of various auditing duties.

An accountant's contract liability is based on the contractual relationship between the accountant and his or her clients. A client can assert breach of contract against an accountant if the client suffers damage because of the accountant's improper or incomplete performance of the accounting engagement. Under certain circumstances, third parties can also assert breach of contract if they can prove that they were intended beneficiaries of the contract between the accountant and the client. For example, an investor who relied on a misleading financial statement including the opinion of an accountant could assert that the accountant breached the contract with the organization whose statement was involved.

Accountants must comply with certain statutory requirements. Primary among those requirements are those imposed by federal and state securities laws, such as the Securities Act of 1933; the Securities Exchange Act of 1934; and, more recently, the Sarbanes-Oxley Act of 2002.

This section discusses accountants' liability loss exposures arising from the following:

- Tax services
- Audit services
- Accounting services
- Securities laws

Tax services are a liability loss exposure for accountants because clients can allege that an accountant is responsible for the late filing of returns, underpayment of estimated tax obligations, and governmental disallowance of the treatment anticipated by the accountant and reported on a tax return prepared by the accountant. Resulting damages can include payment of penalties and interest and other financial harm to the client. Taxation is a broad and complex field that requires both accounting and legal expertise. Accountants must remain current with the Internal Revenue Code and with regulatory changes. Every legislative and regulatory change to the code creates a new element in the standard of professional due care against which the performance of tax practitioners will be judged. Failure to maintain tax expertise creates a liability loss exposure for accountants when clients are harmed by Internal Revenue Service (IRS) penalties and interest charges.

Accounting audits verify the accuracy of accounting information. When applicable, audits are necessary to comply with securities legislation. In the performance of an audit, an accountant will examine an organization's internally prepared financial statements, examine internal accounting controls, and determine whether the organization's accounting methods are consistent with generally accepted accounting principles (GAAP). Audits are conducted to assure investors that the organization's financial statements accurately reflect its financial condition, as well as to disclose fraud and employee embezzlement. Third parties have a right of action against the accountant if they relied on the audit opinion. For example, a creditor could bring a lawsuit against the accountant if negligent auditing failed to disclose material mistakes in the financial statements that were used by the organization to obtain credit.

Accounting services can create liability loss exposures as a result of the accountant's compilation and review (that is, unaudited) work. When performing a compilation or review, the accountant usually acknowledges that no audit was undertaken but that nothing the accountant noticed indicated that entries were not made according to GAAP. The accounting profession has instituted standards for unaudited accounting and review services. Failure to follow these standards may result in legal liability.

Securities laws create liability loss exposures that could involve significant liabilities and defense costs. Complaints based on securities statutes may include allegations of violations of rules that (1) prohibit false or misleading statements made intentionally or recklessly in connection with the offer or sale of securities, (2) govern registration statements and prospectuses, or (3) govern documents required to be filed with the SEC. Allegedly false and misleading statements on which such allegations are based can appear in financial statements, projections, or tax opinions.

Insurance Agents' and Brokers' Professional Liability Loss Exposures

Insurance agents and brokers have professional liability loss exposures that primarily arise out of their failure to obtain the insurance or the correct insurance coverage requested by their client. Consequently, agents' and brokers' professional liability is often referred to as an errors and omissions liability loss exposure. Organizations that employ insurance agents and brokers have this loss exposure. However, risk management professionals for other organizations have a particular interest in this loss exposure because they frequently rely on insurance agents and brokers to place insurance coverages. In effect, the insurance agent or broker functions as the organization's risk manager. Risk management services are beyond the basic duty that insurance agents and brokers owe their clients, and are an additional liability loss exposure that insurance agents and brokers who provide these services face. As with other loss exposures, liability can arise out of tort, contract, or statute. Because the insurance agent's or broker's alleged failure to perform can be characterized in more than one way, legal actions often combine elements of tort, contract, and statute.

Client organizations may bring a tort action against the insurance agent or broker for failing to exercise reasonable care in procuring the insurance coverage requested. Breaching this duty gives rise to a cause of action in negligence.

Courts may find that the insurance agent or broker was contractually obligated to procure insurance on behalf of the client organization. Failure to fulfill that promise may result in an action for breach of contract.

Some states have statutes that require the insurance agent or broker to obtain the insurance coverage requested or inform the client that the insurance coverage cannot be obtained. Client organizations for whom insurance coverage is not obtained can rely on the statute to prove that the defendant (the insurance agent or broker) was negligent per se.

Architects' and Engineers' Professional Liability Loss Exposures

Risk management professionals employed by architectural and engineering organizations need to address the legal liability that may arise out of errors and omissions from these professional activities. Architects and engineers in private practice have exposures to professional liability lawsuits from aggrieved clients and third parties. Architects and engineers frequently perform similar tasks, including designing and drafting plans for a wide variety of structures. They may also supervise the actual construction. Both are exposed to substantial liability in the course of their work. This section will treat architecture and engineering as one profession because the law applies similarly to both.

As with other professionals, architects and engineers are subject to liability loss exposures arising from the duties and requirements imposed by tort, contract, and applicable statutes regulating construction and design.

The common professional liability loss exposures of architects and engineers include the following:

- Practicing beyond the scope of the license
- Conflict of interest
- Negligently prepared plans or designs
- Negligently performed site surveys
- Negligent materials or equipment selection
- Negligent construction supervision
- Increased construction costs

All states require architects to be licensed, however not all engineers need to be licensed to practice. Where state licensing is required, many states recognize licensing in other states through reciprocal agreements. Practicing beyond the scope of a license—which would occur, for instance, if an engineer drafted architectural plans—not only violates a statute but could also be used as evidence against the engineer in a tort action.

When an architect or engineer is hired, the architect or engineer has a duty to engage in activities that are in the best interest of the client. For example, the architect or engineer should not have a financial interest in a contractor or supplier for a project unless this fact is disclosed to the client/project owner. An architect with such a conflict of interest would be liable to the client principal for damages based, at least in part, on the architect's profit.

A significant liability loss exposure comes from allegations that an architect or engineer was negligent in preparing the plans or in the design of a particular structure. Although many courts have held that an architect's work, in the absence of a special agreement, does not imply or guarantee a perfect plan, architects are obligated to prepare plans and drawings that conform to the ordinary expertise and skill of architects. Some cases clearly show negligence, such as when a floor or roof collapses because the design did not provide for adequate structural support. Other cases involve highly subjective determinations. In cases involving negligence of design, damages can be measured in two ways. First, if the defect in the building is minor, damages are usually measured by the cost of repairing the defect. Second, if the defect is major, damages are usually measured by the difference between the value of the building as it was built and the value it would have had if it had been built according to the correct plans and specifications.

Lawsuits against architects and engineers also arise in connection with site surveys, and in particular soil conditions. Soil conditions must be considered in the design of building foundations and other structures. Soft soils, such as silt, may be unsuitable for any structure. Improper evaluation of a site's soil condition frequently generates lawsuits against architects and engineers.

Even if the architect does not warrant the quality of building materials to be used, the architect is still required to select the type of materials and equipment to be used. Most lawsuits alleging negligent specification of materials or equipment are between professionals and their clients, but if a third party brings a lawsuit against the project owner, the project owner may bring the architect or engineer into the litigation.

Negligent construction supervision is the architect's liability loss exposure that arises out of the duty to supervise construction. This duty is separate and distinct from the liability loss exposure of those engaged in the actual construction. The architect's obligation is not inherent in the architect-project owner relationship but is often established by contract. Originally, courts held that the duty to supervise was limited to ensuring that the construction conformed to the specifications and materials contemplated by the plans. More recently, some courts have held that the duty to supervise, once accepted, may include overseeing the construction techniques and procedures. This duty carries with it the responsibility to condemn unfit work. In jurisdictions with structural work laws, this exposure can be significantly increased.

Construction costs may be higher than the architect or engineer anticipated, and consequently the project owner may bring a lawsuit against the architect or engineer for one or more of the following reasons:

- The quantities shown on the plans and specifications were wrong, or the design was defective.
- The designated construction procedures cost the contractor too much money.
- The architect or engineer will not approve the work, the estimate, or the materials or equipment that the contractor has installed.

SUMMARY

This chapter is the third of four chapters that address the liability loss exposures that an organization may face. The following categories of liability loss exposures were addressed in this chapter: (1) workers' compensation, (2) environmental pollution, and (3) professional activities.

Workers' compensation is a comprehensive term used to refer to the statutes that provide financial awards for disability, medical reimbursement, rehabilitation services, and death benefits to employees and their dependents in cases of employment-related injuries and diseases. Workers' compensation laws were enacted as an alternative to a common-law system that did not satisfactorily address work-related injuries. However, employers may still be subject to suit under the common law, so risk management professionals need to know employers' common-law duties and common-law defenses in addition to those under workers' compensation.

Common-law duties include the following:

- Providing a safe place to work
- Providing competent fellow employees
- Providing safe tools and equipment
- Warning employees of inherent dangers
- Making and enforcing rules for the safety of all employees

Common-law defenses include the following:

- Contributory negligence
- Comparative negligence
- Negligence of fellow employees
- Statute of limitations

Workers' compensation laws cover most public and private employments and provide workers with specified benefits and protect employers against tort suits in most cases.

Risk management professionals should understand the following features of workers' compensation laws because they affect the scope of workers' compensation loss exposures.

- Choice of law
- Persons and employments covered
- Injuries and diseases covered
- Benefits provided
- Procedures for obtaining benefits

Workers' compensation statutes provide medical benefits, disability benefits, rehabilitation services, and death benefits.

- Medical benefits cover a broad range of services but may be limited to payment amounts set by a fee schedule that healthcare providers must accept.
- Disability benefits include benefits for temporary total disability, permanent total disability, temporary partial disability, and permanent partial disability. The amount of disability benefits payable is determined using formulas and schedules provided by the relevant workers' compensation statute.
- Rehabilitation services pay for vocational or physical assistance that can shorten an injured employee's disability and therefore reduce the cost of disabling injuries.
- Death benefits consist of income replacement benefits to a deceased employee's surviving family members as well as a burial allowance.

State workers' compensation laws do not apply to all employees. Some employees are covered by the following federal laws:

- Longshore and Harbor Workers' Compensation Act (LHWCA)
- Extensions of the LHWCA
- Federal Employers' Liability Act (FELA)
- Migrant and Seasonal Agricultural Worker Protection Act (MSPA)
- Federal Employees' Compensation Act (FECA)

All organizations potentially have an environmental loss exposure even though it is usually slight. However, some organizations have a significant environmental loss exposure because of the nature of the business they are in. Liability may arise out of tort, contract, or statute. The major federal environmental laws are as follows:

- The National Environmental Policy Act
- Clean Air Act
- Clean Water Act

- Toxic Substance Control Act
- Resource Conservation and Recovery Act (RCRA)
- Motor Carrier Act
- Comprehensive Environmental Response, Compensation, and Liability Act (CERCLA)
- Oil Pollution Act (OPA)

Professional liability arises out of the practice of a profession. Once confined to a few occupations, professional liability insurance now encompasses many. Professional liability loss exposures can arise out of tort, contract, or statute. The chapter highlighted four professions (physicians, accountants, insurance agents and brokers, and architects and engineers) to illustrate the nature of professional loss exposures.

Liability loss exposures deserve extensive treatment because of their potential significance and the difficulty in accurately projecting the occurrence of liability losses.

Risk management professionals are particularly concerned about liability loss exposures because of their severity and unpredictability. These loss exposures can affect both the organization as a whole and its senior management individually. Additional liability loss exposures to which directors and officers are exposed are described in the next chapter.

CHAPTER NOTES

1. U.S. Chamber of Commerce, *2004 Analysis of Workers' Compensation Laws* (Washington, D.C.: U.S. Chamber of Commerce, 2004), p. 6.
2. Lawrence N. Rogak, "When You're Out to Lunch, You're On Your Own," *Insurance Advocate*, November 3, 2003, p. 14.
3. Bruce Hillman, "Positional Risk Doctrine," *National Underwriter*, August 12, 1996, p. 19.
4. *IRMI's Workers Comp: A Complete Guide to Coverage, Laws, and Cost Containment* (Dallas: International Risk Management Institute, 1995), VII.D.4.
5. Environmental Protection Agency, www.epa.gov/superfund/index.htm (accessed December 14, 2004).

Chapter 7

Direct Your Learning

Assessing Management Liability Loss Exposures

After learning the content of this chapter and completing the corresponding course guide assignment, you should be able to:

- Describe the liability loss exposures of a corporation arising out of directors' and officers' responsibilities.

- Describe the liability loss exposures of an organization arising out of its employment practices.

- Describe the liability loss exposures of an organization arising out of its employee benefit plans.

- Define or describe each of the Key Words and Phrases for this chapter.

Develop Your Perspective

What are the main topics covered in the chapter?

This chapter examines liability loss exposures that are specific to management activities. These exposures include directors' and officers' (D&O) liability, employment practices liability (EPL), and fiduciary liability arising from employee benefit plans.

Consider the duties of a corporation's different directors and officers.

- How might the officers breach these duties?
- How has the Sarbanes-Oxley Act of 2002 protected investors in the corporation?

Why is it important to learn about these topics?

Most organizations have some or all of these potentially severe loss exposures and yet often overlook or underestimate them. A risk management professional can provide valuable assistance in properly identifying and managing an organization's D&O, EPL, and employee benefit plan loss exposures.

Critique your organization's employee handbook.

- How might the policies and procedures in the employee handbook affect the organization's employment practices liability loss exposures?
- What changes might you recommend to help mitigate these risks?

How can you use what you will learn?

Imagine that you are approached by the chief financial officer (CFO) of a newly formed corporation for assistance in making sure that the corporation's executives are properly protected against liability claims.

- Explain how the CFO could be held liable for D&O, EPL, and employee benefit plan fiduciary liability claims, and recommend appropriate insurance policies to the CFO for covering these claims.
- Explain how the corporation could provide indemnification for its directors and officers.

Chapter 7

Assessing Management Liability Loss Exposures

This chapter examines the following three related types of loss exposures:

1. Directors' and officers' liability
2. Employment practices liability
3. Fiduciary liability from employee benefit plans

Almost all organizations have some exposure to directors' and officers' liability, employment practices liability, or fiduciary liability under employee benefit plans. Although some organizations overlook or underestimate these loss exposures, the need for applying risk management techniques is pervasive.

As these three types of liability loss exposures have become more prominent in the past few years, the term "management liability" has been increasingly used to categorize them. Accordingly, the loss exposures discussed in this chapter are referred to as management liability. Management liability applies to all organizations. Corporate governance is a more narrowly focused topic in that it is primarily concerned with issues related to how corporations are run. Corporate governance issues are generally concerned with separating oversight and control so that the interests of shareholders remain in the forefront.

DIRECTORS' AND OFFICERS' LIABILITY LOSS EXPOSURES

Being able to identify and analyze directors' and officers' (D&O) liability loss exposures requires an understanding of the following topics:

- The corporation and the role of directors and officers
- Types of lawsuits made against directors and officers
- Directors' and officers' major responsibilities and duties
- Directors' and officers' liabilities under the securities laws
- Indemnification of directors and officers

The Corporation and the Role of Directors and Officers

A corporation is an entity that the law considers to be a person that is distinct from the corporation's owners, called stockholders or shareholders. As such, the corporation has many of the same rights that other persons do, including the right to enter into contracts, own property, and borrow money. Corporations are the predominant form of business organization based on revenues generated. It is easier for corporations to access the capital markets, and the limited liability of shareholders makes corporations more attractive to investors. In general, shareholders' liability is limited to the funds they have invested in the corporation.

A corporation can be either a public corporation or a private corporation. A public corporation (or publicly held corporation) is a corporation whose shares are traded to and among the public on the open market. A private corporation (or privately held corporation) is a corporation whose shares are not traded on the open market.

A corporation is owned by its shareholders but is controlled by its board of directors. The directors (sometimes called trustees) may be major shareholders and executive officers of the corporation, but directors may also include outside business or social leaders who often have little financial stake in the corporation. The board of directors establishes corporate policy, makes major business and financial decisions, and appoints the corporation's executive officers (such as chief executive officer, president, secretary, and treasurer) to manage the daily operations of the corporation. The executive officers are not necessarily the only employees who are officers of the corporation. The corporation's bylaws (the rules by which a corporation governs itself) may specify that employees above a certain level of seniority or holding certain positions are also considered to be officers of the corporation.

A corporation's directors are elected by its shareholders in accordance with the corporation's bylaws. Because few shareholders attend the annual meeting of large corporations in person, voting for directors is done by proxy, meaning that the shareholders who cannot attend the annual meeting authorize representatives (called proxies) to cast votes on their behalf. The statement authorizing a proxy to vote on behalf of an absent stockholder is also called a proxy. Management solicits proxies from the shareholders, at the corporation's expense, and in most cases only one slate (list) of directors is presented. Shareholders can vote for the slate or withhold their vote for either the entire slate or individual directors. Typically, a proxy ballot provides no opportunity for shareholders to vote for other candidates. Contests for control of the board of directors do occur, but they are rare because the opposing group must solicit proxies at its own expense.

Although this chapter focuses on the directors and officers of corporations, the directors and officers of other types of entities have similar loss exposures. These other types of entities include public bodies, not-for-profit organizations, trusts, limited liability companies, and limited partnerships. Although the titles of the officials may differ, their duties are similar to those of corporate directors and officers. Even the directors and officers of not-for-profit charitable organizations can face lawsuits. In one instance, a charity sold an old building that had been used to house the homeless and replaced it with an up-to-date modern facility. Those who believed that the old building was more than adequate sued the directors for wasting the charity's assets.

Many of the liability loss exposures faced by directors and officers are insurable. However, directors' and officers' liability loss exposures are not limited to those that are insurable. For example, in 2003, the Securities and Exchange Commission (SEC) brought criminal proceedings against more than 364 individual directors and officers for fraud. It obtained convictions in 275 cases, with 75 percent resulting in jail sentences. One-fourth received sentences of five years or more, and twenty of those convicted were chief executive officers of the companies.[1]

Types of Lawsuits Made Against Directors and Officers

The legal actions taken against corporate directors or officers as remedies for their breaches of duty are generally classified as either derivative lawsuits or nonderivative lawsuits. Another important concept in understanding D&O suits is a type of suit known as a class action.

A **derivative lawsuit** is a lawsuit brought by one or more shareholders in the name of the corporation. Any damages recovered go directly to the corporation, not to the plaintiff-shareholder(s). However, successful plaintiffs are typically awarded the expenses incurred in bringing the lawsuit, including a reasonable, but often substantial, amount for attorney fees. To be successful, the plaintiff-shareholders normally must establish that the defendants' conduct was outside the permissible boundaries of sound management practice.

Derivative lawsuit
A lawsuit brought by one or more shareholders in the name of the corporation.

Nonderivative lawsuits against directors and officers are brought in the name of the person bringing the suit, not in the name of the corporation. Such lawsuits may be initiated by customers, competitors, employees, creditors, governmental entities, or other persons outside the corporation. Nonderivative lawsuits typically name specific directors or officers and the corporation as co-defendants. The plaintiff must show that an injury or injustice resulted from wrongful acts or omissions of directors and/or officers. Examples are lawsuits for violations of legislative statutes; failure to fulfill legal duties; and intentional, unfair, or harmful conduct.

The frequency of D&O claims by the different types of plaintiffs varies depending on the type of organization. Exhibit 7-1 shows the distribution of plaintiffs bringing lawsuits against directors and officers by type of organization in the United States. As can be seen in the exhibit, over half the lawsuits against directors and officers of corporations with more than 500 shareholders are made by shareholders. Not-for-profit organizations, which usually do not have outside shareholders, receive the bulk of their lawsuits from employees—over 90 percent in the survey. Employees account for 50 percent of the lawsuits against corporations with fewer than 500 shareholders.

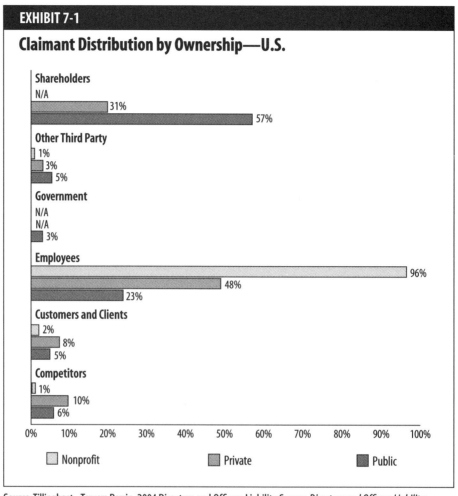

EXHIBIT 7-1

Claimant Distribution by Ownership—U.S.

Source: Tillinghast - Towers Perrin, 2004 Directors and Officers Liability Survey, *Directors and Officers Liability: Understanding the Unexpected*, p. 7.

Examples of Allegations Made Against Directors and Officers

Examples of common allegations made against directors and officers in lawsuits include the following:[2]

- False or inadequate disclosure in connection with stock issuance
- Making or permitting the making of false entries in the corporate books and records
- Preparing and signing false documents filed with regulatory authorities
- Failing to correct inaccurate statements within a prospectus issued by the corporation
- Failing to review annual financial statements and monitor corporate affairs
- Missing an opportunity for expansion, acquisition, or sale of the company

A **class action** (or **class action lawsuit**) is a type of nonderivative lawsuit in which one person or a small group of people represent the interests of an entire class of people in litigation. Class actions are not limited to lawsuits against directors and officers. For example, products liability claims are often brought as class actions. One of the rationales for allowing class actions is that plaintiffs' demands for damages are small relative to the attorneys' fees needed to pursue the lawsuit, so that combining plaintiffs in a class action makes the legal action economically feasible. A hypothetical example is a situation in which one million people have been overcharged $100 each. No one person would sensibly retain an attorney to pursue the lawsuit. However, attorneys are more likely to be willing to represent the entire class.

Class action, or **class action lawsuit**
A lawsuit in which one person or a small group of people represent the interests of an entire class of people in litigation.

Many class actions against directors and officers are based on wrongful acts related to securities. A typical securities class action complaint commonly contains the following allegations:[3]

- The company's public statements (usually either in the company's communications with securities analysts or in the company's periodic reports to shareholders or to the SEC) contained material misrepresentations or omissions.
- The alleged misrepresentations or omissions artificially inflated the company's share price.
- While the share price was artificially inflated, insiders profitably sold their personal holdings in the company's shares.
- After the insider sales were completed, the company's share price dropped sharply when the company divulged information inconsistent with the earlier statements that had inflated the share price.

Securities class actions can result in enormous settlements. For example, Waste Management and Bank of America have settled class actions for nearly $0.5 billion each while Cendant settled a class action for over $3.5 billion. These cases indicate the enormous loss exposure that corporations can face in class actions and the importance of managing these loss exposures.

Directors' and Officers' Major Responsibilities and Duties

D&O liability loss exposures arise out of directors' and officers' legal responsibilities and duties. When directors and officers fail to fulfill these responsibilities and duties, they can be held liable for losses that result. Some major responsibilities of corporate directors are as follows:

- To establish the basic objectives and broad policies of the corporation
- To elect or appoint the corporate officers, advise them, approve their actions, and audit their performance
- To safeguard and approve changes in the corporation's assets

- To approve important financial matters and see that proper annual and interim reports are given to shareholders
- To delegate special powers to others to sign contracts, open bank accounts, sign checks, issue shares, make loans, and conduct any activities that may require board approval
- To maintain, revise, and enforce the corporate charter and bylaws
- To perpetuate a competent board through regular elections and the filling of interim vacancies with qualified persons
- To act as a fiduciary in their relationship to the corporation and its shareholders

Fiduciary duty
The duty to act in the best interests of another.

The fiduciary relationship is the most important in analyzing directors' and officers' liability loss exposures. In addition to performing specific functions, each director and officer occupies a position of trust for shareholders, the board of directors, and the general public. Therefore, directors and officers are said to have fiduciary duties. A **fiduciary duty** is the duty to act in the best interests of another. It is the highest standard of duty implied by law. A breach of fiduciary duties is a common basis for claims against directors and officers. For example, when Advanced Fibre Communications (AFC) was planning to merge with Tellabs, a shareholder filed suit alleging that AFC's directors breached their fiduciary duties because the consideration to be received by company shareholders under the merger was inadequate.[4]

Directors' and officers' fiduciary duties include the duty of care, the duty of loyalty, the duty of disclosure, and the duty of obedience.

Duty of Care

Directors and officers have the duty of care (also called the duty of diligence) in the performance of their corporate functions. A definition of "duty of care" is provided by the Model Business Corporation Act[5] drafted by the American Bar Association to assist states in adopting laws to govern incorporation. The Model Business Corporation Act's definition of duty of care is that directors must discharge their duties with the care that a person in a like position would reasonably believe appropriate under similar circumstances. Directors are considered to have met their duty of care if they do the following:

- Act in good faith and in a manner they reasonably believe to be in the best interests of the corporation
- Discharge their responsibilities with informed judgment and a measure of care that a person in a like position would reasonably believe appropriate under similar circumstances

Business judgment rule
A legal rule that provides that a director will not be personally liable for a decision involving business judgment, provided the director made an informed decision and acted in good faith.

In applying the concept of the general duty to exercise reasonable care, courts have held that directors and officers are not guarantors of the organization's profitability. Nor are directors required to have special business skills. Courts grant directors broad discretion under what is known as the **business judgment rule**, which is a legal rule that provides that a director will not be personally liable for a decision involving business judgment, provided the director made an informed decision and acted in good faith. The business judgment rule means that directors and officers are not liable for honest mistakes of judgment, even if the result is a financial loss, provided they acted with reasonable prudence.

Directors and officers can face lawsuits claiming that their actions do not fall within the protection of the business judgment rule. For example, a plaintiff might allege that the directors did not use reasonable care in making a decision that resulted in a financial loss to the corporation, that they did not use reasonable care in reviewing financial statements, and many other similar allegations.

Directors and officers have a duty to keep themselves informed of the facts and other matters required to make prudent decisions of the types they must make. At a minimum, directors have a duty to attend board meetings and meetings of the committees on which they serve. Many large, for-profit corporations pay their directors substantial fees for participation in board and committee meetings.

Duty of Loyalty

Directors and officers have the general duty of undivided loyalty to the corporation they serve. Accordingly, a director or an officer cannot secretly seize for himself or herself a business opportunity that properly belongs to the corporation. For the same reason, a director or an officer cannot own or operate a business that competes with the corporation. The Model Business Corporation Act provides that directors must discharge their duties, including duties as a member of a committee, "in a manner the director reasonably believes to be in the best interests of the corporation."[6]

Because directors (and sometimes officers) obtain their positions by the vote or consent of the shareholders, they also owe a duty of loyalty to the shareholders. Under the common law and the Securities Exchange Act of 1934, no director or officer (or any other person) may use "insider information" to buy or sell stock of the corporation, whether the information was obtained directly or from others.[7] Insider information is material information about a company that has not been made public. Material information is information that may affect the share price. For example, an organization's plan to merge with another company would be material information. It is illegal for directors and officers to trade shares based on insider information. Under that act, if a director or an officer or an owner of at least 10 percent of the outstanding shares makes a profit within a six-month period by dealing in shares of the corporation, the profit may be taken by the corporation—whether or not such a person actually had insider information. If the person used inside information that was not disclosed, those who bought shares from or sold the shares to the insider may have grounds to sue for damages.

Duty of Disclosure

Directors and officers have the general duty to disclose material facts to all persons who have a right to know such facts and would not otherwise be able to obtain them. Examples include the following:

- The duty of officers to disclose facts that are material to directors
- The duty of officers to disclose facts that are material to various regulatory bodies
- The duty of directors to disclose facts that are material to creditors or potential creditors
- The duty of directors and officers to make public disclosures of facts that are material to shareholders, bondholders, and potential investors in the securities of the corporation

On the other hand, directors and officers also must keep certain matters confidential. Normally, directors are not authorized to act as spokespersons for the corporation. Therefore, some authorities recommend that they not speak to journalists, investors, analysts, or investment advisers about the company, particularly when confidential or market-sensitive information is involved. They should merely refer these inquiries to officers who are authorized spokespersons.

In addition, directors and officers must refrain from discussing confidential or market-sensitive matters with others, including family members and colleagues. If they do, they (and possibly the company, as well as anyone else to whom they tell the information) may become liable under insider trading laws.[8]

Duty of Obedience

Some authorities include a duty of obedience (that is, obedience to the law) in the duties of directors and officers. Directors and officers are required to perform their duties according to the statutes and the terms of the corporate charter. Directors may be liable if they authorize an act that is either illegal or beyond the powers conferred on the corporation by its charter or by the laws of the state. Such acts are known as *ultra vires* acts, which means that they are beyond the scope of authority.

Directors' and Officers' Responsibilities Under the Securities Laws

The two fundamental acts that govern securities transactions, and a director's duties under those transactions, are the Securities Act of 1933 and the Securities Exchange Act of 1934. These acts resulted from the 1929 crash in the financial markets and were designed to protect a corporation's investors. However, over time the securities legislation was increasingly perceived as being abused by shareholders. Consequently, the Private Securities Litigation Reform Act of 1995 was enacted to reform certain aspects of the existing laws. More recently, the Sarbanes-Oxley Act of 2002 (Sarbanes-Oxley) was passed in response to corporate scandals.

Securities Act of 1933

The purposes of the Securities Act of 1933 (the 1933 Act) were to ensure that investors received relevant information about securities being offered for public sale and to prohibit misrepresentation and fraud in the sale of securities.

One of the ways in which the 1933 Act sought to achieve these purposes was through the requirement for securities registration. Section 5 of the 1933 Act requires that when securities (such as stocks, options, bonds, and debentures) are offered for sale to the public in the U.S., they must first be registered with the SEC. The registration must include information about the corporation's management and financial status as well as about the securities themselves.

Some securities are exempt from the registration requirements, including the following:

- Private securities offered to a small number of people
- Securities of a limited size
- Intrastate securities that are offered and sold only in the state where the issuer is incorporated
- Securities from municipal, state, and federal governments

If a security is registered, and the registration document contains an untrue statement about a material fact, the purchaser can bring an action under section 11 of the 1933 Act. If the corporation fails to register a security that is not exempt from the registration requirements, then the corporation may face a suit from a purchaser of that security under section 12(a)(1). If a corporation sells a security that is subject to registration requirements by means of a prospectus or oral communication and makes a material misrepresentation or omission, then the company may face liability under section 12(a)(2).

Section 11 of the 1933 Act enables purchasers of registered securities to recover damages from the corporation's directors if the registration statement contained an omission or a misrepresentation. The omission or misrepresentation must be material, which means the investor must have considered the information important in making the investment decision. In addition, the investor must bring a legal action within three years of purchasing the securities and within one year of discovering the misstatement or omission.

The remedy for a successful section 11 suit is damages. The amount of damages awarded depends on whether the investor sold the security and, if so, the timing of the sale. If the investor did not sell the security, then the damages are the difference between the security's purchase price and the security's value at the time the suit began. If the investor sold the security before the suit began, then the damages are the difference between the security's purchase price and sale price. If the investor sold the security after the suit began, but before the court made its judgment, then the damages are the difference between the security's purchase price and sale price, provided the sale price was less than the security's value at the time the suit began.

The three main defenses available to directors against section 11 suits are as follows:

1. *Due diligence.* Due diligence is the most important defense. Under the due diligence defense, the director must show that he or she made a reasonable investigation and had no reasonable grounds to believe, and did not believe, that the registration statement contained any material omission or misrepresentation. If part of the registration statement was based on an expert's authority, for example, an auditor, the director must show that he or she had no reasonable grounds to believe, and did not believe, that the expert's information contained a material omission or misrepresentation.

2. *No reliance.* Under the no reliance defense, the director must show that the shareholder knew about the material omission or misrepresentation, and therefore acted without relying on it.

3. *No causation.* Under the no causation defense, the director must show that the material omission or misrepresentation did not actually cause a loss to the shareholder. Even if the shareholder lost money, the director is not liable under section 11, provided that the loss was not attributable to a material omission or misstatement.

Section 12(a)(1) of the 1933 Act covers securities sold without the appropriate registration statement or through a nonconforming prospectus. Unlike section 11 liability, section 12(a)(1) imposes strict liability, so the director is liable simply for selling unregistered securities. Whether the director made any material omission or misrepresentation is irrelevant.

A shareholder must bring a section 12(a)(1) suit within a year of the date the securities were offered or sold. The remedy for breach of section 12(a)(1) is either rescission (cancellation of the contract of sale) or damages. If the shareholder chooses rescission, the shareholder returns the securities and any income received (such as dividends) to the corporation, and is entitled to the security's purchase price plus interest. If the shareholder seeks damages, the amount of damages is typically the difference between the security's purchase price and sale price.

Section 12(a)(2) of the 1933 Act covers securities sold through a prospectus or an oral communication. This section only covers public sales of securities that are not exempt from the section 5 registration requirements. A director may be liable under section 12(a)(2) if the prospectus or oral communication contained a material omission or misrepresentation. The shareholder bringing the suit must do so within one year after the shareholder discovered or should have discovered the fraud, or three years after the sale, whichever is shorter.

The remedy for section 12(a)(2) liability is either rescission or damages. If the director can show that the security's decreased value is not the result of the alleged fraud, then the shareholder cannot rescind the security. Similarly, if the shareholder has sold the security and is seeking damages, the director is not liable, provided he or she can show that the security's decreased value is not the result of the fraud. If the shareholder is awarded damages, the amount of damages is typically the difference between the security's purchase price and sale price. Section 12(a)(2) provides a reasonable care defense. If the director can show that he or she did not know, and with reasonable care could not have known, about the fraud, then no liability applies under this section.

Securities Exchange Act of 1934

Whereas the Securities Act of 1933 governs the issuing of securities, the Securities Exchange Act of 1934 (the 1934 Act) governs transactions that occur after securities have been issued. The provisions of the 1934 Act include the following:

- Corporations with publicly traded stock must file periodic financial reports with the SEC.

- Certain types of manipulative or deceptive conduct in the securities markets are prohibited.

- Fraudulent activities are prohibited, such as insider trading done in connection with the offer, purchase, or sale of securities.

Corporations having more than 500 shareholders and more than $10 million in assets are required to file annual and other periodic reports with the SEC. These reports are public documents, and one of the ways in which the public has access to these is through the SEC's Electronic Data Gathering, Analysis, and Retrieval (EDGAR) database, which is accessible from the SEC Web site.[9] Reporting requirements are also imposed on certain directors. If a director owns more than 10 percent of any class of a corporation's stock, then the director must inform the SEC of any change in the director's holdings within ten days of the end of the calendar month in which the security was bought or sold. Liability may arise if the director files a report that is either misleading or false, unless the director acted in good faith and without knowing that the report was misleading or false.

Section 10(b) of the 1934 Act makes it unlawful to engage in manipulative or deceptive conduct in relation to a security's sale or purchase. This section is implemented through a regulation called Rule 10b-5. Rule 10b-5 applies to any communications with investors, including written and oral communications. A director may be liable if he or she attempts to deceive an investor or potential investor by fraud or the misrepresentation or omission of a material fact. A shareholder bringing suit against the director must show that the director acted deliberately or recklessly, that the shareholder acted in reliance of the communication, and that the misrepresentation or omission caused the loss. Once again, the remedy for a suit brought under Section 10(b) is rescission or damages. The suit must be brought within one year after the shareholder discovered or should have discovered the fraud, or three years after the security's sale, whichever is shorter.

Directors and officers are insiders of the corporation for which they work. Two key provisions under the 1934 Act govern the use of inside information when directors trade their corporation's securities to gain a profit. The first relates to short-term trading, and the second relates to manipulative or deceptive conduct.

The first provision, contained in Section 16(b) of the 1934 Act, is intended to prevent insiders from profiting from knowledge that they gained from their positions and that they used in short-term trading. This short-term trading, called **swing trading**, is the sale and purchase, or purchase and sale, of securities within a short period. Proving that a director was acting on inside information is not necessary. Insiders are liable simply for trading within a short period.

Swing trading
A short-term trading strategy that involves the sale and purchase, or purchase and sale, of securities within a short period.

The second provision about insider trading arises from the prohibition of manipulative or deceptive conduct contained in Section 10(b) of the 1934 Act. Under Section 10(b), insiders who have material nonpublic information about their corporation cannot legally buy or sell any of the corporation's securities that they own without first publicly disclosing that information. The restriction may also apply to anyone outside the organization to whom the insider has revealed that nonpublic information. For the outsider to be subject to the same duties as the insider, both must work together to exploit the inside information. In addition, the outsider must have known, or should have known, that the confidential information disclosure was a breach of the insider's fiduciary duty.

Persons convicted of insider trading face substantial fines and up to ten years in prison, as well as the damages available to shareholders bringing legal action.

Martha Stewart

On December 27, 2003, Martha Stewart instructed her broker to sell her 3,928 shares of ImClone Systems. The shares sold at an average price of $58.43. On December 28, the Food and Drug Administration (FDA) announced that it had denied ImClone's application for Erbitux, ImClone's promising cancer drug. ImClone's stock subsequently fell by approximately 70 percent.

Martha Stewart was a friend of Sam Waksal, the former CEO of ImClone. The prosecution argued that Martha found out about the impending FDA announcement from Sam Waksal and that prompted her to sell the stock. Stewart denied any wrongdoing, maintaining that she and her broker had a standing order to sell the shares if the price dropped below $60. Sam Waksal subsequently pleaded guilty to bank fraud, securities fraud, conspiracy to obstruct justice, and perjury.

Ultimately the securities fraud charge against Martha Stewart was dropped. She was, however, found guilty of conspiracy, obstruction of justice, and two counts of making false statements. She was fined $30,000 and sentenced to five months in prison, the minimum penalty that could have been imposed.

Private Securities Litigation Reform Act of 1995

The purpose of the Private Securities Litigation Reform Act of 1995 ("the Reform Act") was to address perceived abuses in securities litigation, particularly in class action suits that forced corporations to settle rather than incur substantial legal defense costs. The Reform Act allows the court to appoint a lead plaintiff in a class action suit who is considered the most capable of representing the interests of the class. The class member with the largest shareholding is most likely to be the lead plaintiff. The lead plaintiff is required to certify that he or she read the complaint and authorized its filing and also that he or she did not buy shares in order to participate in the class action suit. This requirement helps prevent shareholders with limited shareholdings in several companies from adding their names to a class action suit without actually reading the complaint. This provision seems to have increased the number of institutions, rather than individuals, serving as lead plaintiffs. Approximately 30 percent of post-Reform Act settlements have involved institutions serving as lead plaintiffs, an increase over pre-Reform Act figures.[10]

The provisions of the Reform Act were also designed to prevent frivolous lawsuits based on reductions in a corporation's share price rather than on actual evidence of fraud. Previously, a plaintiff could bring a suit based on general allegations. Under the Reform Act, plaintiffs must specifically identify the material omissions or misrepresentations and explain how those omissions or misrepresentations caused their losses.

The Reform Act also introduced the "safe harbor" provision, which provides protection from liability if a director makes a statement about the corporation's future financial performance. Liability for such a statement can be avoided if the director identifies the statement as forward-looking and acknowledges factors that could cause actual financial results to differ materially from those in the statement. Factors that could affect results depend on the nature of the industry but could include new regulations, prices of raw materials, and unusual adverse weather conditions. A forward-looking statement may be one such as "We expect revenues to increase by 5 percent in the next quarter."

The safe harbor provision does not protect against liability for forward-looking statements known to be false. However, the plaintiff must be able to show that the defendant actually knew the statement was false. That the defendant should have known the statement was false is not sufficient.

Although the Reform Act was expected to reduce the number of class action lawsuits, this does not appear to have been the case. The number of lawsuits and total settlement amounts actually increased after the Reform Act.[11] However, the majority of settlement amounts are relatively low.

Sarbanes-Oxley Act of 2002

Whereas the Reform Act was seen as favoring the rights of directors, Sarbanes-Oxley was aimed at protecting investors. Sarbanes-Oxley was enacted in response to corporate scandals such as Enron.

Enron

In November 2001, Enron Corporation restated its earnings downward after admitting accounting errors that led to an overstatement of earnings by almost $600 million. This led to a sharp reduction in share price. Less than a month later, Enron filed for bankruptcy. Many employees lost their jobs, and investors, including employees who had invested their 401(k) funds in Enron stock, lost billions of dollars. The investigation into Enron extended to include Arthur Andersen, Enron's audit firm, and had serious implications for management liability.

Sarbanes-Oxley has created many new obligations and involves significant penalties for noncompliance. Although it applies only to publicly traded companies, most of the requirements are appropriate for other types of companies. Some of the key elements of the legislation from a management liability perspective are as follows:

- Financial reporting and internal controls
- Insider trading
- Personal loans
- Penalties

Sarbanes-Oxley requires the chief executive officer (CEO) and chief financial officer (CFO) to certify the accuracy of the corporation's quarterly and annual financial reports. Specifically, the CEO and CFO must certify that they have reviewed the report and, to the best of their knowledge, the report fairly presents the corporation's financial condition and does not contain any material omissions or misrepresentations. Liability arises only if the CEO and CFO knowingly and intentionally fail to comply with this requirement.

The CEO and CFO are also responsible for establishing, maintaining, and monitoring internal controls to ensure that material information is provided to them. The SEC has recommended the creation of a "disclosure committee" that is responsible for considering the materiality of both financial and nonfinancial information and for ensuring that the corporation meets all disclosure obligations. The SEC recommends that this disclosure committee include directors and employees with an interest and expertise in disclosure controls and procedures. The committee could include a risk management professional as well as the principal accounting officer, general counsel, and investment officer. The CEO and CFO must certify the following in relation to the internal controls:

- That they evaluated the effectiveness of the disclosure controls and procedures as of a date within ninety days before the certification of the financial reports
- That the annual report contains their conclusions about the effectiveness of those controls and procedures

- That they have disclosed to the auditors and audit committee all significant deficiencies in the internal controls that could adversely affect the corporation's ability to record, process, and report financial data, and any fraud involving personnel involved in the internal controls
- Whether any significant changes in internal controls have been made since their most recent evaluation of them

Sarbanes-Oxley prohibits directors from either buying or selling shares that they acquired in connection with their employment as directors during any pension plan blackout period. A pension plan blackout period is a period of more than three consecutive days during which at least half of the pension plan participants may not trade in the corporation's shares that they hold under the plan. If a director does trade shares during a blackout period, the corporation may sue the director for any profits earned by the trade. If the corporation fails to take action, shareholders may do so.

When directors do buy or sell corporate shares, they must file a report of the transaction with the SEC within two business days. The reports must be made available on the corporate Web site.

Sarbanes-Oxley prohibits corporations from making or arranging for personal loans to directors, subject to limited exceptions. This prohibition includes relocation loans, tax loans, and loans to purchase securities. Not only is a corporation not permitted to make a loan to a director, it cannot guarantee a loan made by a third party to a director. Loans that were in place when Sarbanes-Oxley was passed were allowed to remain in place. However, these existing loans cannot be materially altered or renewed.

Indemnification of Directors and Officers

A list of the directors of the 1,000 largest U.S. corporations contains key figures in American business, academia, and society. Even smaller corporations invite outstanding business, academic, and social leaders to join their boards in order to provide the organization with the benefit of their experience, advice, and contacts. However, the risk of being sued based on participation as a board member is a serious concern for prospective directors and can hinder organizations from obtaining the services of qualified people. Indemnification of directors and officers by the corporation—that is, compensating them for the losses they sustain because of lawsuits—is one way that corporations meet these concerns.

At common law, a corporate director or officer who has successfully defended against a derivative suit has a right to indemnification from the corporation to reimburse the director or officer for expenses he or she has paid to defend against the lawsuit. However, defense costs and the amount of time required to prepare an adequate defense can be considerable. Accordingly, corporations in many cases make payment to settle claims against their directors and officers. The result is that the lawsuit is terminated with no determination or admission of wrongdoing—other than what is implicit in a settlement—even when the corporation believes that it might prevail on the merits at trial.

In such situations, the common law is not clear as to whether directors are entitled to indemnification. As a result of the confusion surrounding directors' and officers' common-law right to corporate indemnification, state legislatures enacted statutes granting directors and officers the right to indemnification. Some of the statutes simply permit indemnification, while others require it. Some of the indemnification statutes are "exclusive" in that they authorize indemnification only to the extent provided by the statute. Other statutes permit directors and officers to benefit from any of the rights to which they may be entitled under any bylaw, agreement, vote of shareholders or disinterested directors, or otherwise.

Most states have adopted business corporation legislation modeled after either the Model Business Corporation Act ("the Model Act") or the Delaware Business Corporation Law (because many large corporations are domiciled in Delaware). The Delaware law, in effect, encourages indemnification even when directors only partially vindicate themselves, whereas the Model Act forbids indemnification in such a situation. In derivative lawsuits, the Model Act permits expense indemnification even when the director is liable, but Delaware requires court approval in such a case.[12]

The determination of which rules apply is a matter for qualified legal advice. As added protection for the directors and officers, some authorities recommend that indemnification wording in corporate charters and bylaws *require* indemnification, not just permit it, and require the corporation to reimburse directors and officers for defense costs as they are incurred rather than when the case is resolved.

In most states, the corporation must have adopted some form of contractual provision that sets guidelines for reimbursement. This provision—which can be incorporated in the bylaws, a corporate resolution, or other written agreement such as an employment contract—can obligate the corporation to indemnify the corporate official as long as the requisite standard of conduct is in accord with the statute. Under the laws of some states, corporations can adopt provisions that indemnification will be denied only when the director's or officer's act or omission constitutes gross negligence or willful misconduct.

A related problem for directors and officers is funding defense costs before settlement. Indemnification is retrospective; that is, it takes place after the matter has been concluded. Defense costs can run to hundreds of thousands, even millions, of dollars. Directors and officers generally need advances to cover these expenses before settlement. Most statutes provide that corporations may include provisions for advancing expenses.

Such advances are generally paid subject to the agreement that they will be refunded if the director or officer is ultimately found not to be entitled to indemnification. However, promises to refund advances can be difficult or impossible to enforce. Moreover, some authorities view advancing defense costs as a prohibited loan under Sarbanes-Oxley.

EMPLOYMENT PRACTICES LIABILITY LOSS EXPOSURES

Changes in the relationship between employees and employers and the changing makeup of the workforce have contributed to a rapid expansion in employment practices liability (EPL) loss exposures. In the past, employees expected to work for one employer for their entire careers, whereas it is now typical for employees to work for many employers before they retire. The aging of the baby-boomers coupled with increased immigration has created an older, more diverse worker population. The most important factors, however, are changes in laws. Legislation has greatly expanded the basis for employment-related discrimination claims. Exhibit 7-2 summarizes several U.S. laws that affect EPL loss exposures.

Many states and even some local governments have employment-related laws that are broader than the federal laws. For example, many states and localities have laws that apply labor standards similar to the federal Fair Labor Standards Act (FLSA) to all businesses in the state, regardless of size, and some protect a broader spectrum of rights than those covered by Title VII of the Civil Rights Act of 1964. Although these laws can create EPL loss exposures, not all violations of these laws are covered by EPL insurance. In fact, EPL policies specifically exclude violations of some of these laws. Nevertheless, risk management professionals must be alert to the loss exposures and develop strategies to treat uninsurable exposures as well as insurable ones.

Lawsuits brought by employees alleging that they were subject to discrimination, wrongful termination, or sexual harassment by their employers, supervisors, or fellow-workers were almost unknown before the 1980s. Although Title VII, prohibiting discrimination by employers, was enacted more than forty years ago, EPL claims did not become a major concern for U.S. employers until Title VII was amended in 1991 to include additional recoveries and to allow a jury trial. For example, an employee may sue his or her employer even if that employee resists sexual harassment and therefore suffers no job detriment, such as, being fired. Also, an employer may be responsible for a supervisor's sexual harassment, even if the employer is unaware of the supervisor's actions.

EXHIBIT 7-2

Laws Affecting EPL Loss Exposures

- Title VII of the Civil Rights Act of 1964 prohibits discrimination by employers based on color, race, religion, sex, or national origin. In 1978, the law was amended to bar discrimination on the basis of pregnancy, childbirth, or related medical conditions. The law applies to all employers with fifteen or more employees.

- The Civil Rights Act of 1991 amends Title VII of the Civil Rights Act of 1964. Depending on the size of the employer, the law authorizes damage awards up to $300,000 in lawsuits for intentional gender discrimination and racial discrimination in employment and allows a claimant the right to demand a jury trial.

- The Age Discrimination in Employment Act of 1967 (ADEA) prohibits discrimination against individuals age forty or older based solely on their age. ADEA applies to employers with twenty or more employees.

- The Americans with Disabilities Act of 1990 (ADA) prohibits discrimination against disabled persons and requires an employer to make reasonable accommodations in the workplace for disabled employees. This law applies to employers with fifteen or more employees.

- The Family Medical Leave Act of 1993 (FMLA) requires that all employers with fifty or more employees provide up to twelve weeks of unpaid leave in any twelve-month period to care for a newborn, adopted or fostered child, or to care for oneself, a child, spouse, or parent with a serious illness.

- The Fair Labor Standards Act of 1938 (FLSA) establishes minimum wage and overtime rates and regulates the employment of children. This law applies to employers with at least two employees engaged in interstate commerce and a business volume of over $500,000 a year.

- The Worker Adjustment and Retraining Notification Act of 1989 (WARN) requires employers to provide notice sixty days in advance of covered plant closings and mass layoffs.

- The Consolidated Omnibus Budget Reconciliation Act of 1985 (COBRA) gives workers and their families who lose their health benefits the right to choose to continue group health benefits provided by their group health plan for limited periods of time under certain circumstances.

- The Employee Retirement Income Security Act of 1974 (ERISA) sets minimum standards for most voluntarily established pension and benefit plans.

The major types of EPL lawsuits can be categorized as follows:

- Discrimination lawsuits
- Wrongful termination lawsuits
- Sexual harassment lawsuits
- Retaliation lawsuits

These classifications are not mutually exclusive. An employee may allege that a particular situation involves more than one employment-related offense.

Examples of Large Employment Practices Liability Awards

$7,800,000: Verdict—Age Discrimination

A 56-year-old male electrical engineer sued a medical equipment manufacturer, alleging age discrimination and unlawful retaliation in violation of state law. The engineer alleged that he was laid off because of his age during a companywide downsizing. He also alleged that the company overlooked his application for several open engineering positions when he asked to be rehired.

$4,050,000: Verdict—Retaliation

The EEOC (Equal Employment Opportunity Commission) sued a Virginia medical center, claiming retaliation in violation of Title VII. The EEOC alleged that a former hospital manager was terminated because of counseling a nurse about a complaint involving possible sexual harassment. The plaintiff's award was reduced to $300,000 in accordance with statutory limits.

$4,000,000: Verdict—Sex Discrimination

A female branch manager sued a national janitorial services company, alleging sexual harassment, retaliation, and a hostile work environment based on sex discrimination in violation of state laws. The manager alleged that the company failed to promote her because of her sex, treated her disparately, and retaliated against her for opposing practices that created a hostile work environment. She also alleged that her supervisors made false accusations of sexual harassment against her and that the company demoted her and terminated her while she was on disability leave from job stress.

$3,000,000: Verdict—Disability Discrimination

A fifty-year-old former project engineer sued a nationally-known manufacturer, alleging disability discrimination in violation of the Americans with Disabilities Act. The former engineer contended that the firm failed to accommodate him after surgery for a work accident. He claimed that a short time after his surgery he was terminated because of his disability. The verdict was reduced to $300,000 because of statutory limits.

$2,500,000: Verdict—Whistleblower

A former college vice president sued the college, the former college president, and others, claiming wrongful discharge and retaliation in violation of federal whistleblower laws. The plaintiff alleged that his free speech rights were violated when he was wrongfully terminated in retaliation for notifying the former president, the college chancellor, and the accreditation association of fraud and other illegal academic acts.

Adapted from Jury Verdict Research, *Employment Practice Liability: Jury Award Trends and Statistics*.

Discrimination Lawsuits

Any employer can be sued by an employee for discrimination. A study of verdicts between 1997 and 2003 found that the median compensatory damages in EPL discrimination cases were over $232,000 per claimant.[13] Exhibit 7-3 shows the median awards for various types of discrimination cases from this study. Risk management professionals may want to consider these data when evaluating the adequacy of their organization's insurance program for employment practices liability.

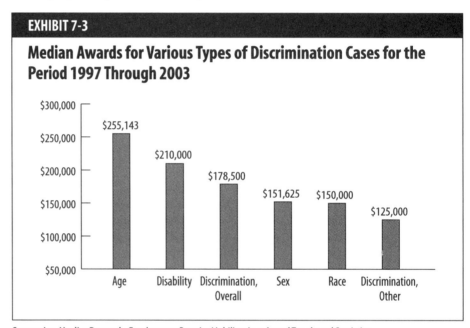

EXHIBIT 7-3

Median Awards for Various Types of Discrimination Cases for the Period 1997 Through 2003

Source: Jury Verdict Research, *Employment Practice Liability: Jury Award Trends and Statistics.*

Overt Discrimination, Disparate Treatment, and Disparate Impact

Many firms that make honest efforts to treat all job applicants and employees equally and never consciously discriminate against individuals based on race, sex, religion, or other grounds, nevertheless have come into conflict with the antidiscrimination rules set down by federal and local laws. Their problems arise because of the difference between overt discrimination, disparate treatment, and disparate impact.

Overt discrimination is a specific, observable action to discriminate against a person or class of persons. This treatment is also referred to as intentional discrimination. An example of overt discrimination is refusing to interview job applicants solely because of their race.

Disparate treatment is unfavorable or unfair treatment of someone in comparison to other similar individuals. Disparate treatment also is referred to as unequal or differential treatment. For example, an employer that reprimands only female employees for taking more than the allotted time at lunch would be guilty of disparate treatment based on gender.

Overt discrimination
A specific, observable action to discriminate against a person or class of persons.

Disparate treatment
Unfavorable or unfair treatment of someone in comparison to other similar individuals.

Disparate impact is indirect discrimination against a group. Disparate impact is an unfair employment practice issue when an employer specifies a job requirement that appears to be fair, but which results in discrimination. For example, an employer that specifies that job applicants be able to lift seventy pounds would limit the number of women who could apply. Such a requirement would be against the law unless the job requirement is necessary for the performance of the job. Other job requirements that have been challenged for having a disparate impact include height and weight requirements, ability on written tests, and educational requirements.

Disparate impact
Indirect discrimination against a group.

Making employment decisions based on stereotypes is also illegal. For example, in one case an employer was held to have violated Title VII when it delayed a female employee's promotion based in part on evaluation comments describing her as "macho" and advising her to "take a course in charm school." This woman was treated differently because, in the opinion of her supervisors, she did not conform to stereotypical female behavior.[14]

Employers must carefully review employment standards to be sure that they are not unintentionally violating the law.

Equal Employment Opportunity Commission

The Equal Employment Opportunity Commission (EEOC) is an independent commission that was created by the Civil Rights Act of 1964. Originally its function was to define acts of employment discrimination and to attempt to mitigate their effects by education and conciliation. In 1972, Congress gave the EEOC authority to sue nongovernmental employers, unions, and employment agencies. As a result, the EEOC could file suits based on pattern or practice, and Title VII coverage was expanded to include the federal government and state and local governments, as well as educational institutions.

Any person who believes that his or her employment rights have been violated may file charges of discrimination with the EEOC. In addition, an individual, organization, or agency may file a charge on behalf of another person in order to protect the aggrieved person's identity. If the charge also involves a state or local law, the EEOC "dual files" with the state or local agency, and vice versa.

The EEOC notifies the employer when a charge of discrimination has been filed against it with the EEOC. The EEOC can investigate and determine whether reasonable cause exists to believe discrimination occurred. The employer may opt to resolve a charge early in the process through mediation or settlement. The EEOC can ask for copies of personnel policies, the complainant's personnel files, the personnel files of other individuals, and other relevant information. An EEOC investigator is allowed to conduct interviews of non-management level employees without the employer's presence or permission.

The charge may be dismissed by the EEOC if it believes no basis exists for proceeding with further investigation. Employees do not have to submit a complaint to the EEOC to sue their employers, and dismissal of a complaint by the EEOC is not a bar to a suit by the employee.

Wrongful Termination Lawsuits

Wrongful termination lawsuits
Lawsuits that arise out of employee claims that an employer has wrongfully discharged the employee.

Wrongful **termination lawsuits** arise out of employee claims that an employer has wrongfully discharged the employee. To bring such a lawsuit, the employee must prove that termination was without cause and that the termination violated an express or implied contract of employment, that the termination was the result of discrimination, or that the termination was against public policy. A termination can be against public policy if it occurs because of an employee's refusal to violate the law for the employer.

At-will employment
Employment for an indefinite duration that can be terminated by either party for whatever reason or no reason at all.

Most employees are "at will" employees. **At-will employment** is employment for an indefinite duration that can be terminated by either party for whatever reason or no reason at all. Although most employee-employer relationships are stated to be "at will," the employer can alter that relationship by creating an implied contract with the employee. An implied contract is formed between an employer and an employee if the employer has made oral or written representations to the employee regarding job security or disciplinary procedures. These representations are held to create a contract of employment even though no written employment contract exists. Many wrongful termination lawsuits have been based on an implied contract created by statements in the organization's employee handbook. For example, an implied contract was said to exist when the employee handbook included the statement that employees would only be terminated for "just cause." Consequently, employers have generally scrutinized employee handbook language as well as other employee communications to ensure that such statements do not inadvertently alter the employee-employer relationship.

As mentioned, wrongful termination lawsuits can also arise out violations of public policy. For example, whistleblowers, or employees who expose wrong-doings within an organization, have filed lawsuits for wrongful termination, as have employees who have refused to be complicit in the questionable acts or crimes of fellow employees.

In addition to the employer altering the employer-employee at-will relationship, various federal and state statutes exist that place limitations on employers' ability to terminate an employee. Because of the potential financial consequences of wrong termination lawsuits, organizations generally have established policies and procedures that guide the organization's managers through the termination process.

Sexual Harassment Lawsuits

The basis for sexual harassment EPL claims developed mainly following the 1980 EEOC publication, *Guidelines on Discrimination Because of Sex*, which defines sexual harassment as "Unwelcome sexual advances...when submission to such conduct is made either explicitly or implicitly a term or condition of an individual's employment."[15]

The EEOC's Web site notes that sexual harassment can occur in a variety of circumstances, including the following:[16]

- The victim as well as the harasser may be a woman or a man. The victim does not have to be of the opposite sex.
- The harasser's conduct must be unwelcome.
- The harasser can be the victim's supervisor, an agent of the employer, a supervisor in another area, a co-worker, or a nonemployee.
- The victim does not have to be the person harassed but could be anyone affected by the offensive conduct.
- Unlawful sexual harassment may occur without economic injury to or discharge of the victim.

A key concept in sexual harassment claims is hostile work environment. A **hostile work environment** exists when an employee is subjected to harassment that is so severe or pervasive that it alters the conditions of his or her employment and creates an abusive working environment. To prove a claim of hostile work environment, an employee generally must show all of the following facts:

- He or she is a member of a protected class.
- He or she was subjected to unwelcome harassment based on the protected characteristic.
- The harassment affected a term or condition of employment.
- The employer knew or should have known about the harassment and failed to take prompt remedial action.

Hostile work environment
An environment that exists when an employee is subjected to harassment that is so severe or pervasive that it alters the conditions of his or her employment and creates an abusive working environment.

Claims of hostile work environment initially were recognized in the context of sex discrimination, but they have since been recognized in other contexts as well, such as discrimination because of race or disability.

Isolated incidents are insufficient to establish a hostile work environment. A hostile work environment exists when an employee experiences workplace harassment and fears going to work because of the offensive, intimidating, or oppressive atmosphere created by the harasser.

Retaliation Lawsuits

Allegations of retaliation by the employer against the employee because of some legitimate act by the employee are another growing source of lawsuits. Such lawsuits may be combined with claims of discrimination based on race, gender, age, or other protected classification. However, they are also brought by employees who, for example, allege that they were discharged because they filed a workers' compensation claim, testified against the employer in a legislative or court hearing, or were whistleblowers. A number of federal laws protect whistleblowers. State and local government employee whistleblowers are constitutionally protected by the First and Fourteenth Amendments and by the Notification and Federal Employee Antidiscrimination and Retaliation Act ("No Fear Act") of 2002. Many states also have laws protecting whistleblowers.

Other Types of EPL Lawsuits

In recent years, employees have made EPL lawsuits that do not fall within the context of discrimination, wrongful termination, sexual harassment, or retaliation. Examples of workplace issues that might lead to such claims are as follows:

- *Mass layoffs.* In many cases, costly litigation has ensued when a firm closed a plant or otherwise discharged large numbers of employees at one time. Congress passed the Worker Adjustment and Retraining Notification Act of 1988 (WARN) to mitigate some of the effects of mass layoffs. Compliance with its terms is another risk management task that employers must manage.

- *Overtime wages.* Class actions on behalf of employees who allege that they did not receive overtime compensation have resulted in substantial awards. The majority of the claims involve improperly categorizing employees as "exempt" rather than "nonexempt." An exempt employee, such as a supervisory or management-level employee, is not entitled to overtime wages, whereas an employer must pay overtime wages to nonexempt employees.

- *Electronic communications.* There have been a growing number of employee claims concerning objectionable e-mail or Web site material.

In addition to D&O loss exposures and EPL loss exposures, directors and officers have legal duties to beneficiaries of the organization's retirement, health, and other employee benefit plans.

FIDUCIARY LIABILITY LOSS EXPOSURES FROM EMPLOYEE BENEFIT PLANS

In addition to fiduciary responsibility owed to shareholders, directors and officers owe fiduciary responsibility to employees as a consequence of the employee benefit plans provided by the employer. Fiduciary liability loss exposures arise mainly out of the possibility that beneficiaries of an employee benefit plan (such as active employees or retirees) may make a claim against the plan officials (or fiduciaries) for breach of their fiduciary duties.

Under defined-contribution retirement plans, such as profit-sharing and 401(k) plans, the size of an employee's benefit depends on the plan's earnings. Some employee retirement plans that were heavily invested in company stock lost millions in value, and attorneys filed class-action fiduciary liability lawsuits against the fiduciaries of these plans.

One of the first fiduciary liability lawsuits was a class action against Rite-Aid Corp. The class bringing suit was composed of employees who participated in Rite-Aid's defined-contribution retirement plans. Attorneys for the class charged that corporate executives knew that the outlook for Rite-Aid's stock was below average but nevertheless invested a portion of the plan's assets in the company's stock. In 2001, Rite-Aid settled with its employees for $67.7 million.[17]

In 2004, insurers paid $85 million under two of Enron's fiduciary liability policies to settle fiduciary liability claims against Enron's board of directors and members of administrative committees. The claims alleged that the directors and administrators imprudently approved or failed to prevent investing in Enron's own shares. Later that year, MCI, part of WorldCom, settled similar lawsuits with its employees for $46.8 million, with insurers paying about half of the settlement. Former WorldCom CEO Bernard Ebbers contributed an additional $4 million to the settlement.[18]

The insurance industry has not been immune to fiduciary liability claims. The drop in the share prices of the insurers and brokers named by New York Attorney General Elliot Spitzer in his 2004 investigation of insurance brokers and insurers was quickly followed by class actions alleging violation of fiduciary responsibilities for investing retirement funds in the companys' own shares.

This section discusses the following topics, which are important for those who seek to identify and analyze fiduciary liability loss exposures:

- Employee Retirement Income Security Act of 1974
- Duties and liabilities of employee benefit plan fiduciaries
- Health Insurance Portability and Accountability Act of 1996

Employee Retirement Income Security Act of 1974 (ERISA)

The federal law that governs retirement and other benefit plans is the Employee Retirement Income Security Act of 1974 (ERISA). It was enacted in response to abuses and underfunding in many benefit plans uncovered by Congressional hearings following the insolvency of several leading corporations. ERISA applies, with only a few exceptions, to everyone involved with the employee benefit plans of employers engaged in interstate commerce or subject to federal minimum wage law. (Federal, state, and local governmental bodies are specifically exempted from ERISA. Religious organizations are exempt from some of the provisions of the law.)

Despite the word "retirement" in the official title of the act, ERISA applies to all types and sizes of employee benefit plans. Plans subject to ERISA range from a customized retirement plan for thousands of employees—having its own trustees, actuaries, and investment advisers—to a group health insurance policy for a small business. The latter type of plan is basically only a contract between the employer and the insurer. An employee benefit does not have to be called a plan, declared to be a plan, or filed with or approved by anyone in order to be subject to ERISA. It only has to be some kind of agreement or arrangement made in advance to provide employee benefits.

Violators of ERISA are subject to such penalties as fines and loss of favorable tax status. However, of particular importance to this discussion are the duties and liabilities imposed on plan fiduciaries.

Duties and Liabilities of Employee Benefit Plan Fiduciaries

As noted previously, a fiduciary duty can be defined in general terms as the duty to act for someone else's benefit. Under ERISA, practically anyone whose role in employee benefits involves discretionary control or judgment in the design, administration, funding, or management of an employee benefit plan or in the management of its assets is a fiduciary. Each fiduciary of an employee benefit plan has the specific duties pertaining to the particular function that the fiduciary is performing under the plan and a general duty (1) to act solely in the interest of plan participants, (2) to abide by the relevant dictates of plan documents, and (3) to avoid acting in ways that are expressly prohibited by ERISA.

The duties of a plan fiduciary are comparable to those of a corporate director. They can be summarized as follows:

- *Care.* A fiduciary must carry out his or her duties with the care, skill, prudence, and diligence of a prudent person familiar with such matters. ERISA specifies that a fiduciary must act with the care, diligence, and skill that would be exercised by a reasonably prudent person in the same or similar circumstances. For instance, a fiduciary who undertakes activities requiring specialized skills, such as investment of plan assets, will be held to the standard of care applicable to professional persons who perform such activities.

- *Loyalty.* A fiduciary's actions must be solely in the best interests of the plan and all of its participants and beneficiaries.

- *Diversification.* A fiduciary must ensure that the plan's investments are sufficiently diversified to minimize the risk of large losses.

- *Obedience.* A fiduciary must act according to the plan documents and applicable law. If the plan document is not in compliance with the law, the fiduciaries must follow the law and bring the plan document into compliance.

These duties imply a relatively high standard of care. The duty of loyalty may present difficult issues for fiduciaries who also are officers, directors, or employees of the employer that sponsors the plan. They cannot take the potential effect on the employer into consideration when making a decision as a prudent independent fiduciary.

If a fiduciary breaches a duty and the breach causes loss to a benefit plan, the fiduciary is personally liable to the plan for the full amount of the loss. The guilty fiduciary may also be subject to a fine and an action for monetary damages brought by an aggrieved plan participant. In addition, a fiduciary may be liable for the breach of a duty by another fiduciary if the first fiduciary knowingly participates in the breach, conceals it, or makes no attempt to correct it.

An employer may be held vicariously liable for breaches of fiduciary duty committed by its employees or agents. The vicariously liable employer may be able to recover its share of the damages from the employee or agent.

Related to fiduciary liability exposures are the loss exposures arising from negligent counseling or administering in connection with employee benefit plans. For example, an employee in human resources may counsel employees to invest their retirement monies in mutual funds that do not perform well.

Health Insurance Portability and Accountability Act (HIPAA)

ERISA was amended by the Health Insurance Portability and Accountability Act of 1996 (HIPAA). Plans sponsored by employers with over fifty employees are subject to HIPAA. In brief, HIPAA does the following:

- Sets standards for health insurance "portability" by providing credit against preexisting condition exclusion periods for prior health coverage
- Limits exclusions for preexisting medical conditions
- Prohibits discrimination in enrollment and in premiums charged to employees and their dependents based on health-related factors
- Improves disclosure about group health plans

Of particular concern from a risk management point of view, HIPAA calls for the protection of employee medical information and subjects the employer and fiduciaries to penalties for failure to comply.

HIPAA penalties can be substantial. Noncompliance with HIPAA results in a $100 penalty per incident, up to an annual maximum of $25,000 for the same incident. Persons who wrongfully disclose health information are subject to fines and imprisonment.

SUMMARY

Management liability loss exposures are loss exposures that arise out of the activities of an organization's management. These loss exposures include directors' and officers' liability, employment practices liability, and fiduciary liability from employee benefit plans. Corporate governance, a related but distinct loss exposure, is primarily concerned with issues related to how corporations are run and is discussed in the next chapter.

Management liability can arise out of the acts or omissions of the organization's directors and officers. Directors and officers are charged with responsibilities and duties that if negligently performed may lead to a lawsuit against the organization, and the directors and officers individually.

Lawsuits against directors and officers are classified as derivative lawsuits or nonderivative lawsuits. Derivative lawsuits are brought against the directors and officers on behalf of the corporation by one or more shareholders. Nonderivative lawsuits are brought against directors and officers by a party or parties other than the corporation, such as customers, employees, and creditors, who are suing on their own behalf.

Directors' and officers' responsibilities include broad mandates such as to safeguard the organization's assets and approve financial matters. Directors and officers also have the fiduciary duties of care, loyalty, disclosure, and obedience. Directors and officers may be protected from personal liability by the business judgment rule, provided the director or officer made an informed decision and acted in good faith.

Directors and officers are also subject to liability arising out of the enforcement of U.S. securities laws that govern securities transactions. The principal acts governing securities are the Securities Act of 1933, the Securities Exchange Act of 1934, the Private Securities Litigation Reform Act of 1995, and the Sarbanes-Oxley Act of 2002. These acts collectively define acceptable security trading by directors and officers in the companies for which they are responsible, and protect investors.

Directors and officers usually seek indemnification from the corporation they serve for damages that they are ordered to pay and for their legal expenses. Most corporations include the indemnification of directors and officers in their bylaws to the extent that directors' and officers' acts or omissions do not violate state statutes, as would be the case with acts of gross negligence or willful misconduct. Most states permit corporations to provide directors and officers with funds to pay for legal expenses.

Management liability can also arise out of an organization's employment practices. Organizations are subject to employee lawsuits for discrimination, wrongful termination, sexual harassment, and retaliation. A growing body of state and federal statutes, regulations, and court cases has more clearly defined unlawful employment practices and increased employers' exposure to such claims.

Directors and officers have a management liability loss exposure under employee benefit plans. These fiduciary liabilities can arise from the Employee Retirement Income Security Act of 1974 (ERISA), duties and liabilities as employee benefit plan fiduciaries, and from the Heath Insurance Portability and Accountability Act of 1996 (HIPAA).

ERISA was enacted in response to employee benefit plan underfunding. ERISA created fiduciary duties for the people who have discretionary control or judgment in the design, administration, funding, or management of an organization's benefit plan.

The duties of a plan fiduciary are comparable to those of a corporate director. If a fiduciary breaches a duty and the breach causes a loss to a benefit plan, the fiduciary is personally liable to the plan for the full amount of the loss, as well as fines and damages sought by plan participants.

HIPAA subjects an organization and its fiduciaries to penalties for disclosing protected employee medical information.

CHAPTER NOTES

1. Michelle Kerr, "Survey: More D&O Precautions Warranted," *Risk & Insurance*, June 2004, p. 13.

2. Adapted from www.esopassociation.org/pubs/insurance.html#doli (accessed May 14, 2004).

3. www.genesismanagers.com/GUM_Cl.nsf/Doc/LPGuide (accessed May 24, 2004).

4. www.americasnetwork.com/americasnetwork/article/articleDetail.jsp?id=97693 (accessed June 15, 2004).

5. American Bar Association, www.abanet.org/buslaw/library/onlinepublications/ mbca2002.pdf (accessed February 8, 2005).

6. Model Business Corporation Act, 3rd ed., § 8.30 (2003).

7. Securities and Exchange Commission, www.sec.gov/divisions/corpfin/34act/ index1934.shtml (accessed February 8, 2005).

8. www.thecorporatecounsel.net/GreatGovernance/member/FAQ/DirectorDuties. htm#dutyofconfident (accessed May 18, 2004).

9. Securities and Exchange Commission, www.sec.gov (accessed November 1, 2004).

10. Cornerstone Research, *Post-Reform Act Securities Lawsuits: Settlements Report through December 2003*, Laura E. Simmons and Ellen M. Ryan, 2004.

11. Cornerstone Research, *Post-Reform Act Securities Lawsuits: Settlements Report through December 2003*.

12. www.bowne.com/newsletters/newsletter.asp?storyID=221 (accessed May 18, 2004).

13. Jury Verdict Research®, *Employment Practice Liability: Jury Award Trends and Statistics* (Horsham, Pa.: LRP Publications, 2004), pp. 7, 15.

14. www.discriminationattorney.com/sex.shtml (accessed February 9, 2005).

15. Title 29—Labor, Chapter XIV—Equal Employment Opportunity Commission Part 1604—Guidelines on Discrimination Because of Sex § 1604.11 available at www. gpo.gov/nara/cfr/waisidx_03/29cfr1604_03.html (accessed February 11, 2005).

16. Equal Employment Opportunity Commission, www.eeoc.gov/facts/fs-sex.html (accessed June 21, 2004).

17. Len Strazewski, "Fiduciary Risk: A Sleeper Awakes," *Risk & Insurance*, August 2004, p. 38.

18. "WorldCom Pension Settlement Reached," *Business Insurance*, July 12, 2004, p. 1.

Chapter 8

Direct Your Learning

Understanding Corporate Governance

After learning the content of this chapter and completing the corresponding course guide assignment, you should be able to:

- Explain how separation of ownership and control leads to agency costs.
- Describe the three categories of agency costs.
- Describe four mechanisms to align manager and shareholder interests.
- Describe the relationship between value maximization and social responsibility.
- Explain how boards of directors are composed to meet corporate governance expectations.
- Describe the five key issues in corporate governance.
- Describe the responsibility of corporate governance as it relates to risk management.
- Define or describe each of the Key Words and Phrases for this chapter.

Develop Your Perspective

What are the main topics covered in the chapter?

This chapter describes corporate governance and its relationship to risk management. Key topics include the role of corporate governance, the board of directors and directors' legal obligations, and other issues faced by organizations as they strive to increase shareholder value.

Consider an organization that has a separation of ownership and control.

- How does the separation of ownership and control create the need for corporate governance?

- What are some of the benefits of the separation of ownership and control?

Why is it important to learn about these topics?

Corporate governance can be a source of loss exposures when corporations fail to meet minimum standards established by regulators and legislators. Understanding corporate governance will help a risk management professional to choose appropriate risk control measures.

Examine the board of directors at the organization previously identified.

- How is the board structured?

- What legal obligations is the board subject to?

How can you use what you will learn?

Evaluate the effectiveness of the corporate governance at the organization previously identified.

- How well do the risk management techniques for corporate governance support organizational risk management goals?

- What suggestions might you make to address the five key issues in corporate governance?

Chapter 8

Understanding Corporate Governance

Medium to large corporations in the United States and many other countries exhibit separation of ownership and control. Separation of ownership and control means that a corporation is owned by its shareholders but controlled by its board of directors and management. The vast majority of shareholders are not actively involved in management of the company they own. Instead, management runs the company with oversight by the board of directors. Corporate governance ensures that management and the board of directors operate with the best interests of the owners in mind. In its broad sense, **corporate governance** encompasses all mechanisms and procedures that determine how corporations are run. The emphasis of corporate governance is on those mechanisms and procedures that affect the investors' well-being. For publicly traded corporations, corporate governance is, in essence, risk control for the management liability loss exposures discussed in the previous chapter. However, corporate governance can also be a source of loss exposures when corporations fail to meet the minimum standards established by regulators and legislators.

Corporate governance
The mechanisms and procedures that determine how corporations are run.

Shareholders and Corporate Governance

Whether corporate governance systems effectively serve investors' interests has been debated for decades. The Enron scandal in 2001 and subsequent major corporate scandals increased the intensity of this debate. Similar to the 1929 stock market crash and subsequent securities legislation, the recent scandals and declines in stock prices produced enormous losses for investors; undermined investor and public confidence in capital markets and corporate behavior; and led to a variety of new practices, rules, laws, and regulations affecting corporate governance. It is difficult to determine the depth and scope of problems in corporate governance. However, widespread belief exists that managers of many corporations can do a better job of increasing the long-term economic value of their corporations and that "business as usual" could produce additional government constraints on corporate decision making.

Risk management is one of the most important concerns of corporate governance. Corporate governance practices should strive to ensure that the corporation is meeting both the spirit and letter of all legal and regulatory requirements in an effort to control management liability loss exposures. This chapter introduces corporate governance and its relationship to risk management. The chapter begins with an overview of the role of corporate governance in market economies.

It then discusses the structure of corporate boards and the legal obligations of directors to shareholders and other stakeholders. The chapter next explores five key issues in corporate governance: pressures from shareholder expectations and behavior, executive incentives and compensation, the accountability of directors, corporate financial reporting, and the importance of integrity in ensuring that corporations serve the interests of shareholders with appropriate consideration for other stakeholders. The chapter concludes with a discussion of the central corporate governance issues related to risk management.

ROLE OF CORPORATE GOVERNANCE

Shareholders of for-profit corporations generally want managers to make risk management and other decisions that maximize the value of their shares, which in turn generally requires maximization of the corporation's total economic value. A corporation's economic value depends on the magnitude, timing, and risk of expected future cash flows. Not-for-profit organizations have different goals. Their broad goal can be viewed as maximizing the value of goods or services provided to their various constituencies. Despite this difference, many corporate governance issues are similar for for-profit and not-for-profit organizations. This section elaborates on the concept of the separation of ownership and control, focusing on for-profit corporations. It discusses whether corporate decision makers generally will pursue the goal of maximizing corporation economic value and whether that goal, appropriately pursued, is likely to conflict systematically with societal goals.

Separation of Ownership and Control

Corporations with publicly traded stock exhibit a separation of ownership and control. Most shareholders are passive, while managers, with oversight by the board of directors, make most of the important decisions that affect the corporation's economic value. Managers, through their executive compensation, are often also shareholders in the corporation. However, for the purposes of this discussion, the term shareholders is used to describe nonmanager shareholders because the benefits of the separation of ownership and control only extend to nonmanager shareholders. Further, the text will not distinguish between managers who are shareholders and those who are not.

Shareholders who are not actively involved in managing the corporation have limited liability for the corporation's obligations. Their liability is limited to the amount they invested in the organization. Therefore, the most that shareholders can lose is the value of their shares. Limited liability of shareholders facilitates the separation of ownership and control. If shareholders had their entire personal wealth at risk from corporate decisions, many more of them would seek to play an active role in corporate decision making.

Separation of ownership and control provides a number of important economic benefits. Decision-making authority rests primarily with managers, who develop substantial expertise in the business's operations and strategy. Shareholders can readily reduce their risk of owning shares by diversifying their investments across many corporations. This diversification reduces corporations' cost of capital, increases productive investment, and provides enormous benefits to consumers through better, more affordable products. Historically, the development of limited liability corporations with separation of ownership and control has widely been accepted as instrumental in the development and growth of modern economies. However, corporate governance is not only concerned with the separation of ownership and control; it is also concerned with the separation of oversight and control as discussed in a subsequent section of this chapter.

As is true for all institutions, the separation of ownership and control in a corporation with publicly traded stock has limitations. In effect, managers and corporate boards are agents of the shareholders; they are the authorized decision makers who act on behalf of shareholders. Shareholders, in turn, want those decisions to increase the value of their shares. Like virtually all principal-agent relationships, managers and nonmanagement board members may be tempted to pursue their own interests (such as, preservation of their own wealth) at the expense of shareholders. That incentive gives rise to agency costs. **Agency costs** are the costs associated with managing the relationship between agent (management) and principal (shareholder).

Agency costs
The costs associated with managing the relationship between agent and principal.

There are three categories of agency costs: monitoring costs, bonding costs, and incentive alignment costs.

Categories of Agency Costs

1. Monitoring Costs

2. Bonding Costs

3. Incentive Alignment Costs

The first category of agency costs is monitoring costs. While various parties incur costs in monitoring corporate decision makers, the majority of monitoring costs are borne by shareholders. An example of monitoring costs is the fee paid to an external auditor to verify the corporation's financial statements.

The second category of agency costs is bonding costs. Managers may have to incur various costs to demonstrate that they are serving (or will serve) the shareholders' interests. In other words, they may incur costs to *bond* their promises to serve shareholders' interests. An example of bonding costs would be the manager's willingness to accept noncash compensation in the form of stock options or restricted stock that link the manager's compensation to the corporation's performance.

The third category of agency costs is incentive alignment costs. Because monitoring and bonding activities are necessarily imperfect (they are not 100 percent effective), corporate decisions will not always benefit shareholders. As a result, corporations

---

Continued on next page.

generally are worth somewhat less than they would be if the incentives of corporate decision makers were perfectly aligned with the interests of shareholders. As an example of the third type of cost in the context of risk management, some managers might tend to be too cautious (risk averse), because their jobs and investment in the corporation's stock are at risk if cash flows from risky investments turn out to be low. Because they may be harmed or even lose their jobs if unfavorable outcomes occur, managers may avoid some projects that are perceived as too risky, even if those projects would increase the corporation's economic value. Similarly, managers may devote more corporate resources to risk reduction or risk transfer than would be necessary to maximize the value of the corporation's stock.

Four main mechanisms are used to help align the incentives of corporate decision makers with shareholders: incentive compensation, legal liability, management reputation, and takeover threats. These four mechanisms— defined in the following text box—serve to reduce the agency costs involved with the separation of ownership and control.

Mechanisms to Align Manager and Shareholder Interests

1. Incentive compensation—linking managers compensation to the corporation's economic performance

2. Legal liability—holding decision makers liable to shareholders for any harm from their decisions

3. Management reputation—management concern about making decisions that do not increase the corporation's economic value and that can develop poor reputations for managers

4. Takeover threats—management concern about the probability that another corporation will acquire their corporation

Exhibit 8-1 depicts the separation of ownership and control, the resulting agency costs, and the four key mechanisms that help align the incentives of corporate decision makers and shareholders, thereby reducing agency costs and increasing the corporation's economic value. Incentive compensation is an important tool that can be used to encourage managers to make decisions that increase the corporation's value to shareholders. By appropriately linking compensation to the corporation's economic performance through incentive compensation, executive compensation systems often help align managerial and shareholders' interests. The question of whether executive compensation effectively serves this goal is controversial and is discussed subsequently in this chapter.

EXHIBIT 8-1

Separation of Ownership and Control

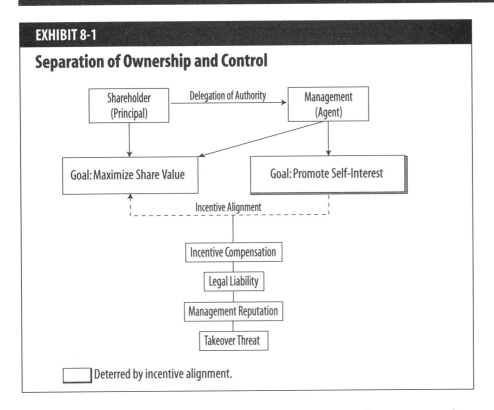

In addition to the influence of incentive compensation, under certain conditions directors and officers can be held personally liable to shareholders for any harm from their decisions. In principle, the risk of legal liability helps align the incentives of directors and officers with those of shareholders and thus reduces the agency costs associated with separation of ownership and control. The employment market for managers also helps align managers' interests with those of shareholders. Managers who make decisions that do not increase the corporation's economic value can develop reputations for being poor managers, with adverse effects on their ability to obtain high-paying positions within the existing corporation or other corporations.

Finally, directors and officers who fail to make decisions to maximize the value of the corporation's stock often increase the probability that another corporation will acquire the corporation and that they will then lose their positions. These types of mechanisms inherent in the marketplace are often generically called market forces.

One market force, takeover threats, can be fundamentally important in aligning the interests of corporate decision makers and shareholders. However, following the wave of hostile corporate takeovers in the 1980s, a variety of impediments were created that reduce the likelihood of corporate takeovers and thus the disciplining effects of takeovers on incumbent directors and officers. Many states enacted "anti-takeover" statutes that made it more difficult for hostile takeovers (that is, takeovers that are not desired by current directors and officers). Many corporations also changed their charters or adopted other strategies to deter takeovers, such as having staggered terms of office for directors, which makes it more difficult and time consuming for an acquirer to replace incumbent directors and officers after a takeover. The reduced threat of takeovers may have contributed to many of the issues in corporate governance.

Value Maximization and Social Responsibility

In part because of corporate scandals, increased media and regulatory attention has focused on whether the goal of maximizing a corporation's economic value (value maximization) appropriately serves the overall interests of society. Some observers argue that value maximization is a flawed goal and that decision makers should place more weight on the effects of their decisions on stakeholders other than shareholders and on the public at large—even if doing so causes the corporation's economic value to decline. Because it has important implications for appropriate corporate governance, it is important to provide some brief perspective on the issues in this debate.

The typical argument in favor of value maximization as an overriding goal for corporate decision makers is that the pursuit of this goal promotes economic efficiency, innovation, and growth, leading to higher standards of living than would otherwise be possible. Increasing economic value is obviously important in its own right. It also generates more resources that can be transferred to citizens who are less fortunate than others through taxes and other mechanisms (such as charitable contributions). In other words, the bigger the economic "pie," the bigger the economic "slices." A strong theoretical and practical case can therefore be made that maximizing corporations' economic value is both economically efficient and also fair—provided that corporations appropriately reflect (internalize) all costs of their decisions. From this perspective, a primary function of legal rules and regulations is to help ensure that corporations consider the full costs of their decisions.

An alternative view is that legal, social, and environmental concerns make it desirable for corporations to give greater weight to the concerns of noninvestor stakeholders than is implied by value maximization. Furthermore, corporations do not always internalize all the costs of their decisions. Some costs are not borne by the corporation but are a result of their decisions. Examples may include costs of pollution or excessive consumption of natural resources.

However, it is also important to emphasize that in most cases no inherent conflict exists between maximizing corporation economic value and societal goals. The value maximization goal does not routinely short-change the interests of noninvestor stakeholders or the interests of the public. Instead, when appropriately pursued, value maximization requires the corporation to carefully weigh the effects of its decisions on employees, customers, suppliers, and lenders in order to attract and retain those stakeholders. Actions that harm those and other noninvestor stakeholders are generally bad for business and therefore bad for shareholders.

The legal system can help mitigate any inherent conflicts that may arise between value maximization and the interests of other stakeholders in ways that could reduce economic efficiency and welfare. In the context of risk management, the legal system helps provide incentives for corporate decision makers to consider the effects of their decisions on noninvestor stakeholders when market forces do not promote such consideration. For example, the threat of liability for injury to consumers or the environment can provide a potent deterrent to harmful activity. In effect, the legal system helps internalize the costs of corporate decisions that otherwise would fall more heavily on other parties. Consequently, value maximizing decisions will carefully consider the risk of harm to noninvestor stakeholders.

In summary, a strong argument can be made that value maximization, properly pursued, *should* be the overriding goal of for-profit corporations, and that the legal system should be designed to influence decisions when value maximization would otherwise lead to excessive costs that fall on noninvestor stakeholders (externalities). The legal system is necessarily imperfect in this regard, as are managerial decision-making and incentive systems. There are decisions that, while they maximize the economic value of a corporation, could result in excessive costs for noninvestor stakeholders or society. Managerial integrity becomes very important under those circumstances because it is nearly impossible to legislate ethics and morality. Regardless of whether this is true, there is widespread belief that directors and officers of many corporations can do a better job of increasing the economic value of their corporations.

BOARD COMPOSITION AND DIRECTORS' LEGAL OBLIGATIONS

Understanding the basics of corporate governance requires knowing how corporate boards are composed and what legal obligations directors have. Similar to the separation of ownership and control found in publicly traded corporations, corporate governance is evolving toward the separation of oversight and control for corporate boards of directors. This separation is accomplished by requiring a majority of directors be outside directors (individuals who are not employees of the corporation), requiring regular meetings of outside directors without management present, and requiring key committees to be composed of only outside directors.

Board Composition

Corporate boards are responsible for overseeing major managerial decisions and protecting shareholders' interests. Shareholders elect directors as discussed in the previous chapter. Corporate boards vary in size, commonly ranging from eight to twenty directors. Boards include both inside directors—the chief executive officer (CEO) and one or more other top officers of the corporation—and outside directors (see Exhibit 8-2). Outside directors often are or have been top officers of other corporations and/or have specialized expertise in the corporation or its industry.

EXHIBIT 8-2

Composition of Corporate Boards

Membership	Key Committees
• Chair (often the CEO)	• Compensation (determines executive compensation arrangements; outside directors only)
• Inside directors (CEO, other officers who serve on board)	• Audit (oversees financial reporting; outside directors only)
• Outside directors (nonemployees)	• Nominations/corporate governance (nominates directors, establishes governance guidelines; can be both inside and outside directors)

Directors elect the board's chair. The corporation's CEO is elected and serves as chair for a significant majority of U.S. corporations. The CEO/chair model is less common in many other countries. Some of the major responsibilities of corporate directors are listed in Exhibit 8-3.

EXHIBIT 8-3

Major Responsibilities of Corporate Directors

- To establish the basic objectives and broad policies of the corporation
- To elect or appoint the corporate officers, advise them, approve their actions, and audit their performance
- To safeguard and approve changes in the corporation's assets
- To approve important financial matters and see that proper annual and interim reports are given to shareholders
- To delegate special powers to others to sign contracts, open bank accounts, sign checks, issue stock, make loans, and conduct any activities that may require board approval
- To maintain, revise, and enforce the corporate charter and bylaws
- To perpetuate a competent board through regular elections and filling interim vacancies with qualified persons
- To act as a fiduciary in their relationship to the corporation and its shareholders

Corporate boards are organized into committees. The most important (as shown in Exhibit 8-2) are the audit committee, the compensation committee, and the nominations/corporate governance committee. The **audit committee**, in conjunction with the corporation's external auditors, oversees preparation and dissemination of the corporation's financial statements. The **compensation committee** determines the compensation arrangements for the CEO and other senior managers, usually with the advice and assistance of outside consultants. The **nominations/corporate governance committee** recommends nominees for election to the board by the shareholders and, in many corporations, establishes corporate governance guidelines.

Directors' Legal Obligations

Corporate directors have two sources of legal liability: common law and statutory law. Common law imposes the four main duties on directors that were discussed in the previous chapter and are listed in Exhibit 8-4.

Audit committee
A board committee that, in conjunction with the corporation's external auditors, oversees preparation and dissemination of the corporation's financial statements.

Compensation committee
A board committee that determines compensation arrangements for the CEO and other senior managers.

Nominations/corporate governance committee
A board committee that recommends nominees for election to the board by the shareholders and, in many corporations, establishes corporate governance guidelines.

EXHIBIT 8-4

Corporate Directors' Duties from Common Law

1. Duty of Care—exercise good faith and reasonable care in supervising corporate activities

2. Duty of Loyalty—place the corporation's interests above own personal interests in financial or other gain

3. Duty of Disclosure—disclose material facts to all who have a right to know such facts and would not otherwise be able to obtain them

4. Duty of Obedience—perform duties according to the statutes and the terms of the corporate charter

---

As described in the previous chapter, investors may sue and directors may be held liable for actions that violate key statutes. In addition to the statutes summarized in Exhibit 8-5, a variety of other federal statutes can create legal liability for officers and directors. In many instances, states have related statutes that also provide a basis for legal liability. Directors and officers may be sued in civil actions for violations of federal antitrust statutes. Those statutes include the following:

- Sherman Antitrust Act, which prohibits business combinations that restrain trade, as well as prohibiting attempts to secure a monopoly

- Clayton Act, which addresses price discrimination, exclusive dealing arrangements, and mergers and acquisitions that substantially reduce competition

- Robinson-Patman Act, which addresses price discrimination and possible predatory pricing

Potential personal liability for directors and officers who violate the Sherman Antitrust and Clayton Acts and harm private entities includes "treble damages" (plaintiff can collect three times their damages) and plaintiffs' attorney fees. Directors and officers also can be held criminally liable under certain conditions.

EXHIBIT 8-5

Statutory Laws Governing Corporate Directors

1. Securities Act of 1933—securities registration
2. Securities Exchange Act of 1934—insider trading and financial reporting
3. Private Securities Litigation Reform Act of 1995—abuses in securities litigation
4. Sarbanes-Oxley Act of 2002—investor protection, internal controls, penalties

---

Some of the federal statutes that may create directors' and officers' liability are directly concerned with risk management issues. If, for example, directors and officers exert extensive control of business operations, they may be deemed employers under the Occupational Safety and Health Act of 1970 (and related state statutes) and held liable for violating the statutory duty of providing a safe working environment or specific regulations governing workplace safety.

Personal liability for violations of environmental statutes and regulations represents a significant source of risk for many directors and officers. The relevant federal statutes include the Comprehensive Environmental Response Compensation and Liability Act of 1980 (CERCLA) and the Resource Conservation and Recovery Act of 1979 (RCRA). Corporate officers have been held personally liable under CERCLA for environmental contamination when the officers had personal knowledge and control of the contamination, and they may be held liable for violations of regulations dealing with transporting and disposing of hazardous waste under RCRA.

KEY ISSUES IN CORPORATE GOVERNANCE

The sharp declines in stock prices and high-profile corporate scandals in the U.S. during the first few years of the twenty-first century produced enormous losses for investors; undermined investor and public confidence in capital markets and corporate behavior; and led to many new practices, rules, laws, and regulations affecting corporate governance. Although the breadth and depth of these problems is debatable, the perception is widespread that many managers and corporate boards can improve their ability to promote and sustain their corporations' long-term economic value. There is also a risk that failure to improve behavior will give rise to more government restrictions on corporate decision making.

Achieving the goal of better managerial performance requires understanding how best to provide directors and officers with incentives for long-term economic value creation and for accurate and transparent (easy for those outside the corporation to understand) reporting of financial results, especially when some investors may focus excessively on short-term corporate earnings and shareholder returns. It also requires considering how integrity affects long-term economic value creation and how directors and officers can instill integrity and ethics at all corporate levels.

This section briefly discusses the following five corporate governance issues that affect long-term economic value creation:[1]

1. Pressures from shareholder expectations and behavior
2. Executive incentives and compensation
3. Accountability of directors
4. Corporate financial reporting
5. Importance of integrity

Pressures from Shareholder Expectations and Behavior

The first corporate governance issue is pressures from shareholder expectations and behavior. The average amount of time that shareholders held a particular stock substantially declined during the late twentieth century. This trend accompanied increased focus on short-term stock returns, quarterly earnings reports, and quarterly earnings projections. Many observers believe that large numbers of individual and/or institutional shareholders focus excessive attention on reported short-term results instead of long-term economic value creation. Whether the incentives and behavior of managers, security analysts, and accountants contribute to a short-term focus is an important issue. Debates about executive incentives and compensation, board incentives and accountability, and the integrity of corporate behavior are linked to the pressures from shareholders expectations and behavior.

Managers of publicly traded corporations generally face strong pressure from shareholders for earnings growth and significant penalties for failure to achieve earnings projections. These influences can produce incentives for managers to increase short-term earnings without adequately considering the effects on long-term economic value and, in some cases, to manipulate reported earnings. Available evidence does not support firm conclusions about the extent to which a short-term focus and unrealistic demands and expectations of some shareholders harm long-term economic value creation. However, there has been a significant increase in the number of restatements of prior reported earnings that were materially misstated.

The substantial increase in stock prices during the 1990s and their subsequent sharp decline also raised the question of whether trading by shortsighted investors produced excessive stock prices in relation to long-term economic value, which could not be reduced through the trading activities of knowledgeable investors.

The Effect of Knowledgeable Investors on the Market

Under normal conditions, knowledgeable investors with substantial resources who believe that a stock is overvalued will "short" the stock (that is, borrow shares of the stock and then sell them, with the obligation to later pay back the shares with newly purchased, lower-priced stock). The sale of large numbers of shorted shares puts downward pressure on the share price. If the price drops, the investor repurchases the stock at the lower price, pays back the borrowed shares, and makes a profit on the difference between the sales price and repurchase price. The strategy is risky because the price might not decline, and shares might have to be repurchased at a higher price to repay the borrowed shares. More important, if investors are not confident that the stock price will fall towards its "correct" value within a reasonable amount of time, they are far less likely to engage in such strategies. That reluctance in turn may allow unreasonably high prices to persist for some period.

Because of these influences, an important issue in corporate governance is how best to achieve long-term economic value creation if many investors have unrealistic expectations, pay too much attention to short-term earnings growth, and sometimes cause the corporation's stock to be overvalued. It is debatable whether long-term economic value creation would be better promoted if corporations downplayed short-term earnings forecasts and informed investors if their expectations for earnings growth were unrealistic. The uncertainty of this issue has also influenced debate and practices related to executive incentives and compensation.

Executive Incentives and Compensation

The second corporate governance issue is executive incentives and compensation. Total compensation of U.S. CEOs rose rapidly in the 1990s. Much of the increase represented growth in nonsalary incentive compensation. Incentive compensation includes stock option grants, restricted stock grants (that is, grants of stock that the executive cannot sell for a specified number of years), performance-related bonuses, and deferred compensation. These forms of compensation can represent more than half of total CEO compensation.[2]

CEO compensation, therefore, became much more sensitive to stock-price performance during the 1990s. Consequently, many executives received enormous, highly valued stock incentives during the strong bull market that characterized the latter part of the decade. Subsequent declines in stock prices and corporate scandals led to shareholder and public criticism that executive incentives and compensation were sometimes grossly excessive. This criticism escalated with the highly publicized debate over the deferred compensation arrangement of the former head of the New York Stock Exchange (Richard Grasso). Some large corporations scaled back deferred compensation, pension arrangements, and option grants to their CEOs, partly because of such criticism.

Two conflicting views exist about these developments in executive incentives and compensation. On the one hand, growth in incentive compensation, and in particular option grants, is thought to help motivate CEOs and other senior executives to maximize long-term economic value. It is also argued that in the late 1980s, executive incentives and compensation were insufficiently sensitive to corporate performance and the return on a corporation's stock. Moreover, compared with requiring executives to maintain large holdings of company stock, it is argued that options improve incentives for value creation with less risk to executives and lower compensation costs to the corporation.

On the other hand, option grants and related forms of incentive compensation sometimes can motivate executives to undertake excessively risky projects that increase the likelihood of making large gains from their options without significant downside risk. In addition, option grants may increase the temptation to manipulate short-term reported earnings to inflate share prices. Some people also believe that the levels and forms of executive incentives and compensation are symptomatic of the basic agency problem that confronts shareholders. They argue that executive incentive and compensation packages are often excessive because of insufficient board oversight and inadequate discipline from the corporate takeover market.

How Should Corporations Account for Stock Options?

Enormous debate has also arisen about whether corporations should be required to expense the estimated value of option grants to executives and other employees when reporting income in their financial statements. Proponents of expensing argue that failure to treat option grants as a current expense overstates income and biases compensation toward the use of such grants. Other observers argue that mandatory expensing of option grants will distort the financial statements of many corporations, that there is no generally accepted method of valuing option grants, and that corporations already report ample information about option grants in their financial statements. As of March 2005, the Financial Accounting Standards Board (FASB), in a revision of FASB Statement No. 123 "Accounting for Stock-Based Compensation," had announced that expensing the estimated value of option grants would be required beginning June 2005 for most public entities. Congress was considering legislation that would limit that requirement to options granted to a few top executives. A number of large corporations have already started expensing option grants.

There is some evidence that total CEO compensation is higher when corporate governance is weak and that earnings "management" is more prevalent when CEO compensation depends more heavily on stock prices.[3] On average, corporations' stock prices have increased when option compensation programs have been introduced (as evidenced by positive "abnormal" stock returns on announcement dates). Although that result could indicate that option programs increase the corporation's long-term economic value, some managers may time the introduction of option grants to correspond with other favorable news that is expected to increase the price of the corporation's stock. The $1 million Internal Revenue Service (IRS) limit, adopted in 1993, on the amount of cash compensation to any one executive that is tax-deductible for a corporation, also appears to have contributed to growth in option grants and other noncash compensation.

A key question in corporate governance is how to best design executive compensation to promote long-term economic value creation. Based on what is currently known, a consensus has yet to emerge about best practices in this regard. Nevertheless, some movement has occurred towards providing fewer option grants, making greater use of restricted stock, and reducing top managers' influence on their own compensation packages.

Accountability of Directors

The third corporate governance issue is accountability of directors. One criticism of the U.S. system of corporate governance of publicly traded corporations is that many outside board directors have been passive and have not provided sufficient oversight of the corporation's management. It is argued that such passiveness and deference is inconsistent with board members' intended role in monitoring and controlling the agency relationship between managers and shareholders, and that board accountability needs to improve to better control the agency relationship.

Partly as a result of provisions of the Sarbanes-Oxley Act, associated Securities and Exchange Commission (SEC) rules, and changes in stock exchange listing requirements, a variety of improvements in board structure have been proposed and in many cases implemented in the U.S. One change involves making a majority or substantial majority of directors outside (independent) directors. A second change involves increasing the independence of audit and compensation committees. A third change is to conduct regular meetings of outside directors without management being present. Although some observers argue against having the CEO serve as board chair, that proposal has thus far had limited traction in the U.S. (such separation is common in the United Kingdom).

While some may argue that earnings management declines as the proportion of outside directors increases, analyses of U.S. data generally have not found a significant relationship between the proportion of outside directors and overall corporate performance (as measured by stock value and accounting measures).[4] Evidence does suggest that U.S. CEOs are more likely to be replaced for poor performance when boards have more outsiders. Some evidence also suggests that overall performance is worse and that CEO compensation is higher when boards are large, suggesting that increases in board size may be accompanied by reduced incentives for board members to monitor corporate performance and executive incentives and compensation.[5]

It is not yet clear whether the evolving roles of corporate boards and their relationships to CEOs will translate into significantly improved corporate performance. Nonetheless, a key corporate governance issue is how best to organize boards and compensate board members to encourage long-term economic value creation.

Corporate Financial Reporting

The fourth corporate governance issue is corporate financial reporting, that is, the extent to which external auditors of corporate financial reports accommodated or even influenced deceptive reporting practices in recent corporate scandals. In some cases, those scandals suggest that close relationships between auditors and their clients compromised the incentives of individual auditors and perhaps entire auditing corporations. Associated debate has questioned whether financial reporting needs to become more transparent and whether the U.S. rules-based accounting system is preferable to principles-based systems as practiced, for example, in the United Kingdom. As noted previously, the Sarbanes-Oxley Act created an accounting oversight board, strengthened independence rules for audit committees, and required more oversight of any nonaudit services that auditing corporations provide to their clients.

Rules-Based Versus Principles-Based Accounting Systems

U.S. corporations use the generally accepted accounting principles (GAAP) system. This system is more of a rules-based system than the type of principles-based system used in other countries. The GAAP system enables investors, when comparing financial statements from various corporations, to compare like with like. That is, the GAAP rules outline what the corporations are reporting and where they are reporting them. A principles-based system would have fewer rules and be more subjective because the corporation would have greater flexibility in interpreting the spirit of the accounting principles rather than having to adhere to specific accounting rules. A principles-based system may make it more difficult for investors to compare corporations' financial statements.

It could be argued that external auditors should not provide nonauditing services to clients (except perhaps for tax services) because providing such services fundamentally compromises their independence. However, cost savings associated with the joint provision of auditing and nonauditing services appear to be sizable, which works against separation of the two.

It also is not clear whether improved transparency of corporate operations would necessarily enhance long-term economic value creation for many or most corporations. Providing more information more quickly could help shareholders and other stakeholders make decisions that are better informed. Also, providing more information more quickly could reduce the likelihood of future scandals and attendant losses by removing the appearance of a corporate cover-up. However, more detailed and timely reporting requirements involve direct and indirect compliance costs. Those costs include the time and effort spent by top executives and board members on financial reporting issues, which may take time away from evaluation and decisions that affect long-term economic value, including risk management decisions.

Rules-based accounting potentially has significant disadvantages compared with principles-based accounting. For example, more detailed rules may lead to increased efforts to circumvent those rules and foster an attitude of complying with the letter of the rules rather than with their spirit. Other notable financial reporting issues include whether traditional accounting rules are appropriate for corporations in the "new economy," in which the principal assets of many corporations are intangible, and whether more tailoring of accounting principles and rules to particular industries would provide information that is more meaningful. In general, how to make financial reports more meaningful in ways that enhance rather than detract from long-term economic value creation is a significant corporate governance issue that boards must address.

Importance of Integrity

The fifth corporate governance issue is the importance of integrity. As discussed earlier, modern analyses of the principal-agent problem that confronts shareholders stress three categories of agency costs: (1) the costs of monitoring managers, (2) the costs of managerial actions to bond their performance, and (3) the reduction in long-term economic value that arises because monitoring and bonding efforts cannot eliminate incentive conflicts. Although carefully planned takeovers, executive incentives and compensation, managers' concerns with reputation, and the threat of legal liability often promote sound corporate governance, their influence is necessarily imperfect.

Corporate scandals and the costs and limitations of mechanisms for reducing conflicts between management and shareholders have led to growing recognition of the importance of integrity to corporate performance. Inherent honesty and integrity of top executives, board members, auditors, securities analysts, and other players serve to reduce conflicts and the associated reductions in corporation value. When integrity is lacking at the top, it generally will be lacking at all corporate levels, undermining public confidence and producing more costly monitoring, more costly rules and regulation, greater penalties for misconduct, and lower corporation values.

A fundamental issue in corporate governance is how to instill integrity throughout the organization. Success in addressing that issue will enhance public confidence and support for private enterprise and initiative. Repeated failures on this issue could easily result in more pervasive government controls on corporate decision making.

CORPORATE GOVERNANCE AND RISK MANAGEMENT

Stock market performance during the first few years of the twenty-first century, corporate scandals, the Sarbanes-Oxley Act, and related changes in securities exchange listing requirements have led corporate boards to have greater concern for risk management issues. It is yet to be seen whether that concern translates into significant improvements in risk management, including integrated risk management at the enterprise level (enterprise risk management). In any event, a central responsibility of corporate governance is to ensure that the corporation practices appropriate risk management.

Directors and officers have the ultimate responsibility for ensuring that the corporation meets or exceeds all legal and regulatory requirements related to risk management, such as environmental law, workplace safety law, other employment law, and compulsory insurance requirements. That responsibility includes ensuring that the corporation has appropriate systems of oversight, compliance, and control. It is also the board of directors' responsibility to disclose material information about the corporation's loss exposures and changes in its loss exposures in a timely manner, including any events or loss exposures that create the possibility of large uninsured losses.

In addition to conscientiously satisfying the letter of regulatory and legal requirements, including appropriate disclosure of loss exposures, boards must strive to satisfy the spirit of those requirements. They must endeavor to balance the benefits and costs of strategic decisions about risk management in order to increase the long-run economic value of the organization. Difficult decisions will often arise and have to be made with limited information. It is therefore all the more important for directors and officers to instill a culture of integrity in which managers and employees strive to behave appropriately under all circumstances. Instilling integrity will help reduce tendencies for managers and other employees to act in ways that might produce short-term increases in reported earnings or managerial incentives and compensation at the expense of long-term economic value.

Directors and officers should play a central role in establishing philosophy and practice about the general choice of risky activities for the corporation to pursue and specific risks to employees, consumers, other stakeholders, and the public. They need to adopt appropriate systems and controls for identifying key risks, understanding their affects on the corporation, selecting risk management techniques, and monitoring their implementation. For example, with respect to loss control, the overall goal of corporate governance should be to ensure that the corporation invests in and employs all risk control techniques for which the expected reduction in harm *to all parties* exceeds the costs of the risk control techniques. Pursuing that goal generally will minimize the corporation's long-term cost of risk and maximize its long-term economic value. As long as the corporation strives to identify the risk of harm to all relevant parties and reflects those risks in the decision-making process, the goal of minimizing the corporation's cost of risk (and therefore maximizing its economic value) is unambiguously in the interest of society, and is consistent with integrity and ethical behavior.

Failure to appropriately weigh the expected harm to employees, customers, or other parties in relation to the costs of risk control exposes the corporation to the risk of having to pay large sums in litigation, including amounts that could cause the corporation to seek bankruptcy protection. The threat of liability helps internalize the cost of risk to the corporation and deter excessive risk taking. However, when cases arise in which incentives do not provide sufficient motivation, the integrity of directors and officers will hopefully encourage them to act in the best interests of all stakeholders.

Boards should also seek to ensure that the corporation's risk financing arrangements provide adequate resources to compensate for any harm that the corporation's activities may cause. Boards should not allow shareholders' limited liability for claims against the corporation—or the potential ability of the corporation to declare bankruptcy and thereby shield certain corporate assets from injured parties' claims—to encourage excessively risky activities in which the ultimate costs could fall on other parties.

In highly competitive markets, the pressure for corporations and their employees to behave in ways that increase short-run earnings at the expense of long-run economic value are often strong. That pressure creates the risk that decisions, including risk control, risk financing, and other risk management decisions, sometimes will cut corners or otherwise sacrifice long-term economic value creation. Major corporate scandals in recent years make it clear that succumbing to such pressure can produce catastrophic consequences for shareholders, managers, directors, employees, and customers. A key dimension of appropriate corporate governance is to instill and oversee strategies and processes that avoid those pressures as they relate to risk management and other corporate decisions.

SUMMARY

Medium to large corporations with publicly traded stock exhibit separation of ownership and control. Most shareholders take a passive role in corporate operations, while managers, with oversight by the board of directors, make most of the decisions that affect the corporation's economic value. Separation of ownership and control gives rise to agency costs, which are the costs associated with managing the relationship between agent (management) and principal (shareholder). The three categories of agency costs are as follows:

1. Monitoring costs
2. Bonding costs
3. Incentive alignment costs

The following four mechanisms, although imperfect, help align the interests of directors and officers with those of shareholders and therefore reduce the agency costs associated with separation of ownership and control:

1. Incentive compensation
2. Legal liability
3. Management reputation
4. Takeover threats

Although gray areas arise in which decisions that maximize the economic value of a corporation could result in excessive costs for noninvestor stakeholders or society, a strong argument can be made that value maximization, properly pursued, should be the overriding goal of for-profit corporations. This goal coupled with the legal system should influence decisions when value maximization would otherwise lead to excessive costs that fall on noninvestor stakeholders (externalities). However, the legal system is necessarily imperfect in this regard, as are managerial decision-making and incentive systems.

Corporate governance is evolving toward the separation of oversight and control for corporate boards of directors. This separation is accomplished by requiring that board composition be made up of a majority of outside directors (individuals who are not employees of the corporation), requiring regular meetings of outside directors without management present, and requiring key committees to be comprised of only outside directors. Furthermore, legal liability is designed to ensure that directors are meeting their legal obligations.

Key issues that confront directors and officers include pressures on directors and officers that arise from shareholder expectations and behavior, executive incentives and compensation, how to determine the accountability of directors to shareholders, how to ensure proper corporate financial reporting, and the importance of integrity to proper governance and long-term economic value creation.

Regarding risk management, boards must strive to make risk management decisions that increase long-term economic corporation value with full consideration of the possible effects of the corporation's actions on shareholders, noninvestor stakeholders, and the public. Directors and officers must also strive to ensure that all decisions related to risk and its management are made with integrity and consistent with high ethical standards.

This chapter described corporate governance and its relationship to risk management. The next chapter discusses assessing personnel loss exposures.

CHAPTER NOTES

1. Adapted from Scott Harrington, Emily Johnson, and David Shrider, "Economics White Paper," *The Forum for Corporate Conscience*, Charlotte, N.C., March 2003.

2. The Wall Street Journal/Mercer Human Resource Consulting, *2003 CEO Compensation Survey and Trends* (New York: Mercer Human Resource Consulting, 2004), p. 2.

3. Antonio Davila and Fernando Penalva, "Corporate Governance and the Weighting of Performance Measures in CEO Compensation," http://ssrn.com/abstract=592045 (accessed February 7, 2005).

4. Margaret M. Blair, "Shareholder Value, Corporate Governance and Corporate Performance: A Post-Enron Reassessment of the Conventional Wisdom," in *Corporate Governance and Capital Flows in a Global Economy*, eds. Peter K. Cornelius and Bruce Kogut (Oxford University Press, 2003).

5. Sanjai Bhagak and Bernard Black, "The noncorrelation between board independence and long-term performance," *Journal of Corporation Law*, vol. 27, issue 2, 2002, p. 231.

Chapter 9

Direct Your Learning

Assessing Personnel Loss Exposures

After learning the content of this chapter and completing the corresponding course guide assignment, you should be able to:

■ Identify the personnel exposed to loss.

■ Describe the causes of loss affecting personnel loss exposures.

■ Describe the workplace hazards affecting personnel loss exposures.

■ Describe the financial consequences of personnel losses.

■ Explain how the following methods help risk managers assess personnel loss exposures:

- Risk assessment questionnaires
- Loss histories
- Other records and documents
- Flowcharts and organizational charts
- Personal inspections
- Expertise within and beyond the organization

■ Explain how demographic trends may affect an organization's personnel loss exposures.

■ Define or describe each of the Key Words and Phrases for this chapter.

Develop Your Perspective

What are the main topics covered in the chapter?

Human assets (personnel) are exposed to a variety of causes of loss and workplace hazards. This chapter describes how to assess those personnel loss exposures.

Consider the different types of personnel exposed to loss and the different causes of loss.

- How might the loss exposures associated with personnel loss vary by the role of the employee?
- How do the effects of a loss vary by the type of loss that is suffered?

Why is it important to learn about these topics?

Determining an individual's worth to an organization is often subjective. Understanding how to identify and analyze personnel loss exposures will enable a risk management professional to recommend effective risk management techniques to apply to losses associated with personnel loss exposures.

Appraise the personnel loss exposures where you work.

- What information would you need to accurately assess personnel loss exposures for your employer?
- What methods might you use to gather this information?

How can you use what you will learn?

Design a risk management plan for the personnel loss exposures you identified above.

- How might you mitigate the financial consequences of the death, disability, or voluntary and involuntary employee separation of a key employee of your organization?
- What recommendations might you make regarding how to mitigate workplace hazards?

Chapter 9
Assessing Personnel Loss Exposures

For many organizations, their most valuable assets are their employees because they add to the value of the organization through their physical and mental labor. Assets, human or otherwise, are used to create net income. The more productive the employees are, the more net income they generate, and the greater their value to the organization. To remain competitive, organizations must be able to attract and retain high quality employees who add value to the organization.

Similar to all of the other organization's assets, human assets are also exposed to loss, that is, organizations face personnel loss exposures. One of the most difficult tasks that a risk management professional faces is to identify and analyze these loss exposures. Personnel losses are difficult to quantify because determining a single employee's value to an organization is often subjective. Just as property has causes of loss such as fire, flood, or human error, personnel are affected by a wide variety of causes of loss, such as death, disability, resignation, layoffs, firing, retirement, kidnap and ransom, war, and terrorism. There are also many workplace hazards that can lead to personnel losses, such as poor work conditions, poor compensation packages, sexual harassment, and workplace violence.

Risk management professionals need to assess the financial consequences of personnel losses. There are a variety of methods that they can use to accomplish this, along with demographic trend data that can assist in forecasting future potential losses.

PERSONNEL EXPOSED TO LOSS

While everyone in an organization has value, some people are more easily replaced than others. A personnel loss exposure was defined in a previous chapter as a condition that presents a potential financial loss caused by the death, disability, retirement, or resignation of an individual that deprives the organization of that individual's special skill or knowledge that cannot readily be replaced. Valuable employees (key employees), who are difficult to replace, present a loss exposure that requires risk management attention. Similarly, groups of employees who perform essential functions, if they are all lost simultaneously, can cause a severe crisis for an organization.

Is That Loss a Personnel, Liability, or Net Income Loss?

Risk management professionals often find that personnel losses overlap with both liability and net income losses. When an accidental loss does occur, risk management professionals usually classify the diminished value of key employee services as a personnel loss. Any compensation owed to that employee through the employers' liability or workers' compensation statutory benefits are classified a liability loss. Finally, any net income that the organization lost because of the accidental loss would be classified as a net income loss.

The most difficult issue for risk management professionals when a cause of loss affects an organization's human assets is to differentiate between a personnel loss and a net income loss. In the insurance field, net income losses are usually defined as the indirect loss of net income because of a cause of loss that results in a direct property loss. For risk management professionals, net income losses can be generated by liability and personnel loss exposures as well as property loss exposures.

For example, if a flood destroyed an organization's production facility and killed some of its senior managers, the organization has suffered a property loss (the production facility), a net income loss (the loss of the income the production facility generated), a personnel loss (the loss of the senior managers' contributions to the organization's value), and a liability loss (any workers' compensation benefits or death benefits the organization must pay). The personnel loss, the loss of the organization's value, often manifests itself as a net income loss. The senior managers' skills contributed to the organization's net income; their loss will reduce the organization's income. The more valuable the employee is to an organization, the larger the net income loss would be without that employee's services, and therefore the larger the personnel loss exposure is.

Identifying key personnel and groups that comprise the personnel loss exposures of an organization is the first step in managing those exposures for a risk management professional. Personnel loss exposures can be comprised of several categories of key personnel including the following:

- Individual employees
- Owners, officers, and managers
- Groups of employees

Individual Employees

The category of individual employees includes employees with unique talents, creativity, or special skills vital to the organization meeting its goals. These employees do not own, manage, or oversee the organization, but they add value to the organization. For example, Jackson Cooper, an engineer working for Danford Oil who specializes in locating and extracting oil from subterranean oil fields, presents a personnel loss exposure to Danford Oil. Engineers skilled in oil location and extraction are in short supply and the skills that Jackson Cooper possesses would not be easy to replace. Similarly, prominent citizens whose leadership contributes to the vitality and success of governmental and civic activities represent personnel loss exposures to their respective organizations. The same can be said for any individual employee whose absence would substantially affect the organization's ability to achieve its goals. In any organization, risk management professionals must identify the key persons whose loss would seriously affect the quantity or the quality of the organization's current or future output.

Owners, Officers, and Managers

Owners, officers, and managers are responsible for making decisions vital to the organization, as well as managing and motivating others. In organizations in which the owner is a key person, that person's activities, health, and managerial competence all influence the organization's value. A sole proprietorship literally ceases to exist as a legal entity when its owner dies or retires. Similarly, partnerships may legally terminate when a partner dies or retires. Even the long-term disability or incompetence of a partner can substantially disrupt a partnership's operations. The same is true in close corporations, in which ownership is typically concentrated in just a few major shareholders, most of whom are also managers. The death or disability of one of these shareholders typically casts doubt over the future control and conduct of the corporation's activities. Therefore, risk management for many private businesses requires careful consideration of how the organization can best survive and remain competently managed even though an owner may die, become disabled, or retire.

Organizations in which ownership and management are separated (for example, many publicly traded companies, public entities, and not-for-profit organizations) have similar exposure to loss of the services of key managers or officers. In addition to the risks of death, disability, and retirement, organizations with separate ownership and management also have to be concerned about officers or managers voluntarily leaving the organization for other employment opportunities.

Groups of Employees

Sometimes a group of employees is critically important to an organization, even if an individual employee in that group is not. An organization may be unable to function without the contributions of an important group. With the exception of layoffs (in which an entire group is usually only laid off if it is considered expendable and not vital to the business), group departure is rare. However, over a short time period, an entire group may leave because of common dissatisfaction (such as poor management), may follow a manager to a new organization, or may be lost because of a catastrophic event, such as a terrorist attack or natural disaster.

Group Loss: An Example

Calder Brokerage (an insurance brokerage organization) relies on teams of employees to service clients. If one individual were to leave the team, the remaining members would be relied on to compensate for that individual's loss without a significant reduction in the service to the client. However, because of the extensive training and research that is required before a brokerage team is fully acquainted with the nuances of its client's operations, if an entire team were to depart (for example, follow the lead broker to a competitor), Calder would have great difficulty in getting another team fully trained to continue the level of service the client expects.

CAUSES OF LOSS

Having identified the personnel exposed to loss, the risk management professional needs to ascertain the causes of loss that affect those personnel. The causes of personnel losses—death, disability, retirement, resignation, layoffs, firing, kidnap, ransom, war, and terrorism—differ considerably in both the media and management attention they attract as well as in their frequency, severity, and predictability. For some of these causes of loss, well-developed data are available to aid the risk management professional in determining the organization's exposure. For example, mortality tables are fairly accurate predictors of death rates. However, for other causes of loss few if any data are available. For example, few data are available on the frequency and severity of kidnapping and ransom demands.

The risk management professional should focus not only on the causes of loss that occur in the workplace, but also those causes of loss that occur outside the workplace. While the causes of loss that occur in the workplace may increase the organization's liability losses, the personnel losses do not vary with the location of loss. For example, the personnel loss arising from the death of a key employee does not vary if the death of that key employee happens at work or away from work. The personnel loss remains the same in both instances.

Personnel Loss Exposures—Causes of Loss

- Death
- Disability
- Resignation, layoffs, and firing
- Retirement
- Kidnap and ransom
- War and terrorism

Death

Unless a disaster occurs, most losses from death are low frequency, with the loss severity (complete, permanent loss of the employee's services) depending on the employee's value to the organization. The predictability of the risk of death, as with all causes of loss, follows the law of large numbers and becomes more predictable as the size of the organization grows. Small and medium-sized organizations have greater difficulty accurately projecting occurrences of death among their employees than large organizations. However, even a large organization will find it difficult to predict the number of employee deaths during a year. An organization with 10,000 employees would normally have only a few deaths per year—a number barely large enough to be statistically reliable for the organization. While the risk of death can vary widely according to the nature of the organization (for example, financial services versus oil exploration and extraction), if the risk management professional is only focused on key employees, then death as a cause of loss will likely be a low frequency event, regardless of the type of organization.

Among the general population in the United States, mortality rates range from 0.96 per 1,000 at age twenty to 17.05 per 1,000 at age sixty-five, with an increasing death rate at each year in between.[1] **Mortality rates** are the death rate per 1,000 population and are usually compiled based on age. Exhibit 9-1 contains the age-specific death rates for the typical age ranges of employees in most organizations. For the most common employment age categories, the probability of death is below 1 percent and is less than one-half of 1 percent for ages 55 and below.

Mortality rate
The death rate per 1,000 population.

The death rates in Exhibit 9-1 vary widely when summarized by geographic location. For example, for the 45–54 age category, death rates were as low as approximately 0.3 percent (3 per 1,000) in Minnesota and as high as approximately 0.9 percent (9 per 1,000) in the District of Columbia. That is, the death rate in the 45–54 age category is three times higher in the District of Columbia than in Minnesota.

EXHIBIT 9-1

Age-Specific Death Rates, United States, 2002

Age Range	Death Rate (per 1,000)
15–24	0.815
25–34	1.036
35–44	2.026
45–54	4.296
55–64	9.538
65–74	23.208

Source: National Center for Health Statistics, "Deaths: Preliminary Data for 2002," *National Vital Statistics Reports*, vol. 52, no. 13, February 11, 2004, p. 7.

Accuracy of Mortality

The statistics provided in Exhibit 9-1 are for the U.S. population as a whole. The group of individuals that make up an organization's employees may not be representative of the general U.S. population. For example, the U.S. population statistics include individuals who are too sick or disabled to work. Therefore, most organizations experience better mortality rates than the U.S. population as a whole. In addition, the type of employee the organization recruits has a large effect on mortality experience. Organizations that employ mainly white collar employees have a better mortality experience than organizations that employ blue collar workers. Also, mortality statistics follow the law of large numbers. The larger the organization, the more accurately the mortality rates of the organization will mirror predicted rates.

Disability

Although death as a cause of loss often attracts more media attention than disability, disability is far more prevalent than death. Therefore, the frequency of personnel losses as a result of disability is much higher than the frequency of personnel losses as a result of death. The severity of personnel losses resulting from disability can be equal to those resulting from death (complete, permanent loss of the employee) if the disability is permanent and total. However, among disabilities, temporary disability is more common than permanent disability, and partial disability is more common than total disability.

Temporary total disability means that for a limited time, the disabled person cannot engage in any productive activity. But because the disability is temporary, the individual is expected to return to work at some point in the near future. For example, some surgeries may cause some employees to be totally disabled for a short time.

Permanent total disability means that the disabled person is unable to engage in any productive work for the rest of his or her life. In addition to severe injuries and illnesses, certain psychiatric conditions, such as schizophrenia, can result in permanent total disability.

Temporary partial disability means that, for a limited time, the disabled person cannot engage in all daily activities, but is only partially prevented from working. A broken finger, for example, might reduce a computer programmer's efficiency at the keyboard, but does not prevent that person from using a computer.

Permanent partial disability means that the disabled person's range of activities is permanently limited, but the person can still perform many types of work. For example, a worker who injured his back lifting boxes in the organization's warehouse may still be able to do office work even though he can no longer do any heavy physical labor.

Organizations can do some things to reduce the frequency of personnel losses resulting from disabilities that occur in the workplace. Workplace injuries are

Temporary total disability
A condition in which, for a limited time, the disabled person cannot engage in any productive activity.

Permanent total disability
A condition in which the disabled person is unable to engage in any productive work for the rest of his or her life.

Temporary partial disability
A condition in which, for a limited time, the disabled person cannot engage in all daily activities, but is only partially prevented from working.

Permanent partial disability
A condition in which the disabled person's range of activities is permanently limited, but the person can still perform many types of work.

often related to companies failing to take adequate safety measures. Examples might include the following:

- Failing to provide protective equipment, such as goggles and gloves, to workers handling caustic materials
- Allowing workers to lift heavy objects without using appropriate lifting techniques or mechanical assistance
- Not providing workers with an ergonomic workspace
- Not allowing workers performing physical labor to take periodic breaks
- Operating an assembly process too quickly, thereby encouraging workers to take chances assembling products and increasing their exposure to potential injury

Rates of workplace injury vary greatly by industry. As expected, more dangerous occupations have higher rates of injuries. In 2002, the average percentage of nonfatal workplace injuries and illnesses for all types of private (nongovernment) workers in the U.S. was 5.3 percent. The rate for manufacturing workers was 7.2 percent (with workers employed in sawmills suffering a higher injury rate of 10.8 percent). By contrast, the injury rate for workers in finance, insurance, and real estate averaged only 1.7 percent. Exhibit 9-2 shows nonfatal workplace injury and illness rates for major industry types.

EXHIBIT 9-2

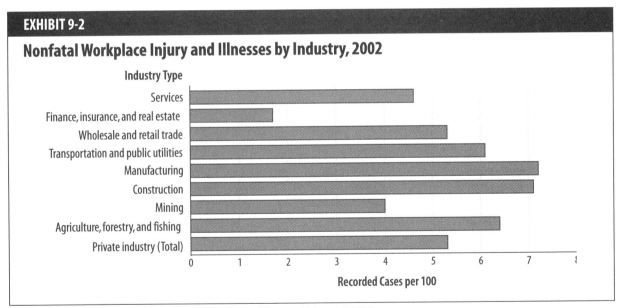

Nonfatal Workplace Injury and Illnesses by Industry, 2002

Adapted from data at www.bls.gov/iif/oshwc/osh/ostb1244.pdf (accessed February 3, 2005).

An unsafe workplace is only one cause of employee disability. Organizations can do little outside the workplace to limit personnel losses caused by disability. In contrast to the rates of workplace injury and illness, the U.S. Census Bureau (2000 U.S. Census) reports that disabilities, regardless of cause, affect one in five Americans and that the rates vary widely with age, gender, racial and ethnic group, and income level. As with many causes of loss, the availability and accuracy of data available regarding disability vary widely. Exhibit 9-3 contains types of disability reported from the 2000 U. S. Census for men and women in the typical working ages of 16–64. This exhibit shows that approximately 10 percent of the population in the 16–64 age range indicated having some type of disability in one of the three categories reported—physical, mental, or sensory. One problem with the data is that the causes of the disabilities are not reported. This lack of detail makes it difficult for the risk management professional to determine what percentage of the organization's workforce is likely to become disabled, and by what cause of loss, over any meaningful time period. The lack of information available to risk management professionals increases the difficulty in accurately analyzing an organization's personnel losses resulting from the disability cause of loss.

EXHIBIT 9-3

Data on Disabilities for the Civilian Noninstitutionalized Population 16–64 Years Old

Sex and Disability Status	Number	Percentage of Population
Both Sexes—Sensory, physical, or mental disability	17,300,050	9.7%
Men—Sensory, physical, or mental disability	8,710,290	9.9% of males
Women—Sensory, physical, or mental disability	8,589,760	9.4% of females

Source: U.S. Census Bureau, Census 2000 PHC-T-32, *Disability Status of the Civilian Noninstitutionalized Population by Sex and Selected Characteristics for the United States and Puerto Rico: 2000*, Table 1.

Resignation, Layoffs, and Firing

Employees may leave for a number of reasons—voluntary (the employee chooses to leave their job) and involuntary (the employee is forced to leave). The Bureau of Labor Statistics (BLS) refers to employees leaving an organization as "employee separations" and compiles statistics in three different categories: voluntary, involuntary, and other (which includes death and disability).

While involuntary employee separations may expose the organization to additional liability loss exposures (such as wrongful termination), generally they are not considered a personnel loss because the organization has determined that it is better off without that employee. For example, a layoff results in the departure of a group of employees. If the layoff occurs because an organization is having financial troubles and cannot afford to keep some employees, even though they add value to the organization, then it could be considered a personnel loss and the loss may be severe. However, if the layoff is the result of a change in the organization's goals—meaning the employees are no longer needed for the organization to operate efficiently—their departure will have minimal effect. The main consequence of the layoff is the immediate financial cost to the organization, in the form of severance pay and the possible rise in its unemployment compensation premiums, neither of which is a personnel loss.

Similar to layoffs, many risk management professionals consider personnel losses resulting from terminations to be a low frequency event. Workers are typically terminated for cause, that is, they are not performing their jobs effectively or they behave in an unacceptable manner. Usually, the organization made a rational decision about the termination and has considered all of the costs and benefits of retaining that employee.

Exhibit 9-4 contains both the voluntary and involuntary annual employee separations in 2003–2004 for a variety of industries. For private industry in the U.S., most employee separations in 2003–2004 were voluntary. The major exception was construction, in which involuntary separations far outpaced voluntary departures.

Resignation (voluntary separation) is an expected part of doing business. The frequency of resignations depends on the type of industry. Some organizations, such as fast food restaurants or construction companies, can expect very high turnover rates, while other industries, such as accounting or government, can expect a low turnover rate. When the turnover frequency increases, this may signify personnel problems that need to be addressed to prevent additional losses. The severity of a resignation depends on who is resigning. If a key person leaves or if a group of employees sharing a similar function departs simultaneously, the severity of personnel losses may be high. In these cases the severity of the potential personnel loss is the same as if the employee were to die.

Exhibit 9-4 shows that voluntary separation rates vary widely by industry. According to the BLS figures, the voluntary separation rates between 2003 and 2004 ranged from 6.8 percent for government employees to 31.9 percent for retailers. The average for all of the U.S. was over 20 percent. This means that the average organization can expect to lose one in five workers every year because of employees voluntarily leaving the organization. Depending on what percentage of the key employees voluntarily separate from the organization, organizations may face substantial personnel losses on a regular basis.

Retirement

While death and voluntary resignation often occur suddenly, retirement is usually planned. Therefore, most personnel losses resulting from retirement can be handled with proper planning from management. With plenty of advance notice, an organization can prepare for the retirement of even key personnel by locating and training replacements. However, as with resignation or death, when a key person decides to retire suddenly, the losses can be severe.

EXHIBIT 9-4

Employee Separations in the United States, 2003–2004

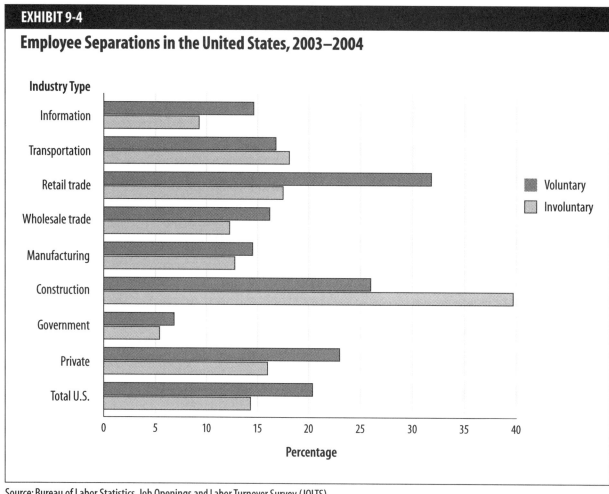

Source: Bureau of Labor Statistics, Job Openings and Labor Turnover Survey (JOLTS).

It is difficult to find reliable statistics about early retirement trends in the U.S. Exhibit 9-5 contains the U.S. labor force participation rates for 2004 in three age categories. The exhibit indicates that approximately 80 percent of adults age 45–54 participate in the workforce, with approximately 60 percent of those age 55–64 working and only about 15 percent of those age 65 and older still participating in the workforce. The 20 percentage point drop in participation rates from the 45–54 age category to the 55–64 age category is likely the result of a variety of factors, including early retirements. Removing economic and demographic factors from this type of aggregate data is often difficult.

Another source of uncertainty about personnel losses resulting from retirement concerns the time at which an employee ceases to be productive. Some employees retire while they are still productive, whereas some remain after their skills deteriorate. While progressive deterioration of aging employees' skills is a concern, a more significant concern may be losing the institutional knowledge and skills of an aging workforce that may be hard to replace because of the lack of younger workers available.

EXHIBIT 9-5

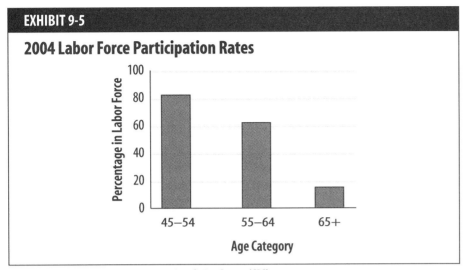

2004 Labor Force Participation Rates

Source: Bureau of Labor Statistics, Current Population Survey (CPS).

Kidnap and Ransom

Kidnap and ransom can be a significant cause of loss for employers with operations outside the U.S. Some kidnappings are politically motivated as a result of political unrest, but employers are more likely to face financially motivated kidnappings, or kidnappings for ransom.

Whether a person is kidnapped for political reasons or for money, kidnapping is still a fairly low frequency event that tends to be localized in some high-risk locations. However, its high severity means that risk management professionals in organizations operating internationally cannot afford to overlook the kidnapping and ransom risk. As with some other causes of loss, reliable data on the frequency and severity of the kidnapping cause of loss are generally unavailable. Experts in security that specialize in the area of kidnap and ransom have rough estimates of frequency for the highest risk locations that range from 10,000 to 20,000 kidnappings per year. However, these experts do not publish such data because it may encourage others to kidnap. High-risk locations include Colombia, Mexico, Argentina, Brazil, Venezuela, the former Soviet Union, and the Philippines.[2]

Kidnappers often target mid-level executives and other important personnel who can be ransomed. In addition, the kidnap victims can be injured or killed during the kidnapping. The most obvious loss that results is the absence of a key employee. In this sense, kidnapping losses are similar to death and disability losses. As noted earlier, their severity depends on the importance of the employee who is lost and how easily he or she can be temporarily or permanently replaced. The uncertain nature of kidnapping—not knowing how long an employee may be unavailable, or even whether he or she will survive—makes it particularly difficult to manage the personnel loss. Under such circumstances, replacing a person may not be considered appropriate until after the situation is resolved.

> ### Kidnapping: Who Is at Risk?
>
> For most organizations, the CEO or other top managers are not located in high risk areas. When they do travel to those areas, they usually have extensive security measures in place to prevent kidnappings from occurring. Therefore, key employees who are most at risk are the experts who are located in the high-risk areas and mid-level managers who are more likely to travel to those areas without the level of security afforded upper management.

War and Terrorism

The war and terrorism causes of loss are often associated with the broader term political risk. Political risk usually refers to the risks that an international organization assumes when operating in a foreign country. This risk could manifest itself in any of the following ways:

- A war in the foreign country that causes significant losses (property, liability, personnel, or net income) to the organization
- An attack on the organization as a political statement
- An expropriation or nationalization of the organization's assets
- A terrorist attack of opportunity (organization is the easiest target)

Some organizations produce political and economic risk maps that attempt to quantify the political and economic risks that a country presents to organizations that operate there.

A significant example of catastrophic personnel loss caused by terrorism is the September 11, 2001, attack on the World Trade Center. With thousands of employees killed, some organizations suffered significant personnel losses. For example, Cantor Fitzgerald, an international financial services provider, lost 658 out of 1,000 people at that location. This event alerted organizations with and without international operations that they are potential terrorist targets in the U.S. as well as internationally.

Consequently, organizations should assess possible future terrorist attacks by evaluating either the nature of the organization, such as a defense contractor, or the location of the organization in a target property, such as the Sears Tower or Empire State Building.

WORKPLACE HAZARDS

An organization may have only limited control over the personnel exposed to loss and the causes of loss to which those personnel are exposed. The area in which organizations can exert the most control over personnel loss exposures is in the workplace. The risk management professional can work to minimize some of the workplace hazards that lead to personnel losses. Poor work conditions, poor compensation packages, sexual harassment, and workplace violence are hazards that can increase the frequency or severity of personnel losses. Any of these workplace hazards may lead employees to voluntarily separate from the organization; some could also lead to death and disability; and some could lead to premature retirement.

Poor Work Conditions

Narrowly defined, "work conditions" typically refers to the physical environment that an organization provides to its employees to help them meet the organization's goals. Physical work conditions are regulated by the Occupational Safety and Health Administration (OSHA) to provide a minimum level of safety and comfort for employees. For example, employers must provide employees with a safe work environment that meets minimum requirements of air quality. Work conditions can also be more broadly defined to include both the physical and psychological aspects of the employer-employee relationship. Therefore, work conditions can include the factors listed in Exhibit 9-6.

EXHIBIT 9-6

Work Conditions

Factor	Concern
OSHA standards	Does the facility meet minimum health and safety standards?
Atmosphere	Does the organization provide a professional atmosphere for employees to fulfill their duties?
Challenging projects	Does the organization provide employees with challenges in the workplace that are appropriate to the employee's skills?
Responsibility level	Does the organization provide employees with the appropriate level of responsibility for the employee's position and skills?
Appearance	Does the organization require that employees dress appropriately for safety?
Opportunity for advancement	Does the organization provide deserving employees the opportunity for advancement?
Equipment	Does the organization provide employees with safe, functioning equipment necessary for the employees to fulfill their duties?
Confidentiality	Does the organization respect the privacy rights of their employees regarding personal matters?
Behavior guidelines	Does the organization provide employees with appropriate guidelines for behavior in the workplace?
Organizational policies	Does the organization provide employees with policies to aid in employee safety and comfort?

Poor Compensation Packages

One aspect of work conditions that is beyond the scope of traditional risk management and that falls under the broader scope of enterprise risk management is employee compensation packages. Attracting and retaining quality employees is directly related in part to the compensation package that an organization is able to offer. Compensation packages include salary and employee benefits. Employee benefits may include health insurance coverage, retirement and pension plans, disability insurance coverage, educational reimbursement, vacation time, fitness facilities, elder and child care services, vision and dental coverage, and stock options. Employee compensation has to meet various state and federal minimums and varies widely by industry and geographic region. Compensation packages should be fair and competitive to help minimize personnel losses.

Sexual Harassment

Sexual harassment affects both women and men and includes any type of unwelcome conduct at work related to an employee's sex that creates a hostile work environment—ranging from offensive humor to sexual assault. Sexual harassment includes any sexual quid pro quo (this for that) in which an employee's promotion, salary, job security, and so on are dependent on sexual favors. In addition, sexual harassment occurs whenever workers experience discrimination because they reject an unwelcome sexual advance, request for sexual favors, or other verbal or physical conduct of a sexual nature.

Sexual harassment is a form of sexual discrimination and is prohibited by Title VII of the Civil Rights Act of 1964. The Civil Rights Act of 1991 ("the 1991 Act") changed the burden of proof regarding sexual harassment. Before the 1991 Act, an employee would have to suffer economic loss to collect any compensation under a sexual harassment complaint. Since the 1991 Act, an employee only needs to show a hostile work environment to collect compensatory and/or punitive damages.

The 1991 Clarence Thomas U.S. Supreme Court nomination hearings brought sexual harassment in the workplace to the media forefront with the testimony of Anita Hill. Anita Hill, a former aide to Clarence Thomas at the Department of Education and the Equal Employment Opportunity Commission (EEOC), and at the time a law professor, testified during the Senate confirmation hearings that she had been sexually harassed by Clarence Thomas. The media attention, along with the 1991 Act, led to an explosion in sexual harassment complaints to the EEOC during the 1990s (37,000 in the 1990s versus 5,800 in the 1980s). As well as the federal statute, a number of states have introduced state laws forbidding sexual harassment. Employers may be held vicariously liable for any sexual harassment or discrimination on the part of their employees.

Exhibit 9-7 shows the number of sexual harassment complaints by year from 1992 through 2003. In 2002, 14,396 charges of sexual harassment were filed with the EEOC or local Fair Employment Practices Agencies (FEPA), nearly 15 percent of which were filed by males. Exhibit 9-7 shows that the number of sexual harassment complaints has been declining since 2000. While many more cases are thought to occur than are filed with the EEOC, employers are most concerned with incidents of sexual harassment that are reported, because they cause direct losses. However, even unreported cases can result in indirect losses in the form of lower morale, reduced productivity, increased sick leave, and higher rates of resignation.

EXHIBIT 9-7

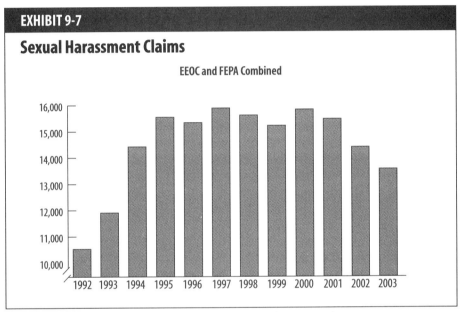

Sexual Harassment Claims

EEOC and FEPA Combined

Adapted from data at www.eeoc.gov/stats/harass.html (accessed February 4, 2005).

Workplace Violence

Another type of workplace hazard is workplace violence. Workplace violence includes any type of violence or threat of violence that occurs in the work environment, including physical and verbal assaults, physical and verbal threats, coercion, intimidation, and all forms of harassment. The term "workplace violence" may evoke images of a disgruntled employee who brings a gun to work and shoots his fellow workers. However, this extreme example is only part of what constitutes workplace violence. In fact not all workplace violence incidences occur at the workplace. It is possible that confrontations, stalking, or harassment that occurs outside the workplace may be considered workplace violence if they are related to employment (for example, if they involve a co-worker, customer, or supplier). Employers are required to provide a safe working environment. This includes protecting employees from both physical violence and mental harm caused by other employees, customers, and other people they come in contact with.

Workplace homicide is a low frequency event—according to the BLS Census of Fatal Occupational Injuries, 639 workplace homicides occurred in 2001. Nonetheless, as shown in Exhibit 9-8, the category of assaults and violence (including homicide) was the third-leading cause of work-related deaths in 2002. However, as a percentage of workplace deaths, homicide has been declining since the mid 1990s. As shown in Exhibit 9-9, between 1993 and 1999 homicide accounted for only 0.1 percent of workplace violence on average. The most common type of workplace violence is simple assault. Workplace violence, narrowly defined as a violent crime, happens to approximately 1.25 percent of the U.S. workforce annually.[3] Obviously, a broader definition of workplace violence, one that included violent threats for example, would have a substantially higher rate of occurrence.

A violent workplace may cause employees to be fearful or depressed, resulting in reduced productivity and increased rates of disability and resignation. Employees who handle money or deal directly with the public are particularly vulnerable to violence during their workday, especially when they work in small groups or late at night. If an employee is injured or harassed by a customer or hurt during the course of a crime, the organization may be liable for failing to provide a safe working environment.

EXHIBIT 9-8

2002 Causes of Workplace Deaths

Cause	Number	Percentage of Total
Transportation	2,381	43%
Contact with objects (equipment)	873	16%
Assaults and violence (includes homicide)	840	15%
Falls	714	13%
Fires and explosion	165	3%

Source: U.S. Department of Labor, Bureau of Labor Statistics, Census of Fatal Occupational Injuries.

EXHIBIT 9-9

Average Annual Number, Rate, and Percentage of Workplace Victimization by Type of Crime, 1993-1999

Category	Average Annual Workplace Victimization	Rate per 1,000 Persons in the Workforce	Percentage of Workplace Victimization
All violent crime	1,744,300	12.50	100.0%
Homicide	900	0.01	0.1%
Rape/sexual assault	36,500	0.30	2.1%
Robbery	70,100	0.50	4.0%
Aggravated assault	325,000	2.30	18.6%

Source: U.S. Department of Justice, Federal Bureau of Investigation, *Workplace Violence: Issues in Response* (Virginia: Critical Incident Response Group, National Center for the Analysis of Violent Crime, FBI Academy, Quantico, 2004).

FINANCIAL CONSEQUENCES OF PERSONNEL LOSSES

Because employees are assets of an organization, the financial effect of the loss of these assets (personnel losses) on an organization is similar to the effect of property and liability losses in that they reduce the value of the organization. The major difference is that personnel losses typically manifest themselves as net income losses. The following are financial consequences of personnel losses:

- Loss of the value the employee contributed to the organization (in cases in which a key person is lost this may be severe, with the organization's value lowered at least for the short term)
- Replacement costs (recruitment, interviewing, and training of replacement personnel)
- Losses to the organization's value caused by negative publicity
- Losses caused by low morale such as reduced productivity or increased illness

In addition, the following costs may also be associated with a personnel loss, but are typically viewed as liability losses:

- Compensation costs (for death or injury)
- Higher costs for insurance premiums (including workers' compensation, unemployment, and liability insurance) resulting from increased claims
- Fines paid for violations of various employment laws
- Amounts paid in settlement of lawsuits brought by employees
- Defense costs

Temporary Versus Permanent Losses

The financial consequences of the loss of a key person depends on whether that person is temporarily or permanently lost to the organization. In some ways, the temporary loss of an employee is more difficult to manage than a permanent loss because of the uncertainty associated with the length of the employee's absence.

Temporary Loss of an Individual

To assess the financial consequences of the temporary loss of an individual, the risk management professional needs to determine the following:

- The length of time the key person will be absent and whether a replacement can be found. For a short-term absence, it may not be cost-effective to replace the employee. In such cases, the work may be allocated among existing employees or potentially outsourced.
- The ease with which the employee can be temporarily replaced. Some employees are not directly replaceable and their loss may require a shift in organizational operations. In that case, someone inside the organization may need to assume the position or someone new may need to be recruited.

- The cost to find and train a suitable replacement, if one is available.
- The length of time it will take to bring the replacement up to the predecessor's competence level.
- The cost to the organization, in extra expenses and reduced revenues, of the replacement's inefficiency and mistakes until the replacement reaches the level of competence of the predecessor.
- The amount that must be added to the organization's total payroll (including salary and employee benefits) to compensate the replacement (after allowing for any adjustment in compensation paid to the "temporarily lost" employee and any current salaries and benefits that the organization may already be paying the replacement if the replacement comes from within the organization).
- The costs of reinstating the regular employee and how to deal equitably with that temporary replacement employee when the regular employee returns to work.

Permanent Loss of an Individual

The permanent loss of a key person may require major changes in an organization's operating procedures. Evaluating the severity of the permanent loss requires determining much of the same preceding information about a temporary loss, but with some modifications as well as some additional information. To determine the financial consequences of this personnel loss the risk management professional will need to determine the following:

- Whether the organization's operations will need to be altered to accommodate the loss. For example, will the organization need to abandon any special projects requiring the lost individual's talents or skills?
- Whether a successor is readily available within or external to the organization and how much recruiting may cost.
- The amount of training the replacement will require to reach the competence level of the predecessor.
- How much must be added to the organization's total payroll (including salary and employee benefits) to compensate the replacement (after subtracting the salary and benefits paid the predecessor.)

Temporary or Permanent Loss of a Group

When an organization suffers the loss of a group, either simultaneously or within a short time period, the organization's concerns are essentially the same as when individuals are lost. With groups as with individuals, the risk management professional should distinguish between temporary and permanent personnel losses.

If the members of the departing group shared a task or an interest, their departure might have a greater financial effect on the organization than if the same number of individuals, randomly selected, left the organization.

For example, if a group of employees all working under the same manager followed the manager to a new organization, the original organization could suffer a severe loss. Furthermore, a trend of voluntary employee separation from a single unit could be a sign of other problems that may exist in that unit, such as managerial issues.

Unique Consequences by Cause of Loss

While the major financial consequences of personnel losses do not vary by cause of loss, there are some unique costs that are associated with each cause of loss. The financial consequences will vary with the employee's position. However, the financial consequences common to all causes of loss include the following:

- Replacement costs, which will include recruiting, interviewing, and training
- Need for a succession plan
- Negative publicity
- Reduced productivity

In addition to the common financial consequences, the cause of loss will also determine whether the personnel losses are temporary or permanent, partial or complete, or whether the organization had some warning that a personnel loss was imminent. Exhibit 9-10 highlights some of the differences in the financial consequences by cause of loss.

METHODS OF ASSESSING PERSONNEL LOSS EXPOSURES

As with property and liability loss exposures, risk management professionals can use a variety of methods to identify and analyze personnel loss exposures. Some of these methods involve information that is unique and proprietary to the organization; others use information that is more standardized and publicly available. Each of the methods described below can be useful in helping to identify and analyze the human assets that are exposed to loss, the causes of loss, or the financial consequences of the loss to the organization.

Methods of Identifying Personnel Loss Exposures

- Risk assessment questionnaires
- Loss histories
- Other records and documents
- Flowcharts and organizational charts
- Personal inspections
- Expertise within and beyond the organization

EXHIBIT 9-10

Unique Financial Consequences of Personnel Losses by Cause of Loss

Cause of Loss	Unique Financial Consequences
Death	Infrequent, permanent, complete loss with no warning.
	Often a shock to other employees within the organization. May have a significant effect on the performance of co-workers, reducing productivity. Individuals often need an adjustment period or period of mourning before being able to fully function. This effect may be more significant if the death occurred in the workplace because the environment may serve as a constant reminder of the event.
Disability	Frequent, temporary or permanent, partial or complete, no warning. Increased expenditures to accommodate disabled employees.
Employee separation—voluntary	Frequent, permanent, complete, may be warning.
	Possibility of the employee going to work for a competitor and attracting some of the organization's current customers to the new organization. This can impose an additional cost on the organization in the form of lost market share.
Retirement	Will become more frequent, permanent, complete, likely will have a warning.
	Personnel loss can be minimized by keeping the retired employee on as a consultant to help smooth the transition for his or her replacement. This can actually reduce the financial loss associated with retirement.
Kidnap and ransom	Infrequent, temporary or permanent, complete, no warning.
	Negative effect on recruitment and retention. Personnel fear traveling to the same dangerous region and require higher compensation. Uncertainty regarding replacement if outcome of kidnapping is not known.
War and terrorism	Infrequent, temporary or permanent, complete, no warning.
	Negative effect on recruitment and retention. Personnel fear traveling to the same dangerous region and require higher compensation.
Workplace hazards	Uncertain frequency, temporary or permanent, partial or complete, uncertain warning.
	Can lead to lower productivity, higher rates of illness and disability, and higher than normal rates of departure.

Risk Assessment Questionnaires

Risk assessment questionnaires are useful in identifying personnel loss exposures because they usually include extensive lists of standardized questions that are designed to aid risk management professionals in developing a better understanding of the organization's loss exposures. Standardization is a strength because the questions are universally relevant. But standardization is also a weakness in that no standardized questionnaire can be expected to uncover all the loss exposures characteristic of a given industry, let alone those unique to a given organization.

Exhibit 9-11 contains a sample question from the International Risk Management Institute (IRMI) questionnaire on personnel and workers' compensation loss exposures. This question is specifically designed to help the risk management professional determine the organization's exposure to personnel losses involving the loss of a group of employees.

EXHIBIT 9-11

Sample Question from IRMI's Exposure Survey Questionnaire

PERSONNEL AND WORKERS COMPENSATION EXPOSURES

17. a. Is there a potential for multiple injuries, illness, death, or disability of employees from:

Event	Max. No. Employees Exposed	Estimate Likelihood			
		Nil	Slight	Mod.	High
Corp. Owned Aircraft Disaster					
Commercial Aircraft Disaster					
Car or Van Pool Accidents					
Rail Travel Disaster					
Other Travel Disasters					
Epidemic					
Sabotage/Assassination					
Exposure to Asbestos, Silicon, Other Harmful Agents					
Industrial Accident (e.g., explosion, building collapse, pollution release, etc.)					

Source: International Risk Management Institute, Inc., *Exposure Survey Questionnaire* (International Risk Management Institute, Inc., 1998), Chapter 15.

Loss Histories

Loss histories are a source of internal information about all of the causes of personnel losses previously discussed. This information can be used to evaluate organization mortality or disability rates as well as retirement trends and voluntary and involuntary employee separation histories. However, although most organizations keep detailed records about death and disability that are work-related, they may not have records indicating death and disability that have occurred outside the workplace. Human resources would be a good source of information about voluntary and involuntary employee separation and retirement trends, provided the data are maintained.

Other Records and Documents

Many of the personnel losses an organization may experience are somewhat projectable by using reliable and widely available public data. These public records help risk managers project future losses. Potential sources of these records include the U.S. Census Bureau, the National Center for Health Statistics, and the BLS.

In the insurance industry, two widely available sources of information are mortality and morbidity tables. Regarding death, an organization should expect its mortality experience to adhere fairly closely to the applicable mortality table. This will be a function of the organization's size, as the law of large numbers would imply. The larger the organization, the closer its mortality rates will be to the applicable mortality table. This holds true as long as the organization does not suffer from adverse selection. That is, as long as the employees of the organization represent a true sample of the general population. An organization may suffer from adverse selection if, for example, the organization offers especially generous life insurance benefits. In this case, potential employees who have a higher risk of dying may find the job offer more beneficial than an average individual. Therefore, the organization would have a higher mortality rate than the standard population. Assuming no adverse selection, the organization should be able to project mortality rates with some accuracy.

Morbidity tables provide data regarding health. Various injury statistics are also available. Previously discussed sources of information on voluntary and involuntary employee separation are available from the BLS. Unfortunately, little publicly available data sources are available on retirement trends.

Flowcharts and Organizational Charts

Flowcharts and organizational charts provide two methods that help risk management professionals identify key persons and key points in an organization's processes. The first method involves identifying key personnel (and, therefore, personnel loss exposures) and is analogous to the flowchart method of analyzing property or net income loss exposures in that it examines how each person's efforts contribute to the organization. This method focuses on how the absence of each person would affect the organization's activities. It is most useful in identifying the persons other than owners, officers, and managers who are essential to the organization. The flowchart method identifies employees in critical junctions in an organization's activities. Each function or operating division should be charted, analyzed, and examined to determine how heavily it relies on key persons at various operational steps. The risk management professional has to identify persons whose loss would seriously affect the quantity or the quality of the organization's output, in the present or in the future.

The second method of identifying personnel loss exposures involves studying organizational charts and the job descriptions that accompany the positions in order to identify the most important positions. This method highlights key persons who (1) exercise unique talents, creativity, or special skills; (2) make decisions vital to the organization; or (3) manage and motivate the acts of others. This approach is comparable to identifying property loss exposures by starting with a list of properties. Such a list is most appropriate for identifying key owners, officers, and managers.

However, merely appearing on an organizational chart does not automatically make an individual valuable or difficult to replace. Identifying these key personnel involves answering the following two questions:

1. What would the organization do if this person suddenly were not available?
2. If this person were unavailable, could the organization achieve its fundamental goals?

The first question helps determine whether, how, and when the key person would be replaced. To manage the risk, a succession policy should be in place. The second question points out what loss of efficiency or profits, if any, would result from the loss of the key person. A risk management professional should consider the following additional questions:

- Are all personnel located in the same facility? Would it be safer to spread out employees over different locations, or will the organization suffer efficiency losses by doing so?

- Are data backed up in an off-site facility? If employees with specialized knowledge were lost, would replacement personnel be able to use these data to recreate their work?

- What would be the effect on the organization if this employee was unavailable for any significant period of time?

Personal Inspections

A personal inspection is a valuable method to help determine the extent of workplace hazards. Risk management professionals can use personal inspections to identify workplace hazards that may lead to the death, disability, or voluntary separation of employees who were not identified by the other methods of assessing personnel loss exposures. Personal inspections also provide the risk management professional with the opportunity to discuss with employees any other issues that may affect employee performance or morale.

Expertise Within and Beyond the Organization

Expertise available within the organization may include human resources, system safety engineers, or senior managers. Interviews with these employees can help the risk management professional gather information about workplace hazards as well as information about employee productivity and morale. An excellent source of information about the organization is former employees. Some organizations use exit interviews to aid in identifying problem areas within the organization. Employees who are leaving the organization often speak more freely than current employees because they do not fear reprisal for any negative comments they may make.

Similar to property and liability loss exposure analysis, the risk management professional always has the option of looking beyond the organization for expertise regarding personnel loss exposures. There are organizations with expertise in personnel loss exposures that specialize in workplace safety and security to help minimize the workplace hazards. There are also outside experts in employee compensation who can aid an organization in building compensation packages that attract and retain quality employees.

TRENDS AFFECTING PERSONNEL LOSS EXPOSURES

Forecasting personnel losses requires attention to demographic trends that affect employee morbidity, mortality, retirement, or employee separations. One of the most significant demographic trends in the U.S. is the aging of the population. Organizations need to be aware of how the demographic changes during the next quarter century are going to affect their personnel needs. Exhibits 9-12 through 9-14 depict the effect of the baby boom generation on U.S. demographics. Comparing these three exhibits, the U.S. population is evolving from a pyramid shape, with a large number of younger citizens supporting a smaller number of older citizens, to a rectangular shape, in which the younger and older citizens are more equally weighted. This type of demographic shift has significant implications for social programs as well as on the labor market for private organizations.

Organizations may find that labor costs are going to rise, as more experienced employees demand higher salaries. As mentioned previously, organizations may have difficulty replacing the intellectual capital lost when older workers retire if there is not a sufficient supply of labor to replace them. Organizations that require younger employees may find it more difficult to recruit and retain quality employees. Furthermore, the retirement cause of loss previously discussed may become a much larger issue over the next twenty-five years.

EXHIBIT 9-12

U.S. Population, 1960

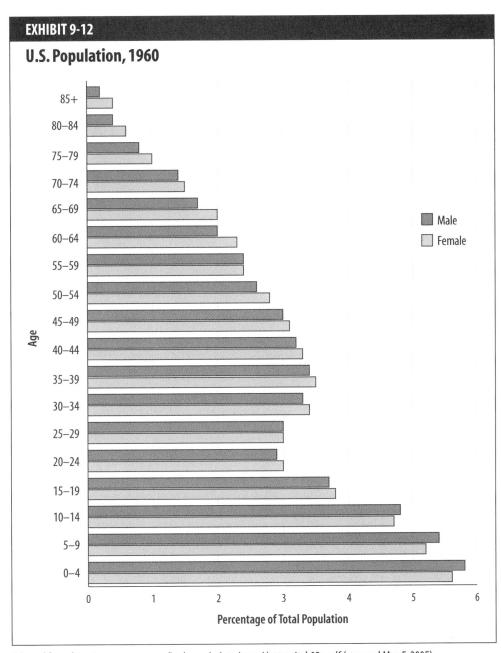

Adapted from data at www.census.gov/ipc/www/usinterimproj/natprojtab02a.pdf (accessed May 5, 2005).

Some other, less publicized, trends may also affect an organization's personnel loss exposures. These include trends in population migration and in education. For example, some organizations in colder climates may find that they are suffering more personnel losses resulting from early retirement because their older employees prefer to live in a warmer climate. Alternatively, some organizations may find that they have been able to retain employees because they have helped them obtain graduate degrees. Exhibit 9-15 contains a list of some other trends affecting personnel loss exposures.

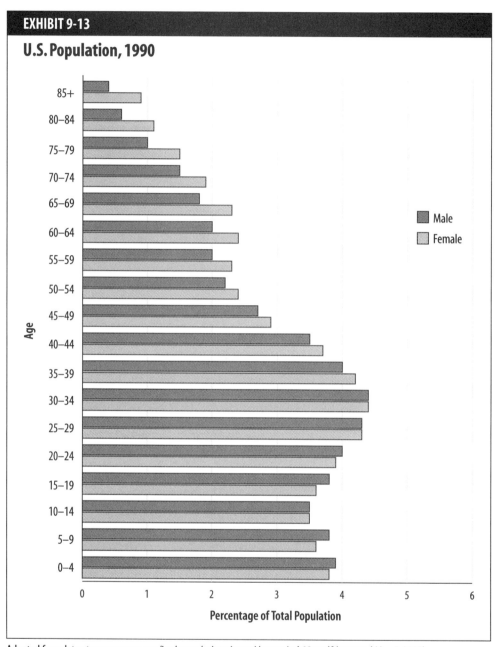

EXHIBIT 9-13

U.S. Population, 1990

Adapted from data at www.census.gov/ipc/www/usinterimproj/natprojtab02a.pdf (accessed May 5, 2005).

EXHIBIT 9-14

U.S. Projected Population, 2020

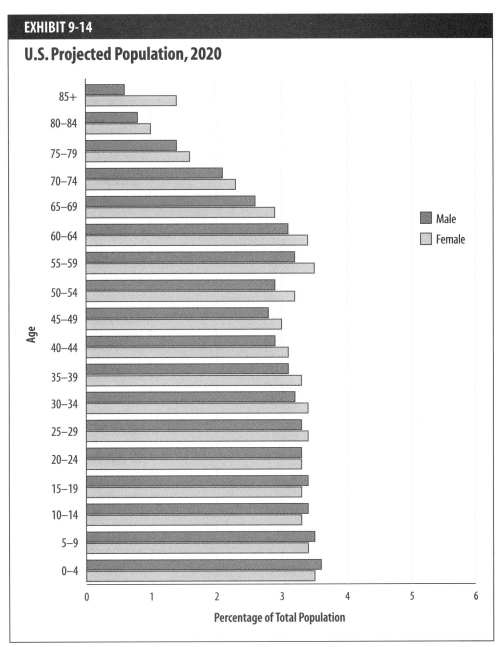

Adapted from data at www.census.gov/ipc/www/usinterimproj/natprojtab02a.pdf (accessed May 5, 2005).

EXHIBIT 9-15

Trends Affecting Personnel Loss Exposures

Trend	Implications
Reduction in the number of jobs that are overtly physically demanding	Reduction in occupations that often produce disabilities related to long-term stress, repetitive motions, or other degenerative forces.
Increase in cumulative injuries to the back, the weakest portion of the human skeleton in relation to the weight it must bear	Increase in lost work time, largely because of inadequate analysis of the back stress inherent in many job duties and daily living conditions and also failure to design furniture and other equipment suitable for these tasks. Back injuries cause employees to lose more work time than all other causes combined.
Increase in alcohol and drug abuse	Abusers of alcohol and drugs have high injury rates, both at and away from work. Increase in monitoring costs for employers who may require random testing. Increase in health insurance costs if plans cover the cost of alcohol and drug treatment.
Increase in obesity and its related conditions (heart disease, diabetes, high blood pressure)	Increase in lost productivity and high levels of health insurance and workers' compensation claims. For this reason, many organizations encourage their employees to adopt a healthy lifestyle by providing information about the benefits of a balanced diet and exercise. Organizations may also provide free gym memberships or on-site exercise facilities and diet programs.

SUMMARY

Organizations face personnel loss exposures from a variety of causes of loss, ranging from the death of a key employee to the kidnap and ransom of international employees. The financial consequences of personnel losses may be severe. Therefore, recognizing and managing personnel loss exposures is an essential component of any organization's risk management program.

The first step in this process is identifying the personnel exposed to loss. Some personnel are more essential than others, as are certain groups within an organization. Organizations should identify key individual personnel; owners, officers, and managers of the organization; and key groups of employees as well as establish procedures for replacing employees so that the organization can continue to function.

Once the personnel loss exposures have been identified, the risk management professional needs to focus on the causes of loss in order to assess the frequency and severity of the personnel losses. These causes of loss include death, disability, resignation, layoffs, firing, retirement, kidnap and ransom, war and terrorism, and workplace hazards. For some of these causes of loss (such as death) there are well-developed data available to aid risk management professionals in determining their organizations' loss exposures. However, for other causes of loss (such as kidnap and ransom) there are few, if any, data available. As the organization's exposure to personnel loss does not vary with the location, it is important for the risk management professional to focus on not only the causes of loss that occur in the workplace, but also those causes of loss that occur outside the workplace. While the causes of loss that occur in the workplace may increase the organization's liability losses, the personnel losses are the same regardless of the location of loss.

Once the causes of loss have been identified, the risk management professional can analyze the financial consequences of personnel losses. Some losses are permanent (such as death, retirement, or permanent disability) while others are only temporary. The consequence of a personnel loss depends both on the cause and the expected duration of the loss. Consequences of personnel loss include the loss of the value the employee contributed to the organization, the costs of replacing the employee (recruitment and training), increased insurance premiums (workers' compensation, unemployment, and liability insurance), negative publicity, and reduced productivity.

Risk management professionals have a variety of methods available to them to aid in identifying and analyzing personnel loss exposures. They include risk assessment questionnaires, loss histories, other records and documents, flow-charts and organizational charts, personal inspections, and expertise within and beyond the organization. Finally, the risk management professional needs to remain current on any trends (such as demographics) that may affect the organization's personnel loss exposures.

This chapter described assessing personnel loss exposures. The next chapter discusses assessing net income loss exposures.

CHAPTER NOTES

1. U.S. Census Bureau, *Statistical Abstract of the United States* (Washington, D.C.: U.S. Census Bureau, 1999), p. 94.

2. www.aon.com/risk_management/crisis_management/kidnap_ransom_protection. jsp (accessed February 3, 2005).

3. U.S. Department of Justice, Federal Bureau of Investigation, *Workplace Violence: Issues in Response* (Virginia: Critical Incident Response Group, National Center for the Analysis of Violent Crime, FBI Academy, Quantico, 2004), p. 12.

Chapter 10

Direct Your Learning

Assessing Net Income Loss Exposures

After learning the content of this chapter and completing the corresponding course guide assignment, you should be able to:

- Explain how business risk and hazard risk can result in net income losses.

- Describe the three types of loss exposures that can lead to a net income loss.

- Explain how property losses, to an organization's property or other's property, can lead to net income losses.

- Describe the financial consequences of net income losses stemming from business interruption.

- Explain how the following methods help risk management professionals assess net income loss exposures:
  - Risk assessment questionnaires
  - Loss histories
  - Financial statements and underlying accounting records
  - Other records and documents
  - Flowcharts and organizational charts
  - Personal inspections
  - Expertise within and beyond the organization

- Given a case, analyze the income statement to measure net income loss exposures.

- Define or describe each of the Key Words and Phrases for this chapter.

Develop Your Perspective

What are the main topics covered in the chapter?

This chapter describes how to identify and analyze an organization's net income loss exposures. The topics discussed include business risk and hazard risk, the financial consequences of business interruption, and the methods of assessing net income loss exposures.

Identify net income loss exposures facing your organization.

- Which exposures are unexpected drops in revenues?
- Which exposures represent possible unexpected increases in expenses?
- Are any exposures combinations of both?

Why is it important to learn about these topics?

Risk management professionals must understand the net income losses that result from hazard risk (the focus of this chapter) as well as business risk because the risk management professional may be working with other managers to address both types of risk as part of an overall enterprise-wide risk management program.

Analyze the loss exposures at your organization.

- What information would you need to accurately estimate net income losses?
- Which property, liability, or personnel loss exposures would generate the largest net income losses for your organization? Why?

How can you use what you will learn?

Formulate a risk management plan for the exposure you identified above.

- What would be the financial consequences of a long-term business interruption resulting from this exposure?
- What technique(s) might you choose to manage this exposure? Why?

Chapter 10
Assessing Net Income Loss Exposures

Net income is the difference between an organization's total revenues and its total expenses. Net income losses are unanticipated reductions in an organization's net income. To identify and analyze potential net income losses, revenues and expenses must be projected without considering the effect of losses. Once the loss occurs, the difference between the projected net income and the actual net income earned after the accident is the net income loss.

Net income losses can be caused either by unexpected drops in revenues, unexpected increases in expenses, or a combination of both. While the term "net income loss" implies negative net income (that is, expenses exceeding revenues), any reduction in anticipated net income could be considered a net income loss in the sense that the organization ends up with less net income than it would otherwise have had. For example, an organization that had planned for net income of $100 million but subsequently earned only $10 million has suffered a net income loss of $90 million, even though net income is still positive.

Direct Versus Indirect Losses

Net income losses are usually the result of losses to property, liability, or personnel. Therefore, the property, liability, and personnel loss exposures present the possibility of *direct* losses to an organization, whereas the net income loss exposures present the possibility of *indirect* losses. A direct loss is a loss that occurs as the result of a particular cause of loss, such as the loss of a building destroyed by fire. An indirect loss is a loss that occurs as the result of a direct loss, such as the loss of revenues an organization suffers as a result of losing one of its buildings in a fire.

Pre-loss analysis of potential indirect losses is often challenging to risk management professionals because of the difficulty in projecting the effects that a direct loss will have on revenues or expenses. For example, a risk management professional working at a restaurant chain may be able to project the amount needed to settle a lawsuit brought by a customer accusing the restaurant of food poisoning (direct loss) with some certainty. However, it would be very difficult to project the effect that any negative publicity relating to the lawsuit would have on future restaurant sales (indirect loss).

In a broad sense, a net income loss could involve any decrease in net income that an organization incurs, for whatever reason. Whether the loss of net income is caused by a tornado that destroys the organization's facilities or by the products of a new competitor, the organization's financial results are still affected. Consequently, advocates of enterprise risk management believe that all loss exposures (including net income loss exposures) should be treated regardless of their source (business risk or hazard risk).

Net Income and Commercial Property Coverages

In the context of commercial property insurance, net income loss is narrowly defined as a loss of net income that results from accidental loss to property, which involves one specific type of loss exposure (property loss exposure). In addition to the property loss exposures that are the focus of commercial property insurance, this chapter also discusses net income losses that result from liability and personnel loss exposures.

Net income can be higher or lower than expected as a result of either the business environment or accidental events. Therefore, net income loss exposures stem from two types of risk: business risk and hazard risk. Similar to the rest of this text, this chapter focuses mainly on net income loss exposures resulting from hazard risk. However, risk management professionals should also understand net income loss exposures resulting from business risk because they may be asked to work with other managers to address both types of risk as part of an overall enterprise risk management program.

Identifying the loss exposures arising from business risk and hazard risk is the first step in assessing net income loss exposures. The risk management professional then needs to analyze these loss exposures by determining the financial consequences of business interruption. A risk management professional can then use a variety of methods to assess the net income loss exposures faced by his or her organization.

BUSINESS RISK

Business risks can result in either positive or negative changes in an organization's net income. Examples of business risk include seasonal and cyclical demand for the organization's products or services; unanticipated changes in the cost of raw materials or labor; and new government regulations, taxes, or tariffs.

The main business risks to net income are price risk and production risk. Price risk is unanticipated variability in the cost of a product's inputs or in the product's output price. Production risk is unanticipated variability in the product's production level.

The business risks that organizations face can be general or organization-specific, although both represent net income loss exposures to the organization. General business risk is a risk that affects all organizations at the local, national, or global level and it often results from changes in information, attitudes, technology, or general economic conditions. Organization-specific business risk is a risk that affects a single or small group of organizations. The distinction is important in determining the risk control or risk financing techniques that may be available to manage the business risks that can lead to net income losses. For example, hedging often works well with general business risk but not as well for organization-specific business risk. Organization-specific business risk often has to be managed through careful planning or contractual transfers.

General Business Risk

As said previously, net income losses may be caused by reductions in revenues, increases in expenses, or a combination of the two. Revenue reductions may be caused by price risk or production risk. For instance, revenues may drop as a result of a decrease in demand because of a cyclical slowdown or recession, which will lead to lower prices (price risk).

The degree of exposure to general business risk differs by organization. Some organizations are much more susceptible to business cycles than others. For example, in the trough of a business cycle, the demand for consumer durables such as refrigerators or vacuum cleaners is expected to drop, causing reduced revenues for manufacturers and retailers. Service organizations such as business consulting are also particularly susceptible to business cycles because outside consulting services are one of the first things that businesses cut when faced with revenue reductions. Other organizations, such as electric utilities and food producers, are less susceptible to business cycles because people continue to use their products even in the worst economic times.

While some general business risk is cyclical or temporary, some is permanent or irreversible. Revenues may drop because the entire product line or service falls out of favor and customers stop buying the product. For example, the reduction in sales of video cassette recorders (VCRs) as a result of the popularity of DVD players demonstrates how technological advances can make products obsolete. Similarly, the role of travel agents has been greatly diminished by the availability of travel information on the Internet. Unlike the revenue decreases arising from business cycles, these risks are longer term and may never reverse themselves. Still, these types of risk are the normal risk associated with doing business. These risks can be managed, although the techniques used are in the enterprise risk management field and are different from those traditionally used by risk management professionals. However, the risk management concepts are for the most part the same as those discussed in previous chapters.

Net income losses can also stem from increased expenses. As with reductions in revenue, increases in expenses could be the result of price risk or production risk. For example, healthcare cost inflation, which affects the price of employee benefits, has been in the double digits for the past several years. That increases the cost of labor, a key expense input to virtually all organizations. If these expenses cannot be passed on to the end consumer through price increases, the organization's net income is reduced and a net income loss can occur.

Organization-Specific Business Risk

Similar to general business risk, organization-specific business risk may be caused by price or production risk, and can lead to net income losses as a result of reductions in revenue, increases in expenses, or a combination of the two. Organization-specific business risk can be caused by the actions of competitors, regulators, or government organizations as well as by the actions of the organization. Competitors offering new or better products or services, regulators limiting pricing or production, or government restricting an organization's operations can all cause a net income loss for an organization.

An organization's own decisions or activities are also a major source of organization-specific business risk. One example is poor product planning. A manufacturer may be unable to meet demand for some of its products or may be producing product lines that do not interest consumers. Both examples result in a net income loss resulting from a reduction in revenue. To illustrate, a toy manufacturer may be unable to predict the "hot" holiday toy. It may lose revenue because it underestimated the demand for its product and could not fill the orders that were placed.

Another example of a net income loss resulting from a reduction in revenue involves credit risk. Credit risk is the inability to collect money that is owed to the organization. If an organization is unable to collect on its accounts receivable, regardless of the reason, it incurs a net income loss.

An organization's net income can also drop because of increased expenses. Any unexpected expense increases for inputs or production functions that cannot be passed on to customers represent a net income loss. For example, an unanticipated increase in lumber prices can reduce the net income of a furniture manufacturing enterprise by increasing the cost of making furniture. Conversely, if the price of lumber drops unexpectedly, the furniture manufacturer's expenses drop and net income can actually increase.

Social or Political Actions and Net Income Losses

Social or political actions (events) can result in net income losses for an organization. These actions vary widely and can include social events such as Mardi Gras in New Orleans; a sporting event such as the Super Bowl or the Olympics; or political actions such as rallies, conventions, or protests. Alternatively, actions could be undesirable, such as riot, civil commotion, or political unrest, turmoil, or overthrow. All are examples of actions that could lead to net income losses.

Some of the examples previously mentioned may appear to have only a positive effect, such as the Olympics, a Super Bowl, or a political convention. However, they can have a negative effect on organizations that do not directly deal with the influx of visitors to the area. Some manufacturing organizations, or those that offer business-to-business related services in the host city, could incur productivity and net income losses. For example, these organizations may have to spend more on security, reduce production because of increased employee leave time, or delay shipping and receiving because of increased traffic. To illustrate, in Atlanta during the 1996 Olympics, local employers were encouraged to allow their employees to telecommute if possible because of the congestion that was expected during the Olympic Games. For many organizations, this resulted in the additional expenses of setting up telecommuting infrastructure and lost productivity of some of their workforce, leading to net income losses.

HAZARD RISK

Other sources of risk that lead to net income losses are hazard risks—those that can result in losses but not in gains. Examples include risks that cause accidental (from the insured's standpoint) losses because of industrial accidents, fires, work stoppages, and employee dishonesty. These risks cause direct losses (such as fire damage) as well as indirect losses (such as interruptions in the production flow) that both lead to net income losses. Distinguishing between business risk and hazard risk is important because the risk management techniques that can be used to control or finance these risks are very different. For example, price risk for inputs can be managed through hedging, whereas hazard risk is more often managed through insurance. Additionally, many of the risk control efforts that are intended to limit the loss frequency or severity of hazard risk may actually increase an organization's exposure to business risk. For example, a manufacturing organization may require extensive employee training in an effort to reduce employee injuries at work. If that organization is spending more than its competitors on worker safety, and not saving more on workers' compensation expenses, this could drive up the organization's manufacturing costs and reduce profits.

Any disruption of a normal production process—not just physical damage to the process—causes a net income loss. The following three types of hazard risk loss exposures can cause net income losses:

1. Property loss exposures
2. Liability loss exposures
3. Personnel loss exposures

Property Loss Exposures

A previous chapter presented a detailed assessment of property loss exposures. This section focuses on the financial consequences of a property loss specifically related to net income loss exposures and divides the property loss exposures into two groups: damage to the organization's property and damage to the property of others.

Damage to the Organization's Property

In the commercial property insurance context, most net income losses arise as a consequence of physical damage to property at the organization's own premises that either prevents the organization from operating or that reduces its capacity to operate. Therefore, identifying an organization's property damage loss exposures also reveals potential net income loss exposures. Any risk control technique to reduce the frequency or severity of property losses affecting the organization can also reduce the frequency or severity of net income losses.

It is important not to overlook loss exposures that involve damage to an organization's property while off premises, perhaps while in transit or while being stored or worked on at the premises of a bailee. For example, the damaged property could be essential components in a manufacturing process. Without those components, production might be curtailed until the components can be replaced.

In addition to tangible property, many organizations also own and rely on intangible property. For example, licenses, permits, copyrights, patents, trademarks, and service marks confer commercially valuable legal rights on their holders. Such intangible property entitles their owners to engage in licensed activities, produce and market patented products or copyrighted works, or use particular trademarks or service marks to the exclusion of others who do not own these marks. Intangible property is typically evidenced by a certificate or other documentation, but the property's value does not depend on that evidence. Nonetheless, intangible property can suffer loss. Examples of intangible property loss include the following:

- A permit may be inoperative because of a procedural flaw in how it was issued.
- The ideas underlying patented, copyrighted, or otherwise legally protected materials may be stolen, imitated, and marketed by a competitor.
- A trademark or a service mark may be infringed by a close imitation.

Any losses to intangible property reduce the value of its exclusive rights and allow competitors to gain a share of the market (and the revenue) that the property holder formerly enjoyed. Even if the property holder can legally defend the rights represented by the intangible property, the legal and other expenses it incurs in doing so reduce its net income.

Damage to the Property of Others

The net income loss exposure is not limited to the organization's own property. An organization can also suffer a net income loss because of damage to property that the organization does not own or control. This type of loss can result from the following three types of damage:

1. Damage to other businesses on which the organization depends
2. Damage resulting from acts of civil authorities
3. Damage interrupting utility services

Risk management professionals must carefully consider how damage to the property of others can affect their own organizations, particularly as these loss exposures are not as obvious as those posed by damage to the organization's own property.

Contingent net income loss exposure
A loss exposure for which the interruption of the organization's operations is conditional on another organization's ability to fulfill its duties.

The first type of damage to property of others that can cause a net income loss is damage to other businesses on which the organization depends. These dependency loss exposures are sometimes called contingent net income loss exposures. A **contingent net income loss exposure** is a loss exposure for which the interruption of the organization's operations is conditional on another organization's ability to fulfill its duties.

The contingent net income loss exposure has increased because of the growing reliance on external suppliers. Even the largest corporations find that outsourcing some of their operations is more cost-effective than performing those operations themselves. In addition, the large inventories of raw materials and components that once served to cushion the effect of supply interruptions have been eliminated by the just-in-time inventory systems that organizations have adopted to reduce costs.

Organizations tend to depend on the following types of businesses:

- Key suppliers
- Key buyers
- Leader properties

Key suppliers for an organization vary widely based on the organization's activities. For an organization that depends significantly on a supplier for key materials or services, a business interruption of the supplier's operation may reduce or stop the organization's operations as well. How soon or for how long the organization's operations are reduced or stopped depends on various factors, including what material stockpile the organization has when the loss occurs, what options the supplier has to continue or resume supply, and whether other suppliers are available to provide the same material.

Organizations that sell products manufactured by others face a similar dependency loss exposure. Generally called manufacturers' representatives, these organizations act as the sales force for a number of different manufacturers but are not employees of any of them. Damage to a manufacturer's facilities could leave its representative without a source of production for the items it sells.

Key buyers can also expose an organization to net income loss. For example, a small manufacturer might sell more than half of its output of automobile parts exclusively to one auto manufacturer. If a major property loss shuts down the auto manufacturer's plant, the supplier will suffer a loss of net income because the parts it manufactures will not be needed again until the auto manufacturer's production is resumed.

Organizations may depend heavily on leader properties. For example, many small businesses in or near a shopping mall, typically stores, depend on customers who are drawn to the mall by a major department or discount store, which is sometimes called a magnet or anchor store. If a property loss shuts down the magnet store, the customers shop elsewhere, and the smaller businesses (satellite stores) lose customers and net income even though the satellite stores themselves have suffered no property damage. These contingent net income loss exposures can often be overlooked when assessing net income loss exposures.

The second type of damage to property of others that can cause a net income loss results from acts of civil authorities. In some cases, damage to nearby property creates such a hazardous loss exposure to a wider area that the police or fire departments prohibit access to the area. Even though a particular organization in the affected area may have sustained no property damage, the act of the civil authority prevents occupancy, resulting in a net income loss.

The destruction of the World Trade Center on September 11, 2001, provides a dramatic example of this type of loss. As shown in Exhibit 10-1, civil authorities closed most of the area below Canal Street in Manhattan—more than two square miles—to all but essential traffic until September 19, 2001. The restricted area was gradually reduced, but more than thirteen square blocks, in addition to the former World Trade Center site, were closed for two months, and small portions of the area remained closed for more than eight months. These closures resulted in net income losses for many of the organizations in the affected area.

The third type of damage to property of others that can cause a net income loss is damage interrupting utility services, which usually refers to damage to utility services such as power transmission lines or generating stations. The resulting loss of power or other utilities (such as telephone service or water) can shut down almost any organization that uses those services.

Liability Loss Exposures

Liability loss exposures are conditions that present the possibility of financial losses that can be caused by a claim of legal liability by someone seeking monetary damages or some other legal remedy against the organization. When an organization suffers a liability loss, it is often difficult to discern when the liability loss ends and when the net income loss begins. A good guideline to follow is often that any direct costs associated with liability are considered liability losses and any indirect or consequential losses are considered net income losses.

As with property loss exposures, liability loss exposures can create both direct and indirect costs. The direct costs that an organization incurs as a result of liability claims include defense costs, verdicts or negotiated settlements, and the costs of complying with any injunction requiring that a current activity be abandoned or modified. Those costs are liability losses and are typically insured. In addition, costs to reduce the frequency or severity of future liability claims—such as a polluter's voluntary investment in a new pollutant disposal system—are liability risk control costs. Neither the liability losses nor liability risk control costs are net income losses stemming from liability. They are the direct costs associated with liability loss exposures.

Indirect costs associated with liability could include the loss of reputation or market share as a result of the liability incurred by the organization. For example, human resources may find it difficult to attract qualified employees, product sales may be affected, or suppliers may be unwilling to continue doing business with the organization. All of the above examples would reduce the organization's net income either by reducing revenues or increasing expenses and are an indirect result of liability. These indirect costs are often difficult

EXHIBIT 10-1

Restricted Area Following September 11, 2001

Prohibited Zone
September 14 to September 18

City of New York
Emergency Mapping Center
Michael R. Bloomberg, Mayor

Map Reviewed
3/1/02

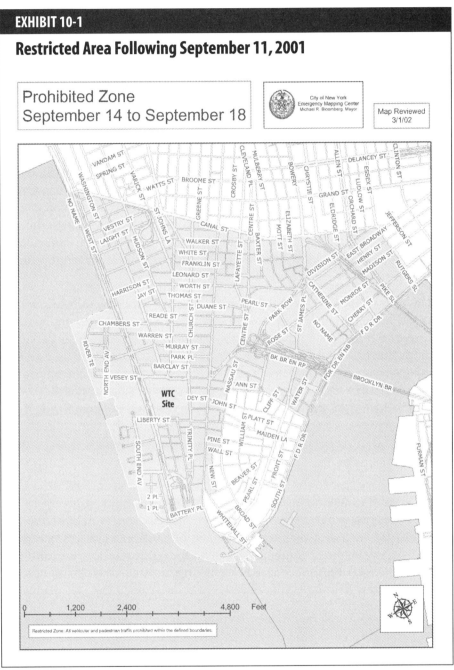

Source: City of New York Emergency Mapping Center, "Prohibited Zone September 14 to September 18,"
http://home.nyc.gov/html/oem/html/other/restricted_zones/frozen_zone_history_pdf_page.html
(accessed January 15, 2003).

to quantify. However, the risk management professional needs to account for both the direct and indirect costs of liability loss exposures. Some questions may arise about whether those costs should be considered as liability costs or net income costs. Regardless, it is important for the risk management professional to recognize these costs and the fact that liability losses can lead to net income loss exposures is more important than classifying them.

Personnel Loss Exposures

Personnel loss exposures are also often difficult to quantify. An organization can suffer a personnel loss through the death, disability, retirement, or resignation of one of its key employees. A key employee is an employee who has special skills, talents, or other characteristics that are valuable to the organization and that cannot be readily replaced. A net income loss occurs if the loss of that key employee causes the organization to lose revenue or incur extra expenses.

Again, it is often difficult to discern where the personnel loss (direct loss) ends and when the net income loss (indirect loss) begins. For example, the organization might experience decreased efficiency of remaining employees, a net income loss. The organization may also incur the cost of finding and training a competent replacement and perhaps paying additional compensation to attract a qualified replacement from a competing organization, a personnel loss. The real problem is that personnel losses often manifest themselves in the same ways that net income losses do, through reduced revenues and increased expenses. The risk management professional must recognize the loss exposure and all of the costs associated with that exposure, whether classified as personnel or net income costs.

Once a risk management professional has recognized that net income loss exposures can be generated by property, liability, and personnel loss exposures, the net income loss exposures need to be analyzed. The following section on the financial consequences of business interruption, regardless of whether the interruption is caused by property, liability, or personnel losses, is designed to help a risk management professional assess the net income loss exposures.

FINANCIAL CONSEQUENCES OF BUSINESS INTERRUPTION

To assess the financial consequences of a net income loss from a business interruption, a risk management professional should systematically identify and separately consider each of the following five factors that affect the severity of a net income loss:

1. Length of business interruption
2. Degree of business interruption
3. Changes in revenues

4. Changes in expenses
5. Restoration to normal income

While most of the following discussion focuses on net income losses resulting from a property loss, these factors apply to a net income loss from any accident, whether it involves property damage, liability claims, or personnel losses.

Length of Business Interruption

A business interruption refers to a disruption (reduction or ceasing) of operations, usually temporary, with the intent of reestablishing normal operations. One of the most significant factors affecting the extent of net income losses is the time it takes to restore the disrupted operations after a business interruption. For example, consider a net income loss exposure related to a property loss exposure. The risk management professional is concerned with restoring operations, not just with restoring property. In fact, the optimal solution is not always the restoration of the damaged property. The organization may be able to restore operations with a new location or new technology that renders the damaged property obsolete and unnecessary.

However, in most cases, the length of a business interruption depends principally on how long it will take to restore damaged property. The risk management professional must project, as accurately as possible, the length of time it would take in a particular case to repair or reconstruct essential facilities. Estimating the time to repair facilities is difficult. Therefore, it may be helpful to consult with experts in the property restoration field. For example, consider a fire at a local restaurant. Reconstruction could be subject to disruption by weather, strikes, and other unpredictable events. Delays are common, and the availability of equipment and furnishings could be a factor in reopening the restaurant. In addition, once the work has been completed, the equipment must be tested and approved before it can be used.

If the loss is more widespread, for example if an earthquake, flood, or hurricane inflicts major damage to many structures in one area, any damage to the infrastructure (such as roads, bridges, pipelines, and utility lines) must be repaired before work can begin on any one building. The length of business interruption under such circumstances would be longer than if only a single building were involved. Construction delays can also be expected in the aftermath of major hurricanes, earthquakes, or other events that cause extensive damage over a widespread area. In such instances, transportation and communications are disrupted, and the people and materials needed for repair and replacement are in short supply. Consequently, reconstruction can take weeks or even months longer than would be anticipated for a single building.

Certain organizations have special circumstances that lengthen their business interruption periods—for example, private schools that charge tuition. Private schools typically contract with their professional staff on a school-year basis and tuition is calculated annually to support the school's projected expenses. If such a school were damaged by an accident during the summer and repairs were completed before school reopened in the fall, the school would not suffer a net income loss. Tuition and expenses would be unaffected by the damage to the school, which would be closed for vacation regardless of the damage. However, if the accident closed the school in October, students and their parents would need to make alternative arrangements. The school would likely have to refund tuition. Once enrolled elsewhere, students probably would not return to the original school until at least the following school year. Therefore, the school would lose the tuition revenue for the remainder of the school year, forcing it to extend its period of business interruption well beyond the time needed to repair the damage.

Small Physical Damage Loss, Long Business Interruption

Net income loss exposures would be easier to handle if physical damage losses and net income losses were always proportionate, meaning that a small physical loss only resulted in a small net income loss. Because these losses are not proportionate, risk management professionals should be alert to situations in which a relatively small physical damage loss could cause a long business interruption and therefore a large net income loss. The following are examples of situations in which a long business interruption can result from a relatively small physical damage loss:

- Information technology (IT) equipment
- Bottlenecks
- Pollution losses

Information technology (IT) equipment may not represent a large percentage of the total value of an organization's physical assets, but even a small loss to such equipment can have devastating results. E-commerce businesses, banks, stock brokerages, and airlines are common examples of organizations that depend heavily on IT. However, the decreasing cost and increasing power of computer systems have made almost every business dependent on IT to some extent. IT systems can be subject to viruses, denial of service attacks, fires, water damage, and other causes of loss that can result in large net income losses, despite relatively minor property damage.

Blockages (bottlenecks) in business operations can cause the business process to slow down or even stop. The term "bottleneck" is often applied to situations in which work from several assembly lines or processes either flow through, or depend on continued operation at, a single job site or position. A relatively small physical damage loss at this bottleneck position could shut down several assembly lines. Production bottlenecks are easiest to imagine, but bottlenecks can also exist in almost any operation.

Some organizations manufacture a product assembled in a long series of steps that must be performed in sequence. Autos, for example, are assembled in the sequence dictated by the assembly line, which usually has many potential bottlenecks. Other organizations manufacture products that can be completed in steps that have no necessary sequence. These organizations are less prone to production bottlenecks because no one position has a disproportionate effect on operations at other positions.

Flowcharts are often effective in identifying bottlenecks. However, even when bottlenecks are properly identified, the organization is not necessarily able to eliminate those bottlenecks.

Relatively small fires in buildings can cause significant pollution and contamination problems that take a great deal of money and time to clean up. For example, in 1990 a minor fire occurred in the research lab at a large factory. The fire itself was confined to a single room, but smoke and soot spread throughout the factory. The ceiling paint in the lab contained a large amount of polychlorinated biphenyls (PCBs), a suspected carcinogen and a common ingredient in some old paints. The fire volatilized the PCBs and spread them throughout the factory in the smoke and soot. What was initially thought to be a $100,000 fire loss turned out to require more than $50 million to clean up properly. The factory was closed for more than one year and the organization suffered over $10 million in lost net income.

IT equipment, bottlenecks, and pollution losses are not the only examples of small physical losses that can lead to large net income losses. The risk management professional needs to be aware of any unique characteristics of his or her organization that offer the possibility of a disproportionate loss occurring. Conversely, major property damage sometimes does not disrupt operations and therefore causes no net income loss. For example, if an organization with multiple production facilities lost one facility because of property damage, provided that organization had enough excess capacity at other production plants, net income losses may be avoided.

Seasonal Fluctuations

Another factor affecting the length of business interruption is seasonal fluctuations. Some organizations earn significantly different amounts of net income at different times of the year. For example, retailers may transact as much as half their annual business during their peak three months. Businesses with an even more seasonal pattern (such as vegetable and fruit packers, summer camps, and ski resorts) might generate their entire annual net income within a three-month period.

For these businesses, the net income loss resulting from a business interruption could vary considerably depending on when during the year it occurred. Consequently, anyone analyzing net income loss exposures needs to consider seasonal net income differences.

Suppose a maximum business interruption of six months is projected for a particular organization. Which six months of the year would the organization be shut down? Determining when an interruption will occur is impossible, but the question is important for an organization whose revenue varies substantially by month. The most conservative assumption is that the interruption will occur at the worst possible time, that is, during the organization's peak season.

If a seasonal pattern exists, the pattern of fluctuation in revenue should be identified—either by studying the business's past seasonal revenue or by using figures that show typical seasonal patterns for the same type of business as that being analyzed.

Degree of Business Interruption

The degree of business interruption is the second factor that affects the severity of a net income loss. Operations can be either partially or fully shut down by an accident. If an operation can partially continue, then the organization's net income loss will not be as severe as with a full shutdown. In cases of partial shutdown, an organization can often supplement its own operations with outside resources and therefore avoid losing significant revenue. However, an accident that slows but does not disrupt operations still reduces an organization's revenue or increases expenses and therefore produces a net income loss.

An example of a partial business interruption, as opposed to a full business interruption, is a jewelry manufacturer that is forced to limit production because a labor dispute at the overseas mine has resulted in limited output. The jewelry manufacturer is still functioning, but at a reduced rate. The reduction in output and sales may reduce the jeweler's income because expenses remain essentially fixed while revenues are reduced.

If the jewelry manufacturer arranged for an alternative source of supply, operations could resume at their normal pace but costs would be higher by any extra amount paid to have the substitute jewels. Although sales could continue at the same rate based on full production, the jeweler would incur a net income loss because expenses would be higher than at the normal level of manufacturing activity.

Some large organizations perform the same activity at multiple facilities and may, therefore, be able to shift production from a damaged facility to one that is undamaged. If idle capacity exists at the second facility, the shift might be made with little or no additional expense. If, however, the second facility is already producing at or near full capacity, such a shift in operations would probably increase costs and lower net income.

While a fire at a restaurant typically leads to a complete shutdown, large, more complex organizations can often continue part of their operations despite damage that inhibits or prevents some aspects of production. Additionally, some businesses are not tied to their locations to the same degree as a restaurant. For example, business activities that do not deal directly with the public can shift locations more easily than can some retail businesses. Manufacturing and processing operations can often find suitable facilities away from their damaged ones for at least some of their operations.

Changes in Revenues

Changes in revenues is the third factor that affects the severity of a net income loss. Determining how much revenue an organization loses because of an accident involves calculating that organization's actual revenues and determining what that organization's normal level of revenues would have been had no accident occurred.

When operations are disrupted, the risk management professional can choose from among three appropriate techniques to determine revenue losses. For a mercantile business—that is, one that markets a service or product it does not manufacture—the measure of net income loss exposure is based on the projected revenue from sales. For a manufacturer, it is based on the sales value of production. For investors who have not yet received a return on their investments, it is based on anticipated return on investments.

Revenue From Sales

The net income loss exposure for a mercantile business is the difference between the projected level of sales before the disruption in operations and the projected level of sales after the disruption in operations. That projection should include earnings derived from all operations. In the case of the fire at the restaurant, revenue loss could be estimated by taking the average daily sales totals (adjusting for seasonal variances or other factors) and then multiplying the result by the number of days the restaurant was closed. If the restaurant's overall volume of business were steadily trending upward or downward, those results should be similarly trended to more accurately calculate the actual revenue loss.

In the case of a rental property, the measure of revenue loss for a landlord is the rent not collected because the property is untenantable. In some cases, this is a fixed amount stated in the lease. In other cases, adjustments are made to a base rental amount, such as a percentage of sales or a share of the landlord's increased costs to operate the building. If the lease includes rent adjustments, these must be estimated in the same manner as lost sales.

Sales Value of Production

For a manufacturer, the change in the revenue that affects net income is the lost sales value of production. Valuing the reduction in revenues for a manufacturing organization is more complex than for many other organizations because a manufacturer cannot replace its product by buying it from other sources. The **sales value of production** is the value of what would have been produced had the manufacturing plant continued its normal operations. To determine that value, adjustments must be made for the levels of inventory available at the time of the loss. Sales value of production is the measure of producing capacity rather than the amount produced in a prior period. It is the revenue that an organization could have generated by selling the maximum potential volume of

Sales value of production
The value of what would have been produced if a manufacturing plant had continued its normal operations.

product that the organization could have produced during a given period. For a full business interruption, the total sales value of production will be lost. For a partial business interruption, only a portion of the sales value of production will be lost.

Anticipated Return on Investments

In some situations, an organization can forecast a net income loss even though it has no current revenue. Such net income losses are called losses to an organization's anticipated return on investments. The net income loss for these organizations is the difference between the anticipated net income from the operations before a disruption and the actual net income after a disruption.

For example, consider a venture capital organization that invests in a company engaged in research involving a new technology. The research and development facility is funded as an investment and currently produces no revenue. Suppose the facility, and therefore the entire operation, is destroyed. What would be the loss of revenue? One answer may be none at all if the progress of the research was insignificant. But if the researchers were on the brink of a major revenue-producing development, a revenue loss would occur even though no revenues were earned before the disruption. Revenues could have been anticipated in the immediate future, and the result of the disruption would be a reduction in those anticipated revenues.

Once the effect that change in revenues has on the severity of net income losses has been determined, the risk management professional needs to determine the effects that changes in expenses will have on the severity of net income losses.

Changes in Expenses

The fourth factor that affects the severity of a net income loss is changes in expenses. After an accident, an organization may either be shut down or be able to continue partial or full operations. In either case, an increase in expenses will almost surely be a part of that organization's net income loss. If the organization is shut down, some continuing expenses will be incurred for items such as payroll or utilities. Some major expenses do not continue; for example, the cost of a manufacturer's raw stock or of retailers' or wholesalers' merchandise. That stock or merchandise does not need to be replenished while the organization cannot function. Other expenses that do not normally continue include supplies of most materials used in normal daily operations, such as packaging and office supplies. If the organization continues, it is likely to incur some additional expenses because of the hardships of continuing despite the accident. Regardless of whether a business interruption occurs, the organization may choose to pay extra expenses to expedite restoration of any damaged property and shorten the time until normal operations can resume.

Continuing Expenses

Certain expenses are considered continuing expenses. Continuing expenses are expenses that continue even when an organization's operations are impaired (when the organization suffers a business interruption). If the organization is shut down, some continuing expenses will be incurred for items such as payroll, utilities, and taxes. Exhibit 10-2 summarizes the common continuing expenses incurred.

EXHIBIT 10-2

Common Continuing Expenses

- Payroll
- Utilities
- Services performed by independent contractors
- Leases, rents, or mortgages
- Taxes
- Advertising
- Franchise and license fees and royalties
- Professional fees
- Insurance premiums
- Depreciation

- *Payroll.* The extent to which payroll expenses continue during a business interruption depends on several factors, such as the duration of the business interruption, the number of employees who are of special value to the organization, conditions in the local labor market, union contracts, severance pay policies, and obligations to continue providing employee benefits.

  How long employees will be kept on the payroll during a business interruption also depends on several factors. Some employees are paid by the hour, and when they do not work, they are not paid. Other employees are promised or have some reason to expect regular paychecks. If a long business interruption is expected, the organization will probably discontinue payroll expense for many employees. However, it is rare for all employees to be dismissed, even during a prolonged business interruption. Retaining some employees is usually necessary (or desirable) to ensure a smooth transition back to normal operations. In addition, many organizations have employees with special skills, such as designers or tool and die makers, who could not be easily replaced and who may find other jobs if they are eliminated from the payroll. Furthermore, some employees are usually required to manage the process of repair and reconstruction and to prepare for successful operations after reopening. In practice, officers' salaries are usually continued regardless of the duration of a business interruption. Salaries may also be continued for department managers and supervisors.

- *Utilities.* Utility costs for heat, light, and power would probably be affected only minimally during short business interruption periods. During longer periods, the expense might be discontinued or greatly reduced until shortly before reopening. For organizations that normally have small utility bills, the difference may be insignificant. However, those that normally use a large amount of electricity, such as many manufacturers, may see a substantial drop in utility expenses. However, some may be obligated to pay a minimum charge to the utility company regardless of their power consumption.

  Communication expenses would probably continue in full during a short business interruption. During a prolonged business interruption, these expenses would probably be reduced or discontinued and then be resumed shortly before operations resume.

- *Services Performed by Independent Contractors.* Many organizations hire independent contractors to perform some functions or services. In addition, many retailers, such as hardware, appliance, or jewelry stores, hire outsiders to perform alteration, installation, or repair work. Restaurants and bars often hire musicians and other entertainers. An organization may be obligated by contract to make payments to these independent contractors, even when no services are rendered during a business interruption. However, it is more likely that services performed by independent contractors will not be continued and that, therefore, payments will not be required.

- *Leases, Rents, or Mortgages.* Whether lease or rental expense for buildings and equipment would continue during a business interruption depends on the terms of the lease or rental agreement. An undesirable long-range outcome might be cancellation of a favorable lease. Generally, if the lease agreement provides for abatement of rent, it does so only when the rented property itself is damaged and made unusable. Therefore, rent on branch offices, warehouses, and storage facilities normally continues during a business interruption at the main location. Likewise, a business interruption does not normally free a lessee from rental payments for equipment rented on a long-term basis, such as copy machines, telephone systems, autos, and trucks.

  Mortgage interest payments generally are a continuing expense, with some exceptions. If a building is destroyed, the mortgage debt probably will be paid off with property insurance proceeds. Although new loans may be needed to finance a new building, mortgage interest expense will be reduced until borrowing reaches the previous level. Business interruptions do not affect interest on other loans and mortgages on property away from the damaged premises, so interest payments on such loans will necessarily continue.

- *Taxes.* Taxes affect the net income loss exposure in various ways. Among the taxes to be considered are real and personal property taxes, Social Security taxes, unemployment insurance taxes, and income taxes.

A conservative assumption is that property taxes will be a continuing expense. Depending on the situation, major losses may reduce taxable real property values. However, in many areas, taxes are assessed as of a given date; for example, January 1. If an organization has a loss immediately after that date, it could be a year or more before any property tax relief is given. If the insured rebuilds before the next January 1, a reduction in assessments will usually not be allowed. Similarly, partial losses may cause a business interruption but entail little, if any, reduction in taxable property values.

The same reasoning applies to personal property taxes based on inventory. These taxes may continue at the same level, or nearly so, even though operations are shut down. Employer contributions for Social Security and unemployment compensation continue only to the extent that employees are paid during the business interruption.

In the analysis of net income loss exposures, the effect of income taxes might also be considered. For example, an organization with a marginal tax rate of 30 percent that projects a $1,000,000 reduction in net income will sustain only a $700,000 reduction in income after taxes.

- *Advertising.* To determine whether advertising expense would be continued during a business interruption, the organization's advertising policy must be considered. Some advertising is intended to stimulate sales in the short run. Other advertising is intended to enhance the organization's image, and no short-run benefits are expected.

  If advertising has been contracted in advance and cannot be canceled, it is a continuing expense. Otherwise, advertising to stimulate sales is unnecessary except perhaps shortly before the operations resume. However, organizations often choose to maintain their image-enhancing advertisements even during a long business interruption. Such advertising may help to reduce the residual loss of net income after the business interruption ends.

  Organizations that relocate to temporary locations while repairs are being made at the damaged location usually advertise their temporary location. In so doing, they may incur greater advertising expense than normal. This advertising expense can be classed as an extra expense.

- *Franchise and License Fees and Royalties.* If payments of franchise fees, license fees, and royalties are based on sales or production, such fees cease when operations shut down. However, these fees might continue if a minimum or a flat fee is guaranteed.

- *Professional Fees.* Professional fees such as those for accounting and legal services normally continue if paid on a retainer basis. In fact, extraordinary legal and accounting services may become necessary as a result of the loss. These expenses can also be classified as extra expenses.

- *Insurance Premiums.* Some insurance premiums may be reduced during a business interruption. Coverage on property that is destroyed can be eliminated and the premium for property insurance arranged on a reporting form basis (premium is based on reported values) will be reduced if lower values are reported because of the loss. Both workers' compensation premiums based on payroll and liability premiums based on payroll or sales are reduced commensurate with any reduction in payroll or sales caused by the business interruption.

- *Depreciation.* In accounting, if an asset is expected to have a useful life greater than one year, organizations can depreciate the purchase price over the useful life of the asset rather than expensing it in the year of the investment. Depreciation expense is the allocation of a capital expenditure over the useful life (usually a schedule set by tax codes) of the asset. Although it does not represent a current outflow of cash, depreciation expense does reduce net income. In general, depreciation would be a continuing expense during a business interruption. For any physical assets destroyed during the year, the remaining book value (the amount of the capital expenditure in the asset that you have not yet depreciated) is included in any depreciation expenses that year. If that physical asset was insured, the remaining book value would be offset by any insurance proceeds collected.

While the assessment process for determining continuing expenses does not vary much from organization to organization, the magnitude of the continuing expenses will vary widely. For some organizations, payroll may be the largest continuing expense; for others, it may be advertising. The assessment of continuing expenses for an organization is just one assessment that a risk management professional needs to do related to changes in expenses. The next step is determining the extra expenses that an organization may incur during a business interruption.

Economic Depreciation

The accounting depreciation discussed in this section is vastly different from the economic depreciation of a capital expenditure. Economic depreciation is the difference between the initial capital expenditure and the current market value of an asset. Economic depreciation is typically the result of physical or functional depreciation.

Physical depreciation is the wear and tear of the asset and is usually reflected in a reduction in the asset's ability to perform its intended function. For example, a building will continue to depreciate (the roof will wear, the paint will age, and so on) even if operations are shut down. In contrast, the depreciation of some equipment is clearly related to use. Motors that must be rebuilt after a stated number of hours of use may depreciate little during a business interruption.

Functional depreciation is usually the result of technological advances that mean that the function performed by the capital expenditure is no longer needed or can be performed better by other methods. For example, personal computers that an organization purchased three years ago would have a greatly reduced value today, even if they had never been taken out of their original cartons.

Extra Expenses

Another change in expenses that may result from business interruption is extra expenses that are incurred by the organization to remain in operation. Some organizations cannot or choose not to shut down after a major business disruption. Those organizations continue to provide their goods or services and elect to incur additional costs, called extra expenses, to remain in operation. Their net income loss then includes those extra expenses. **Extra expenses** are expenses that an organization incurs in addition to ordinary expenses to mitigate the effects of a net income loss. For example, extra expenses could include items such as rental of temporary substitute buildings and equipment, excess transportation charges to relocate to the new location, employees' travel expenses to the new site, advertising and public relations expenditures to alert the public to the new location, and higher raw materials costs necessitated by purchasing in smaller-than-normal lots.

Extra expenses
Expenses that an organization incurs in addition to ordinary expenses to mitigate the effects of a net income loss.

Whether it has shut down or is continuing to operate under adverse conditions, an organization may choose to incur extra expenses, known as expediting expenses, to hasten its return to normalcy. **Expediting expenses** are extra expenses incurred to hasten the return to normal operations after a net income loss. Expediting expenses could include premium prices paid for immediate salvage and other costs associated with disposing of damaged property, speedy reconstruction or repair of damaged property, increased shipping costs for express delivery of replacement parts or new materials, and overtime payroll expenses. Incurring these expediting expenses is justified when these expenditures reduce the net income loss that the organization would have suffered had it allowed recovery to proceed at its normal pace.

Expediting expenses
Extra expenses incurred to hasten the return to normal operations after a net income loss.

Once the risk management professional has determined the length and degree of the business interruption, as well as the changes in revenues and expenses the organization can expect to incur, he or she needs to assess the final factor in the severity of net income loss exposures, the time required to restore normal income.

Restoration to Normal Income

Not all net income losses cease when the operations have been restored. In some cases, businesses lose their existing customers and potential new customers to competitors after a long business interruption, and it can take time to win them back. In other cases, businesses lose important licenses, leases, or contracts as the result of a business interruption. A business interruption can also lead to loss of customer goodwill and market share.

In this context, normal income means the amount of income that would have been earned had no business interruption occurred. This is not necessarily the level of business as of the accident's date, but rather the level of activity that would have been expected on resuming operations had the accident not occurred. For example, if a business interruption occurs during an organization's slow season and it reopens during its peak season, normal activity would be peak-season activity.

Some types of businesses are more susceptible than others to loss of customers. A convenience store in a favorable location might experience normal revenues shortly after reopening after a lengthy business interruption. In contrast, a self-storage facility may need many months to locate enough new tenants to restore profitability. Schools and colleges may lose tuition for an entire academic year or longer if the campus is unusable when students are enrolling or are making financial commitments for the school year. When a restaurant or store is closed, its customers may start eating or shopping elsewhere and may not return to those establishments as soon as they are restored. Many other organizations also lose customers during a business interruption, though not necessarily to the same degree. Most organizations will need additional time to recapture lost business even after operations have been completely restored.

Another aspect of restoring normal income involves the cancellation of a license, lease, or contract. A license to serve as the exclusive distributor of a product may be contingent on the licensee's selling a minimum quantity. Loss of the license because of failure to meet this requirement might reduce an organization's income long after its facilities are restored if it cannot obtain a replacement product to sell.

A business interruption may also reduce an organization's market share or erode carefully developed customer goodwill. Market share and goodwill are valuable in their own right, even though it is difficult to assign a monetary value to them.

Once the risk management professional has determined the financial consequences of a business interruption using the five factors—length and degree of business interruption, changes in revenues and expenses, and restoration to normal income—he or she needs to know where to find the information that will help in assessing the sources of net income loss exposures.

METHODS OF ASSESSING NET INCOME LOSS EXPOSURES

The seven widely used methods for assessing (identifying and analyzing) any loss exposure are also useful in assessing an organization's net income loss exposures. These methods can be used to determine the frequency of the various types of accidents that might result in net income losses and the potential severity of these net income losses. The seven widely used methods are as follows:

1. Risk assessment questionnaires
2. Loss histories
3. Financial statements and underlying accounting records
4. Other records and documents
5. Flowcharts and organizational charts

6. Personal inspections
7. Expertise within and beyond the organization

Financial statements; underlying accounting records; and other, both public and private, records and documents are useful for assessing potential net income losses before they occur, while loss histories are useful for assessing potential net income losses based on what has happened in the past. Risk assessment questionnaires may be used to uncover potential net income losses that have not happened before and are therefore not reflected in either loss histories or financial statements. These are also useful when assessing newly created loss exposures. Flowcharts and organizational charts provide insight into the potential length of any business interruption that might affect revenues or expenses and are therefore useful in quantifying the extent of potential losses. They also provide a basis for identifying bottlenecks in the organization's operations that can exacerbate net income losses through prolonged business interruptions.

Personal inspections help reveal hazards that affect property, liability, and personnel loss exposures that are related to net income loss exposures. Expertise within the organization is an invaluable source for assessing net income loss exposures. The line managers should be intimately familiar with the organization's input costs and price structure. Managers may also have experience from prior work at other organizations, and that external experience may be useful in quantifying risk at this organization. Expertise outside the organization can also provide insights into the effect of both business-risk-related and hazard-risk-related net income loss exposures. These and other sources can be used to both identify and quantify potential net income losses, either from increases in expenses or reductions in revenues.

Risk Assessment Questionnaires

The first method of assessing net income loss exposures is using a risk assessment questionnaire. Although most standardized surveys and questionnaires have an insurance orientation (focusing on insurable loss exposures), the typical risk assessment questionnaire contains one or more worksheets that can help develop historical perspectives on net income loss exposures. Used in conjunction with internal documents and financial records, risk assessment questionnaires can be useful starting points for assessing the potential severity of business interruptions from hazard risk.

A portion of one such work sheet, often called a business income report sheet or business income work sheet, is shown in Exhibit 10-3. This exhibit provides a format to record revenues and expenses for a given time period for the organization as a whole or, with some modifications, for any department within that organization. (This particular exhibit applies to a mercantile or another nonmanufacturing operation. Slightly different forms are available that apply to

EXHIBIT 10-3

Business Income Report/Work Sheet

POLICY NUMBER:

COMMERCIAL PROPERTY
CP 15 15 06 95

BUSINESS INCOME REPORT/WORK SHEET

Your Name _____   Date _____

Location _____

_____

This work sheet must be completed on an accrual basis.

The beginning and ending inventories in all calculations should be based on the same valuation method.

_____

APPLICABLE WHEN THE AGREED VALUE COVERAGE OPTION APPLIES:

I certify that this is a true and correct report of values as required under this policy for the periods indicated and that the Agreed Value for the period of coverage is $ _____ , based on a Co-insurance percentage of _____%.

Signature _____
Official Title _____

_____

APPLICABLE WHEN THE PREMIUM ADJUSTMENT FORM APPLIES:

I certify that this is a true and correct report of values as required under this policy
for the 12 months ended _____

Signature _____

Official Title _____

Agent or Broker _____

Mailing Address _____

BUSINESS INCOME REPORT/WORK SHEET
FINANCIAL ANALYSIS

Income and Expenses	12 Month Period Ending _____		Estimated for 12 Month Period Beginning _____	
	Manufacturing	Non-Manufacturing	Manufacturing	Non-Manufacturing
A. Gross Sales....................................	$_____	$_____	$_____	$_____
B. DEDUCT: Finished Stock Inventory (at sales value) at Beginning................	– _____	XXXXXXXX	– _____	XXXXXXXX
	_____	XXXXXXXX	_____	XXXXXXXX
C. ADD: Finished Stock Inventory (at sales value) at End.........................	+_____	XXXXXXXX	+_____	XXXXXXXX
D. Gross Sales Value of Production....................................	$_____	XXXXXXXX	$_____	XXXXXXXX
E. DEDUCT: Prepaid Freight – Outgoing........	– _____	– _____	– _____	– _____
Returns & Allowances................	– _____	– _____	– _____	– _____
Discounts...................................	– _____	– _____	– _____	– _____
Bad Debts..................................	– _____	– _____	– _____	– _____
Collection Expenses..................	– _____	– _____	– _____	– _____
F. Net Sales.......................................		$_____		$_____
Net Sales Value of Production........	$_____		$_____	
G. ADD: Other Earnings from your business operations (not investment income or rents from other properties): Commissions or Rents	+_____	+_____	+_____	+_____
Cash Discounts Received.............................	+_____	+_____	+_____	+_____
Other..	+_____	+_____	+_____	+_____
H. Total Revenues.............................	$_____	$_____	$_____	$_____

         CP 15 15 06 95

Continued on next page.

		12 Month Period Ending _____		Estimated for 12 Month Period Beginning _____	
Income and Expenses		Manufacturing	Non-Manufacturing	Manufacturing	Non-Manufacturing
Total Revenues (Line **H.** from previous page).............................		$ _____	$ _____	$ _____	$ _____
I. DEDUCT: Cost of goods sold (see next page for instructions).....................		– _____	– _____	– _____	– _____
Cost of services purchased from outsiders (not your employees) to resell, that do not continue under contract.............		– _____	– _____	– _____	– _____
Power, heat and refrigeration expenses that do not continue under contract (if **CP 15 11** is attached)..		– _____	XXXXXXXX	– _____	XXXXXXXX
All ordinary payroll expenses or the amount of payroll expense excluded (if **CP 15 10** is attached)....................................		– _____	– _____	– _____	– _____
Special deductions for mining properties (see next page for instructions)..............................		– _____	– _____	– _____	– _____
J.1. Business Income exposure for 12 months.....................................		$ _____	_____	_____	_____
J.2. Combined (firms engaged in manufacturing & non-manufacturing operations)..............		$_____		$_____	

The figures in **J.1.** or **J.2.** represent 100% of your actual and estimated Business Income exposure for 12 months.

K. Additional Expenses:

1. Extra Expenses – form **CP 00 30** only (expenses incurred to avoid or minimize suspension of business & to continue operations)................. | | | | $ _____ | $ _____ |

2. Extended Business Income and Extended Period of Indemnity – form **CP 00 30 or CP 00 32** (loss of Business Income following resumption of operations, up to 30 days or the no. of days selected under Extended Period of Indemnity option)...................... | | | | + _____ | + _____ |

3. Combined (all amounts in **K.1.** and **K.2.**).................................. | | | | $ _____ | |

"Estimated" column

L.   Total of **J. and K.** .... $ _____

The figure in **L.** represents 100% of your estimated Business Income exposure for 12 months, and additional expenses. Using this figure as information, determine the approximate amount of insurance needed based on your evaluation of the number of months needed (may exceed 12 months) to replace your property, resume operations and restore the business to the condition that would have existed if no property damage had occurred.

Refer to the agent or Company for information on available Coinsurance levels and indemnity options. The Limit of Insurance you select will be shown in the Declarations of the policy.

Supplementary Information

	12 Month Period Ending _____		Estimated for 12 Month Period Beginning _____	
	Manufacturing	Non-Manufacturing	Manufacturing	Non-Manufacturing
CALCULATION OF COST OF GOODS SOLD				
Inventory at beginning of year (Including raw material and stock in process, but not finished stock, for manufacturing risks)..............	$ _____	$ _____	$ _____	$ _____
Add: The following purchase costs: Cost of raw stock (including transportation charges)........................	+ _____	XXXXXXXX	+ _____	XXXXXXXX
Cost of factory supplies consumed..	+ _____	XXXXXXXX	+ _____	XXXXXXXX
Cost of merchandise sold including transportation charges (for manufacturing risks, means cost of merchandise sold but not manufactured by you)......................	+ _____	+ _____	+ _____	+ _____
Cost of other supplies consumed (including transportation charges)..........	+ _____	+ _____	+ _____	+ _____
Cost of goods available for sale.............	$ _____	$ _____	$ _____	$ _____
Deduct: Inventory at end of year (Including raw material and stock in process, but not finished stock, for manufacturing risks)..............	– _____	– _____	– _____	– _____
Cost of Goods Sold (Enter this figure in Item I. on previous page).........	$ _____	$ _____	$ _____	$ _____

other types of organizations.) Another portion of the questionnaire, as shown in Exhibit 10-3, is a guide to help identify the extra expenses an organization could incur to maintain continuous operations despite an accidental loss. Therefore, Exhibit 10-3 suggests values exposed to net income loss if an accident forces the organization to shut down wholly or partially.

A number of insurance organizations have also developed their own extra expense work sheets to help risk management professionals quantify the net income consequences of attempting to stay open despite an accidental loss. Exhibit 10-4 shows a sample extra expense work sheet. Because net income loss exposures are future values, the historical data developed through such work sheets may need to be adjusted to reflect future projections.

In addition to providing formats to calculate net income losses from business interruptions, a typical risk assessment questionnaire will identify each of the organization's locations that produce revenue, either through a product or service or through rental income. Annual or other periodic revenues may be specified for each location. That information can help identify specific locations at which disruption is likely to cause a significant net income loss.

Loss Histories

The second method of assessing net income loss exposures is reviewing loss histories. Because a variety of events occurring on or off an organization's premises may cause several forms of net income loss from reduced revenues or increased expenses, an organization's loss history tends to be a series of episodes rather than a source of credible net income loss exposure statistics. Therefore, these net income loss histories are useful for identifying net income loss exposures but may not be as useful for quantifying frequency or severity of future losses. For example, property damage at a location may have been easily repaired in the past so that little or no net income loss actually occurred. The loss exposure from a similar incident still exists but the potential amount of loss may now be much greater than it was in the past.

While loss histories are more useful as measures of potential frequency than as measures of potential severity, they can still be used to assess potential severity of an organization's net income loss from current events. For example, a net income loss history may indicate the length of time required to make repairs or otherwise return to normal operations after an accidental loss. Knowing from experience how long it takes to restore operations could help a risk management professional to project the severity of future business interruptions based on current operations and prices. In short, records of the severity of net income losses can help estimate the size of potential net income losses from similar occurrences. Even for this purpose, however, such records may not be fully reliable because many things may have changed since those losses occurred.

EXHIBIT 10-4

Sample Extra Expense Work Sheet

	1st Month	2nd Month	3rd Month	Additional Months
Temporary Location and Equipment Expenses				
Location Rent or Lease	$_____	$_____	$_____	$_____
Equipment Rent, Lease, or Purchase	_____	_____	_____	_____
Security Expenses	_____	_____	_____	_____
Janitorial Expenses	_____	_____	_____	_____
Moving Expenses				
Set-up/Installation of Equipment	_____	_____	_____	_____
Move out/Removal of Equipment	_____	_____	_____	_____
Utility Expenses				
Water	_____	_____	_____	_____
Electricity/Gas	_____	_____	_____	_____
Communication: Telephone, Internet	_____	_____	_____	_____
Postage	_____	_____	_____	_____
Employee Expenses				
Additional Employee Travel	_____	_____	_____	_____
Temporary Labor	_____	_____	_____	_____
Special Bonuses and Overtime to Employees	_____	_____	_____	_____
Miscellaneous Expenses				
Advertising Expenses	_____	_____	_____	_____
Additional Delivery Expenses: Raw Materials	_____	_____	_____	_____
Additional Delivery Expenses: Finished Products	_____	_____	_____	_____
Expediting Expenses for Professional Services	_____	_____	_____	_____
Total Extra Expense	$_____	$_____	$_____	$_____

The usefulness of loss histories in identifying and quantifying net income exposures varies by the accuracy and detail of recordkeeping within the organization. Many loss histories are biased by the existence of traditional business income insurance, and records apply only to the insurable portion of those net income losses rather than to the complete insured and uninsured losses. Therefore, an organization's history of net income losses probably has some significant limitations for risk management purposes.

Financial Statements and Underlying Accounting Records

The third method of assessing net income loss exposures is reviewing the organization's financial statements and underlying accounting records. The financial statements can provide information not only on the values exposed to loss, but also the potential severity of a net income loss. The three primary financial statements are the income statement, the balance sheet, and the statement of cash flows.

Income Statement

The income statement, sometimes called a profit and loss statement, shows the organization's total revenues and expenses for a specific time period. The income statement is the most useful of the financial statements for measuring potential net income loss exposures. The values on the statement are laid out in a systematic manner that is common to all organizations. While variations in the level of detail exist, all income statements follow the same basic format, as follows:

$$\text{Net income} = \text{Sales} - \frac{\text{Cost of goods or}}{\text{services sold}} - \frac{\text{Cost of}}{\text{sales}} - \frac{\text{Other}}{\text{expenses}} - \frac{\text{Income}}{\text{taxes}}.$$

Income statement values are not to be confused with the flow of actual cash and in fact may differ significantly from the inflows and outflows of cash an organization actually experiences. For example, sales made on credit are recorded at full value on the income statement, even though the organization has not yet actually received any money. Indeed, the sale on credit has introduced a new element of risk into the organization's operations, the credit risk that the organization will not be paid by its customer. Risk management professionals must understand how financial statements are created so that they can effectively use these statements to assess net income loss exposures.

A simplified income statement constructed on an accounting basis is shown in Exhibit 10-5 for Atley Tractors. The income statement in Exhibit 10-5 is based on generally accepted accounting principles (GAAP) as prepared by an accountant. The first line of the statement is net sales, which is the value of the products sold or the services provided by the organization during the period. This chapter uses annual income statements, but income statements can also be produced on a monthly or quarterly basis. For simplicity, assume that Atley Tractors sells a single product, lawnmowers. Each lawnmower sells for $500, and the organization sold 20,000 units last year. Sales are 20,000 units sold (quantity, or "Q") multiplied by $500 (average price, or "$P$"), for a total sales volume of $10 million ($P \times Q$).

EXHIBIT 10-5

Atley Tractors Income Statement, Accounting Basis

	Year Ended 12/31/XX
Net sales	$ 10,000,000
Cost of sales	(6,000,000)
Gross profit	4,000,000
Selling, general, and administrative costs	(3,000,000)
Operating profit	1,000,000
Interest expense	(300,000)
Taxable income	700,000
Income taxes at 40%	(280,000)
Net income	$ 420,000

Atley Tractors buys the lawnmowers from a manufacturer for $300 each, so the cost of sales for 20,000 units is $6 million (20,000 units sold multiplied by $300). Atley Tractors has selling, general, and administrative expenses (such as worker salaries, utilities, insurance premiums, and rent on floor space) of $3 million. Some of those operating expenses vary with the number of units sold (sales commissions, for example) but other operating costs are independent of the number of lawnmowers sold (for example, salaries for clerical staff). Therefore, after selling its product and paying all of its expenses, Atley Tractors had $1 million of operating profit with which to pay any interest expenses on borrowed money and taxes to the government.

Alternative Form of the Income Statement

Alternatively, the income statement can be rearranged to classify the operating expenses (both cost of sales and general, selling, and administrative costs) into two different sets of figures: those expenses that vary directly with the number of units sold (variable costs) and those expenses that are independent of the number of units sold (fixed costs). For example, utilities are largely independent of the number of units sold. While Atley Tractors' showrooms are open, the lights are turned on, regardless of whether ten customers make purchases or whether one hundred customers make purchases. On the other hand, for every lawnmower sold, Atley has incurred a cost of $300 that it paid to the lawnmower's manufacturer. If it sells 100 lawnmowers today, that is a cost of $30,000 for the units sold. If it sells 101 lawnmowers, the cost goes up by another $300 to $30,300. Therefore, the cost of the products sold varies directly with the number of units sold. The information necessary to reconfigure the income statement is readily available within the organization and can be estimated in consultation with the line managers, accounting staff, and others. Exhibit 10-6 restates the income statement into costs that vary directly with units sold and costs that do not vary with units sold.

The most important variables in assessing the net income loss exposure are usually price (P), quantity of units sold (Q), variable cost per unit sold (V), and fixed costs (F).

EXHIBIT 10-6

Atley Tractors Income Statement, Expense Category Basis

	Year Ended 12/31/XX	Algebraic Notation
Net sales	$ 10,000,000	$P \times Q$
Variable costs	(8,000,000)	$V \times Q$
Fixed costs	(1,000,000)	F
Operating profit	1,000,000	OP
Interest expenses	(300,000)	I
Taxable income	700,000	$OP - I$
Income taxes at 40%	(280,000)	$(OP - I) \times t$
Net income	$ 420,000	$(OP - I) - [(OP - I) \times t]$

P = Average price of product
Q = Units of product sold
V = Variable cost per unit of product sold
F = Overhead costs (independent of number of units sold)
OP = Operating profit = $PQ - VQ - F$
I = Interest expenses
t = Average tax rate

Relationship Among Production, Cost, and Net Income

Restating the income statement in algebraic form can help a risk management professional to assess the net income loss exposures more accurately. Holding all other variables constant, if the price (P) is reduced, then net income will be reduced. Again, holding all other variables constant, increases in the variable costs per unit (V) reduce net income. Similarly, if the fixed operating costs (F), interest expenses (I), or average tax rate (t) are increased, net income is reduced. In this example, all the other variables are constant. However, in the real world that is not always the case. Increases or decreases in expenses can occur simultaneously with changes in prices or interest expenses.

Other Financial Statements

The balance sheet is a snapshot at a point in time of the assets that an organization owns as well as the liabilities that it owes to others. The difference between assets and liabilities is the organization's equity or net worth. While the balance sheet does not directly measure net income loss exposures, it does provide useful information about changes in the organization's assets or liabilities that could exacerbate net income losses that may occur. For example, the balance sheet shows the level of inventory as of the date of the balance sheet.

If inventory is down from its historic levels, or the organization has adopted a just-in-time delivery system, then a disruption in transportation or manufacturing processes could trigger an inventory shortage and lost sales. On the other hand, excessive levels of inventory may signal changes in the organization's business operations that may have an effect on the potential for net income losses in the future.

Another useful financial statement is the statement of cash flows, which is similar to the income statement in that it tracks revenues and expenditures over a specific time period. However, unlike the income statement, the values reported in the statement of cash flows are changes in actual cash values instead of accounting values. For example, the statement of cash flows would record the revenue generated by a sale or credit not when the sale is made (as is done on the income statement) but when the payment is received from the customer. This can be useful when evaluating the potential cash flow needs that might be associated with losses, as it will help the risk management professional determine if the organization can meet its cash flow needs during the period immediately following a net income loss. The statement of cash flows is like a condensed version of the corporate checkbook, showing total deposits to the organization's checking account during the period as well as major expense categories over the same time period. The values in the statement of cash flows can be significantly different from those shown in the financial statements because they do track only cash expenditures.

Although the organization's income statement and balance sheet are usually public records, some details of the organization's business operations are considered trade secrets and therefore are not available to the general public. The information in those records can be useful in assessing the organization's potential net income loss exposures. For example, budgets and sales forecasts are generally closely held, as are marketing plans and strategies. The risk management professional can use these documents as the basis for assessing potential net income loss exposures, whether from business risk or hazard risk.

The income statement provides information over a period of time, typically one year, but loss exposures may be cyclical or seasonal. Many organizations have seasonal fluctuations in sales or in expenses, and those fluctuations should be available in internal financial records. Some organizations also have revenues or expenses that are tied to a specific event, and those revenues and expenses could be disrupted by unforeseen events. For example, a town may sponsor an annual outdoor fair that is subject to disruption by unforeseen events, especially weather. Sponsors of such events typically purchase weather insurance or use weather-based financial derivatives (a contract that pays when a specified weather event such as rain or snow occurs) to protect themselves from unexpected decreases in revenues. For such events, risk management professionals have access to gate receipts, attendance records, and expense records for past events and can use that information to estimate the potential severity of a weather-related loss exposure.

Net Income Loss Comparison

To see how net income loss exposures vary based on an organization's revenue and expense structures, a comparison of two similar organizations is helpful. Exhibit 10-7 shows a comparative income statement for Atley Tractors and Zelles Tractor Equipment, which, like Atley Tractors, is also in the lawn-mower business. The primary difference between the two organizations is that Zelles Tractor Equipment builds its own lawnmowers rather than purchasing them from a manufacturer. Both Atley Tractors and Zelles Tractor Equipment have the same level of sales, charge the same prices for their lawnmowers, have the same interest expenses and tax rates, and earn the same amount of net income. The difference between the two organizations is in the composition of their expenses. While Atley Tractors has variable expenses per unit equal to 80 percent of its average price ($400 ÷ $500) and fixed expenses of $1 million, Zelles Tractor Equipment has variable expenses per unit equal to 50 percent of the sales price ($250 ÷ $500) and fixed expenses of $4 million. These differences alter the loss exposure of the two organizations.

Suppose that both organizations suffer a ten-week business interruption in the wake of a hurricane. As shown in Exhibit 10-8, both organizations lose 20 percent of their sales during the business interruption period, so that the number of lawnmowers sold drops from 20,000 units to 16,000 units for the year. Zelles Tractor Equipment suffers a greater net income loss than Atley Tractors because of its cost structure. The operating profit at Atley Tractors drops from $1 million to $600,000 while the operating profit at Zelles Tractor Equipment drops from $1 million to zero. Atley Tractors ends up with a net income loss of $240,000 because net income falls from $420,000 to $180,000, although there is sufficient operating profit to pay the interest expenses and still generate a positive net income for the owners. The total net income loss for Zelles Tractor Equipment, on the other hand, is $720,000. In addition, the operating profit is not sufficient to cover the interest expenses, and Zelles Tractor Equipment ends up with negative net income.

The difference in the level of net income loss exposure is caused by the organizations' cost structure. Zelles Tractor Equipment has relatively more fixed expenses that must be paid regardless of the level of sales. Therefore, Zelles Tractor Equipment has more exposure to net income losses from reductions in the level of sales. Atley Tractors, on the other hand, can tolerate a relatively larger reduction in sales (either through a reduction in price or a reduction in units sold) before its net income becomes zero or negative.

EXHIBIT 10-7

Comparative Income Statements for Atley Tractors and Zelles Tractor Equipment, Expense Category Basis

	Atley		Zelles
Price per unit	$500	P	$500
Quantity of units sold	20,000	Q	20,000
Variable cost per unit	$400	V	$250
Fixed cost	$1,000,000	F	$4,000,000
Interest expense	$300,000	I	$300,000
Average tax rate	40%	t	40%

	Year Ending 12/31/XX		Year Ending 12/31/XX
Net sales	$10,000,000	$P \times Q$	$10,000,000
Variable costs	(8,000,000)	$V \times Q$	(5,000,000)
Fixed costs	(1,000,000)	F	(4,000,000)
Operating profit	1,000,000	OP	1,000,000
Interest expense	(300,000)	I	(300,000)
Taxable income	700,000	$OP - I$	700,000
Income taxes	(280,000)	$(OP - I) \times t$	(280,000)
Net income	$ 420,000	$(OP - I) - [(OP - I) \times t]$	$ 420,000

To assess the effect of a reduction in sales, an organization can calculate its breakeven sales point. The breakeven sales formula is a mathematical formula used to estimate the level of sales at which the organization breaks even—that is, the point at which sales equal costs and therefore net income equals zero. It is calculated by dividing fixed costs by the contribution margin. The contribution margin is the portion of each sales dollar that is left over after paying variable costs (those costs that vary directly with the number of units sold). The contribution margin for Atley Tractors is 20 percent because variable costs are 80 percent of sales. Similarly, the contribution margin for Zelles Tractor Equipment is 50 percent. Atley Tractors' fixed costs are $1 million of operating expenses plus $300,000 of interest expense, so its breakeven sales level is calculated as $1,300,000 ÷ 0.20 = $6,500,000. At $6.5 million of sales, holding all else constant, Atley Tractors will have a net income of exactly zero. Sales above $6.5 million will generate positive net income. Sales less than $6.5 million will generate negative net income. Zelles Tractor Equipment's fixed costs are $4 million of operating expenses plus $300,000 of interest expense, so its breakeven sales level is calculated

EXHIBIT 10-8

Comparative Income Statements for Atley Tractors and Zelles Tractor Equipment Following a Drop in Quantity Sold

	Atley		Zelles	Percentage Change Atley	Zelles
Price per unit	$500	P	$500	0.00%	0.00%
Quantity of units sold	16,000	Q	16,000	−20.00%	−20.00%
Variable costs per unit	$400	V	$250	0.00%	0.00%
Fixed costs	$1,000,000	F	$4,000,000	0.00%	0.00%
Interest expense	$300,000	I	$300,000		
Average tax rate	40%	t	40%		

	Year Ending 12/31/XX		Year Ending 12/31/XX		
Net sales	$ 8,000,000	$P \times Q$	$ 8,000,000	−20.00%	−20.00%
Variable costs	(6,400,000)	$V \times Q$	(4,000,000)	−20.00%	−20.00%
Fixed costs	(1,000,000)	F	(4,000,000)	0.00%	0.00%
Operating profit	600,000	OP	0	−40.00%	−100.00%
Interest expense	(300,000)	I	(300,000)	0.00%	0.00%
Taxable income	300,000	$OP - I$	(300,000)	−57.14%	−142.86%
Income taxes	(120,000)	$(OP - I) \times t$	0	−57.14%	−100.00%
Net income	$ 180,000	$(OP - I) - [(OP - I) \times t)]$	$ (300,000)	−57.14%	−171.43%
Net income @ 20,000 units	420,000		420,000		
Net income @ 16,000 units	180,000		(300,000)		
Change	$ −240,000		$ −720,000		

as $4,300,000 ÷ 0.50 = $8,600,000. Therefore, Zelles Tractor Equipment has more loss exposure to decreases in the level of sales. In other words, the severity of a net income loss from reductions in P or Q will be greater for Zelles Tractor Equipment than for Atley Tractors.

Note that although Zelles Tractor Equipment is more susceptible to losses in the event of a decline in sales, Zelles Tractor Equipment also generates more profit with increased sales because each dollar of sales over $8.6 million generates 50 cents towards taxable income. For Atley Tractors, each sales dollar above $6.5 million contributes only 20 cents towards taxable income. Therefore, such a level of business risk is often considered good for an organization because of the potential for higher profits. On the other hand, a greater level of business risk means that the organization must make greater efforts in its risk management of hazard risk net income loss exposures to alleviate the greater degree of exposure to business risk.

Increases in the variable costs per unit sold (V), which is a business risk, can also reduce net income. Increases in variable costs are either the result of increases in raw materials and labor costs that comprise the cost of manufacturing the product or increases in the costs of wholesale products that the organization retails. Generally, those increases are faced by all the competing organizations in an industry and are not specific to a particular organization. For example, all airlines face the risk that the cost of fuel, which is tied to the market price of oil, will increase and therefore reduce net income. Most airlines manage such risk by hedging to reduce or eliminate it. However, other risks increase the costs of inputs that only affect a single organization, and that organization's ability to hedge those types of risk is severely limited.

To illustrate, Atley Tractors and Zelles Tractor Equipment have different variable cost risks. Atley Tractors buys its lawnmowers exclusively from a single manufacturer, ABC Mowers (ABC), which operates three factories in Alabama, Vermont, and Oregon. Zelles Tractor Equipment manufactures its own lawnmowers. Part of the variable cost for Atley Tractors is the transportation costs of moving the assembled mowers from ABC's plant to Atley Tractors's warehouse and from there to the sales showroom. Suppose that ABC's factory in Oregon was damaged and had to suspend operations, which is a hazard risk. Atley Tractors could still buy its mowers from the remaining plants, but the average shipping cost per mower could increase. That increased cost would affect Atley Tractors, but not its competitor, Zelles Tractor Equipment. Atley Tractors might not be able to pass the increased costs on to its customers if it wanted to remain price competitive. Atley Tractors would then suffer a net income loss because the variable cost per unit sold (V) would increase. The degree of the net income loss would depend on how long it took ABC to return to full operations at its Oregon plant.

Atley Tractors also faces a business risk related to its variable costs, the risk that ABC could simply raise the price of its products. While that would cause short-term net income losses, Atley Tractors could address that risk by switching to an alternative manufacturer, diversifying its product line, or perhaps by using its marketing skills to convince customers to pay more for ABC-brand mowers. These types of general business risks are addressed through general business risk management techniques. However, it may not be appropriate to use these techniques to address a hazard risk like the increased transportation costs. The line between business risk and hazard risk is sometimes blurry, which emphasizes the need for coordinated risk management efforts throughout the organization.

Risk management professionals need to be able to read and understand financial statements to accurately assess net income loss exposures. While the most important financial statement in assessing net income loss exposures is the income statement, the ability to understand other financial statements is also important. Besides the financial statements, the risk management professional will need to use other public and private records and documents to ensure the accurate assessment of net income loss exposures.

Other Records and Documents

The fourth method of assessing net income loss exposures is reviewing public and private records and documents. Because net income loss exposures are most directly and accurately portrayed in financial statements and records, other nonfinancial records are typically less important in analyzing these loss exposures. Nonetheless, the risk management professional should consider the net income loss implications reflected in other records and documents. Those records could include minutes of the organization's board of directors that refer to plans to change the mix of products, production processes, or key customers or suppliers. Those changes might affect future normal streams of revenues and expenses, which must be protected through the risk management process. Accident, maintenance, and repair records may also highlight past or potential breakdowns in operations that could be sources of business interruptions.

A vast array of public information also is available on input prices and product demand. For example, a bakery is able to obtain historical wheat prices, as well as information on the variation of wheat prices, using the Internet. This information can be used to estimate potential changes in net income, either positive or negative, that arise from general business risk.

Financial services organizations are especially sensitive to changes in interest rate levels, and a wealth of information is available in easy-to-use form. The Federal Reserve Bank of St. Louis maintains an extensive database of information on interest rates and commodity prices, inflation rates, and credit levels in its Federal Reserve Economic Data (FRED) database, available on the Internet. For financial services organizations, interest rate risk is a key element in managing the organization's overall risk. However, even nonfinancial services organizations are subject to interest rate risk because the cost of borrowing is driven by interest rates and by the supply of and demand for loanable funds.

In addition to input price information, organizations also have access to information on competitors and potential competitors and on cost structures and normal profit margins, through public documents available at local libraries or on the Internet. An organization may evaluate financial information on similar organizations to determine its own susceptibility of net income to changes in input or output prices, consumer tastes, or business cycles.

In addition to the free services available through the Internet or through libraries, a large number of data services provide information services for a fee. Trade associations and affinity groups are another reliable source of information. For example, the National Association of Home Builders reports annually on the costs of the component parts of residential construction. A home construction company can use this information to assess its loss exposure to general business risk. Cost of risk surveys are published by the Risk and Insurance Management Society (RIMS), and insurance industry financial information is published by A.M. Best Company. While these sources are not free, they are a relatively inexpensive source of risk management information. Industry trade associations are present in all industries, and risk management professionals should look to both public and private information sources for data on general business risk in their industry.

Public information is available on hazard risk as well as business risk, but the information on hazard risk is not as extensive. Nonetheless, risk management professionals can look to public records and documents to supplement the information on hazard risk found in internal records and documents.

Flowcharts and Organizational Charts

The fifth method of assessing net income loss exposures is reviewing flowcharts and organizational charts. One of the most significant factors affecting the extent of the net income loss is the time it takes to restore disrupted operations. Flowcharts and organizational charts are particularly useful for assessing the effect of business interruptions on the organization's net income. A flowchart can be used to identify bottlenecks and critical processes. Organizational charts, including personnel charts, can identify key personnel that are essential to the delivery of products or services and whose loss could lead to a production business interruption. Risk management professionals can use these charts to assess what would be required to restore operations, not just to restore the property itself.

Personal Inspections

The sixth method of assessing net income loss exposures is by personal inspections. Some loss exposures are apparent only after inspecting the premises involved. Personal inspections are information-gathering visits to critical sites both within and outside the organization. These visits provide a firsthand look at loss exposures to determine what is subject to loss and what causes of loss are likely to strike. For some loss exposures, nothing is as effective as personal inspections, especially those conducted by individuals whose background and skills equip them to identify the unexpected, but possible, loss exposures. Therefore, personal inspections should lead to better forecasts of potential property, liability, or personnel losses that could lead to net income losses.

Expertise Within and Beyond the Organization

The seventh method of assessing net income loss exposures is expertise within and beyond the organization. The risk management professional should rely on others within the organization who have more specific expertise in areas outside of risk management. The accounting department is particularly helpful in assessing net income loss exposures. It is the logical contact from which to obtain details about the organization's financial operations. A general overview of the organization's financial plans and the major sources of revenue and expenses that those plans entail might be available to the risk management professional from the organization's senior financial or planning executives. Additionally, information about leases or other contracts can be obtained from attorneys. Furthermore, the finance department may be able to provide information on anticipated projects and financial costs, as well as projections for interest rates and other capital costs. Many organizations use internal tax specialists, and those experts can provide information on the tax issues affecting the risk management techniques.

Because budgets are vital in projecting future net income losses, the risk management professional should confer with those involved in budgeting. Beyond accountants and senior financial personnel, operating managers can give detailed information about net income loss exposures arising within their particular departments. In manufacturing operations, line managers are a useful source of information on bottlenecks, critical processes, and possible alternative risk management techniques.

The risk management professional should also be able to access the special knowledge of experts outside the organization for its net income loss exposures. This involves maintaining regular communication with practitioners in such fields as law, finance, statistics, accounting, auditing, and the technology of the organization's industry.

Outside certified public accountants are helpful in analyzing net income loss exposures. They can supplement the information from internal accounting and provide general insights on the loss exposures faced by similar organizations. Many organizations use outside accountants for tax work as well.

Outside consultants may be approached for advice on specific issues, including risk management. Insurance brokerage organizations may supply consulting services as well as provide risk management products. Insurers provide loss control advice, although their services are generally limited to insurable loss exposures.

Outside experts such as architects, engineers, building contractors, equipment vendors, and key suppliers can provide advice about the time necessary to repair or replace damaged equipment and inventory. The lead time that those experts can estimate for many construction projects and for the replacement of equipment and inventory should be incorporated into the organization's recovery plans.

SUMMARY

This chapter explained the basics of identifying and analyzing net income loss exposures for an organization. Net income is the difference between an organization's total revenues and its total expenses. Net income losses are unanticipated reductions in an organization's net income.

Net income can be higher or lower than expected as a result of either the business environment or accidental events. Therefore, net income loss exposures stem from two types of risk: business risk and hazard risk. The main business risks to net income are price risk and production risk. Price risk is unanticipated variability in the cost to a product's inputs or in the product's output price. Production risk is unanticipated variability in the product's production level. Business risk can be either general or organization-specific.

The three types of hazard risk loss exposures that can lead to net income loss exposures are property, liability, and personnel loss exposures. Property loss exposures related to net income loss exposures can be divided into two groups: damage to the organization's property and damage to the property of others. Liability loss exposures can be caused by a claim of legal liability by someone seeking monetary damages or some other legal remedy against the organization. When an organization suffers a liability loss, it is often difficult to discern when the liability loss ends and when the net income loss begins. However, it is important to recognize these costs and to recognize the fact that liability losses can lead to net income loss exposures. A personnel loss can occur through the death, disability, retirement, or resignation of an employee who has special skills, talents, or other characteristics that are valuable to the organization and cannot easily be replaced. A personnel loss results in a net income loss if the loss of a key employee causes the organization to lose revenue or incur extra expenses.

The five factors that affect the severity of net income losses are as follows:

1. Length of business interruption
2. Degree of business interruption
3. Changes in revenues
4. Changes in expenses
5. Restoration to normal income

The seven widely used methods for assessing any loss exposure can be used to determine the frequency of the types of accidents that might result in net income losses and potential severity of these net income losses. These seven methods are as follows:

1. Risk assessment questionnaires
2. Loss histories
3. Financial statements and underlying accounting records
4. Other records and documents
5. Flowcharts and organizational charts
6. Personal inspections
7. Expertise within and beyond the organization

Chapter 11

Direct Your Learning

Understanding Forecasting

After learning the content of this chapter and completing the corresponding course guide assignment, you should be able to:

- Explain why loss forecasts are important to organizations, risk management professionals, and the risk management process.

- Explain how relevant, complete, consistent, and organized loss data are developed and why such data are important.

- Explain probability distributions and their characteristics.

- Contrast theoretical and empirical probability distributions.

- Use the standard deviation of a normal probability distribution to calculate probabilities based on integer values (whole numbers) of standard deviations.

- Describe the risk management significance of trend analysis and the two methods of trending loss data.

- Given a case, analyze past data using the appropriate forecasting technique to project the expected value of the accidental losses that an organization will incur during a given time period.

- Define or describe each of the Key Words and Phrases for this chapter.

Develop Your Perspective

What are the main topics covered in the chapter?

The second step of the risk management process is analyzing loss exposures. One method of analyzing loss exposures is forecasting accidental losses. This chapter describes how probability analysis and trend analysis are used to forecast accidental losses.

Gather data from past losses from your organization.

- Are the data relevant to project future losses? How do you know?
- How might you ensure that the data are complete and consistent?
- What affects the organization of the data?

Why is it important to learn about these topics?

Forecasts help risk management professionals estimate the costs and benefits of various risk management alternatives, enabling them to choose the ones whose benefits most exceed their costs.

Analyze the loss data you gathered.

- What patterns do you see?
- How might these patterns predict the frequency or severity of the potential future losses?

How can you use what you will learn?

Choose an appropriate risk management technique to manage a particular workers' compensation exposure.

- What information would you need to accurately forecast workers' compensation losses for your organization?
- How effectively is your organization using this information to forecast future losses?
- Should your organization's workers' compensation loss exposures be transferred or retained?

Chapter 11

Understanding Forecasting

Risk management decisions are based on information about potential future losses. This information includes forecasts of the size (severity) of losses that could occur, as well as the number (frequency) of those losses occurring. A **forecast** is an estimate of some future value, amount, or quantity calculated by mathematical techniques or determined by intuition. The development of accurate forecasts takes place during the second step of the risk management process—analyzing loss exposures.

Forecast
An estimate of some future value, amount, or quantity calculated by mathematical techniques or determined by intuition.

Forecasts are important to organizations, risk management professionals, and the risk management process. Organizations use forecasts because they allow the organization to make more informed decisions about future activities. Risk management professionals can use forecasts to help determine the costs and benefits of various risk management techniques, which in turn enables them to make more informed decisions in the later steps of the risk management process. Forecasts are important to the risk management process because they are vital to the accuracy of the analysis of the loss exposures. Without proper forecasts, inaccurate analysis would lead to poor decisions in the remaining steps of the risk management process.

Projecting accidental losses is one of the biggest risk management challenges. Therefore, organizations must develop sound forecasts of their property, liability, personnel, and net income losses, just as they forecast their sales or production costs. To conduct these forecasts, risk management professionals must examine data on past losses. They can then subject these data to probability analysis and/or trend analysis to project the expected value of accidental losses. These projections can then be used to help management make cost-effective risk management decisions. These risk management decisions should be made like other business decisions—by determining the benefits and costs of each alternative and choosing the one(s) with the greatest benefits over costs.

DATA ON PAST LOSSES

To obtain information about future losses, forecasters analyze data about past (historical) losses. Provided that the underlying structural relationships are stable (that is, major changes have not rendered the older data irrelevant), past losses can reveal patterns that can be used to forecast the frequency and severity of potential future losses. The pattern could be as simple as "no change." Alternatively, information could indicate change. For example, past data on output levels and the frequency of employee injuries may indicate that plans to increase factory output could produce a greater number of employee injuries than in the past. Similarly, if data on wages and healthcare inflation indicate that inflation will continue, any future injuries that employees sustain would likely be more costly than past injuries.

To find patterns in past losses, a risk management professional must obtain data that are as follows:

- Relevant
- Complete
- Consistent
- Organized

Relevant Data

In order to project future losses based on past data, the past data must be relevant to the type of loss exposure being assessed. In addition, past losses should be valued on the basis that is most appropriate to risk management—usually an organization's cost of restoration after a loss. For property losses, these relevant data are the repair or replacement cost of the property at the time it is to be restored, not the property's book value. For liability losses, the relevant data include not only details of any claims paid but also the cost of investigating and defending or settling those claims. The relevant data for both personnel and net income losses include not only the reductions in revenue from any disruption of operations but also any extra expenses that an organization incurs while trying to return the business to normalcy.

Complete Data

To obtain data about past losses, risk management professionals often must rely on others, both inside and outside their organization. When gathering these data, risk management professionals must ensure that the data provided are complete. Consider, for example, the loss data for machinery damage presented in Exhibit 11-1. As the note to the exhibit indicates, the data for Year 2 (2002) were omitted from the accounting department's original report. Without that 2002 data, the forecast for machinery damage may be inaccurate.

A risk management professional often finds factors relating to each loss to be useful. Factors such as the affected employees' experience and training, the time of day that the machinery damage or breakdown occurred, the task being performed, and the supervisor on duty at the time of injury can be helpful in isolating and correcting the causes of each incident of machinery damage or breakdown.

In addition, having reliable estimates of the dollar amounts of the various elements of each loss is useful. For example, for each incident, the risk management professional would ideally like to know the cost of repairing or replacing the damaged or inoperative machinery, the resulting loss of revenue, any extra expense, and any overtime wages paid to maintain production levels. All of these details go into making the data complete.

EXHIBIT 11-1

Calendar of Historical Losses Resulting From Machinery Damage

	Date	Historical Amount		Date	Historical Amount
Year 1	4/21/01	$ 1,008	Year 3	2/8/03	$ 5,189
	5/3/01	4,651		5/17/03	7,834
	9/29/01	155		7/27/03	3,774**
	12/4/01	1,783		8/4/03	12,925**
				12/19/03	12,830
Year 2	3/18/02	$ 1,271*	Year 4	1/2/04	$ 6,782
	7/12/02	6,271*		1/9/04	21,425
	8/15/02	7,119*		4/22/04	4,483
	11/1/02	13,208*		6/10/04	9,059
				6/14/04	4,224
				10/23/04	35,508

*   Originally omitted from listing by accounting department.

** Originally reported by the accounting department as $2,100 and $15,000, respectively.

Consistent Data

To reflect past patterns, loss data must also be consistent in at least two respects. First, the loss data must be collected on a consistent basis for all recorded losses. Second, data must be expressed in constant dollars, to adjust for differences in price levels.

When Is a Dollar Not Worth a Dollar?

When referring to historical values, risk management professionals will often hear a variety of terms such as nominal dollars, current dollars, constant dollars, or real dollars. Remembering some very general definitions will help ensure consistent data and avoid some confusion.

Nominal dollars—dollar values that are the value at the time of the loss. For example, if a fire destroyed a building in 1995 and it cost $100,000 to repair the building in 1995, the $100,000 is in nominal dollars.

Current dollars—dollar values in today's dollar values. This value involves inflating all historical dollar values to today's value by using some measure of inflation (such as the Consumer Price Index).

Continued on next page.

For example, the $100,000 loss in 1995 would actually be a $125,000 loss in current dollars.

Constant or real dollars—dollar values in some base year. This value enables comparison of losses that have occurred in different time periods. As a matter of convenience, the most recent year is often chosen. For example, if a risk management professional had losses reported over the four year window 2001–2004, he would have to multiply 2001 values by 1.08 (to account for the 8% increase in prices from 2001 to 2004) to get the 2001 values into 2004 values for comparison. Similarly, 2002 losses would have to be multiplied by 1.06, and 2003 losses, by 1.04.

Consistent Basis for Data Collection

Loss data are often collected from different sources using different methods. Consequently, the possible sources of inconsistency are numerous. One common source of inconsistency results from some loss amounts being reported as estimates and others being reported as actual paid amounts. For example, in examining the loss amounts in Exhibit 11-1, the risk management professional noticed that two losses, those whose amounts are marked with two asterisks, were originally reported in even hundreds of dollars. The other loss amounts were not. This alerted the risk management professional to a potential issue.

Although a dollar amount ending in "00" or "000" is just as likely as an amount ending in any other two or three digits, a risk management professional should be aware of the common tendency to use round numbers when exact figures are not known. An inquiry to the accounting department revealed that these two asterisked amounts were estimates, made by the machinery maintenance department at the time of the accident. Therefore, while not to be ignored, these amounts are likely to be less credible than the other loss figures in Exhibit 11-1. So that all the data were consistent, the risk management professional asked the accounting department to provide the actual property, revenue, and extra expense costs resulting directly from these two incidents. Reconstructed to be consistent with the other data, these amounts were changed from $2,100 to $3,774 and from $15,000 to $12,925. These revised figures are used in all subsequent calculations involving those two losses.

Amounts of Loss Adjusted for Price Level Changes

For consistency, historical losses should be adjusted (or indexed) for price level changes. Otherwise, the reported amounts of two physically identical losses occurring in different years probably will be different. Inflation makes the later loss appear larger because it is measured in less valuable dollars. To prevent this distortion, risk management professionals must use loss data expressed in constant dollars. Data from different time periods are expressed in constant dollars when the amounts reported are comparable in terms of the value of goods and services that could be purchased in a particular benchmark year. Although any year could be chosen as the benchmark year, standard practice is to use the most recent complete year—in this case, Year 4—as the benchmark year. Therefore, data are reported in constant Year 4 dollars so that each amount reflects what could be purchased in Year 4.

Price indices are used to adjust data so that they are in constant dollars. A **price index** for a year indicates the price of a particular basket of goods and services relative to some base year, when the price index for the base year is set to be 100. For example, if the price index in Year 4 equals 148.6 and the base year is Year 0, then a basket of goods and services that cost $100 in year 0 would cost $148.60 in Year 4. Stated differently, the basket of goods and services would cost 48.6 percent more in Year 4 than in Year 0. Exhibit 11-2 provides hypothetical price indices for Year 1 through Year 4. The price index in Year 1 is 115.2 and the price index in Year 4 is 148.6. Therefore, a price of $115.20 in Year 1 is equivalent to a price of $148.60 in Year 4. Some common price indices used by risk management professionals include the Consumer Price Index, medical cost inflation indices, and real estate price indices.

To put the loss data in constant Year 4 dollars, historical amounts of all past losses must be inflated by multiplying the historical amount of each loss in a given year by an indexing factor appropriate for that year. The indexing factor appropriate for a given year is equal to the price index in the benchmark year (Year 4) divided by the price index for the given year. For example, the indexing factor used to put Year 1 losses into Year 4 dollars is calculated as follows:

Indexing factor for Year 1 losses = Year 4 price index ÷ Year 1 price index

= 148.6 ÷ 115.2

= 1.29.

As well as showing the price indices, Exhibit 11-2 shows how an appropriate indexing factor for each year is calculated. Year 1 losses should be multiplied by the indexing factor for Year 1 losses (1.29).

Price index
The price of a particular basket of goods and services relative to some base year, when the price index for the base year is set to be 100.

EXHIBIT 11-2

Indexing Factors for Adjusting Losses to Year 4 Dollars

	Base Year			Benchmark Year	
	Year 0	Year 1	Year 2	Year 3	Year 4
Price index	100	115.2	125.9	140.2	148.6

Year	Price Index ($P_0 = 100$)		Indexing Factor	
1	P_1	115.2	$P_4 \div P_1$	1.29
2	P_2	125.9	$P_4 \div P_2$	1.18
3	P_3	140.2	$P_4 \div P_3$	1.06
4	P_4	148.6	$P_4 \div P_4$	1.00

Exhibit 11-3 shows both historical and adjusted loss amounts for the machinery damage outlined in Exhibit 11-1. Each adjusted loss amount was calculated by multiplying the loss by the indexing factor for the year in which the loss occurred.

To illustrate, the first loss amount in Exhibit 11-3 had a historical value of $1,008 on April 21 of Year 1. When multiplied by the Year 1 indexing factor

EXHIBIT 11-3

Adjustment of Historical Losses to Year 4 Price Levels

Date	Historical Amount	Indexing Factor	Adjusted Amount	Annual Total	Annual Frequency
4/21/01	$ 1,008	1.29	$ 1,300		
5/3/01	4,651	1.29	6,000		
9/29/01	155	1.29	200		
12/4/01	1,783	1.29	2,300	$ 9,800	4
3/18/02	1,271	1.18	1,500		
7/12/02	6,271	1.18	7,400		
8/15/02	7,119	1.18	8,400		
11/1/02	13,208	1.18	15,585	$ 32,885	4
2/8/03	5,189	1.06	5,500		
5/17/03	7,834	1.06	8,304		
7/27/03	3,774	1.06	4,000		
8/4/03	12,925	1.06	13,701		
12/19/03	12,830	1.06	13,600	$ 45,105	5
1/2/04	6,782	1.00	6,782		
1/9/04	21,425	1.00	21,425		
4/22/04	4,483	1.00	4,483		
6/10/04	9,059	1.00	9,059		
6/14/04	4,224	1.00	4,224		
10/23/04	35,508	1.00	35,508	$ 81,481	6
			Total number of losses:		19
			Total dollar losses:	$169,271	

Mean frequency (per year) = Total number of losses ÷ number of years = 4.75.

Mean severity (per loss) = Total dollar losses ÷ Total number of losses = $8,909.

of 1.29, the adjusted loss amount becomes $1,300 rounded to the nearest dollar. This figure is shown in the "Adjusted Amount" column of Exhibit 11-3. Similarly, the November 1, Year 2 loss, with a historical value of $13,208, adjusts to $15,585.

These examples used one price index for the total loss for each accident. Ideally, separate price indices for each cost element of each loss would be used to adjust the data. For example, a price index for machinery replacement costs would be used to adjust the machinery replacement costs and a different price index for wages would be used to adjust the overtime wage costs.

These examples also follow the usual practice of applying all indexing factors on an annual basis, even though losses occurred at different times of the year. If monthly price index figures are available, improved accuracy could be gained by applying this indexing procedure on a monthly basis, starting with the month in which each loss occurred.

Organized Data

As well as being relevant, complete, and consistent, data must be organized in order to accurately project future losses. Data can be organized in different ways, with some ways being more useful to project future losses than others. For example, listing losses by calendar dates, as in Exhibits 11-1 and 11-3, may not disclose patterns that could be revealed by listing losses by size. An array of losses—amounts of losses listed in increasing or decreasing value—could reveal clusterings of losses by severity and could also focus attention on large losses, which are often the most important for risk management decisions. Organizing losses also is the first step in charting losses by size to develop loss severity distributions or loss trends over time.

An array of the nineteen major machinery damage losses suffered in Year 1 through Year 4 appears in Exhibit 11-4. Column 3 indicates the adjusted loss amounts, with the other columns showing the dates, historical (unadjusted) amounts, and rank of each arrayed loss, respectively. Notice that the numbers in Column 4, "Rank," of Exhibit 11-4 are arranged so that the largest loss, potentially the most important, has a rank of "1" (largest), while the smallest loss has a rank of "19" (smallest). Finally, notice that ranking losses by adjusted price-indexed amounts rather than historical amounts eliminates distortions caused by price level changes and is therefore more useful in identifying the actual effect of each loss.

Adjusted and organized, historical loss data provide an important basis for forecasting losses. The following discussion explains how to make such forecasts, first by using probability analysis (which presumes an unchanging environment) and then by using trend analysis (which presumes a changing environment, but one that is changing predictably).

EXHIBIT 11-4

Array of Historical and Adjusted Losses

[1]	[2]	[3]	[4]
Date	Historical Amount	Adjusted Loss Amount	Rank
9/29/01	$ 155	$ 200	19
4/21/01	1,008	1,300	18
3/18/02	1,271	1,500	17
12/4/01	1,783	2,300	16
7/27/03	3,774	4,000	15
6/14/04	4,224	4,224	14
4/22/04	4,483	4,483	13
2/8/03	5,189	5,500	12
5/3/01*	4,651	6,000	11
1/2/04*	6,782	6,782	10
7/12/02	6,271	7,400	9
5/17/03*	7,834	8,304	8
8/15/02	7,119	8,400	7
6/10/04	9,059	9,059	6
12/19/03	12,830	13,600	5
8/4/03	12,925	13,701	4
11/1/02	13,208	15,585	3
1/9/04	21,425	21,425	2
10/23/04	35,508	35,508	1

* Loss for which adjustment of historical amount to Year 4 constant dollars changes ranking in array

Probability analysis
A technique for forecasting events, such as accidental and business losses, on the assumption that they are governed by an unchanging probability distribution.

Probability distribution
A presentation (table, chart, or graph) of probability estimates of a particular set of circumstances and of the probability of each possible outcome.

PROBABILITY ANALYSIS

Probability analysis is a technique for forecasting events, such as accidental and business losses, on the assumption that they are governed by an unchanging probability distribution. A **probability distribution** is a presentation (table, chart, or graph) of probability estimates of a particular set of circumstances and of the probability of each possible outcome.

Probability analysis is particularly effective for predicting accidental losses in organizations that have a substantial volume of data on past losses and fairly stable operations so that (except for price level changes) patterns of past losses presumably will continue unchanged in the future. In such an unchanging environment, past losses can be viewed as a sample of all possible losses that the organization might suffer. The larger the number of past losses, the larger the sample of losses. Consequently, the environment that produces those losses is more stable, and the forecasts of future losses are more reliable.

The Nature of Probability

The probability of an event is the relative frequency with which the event can be expected to occur in the long run in a stable environment. For example, given many tosses, a coin can be expected to come up heads as often as it comes up tails. Given many rolls of one die from a pair of dice, a 4 can be expected to come up one-sixth of the time. According to one standard mortality table, slightly more than 0.3 percent of males age sixty-seven can be expected to die before reaching age sixty-eight.[1] Finally, statistics in 2001 indicated that of the automobiles on the road, 1 out of every 194 could be expected to be stolen within the year.[2]

Any probability can be expressed as a fraction, a percentage, or a decimal. The probability of a head on a coin toss can be expressed as ½, 50 percent, or .50. The probability of a 4 on one roll of one die can be written as ⅙, 16.67 percent, or .167. Similarly, ¹⁄₁₉₄, 0.516 percent, and .00516 are all proper ways of indicating the probability that an automobile would have been stolen during 2001.

The probability of an event that is totally impossible is 0, the probability of an absolutely certain event is 1, and the probabilities of all events that are neither totally impossible nor absolutely certain are greater than 0 but less than 1.

Probability distributions can be developed either from historical (empirical) data or from theoretical considerations. Probabilities associated with coin tosses or dice throws can be developed and are unchanging. From a description of a fair coin or die, a person who has never seen either a coin or a die can calculate the probability of flipping a head or rolling a 4. Such probabilities are known as theoretical probabilities because they are based on theoretical principles rather than on actual experience.

In contrast, the empirical probability that a sixty-seven-year-old male will die or that a car will be stolen during a particular year cannot be deduced theoretically but must be estimated by studying the loss experience of a sample of men age sixty-seven or a sample of cars. The empirical probabilities deduced solely from historical data may change as new data are discovered or as the environment that produces these events changes. For example, data from 2001 indicated that 1 vehicle in 194 could be expected to be stolen, whereas data from 1970 might have indicated that 1 vehicle in 121 could be expected to be stolen. Therefore, empirical probabilities are only estimates whose accuracy depends on the size and representative nature of the samples being studied. On the other hand, theoretical probabilities are constant as long as the physical conditions that generate them remain unchanged.

Data Sources for Calculating Empirical Probabilities

For most of the situations that risk management professionals encounter, theoretical probabilities of events are not available. When appropriate to do so, risk management professionals must therefore rely on empirical probabilities, even though these probabilities are estimates of some hypothetical probability that will never be known.

Although empirical probabilities are estimates, they are more reliable when they are calculated using a substantial volume of data on past losses and when the organization faces fairly stable operations so that (except for price level changes) patterns of past losses presumably will continue in the future. In such an unchanging environment, past losses can be viewed as a sample of all possible losses that the organization could suffer in the future.

Risk management professionals often have difficulty developing empirical probability distributions of accidental losses. The organization's own loss data are often not substantial enough to be reliable, and the data on the combined experience of other organizations, if available, may not be sufficiently specific or current to be useful. In these situations, other sources of data can be used to estimate empirical probabilities, including loss experience from regional or nationwide insurers, or from organizations such as the National Safety Council or the National Fire Protection Association.

Probability Distributions

Once empirical probabilities have been determined, probability distributions can be constructed. Because every probability distribution includes the probability of every possible outcome (making it certain that one of these outcomes and only one will occur), the sum of the probabilities in a probability distribution must be 1.0.

The definition of a probability distribution applies to both theoretical probabilities (such as those involved in tossing coins or rolling dice) and empirical probabilities (such as of the number or size of accidental losses). For example, in flipping a fair coin, each of the two possible outcomes, heads or tails, has an equal probability of one-half, or 50 percent. Because, on a particular flip of a coin, only one outcome is possible, these outcomes are mutually exclusive. Similarly, these two outcomes are the only possible outcomes and, therefore, are collectively exhaustive. A properly constructed probability distribution always contains outcomes that are both mutually exclusive and collectively exhaustive. For example, take the probability of the number of hurricanes making landfall in the state of Florida during any given hurricane season. The frequency probability table may look like the one shown in Exhibit 11-5. To aid in visualizing the mutually exclusive and collectively exhaustive nature of a probability distribution, Exhibit 11-6 shows the distribution as a pie chart.

EXHIBIT 11-5

Number of Hurricanes Making Landfall in Florida During One Hurricane Season

Number of Hurricanes Making Landfall	Probability
0	.300
1	.350
2	.200
3	.147
4	.002
5+	.001

EXHIBIT 11-6

Florida Hurricane Season: Number of Hurricanes Making Landfall

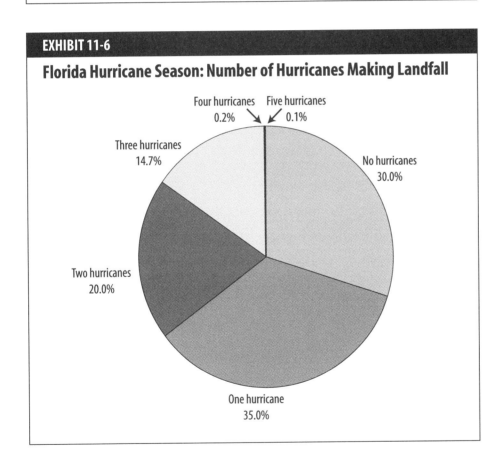

Discrete Versus Continuous Probability Distributions

Probability distributions come in two forms: discrete probability distributions and continuous probability distributions. A discrete probability distribution is a table listing the probability of every possible outcome. Discrete probability distributions are typically used as frequency distributions—that is, to analyze how often something will occur. For example, what is the probability that a building will suffer zero fires this year? One fire? Two fires? Discrete probability distributions have values that are whole numbers. It is impossible to have 2.5 fires.

Continuous probability distributions are typically used for severity distributions in which the value lost can take any value between $0.00 and some upper limit (such as $1,000,000). The loss can be $1.50 or $4,567.51. Continuous probability distributions generate a probability of an outcome being in a certain range. For example, a discrete frequency distribution may show that the probability of a building not having a fire (0 fires) is .50, of having one fire is .35, and of having two fires is .15. If a fire occurs, a continuous severity distribution may show the damage to be anywhere between $0.00 and $1,000,000, with the probability of the damage between $1,000 and $5,000 being .25, between $10,000 and $20,000 being .30, and so on.

An example of a theoretical probability distribution is the distribution of the total number of pips on one throw of two dice, one red and one green. The thirty-six equally likely outcomes (green 1, red 1; green 1, red 2;…green 6, red 6) are shown in Exhibit 11-7. Eleven pip values are possible (ranging from a total of two pips to a total of twelve pips), and the probability of each of these eleven possible pip values is proportional to the number of times each pip value appears in the table of outcomes. As the chart in Exhibit 11-7 indicates, the probability of a total of two pips is 1/36 because only one of the thirty-six possible ways that the dice may fall (green 1, red 1) produces a total of two pips. Similarly, 1/36 is the probability of a total of twelve pips. The most likely total pip value, seven pips, has a probability of 6/36, represented in the table of outcomes by the diagonal southwest-northeast row of sevens.

In the graph showing each possible outcome, the height of the vertical line above each outcome is proportional to the probability of that outcome. Exhibit 11-7 presents three views of a complete probability distribution. All possible outcomes are accounted for (they are collectively exhaustive), and the occurrence of any possible outcome (such as green 1, red 1, or alternatively, a point total of 2) makes impossible (or excludes) any other outcome.

Empirical Probability Distributions

Empirical probability distributions (estimated from historical data) are constructed in the same way as theoretical probability distributions. Exhibit 11-8 shows an empirical probability distribution for the machinery damage losses from Exhibit 11-4. Because a probability distribution provides a mutually exclusive, collectively exhaustive list of outcomes, loss categories (bins) must be designed so that all losses can be included. One method is to divide the bins into equal sizes, similar to Exhibit 11-8, in which each bin size is standard (in this case $5,000).

EXHIBIT 11-7

Probability Distribution of Total Pips on One Roll of Two Dice

A. Table of Outcomes

		Red Die					
		1	2	3	4	5	6
Green Die	1	2	3	4	5	6	7
	2	3	4	5	6	7	8
	3	4	5	6	7	8	9
	4	5	6	7	8	9	10
	5	6	7	8	9	10	11
	6	7	8	9	10	11	12

B. Chart Format

Total Pips—Both Dice	Probability				
2	1/36	or	.028	or	2.8%
3	2/36	or	.056	or	5.6%
4	3/36	or	.083	or	8.3%
5	4/36	or	.111	or	11.1%
6	5/36	or	.139	or	13.9%
7	6/36	or	.167	or	16.7%
8	5/36	or	.139	or	13.9%
9	4/36	or	.111	or	11.1%
10	3/36	or	.083	or	8.3%
11	2/36	or	.056	or	5.6%
12	1/36	or	.028	or	2.8%
Total	36/36	or	1.000	or	100.0%

Totals may not sum to 1 or 100% because of rounding.

C. Graph Format

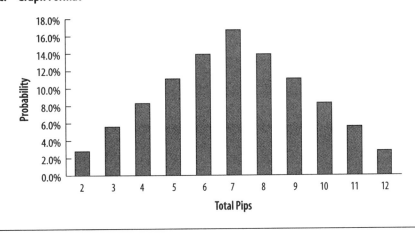

The second component of a probability distribution is the set of probabilities associated with each of the possible outcomes. Column 3 of Exhibit 11-8 shows empirical probabilities for each size category. The empirical probability for each category is the relative frequency with which historical losses fell into each of the categories and is calculated by dividing the number of losses in a category by the total number of losses. Notice that the sum of the resulting empirical probabilities is 100.00 percent (the outcomes are collectively exhaustive) and that any given loss falls into only one category (the outcomes are mutually exclusive). Therefore, the empirical probability distribution for losses shown in Columns 1 and 3 of Exhibit 11-8 satisfies the requirements of a probability distribution.

EXHIBIT 11-8

Empirical Probability Distribution of Loss Severity Developed from Year 1 through Year 4 Adjusted Machinery Losses

[1]	[2]	[3]	[4]	[5]
Size Category	No. of Losses	Percentage of Total No. of Losses	Dollar Amount of Losses	Percentage of Total Dollar Amount
$0–$5,000	7	36.84%	$ 18,007	10.64%
$5,001–$10,000	7	36.84%	$ 51,445	30.39%
$10,001–$15,000	2	10.53%	$ 27,301	16.13%
$15,001–$20,000	1	5.26%	$ 15,585	9.21%
$20,001–$25,000	1	5.26%	$ 21,425	12.66%
$25,001+	1	5.26%	$ 35,508	20.98%
Total	19	100.00%	$169,271	100.00%

Percentages may not equal totals because of rounding.

Columns 4 and 5 of Exhibit 11-8 present some additional information that a risk management professional may use to supplement the probability distribution in Columns 1 and 3. Each dollar amount in Column 4 shows the total of the losses per size category in Column 1. The adjusted amounts of these losses, which total $169,271, are taken from Exhibit 11-3. Column 5 of Exhibit 11-8 expresses the dollar amounts in Column 4 as percentages of this $169,271 total.

Columns 4 and 5 show that, although large dollar losses are individually infrequent, they usually account for most of the dollar total of losses. For example, the three losses that are greater than $10,000 but less than or equal to $20,000 total $42,886, or about 25 percent of the total dollar amount of losses. The five losses that exceed $10,000 total $99,819, or about 59 percent of the total dollar amount of machinery losses.

The empirical probability distribution for machinery losses presented in Exhibit 11-8 differs in two ways from the theoretical probability distributions of coin tosses and dice rolls calculated earlier. First, the outcomes shown in Column 1, size categories of losses, are somewhat arbitrary and are not as evident as the heads/tails outcomes in tossing coins or the two through twelve total pip scores in rolling two dice. Second, the highest possible dice total is twelve, while the largest-size category of machinery losses, those exceeding $25,000, is open-ended, with no evident upper limit.

Law of Large Numbers

A risk management professional would have increasing confidence in the estimates in the empirical probability distribution in Exhibit 11-8 as more loss data were included. Such confidence is supported by the law of large numbers. The law of large numbers indicates that as the number of independent events increases, the actual relative frequency (percentage) of each of the possible outcomes more nearly approaches the underlying true or theoretical probability of that outcome. Essentially, the law of large numbers says that the accuracy of the relative frequencies of outcomes increases as the number of independent observations increase.

The law of large numbers does not imply that a larger sample size *always* produces a smaller estimate error; it states that *on average* the relative error will be lower as the sample size increases. Nonetheless, when constructing empirical probability distributions, a greater sample size is better, assuming that the underlying structural relationships remain relatively stable. In risk management, samples can be exposure units, losses, events, time periods (such as days, months, or years), or other units that are essentially similar to one another.

There are some limitations to the law of large numbers. It applies to forecasts of future events only when those events meet all three of the following criteria:

1. The events have occurred in the past under substantially identical conditions and have resulted from unchanging, basic causal forces.
2. The events can be expected to occur in the future under the same unchanging conditions.
3. The events have been, and will continue to be, both independent of one another and sufficiently numerous.

Continuous Probability Distributions

Each of the probability distributions discussed so far is an example of a discrete distribution—that is, a countable number of possible outcomes exists. For example, the probability distribution for the number of points on two dice presented in Exhibit 11-7 has eleven possible outcomes—any whole number between 2 and 12. The empirical probability for machinery losses in Exhibit 11-8 has five possible outcomes described by various ranges of losses.

It is also possible to model continuous probability distributions for losses; that is, outcomes can be any number falling within some range. For example, losses on property worth $100,000 can take any value between $0 and $100,000.

Exhibit 11-9 illustrates continuous probability distributions. The possible outcomes are presented on the horizontal axis and the height of the line above the outcomes indicates the likelihood of those outcomes. These outcomes are called probability density functions. Figure (a), which has a flat line above the interval $0 to $1,000, illustrates that all of the outcomes between $0 and $1,000 are equally likely. Figure (b), which has a curve that starts at $0 and increases until it reaches a peak at $500 and then declines to zero again at $1,000, illustrates that the very low (close to $0) and very high (close to $1,000) outcomes are unlikely to occur and that the outcomes around $500 are much more likely to occur.

For continuous probability distributions, as with discrete probability distributions, the probability density functions must sum to one.

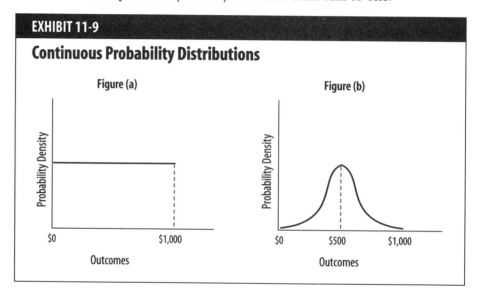

EXHIBIT 11-9

Continuous Probability Distributions

Characteristics of Probability Distributions

One important characteristic of all probability distributions has already been noted: every distribution must assign relative frequencies (probabilities) to all of the possible outcomes. No possible outcome can be omitted. Consequently, the outcomes in a valid probability distribution must be mutually exclusive and collectively exhaustive.

Probability distributions also summarize important information about distribution characteristics. These characteristics, which include skewness, central tendency, and dispersion, are often used to compare distributions.

Skewness
A measure of whether a probability distribution is symmetrical.

Symmetrical distribution
A distribution that, when bisected by a vertical line, is identical on both sides.

Skewness

Skewness is a measure of whether a probability distribution is symmetrical. A **symmetrical distribution** is a distribution that, when bisected by a vertical line, is identical on both sides. Figure (a) in Exhibit 11-10 illustrates a symmetrical distribution. The probabilities of less likely outcomes decline at the same rate on both sides of the distribution. A symmetrical distribution has a skewness of zero. Figures (b) and (c) in Exhibit 11-10 provide other examples of symmetrical distributions.

In each case, the area to the right of the vertical line is a mirror image of the area to the left. The bar chart in Exhibit 11-7 of a probability distribution of the total points on a single roll of two dice also illustrates a symmetrical distribution.

A distribution that is not symmetrical is **skewed**. Therefore, a distribution that has outcomes clustered to the left or right of the distribution, with a long, thin tail extending to the other side, is skewed.

Skewed
A distribution that is not symmetrical.

EXHIBIT 11-10

Typical Shapes of Symmetrical and Skewed Distributions Showing Relative Locations of Mean, Median, and Mode

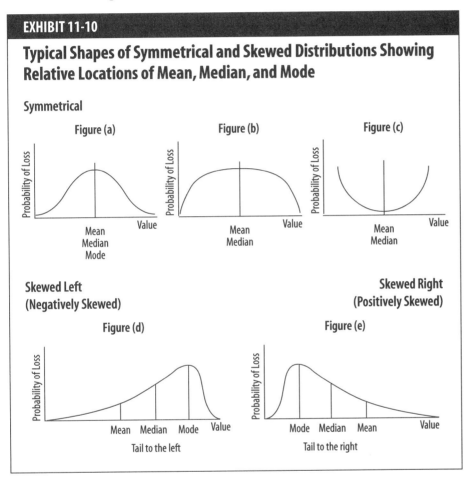

Symmetrical

Skewed Left
(Negatively Skewed)

Skewed Right
(Positively Skewed)

Skewed probability distributions are sometimes described by the direction in which their tails point. In a negatively skewed probability distribution (skewness is less than zero), the most frequent outcomes are clustered on the right side of the distribution. A thin tail of low probability outcomes extends to the left. Although relatively rare in risk management, such distributions could apply to circumstances such as cargo thefts for which most losses are generally presumed to be total rather than partial. A probability distribution of such losses might follow the general shape of the negatively skewed distribution shown in Exhibit 11-10, Figure (d).

In a positively skewed probability distribution (skewness is greater than zero), the most frequent outcome is centered over the outcomes clustered on the left side of the distribution. A thin long tail of low probabilities outcomes extends to the right. For example, with protected properties, a distribution of loss size by fire, theft, or flood is generally presumed to follow the shape of the positively skewed distribution in Figure (e) in Exhibit 11-10 because small losses tend to be more frequent than large ones.

Central Tendency

Central tendency
The single outcome that is representative of all possible outcomes included within a probability distribution.

The **central tendency** is the single outcome that is representative of all possible outcomes included within a probability distribution. Many probability distributions cluster around a particular value, which may or may not be in the exact center of the distribution's range of values. The three most widely accepted representative outcomes are the expected value (or mean from an empirical distribution), the median, and the mode. For any particular distribution, the relationship of these values to one another and to the other values in the distribution depends on the distribution's skewness.

Expected value
The weighted average of all of the possible outcomes of a probability distribution.

The **expected value** is the weighted average of all of the possible outcomes of a probability distribution. The weights are the probabilities of the outcomes. The outcomes of a probability distribution are symbolized as $x_1, x_2, x_3, \ldots x_n$ (x_n represents the last outcome in the series), having respective probabilities of $p_1, p_2, p_3, \ldots p_n$. The expected value of the distribution is $(p_1 x_1) + (p_2 x_2) + (p_3 x_3) \ldots + (p_n x_n)$. In the dice example, the calculation of the expected value of the distribution is shown in Exhibit 11-11. The procedure for calculating the expected value applies to all discrete probability distributions regardless of their skewness or dispersion. For continuous distributions, the expected value is also a weighted average of the possible outcomes. However, calculating the expected value for a continuous distribution is much more complex and is beyond the scope of this text.

Probabilities are needed to calculate the expected value of a distribution. When considering an empirical distribution constructed from historical data, the distribution's expected value is estimated using the mean or average of the outcomes. The **mean** is the numeric average; calculated by summing all observed values and dividing by the number of observations. For example, if the observed values are 2, 3, 4, 4, 5, 5, 5, 6, 6, and 8, then the mean equals 4.8, which is the sum of the values, 48, divided by the number of values, 10. Just as the expected value is calculated by weighting each possible outcome by its probability, the mean is calculated by weighting each observed outcome by the relative frequency with which it occurs.

Mean
The numeric average; calculated by summing all observed values and dividing by the number of observations.

Using the machinery loss example presented in Exhibit 11-3, the average number of machinery losses per year can be estimated by calculating the mean number of machinery losses per year using data from Years 1 through 4. The number of losses in each of these years is 4, 4, 5, and 6, respectively. Consequently, an estimate of the expected number of losses per year is the mean number of losses observed, which equals 4.75 (19 ÷ 4). Of course, this is only a good estimate of the expected number of losses if the underlying conditions determining losses remain constant over time.

EXHIBIT 11-11

Calculating the Expected Value of a Probability Distribution— The Example of Two Dice

Total Pips—Both Dice (x)	Probability (p)	$p \times x$
2	1/36	2/36
3	2/36	6/36
4	3/36	12/36
5	4/36	20/36
6	5/36	30/36
7	6/36	42/36
8	5/36	40/36
9	4/36	36/36
10	3/36	30/36
11	2/36	22/36
12	1/36	12/36
Total	36/36	252/36

Expected Value = 252/36 = 7.

The **median** is the midpoint of a sequential set of values. For an even number of values, the median is the average of the two middle values. Values must be arranged by size, from highest to lowest or lowest to highest. The median has the same number of values above it or below it. Therefore, in the array of nineteen machinery losses in Exhibit 11-4, the median adjusted loss has a value of $6,782. This tenth loss (counting from either the top or the bottom of the array) is the median because nine losses are smaller and nine losses are larger.

For Year 2 losses in Exhibit 11-3, the median is the average of $7,400 and $8,400, or $7,900. This is true for the median of any even number of outcomes, even if two or more of them are the same. In another example, for Year 4 losses in Exhibit 11-3, the median is the average of the third and fourth losses. The third and fourth losses in this array are $6,782 and $9,059, so the median of all six Year 4 losses is $7,920.50, calculated as ($6,782 + $9,059) ÷ 2. If two or more of these six losses had been the same, such as if the $21,425 loss had instead also been $9,059, the median still would have been calculated as ($6,782 + $9,059) ÷ 2, or $7,920.50.

The median of a probability distribution can also be determined by summing the probabilities to find the value for which a cumulative probability of 50 percent is reached. For example, 7 is the median of the probability distribution of pips in rolling two dice because 7 is the only number of pips for which

Median
The midpoint of a sequential set of values. For an even number of values, the median is the average of the two middle values.

the probability of higher observations (15/36) is equal to the probability of lower observations. That is, there are fifteen equally probable ways of getting a result higher than 7 and fifteen equally probable ways of getting a result lower than 7.

This same result can be confirmed by summing the probabilities of outcomes equal to or less than a given number of pips in rolling two dice, as in Exhibit 11-12. The cumulative 50 percent probability (18/36) is reached with 7 pips (actually, in the middle of the 7-point class of results). Therefore, 7 is the median of this distribution.

The cumulative probabilities in Column 3 of Exhibit 11-12 indicate the probability of a die roll yielding a certain number of pips or less. For example, the probability of rolling a 3 or less is 3/36 (or the sum of 1/36 for rolling a 2 plus 2/36 for rolling a 3). Similarly, the probability of rolling a 10 or less is 33/36, calculated by adding the individual Column 2 probabilities of outcomes of 10 pips or less. With probability distributions of losses, calculating probabilities of losses equal to or less than a given number of losses or dollar amounts of losses, individually and cumulatively, can be helpful in selecting retention levels and insurance deductibles. Similarly, calculating individual and cumulative probabilities of losses equal to or greater than a given number of losses or dollar amounts can help in selecting upper limits of insurance coverage.

EXHIBIT 11-12

Cumulative Probability Distribution of Total Pips in Rolling Two Dice

	Cumulative Probability	
[1]	[2]	[3]
Total Pips—Both Dice (x)	Probability (p)	Sum of Probabilities
2	1/36	1/36
3	2/36	3/36
4	3/36	6/36
5	4/36	10/36
6	5/36	15/36
7	6/36	21/36
8	5/36	26/36
9	4/36	30/36
10	3/36	33/36
11	2/36	35/36
12	1/36	36/36

For example, the probability of rolling a 3 or less is 3/36, or the sum of 1/36 for rolling a 2 plus 2/36 for rolling a 3.

Exhibit 11-13 shows how to derive a cumulative probability distribution of loss sizes from the individual probabilities of loss size in Exhibit 11-8. Examining the $0–$5,000 size category on the basis of the available data, 5.26 percent of all losses are less than or equal to $1,000 (1 loss out of 19) and another 31.58 percent are greater than $1,000 but less than or equal to $5,000 (6 losses out of 19). Therefore, the probabilities of a loss being $5,000 or less are calculated as the sum of these two probabilities, or 36.84 percent, as shown in Column 3. Similarly, as shown in Column 6, losses of $5,000 or less can be expected to account for 10.64 percent of the total *dollar* amount of all losses.

The summed probabilities in Column 3 indicate that the median individual loss is between $5,001 and $10,000, the category in which the 50 percent cumulative probability is reached. This result is consistent with the $6,782 median loss found earlier by examining Exhibit 11-4.

Beyond locating the median loss, Exhibit 11-8 and Exhibit 11-13 have some implications for risk management decisions. For example, if the organization had insured its machinery losses subject to a $5,000 per accident deductible, the organization would have retained the full amount of more than one out of every three losses (36.84 percent of the number of losses in Column 3 of Exhibit 11-13). The organization would also have retained the first $5,000 of every larger loss (an additional $60,000 for the twelve losses in Column 2

EXHIBIT 11-13

Cumulative Probabilities That Machinery Losses Will Not Exceed Specified Amounts

[1] Size Category	[2] No. of Losses	[3] Percentage of No. of Losses	[4] Cumulative Percentage of No. of Losses Not Exceeding Category	[5] Dollar Amount of Losses	[6] Percentage of Dollar Amount	[7] Cumulative Percentage of Dollar Amount of Losses Not Exceeding Category
$0–$5,000	7	36.84%	36.84%	$18,007	10.64%	10.64%
$5,001–$10,000	7	36.84%	73.68%	$51,445	30.39%	41.03%
$10,001–$15,000	2	10.53%	84.21%	$27,300	16.13%	57.16%
$15,001–$20,000	1	5.26%	89.47%	$15,585	9.21%	66.37%
$20,001–$25,000	1	5.26%	94.73%	$21,425	12.66%	79.03%
$25,001+	1	5.26%	100.00%	$35,508	20.98%	100.00%
Total	19	100.00%		$169,270	100.00%	

Column 4 indicates that, based on historical data, 36.84% of all losses are less than or equal to $5,000 and that another 36.84% are greater than $5,000 but less than or equal to $10,000.

The probability of a loss being less than or equal to $10,000 is 73.68%.

Percentages may not equal totals because of rounding.

of Exhibit 11-8 that exceed $5,000). Therefore, total retention of machinery losses with a $5,000 deductible would have been the full amount of all losses not exceeding $5,000 ($18,007 from Exhibit 11-8, Column 4) plus $60,000 ($5,000 × 12, the number of such larger losses from Exhibit 11-8, Column 2). This makes a total of $78,007. This retention would have been about 46 percent of the $169,271 total of all of the organization's machinery losses. This is the amount that the organization might budget over the four years for retained machinery losses or use as a comparison against the insurance premium credits for a $5,000 deductible policy over the same time period.

Alternatively, if the organization were to adopt a $10,000 deductible, it could expect to retain the full amount of more than seven out of every ten losses (73.68 percent of the number of losses in Exhibit 11-13, Column 4), or, from Exhibit 11-8, $119,452 of the losses (consisting of the $69,452 full expected value of losses not exceeding $10,000 ($18,007 + $51,445) plus $10,000 for each of the five expected larger losses). This expected retention would be approximately 71 percent of the total amount of all machinery losses.

Mode

The most frequently occurring value in a distribution.

A distribution's **mode** is the most frequently occurring value in the distribution. For a continuous distribution, the mode is the value of the outcome directly beneath the peak of the probability density function. In the distribution of the total points of two dice throws, the mode is seven points. In the empirical distribution of machinery losses shown in Exhibit 11-8, the mode is the $0–$5,000 range or the $5,001–$10,000 range because those ranges have the highest frequency of losses (seven).

In most distributions that have only one peak, the direction of skewness determines the relative locations of its mean, median, and mode. In a positively skewed distribution, the tail extends to the right, and the three measures of central tendency are positioned in mode-median-mean order when reading from left to right. In a negatively skewed distribution, the tail extends to the left and the three measures of central tendency are positioned in mean-median-mode order when reading from left to right. Exhibit 11-10 illustrates these locations.

The mode of a skewed unimodal distribution corresponds to the highest point on the probability density function. The median falls between the mode and the mean. In a symmetrical unimodal distribution, the mean, median, and mode have the same value.

Dispersion

The variability, or scatter, among the values of a data set.

Dispersion

Dispersion is the variability, or scatter, among the values of a data set. Dispersion describes the extent to which the distribution is spread out rather than concentrated around a single outcome. It is the degree of variability from the distribution's mean. The less dispersion around the distribution's mean, the greater the likelihood that actual results will fall within a given range of that mean. With less dispersion, less uncertainty is involved in determining that a result close to the mean will actually occur.

Two widely used measures of dispersion are standard deviation and coefficient of variation. A **standard deviation** is the average of the differences (deviations) between the possible outcomes and the expected value of those outcomes. To calculate the standard deviation, one must carry out the following six steps:

Standard deviation
The average of the differences (deviations) between the possible outcomes and the expected values of those outcomes.

1. Calculate the distribution's expected value
2. Subtract this expected value from each distribution value to find the differences
3. Square (multiply a number by itself) each of the resulting differences
4. Multiply each square by the probability associated with the value
5. Sum the resulting products
6. Find the square root of the sum

Exhibit 11-14 illustrates this procedure for the distribution of values in rolling two dice. This distribution's mean, written $\bar{x}$, was calculated in Exhibit 11-11 to be 7. Column 3 of Exhibit 11-14 subtracts 7 from the values in Column 1, Column 4 squares the differences shown in Column 3, and Column 5 multiplies each of these differences by the probability of the respective values. The sum of the products in Column 5, 210/36, or 5.83, is the square of the standard deviation. The square root of this number, approximately 2.4, is therefore the standard deviation. (The square root of any number is another number that when multiplied by itself equals the original number. For example, the square root of 16 is 4.)

A method of estimating the standard deviation of machinery losses is to use the individual loss data reported in Exhibit 11-4. The procedure for calculating a standard deviation using an actual sample of observations (as opposed to a probability distribution) is as follows:

1. Calculate the mean of the observations (the sum of the observations divided by the number of observations)
2. Subtract the mean from each of the observations
3. Square each of the resulting differences
4. Sum these squares
5. Divide this sum by the number of observations minus one (to obtain a quotient)
6. Calculate the square root of the quotient

Exhibit 11-15 shows how to apply this procedure to the actual loss data in Exhibit 11-4.

A variation on calculating the standard deviation using the individual observations is to estimate an empirical probability distribution for the individual observations (similar to Exhibit 11-8) and then calculate the standard deviation of the empirical probability distribution. (These calculations are not shown in the text.) The standard deviation calculated using the nineteen individual losses would differ slightly from the standard deviation calculated using the empirical probability distribution because that distribution uses the midpoint of each size class to represent all losses in that size class. A standard deviation, or any other statistic that has been calculated directly from individual data, can be expected to be more accurate than that calculated from grouped data.

Standard deviation is the first widely used measure of dispersion. The second is the coefficient of variation. If two distributions have the same mean, then the one with the larger standard deviation has the greater variability. If two distributions have different means, the coefficient of variation is often used to compare variability.

EXHIBIT 11-14

Calculation of the Standard Deviation of a Probability Distribution—Example of Two Dice

[1] Pips (x_i)	[2] Probability (p)	[3] ($x_i - \bar{x}$)	[4] ($x_i - \bar{x})^2$	[5] $p \times (x_i - \bar{x})^2$
2	1/36	−5	25	$1/36 \times 25 = 25/36$
3	2/36	−4	16	$2/36 \times 16 = 32/36$
4	3/36	−3	9	$3/36 \times 9 = 27/36$
5	4/36	−2	4	$4/36 \times 4 = 16/36$
6	5/36	−1	1	$5/36 \times 1 = 5/36$
7	6/36	0	0	$6/36 \times 0 = 0$
8	5/36	+1	1	$5/36 \times 1 = 5/36$
9	4/36	+2	4	$4/36 \times 4 = 16/36$
10	3/36	+3	9	$3/36 \times 9 = 27/36$
11	2/36	+4	16	$2/36 \times 16 = 32/36$
12	1/36	+5	25	$1/36 \times 25 = 25/36$
				$\overline{}$ 210/36

$\bar{x}$ = mean of distribution = 7 (previously calculated).

$$s = \sqrt{210/36}$$
$$= \sqrt{5.83}$$
$$= 2.4.*$$

* Rounded

EXHIBIT 11-15

Calculating a Standard Deviation—Individual Observations

[1] Adjusted Loss Amount	[2] Deviation From Mean Loss	[3] Squared Deviation
$200	−8,709	$ 75,846,681
1,300	−7,609	57,896,881
1,500	−7,409	54,893,281
2,300	−6,609	43,678,881
4,000	−4,909	24,098,281
4,224	−4,685	21,949,225
4,483	−4,426	19,589,476
5,500	−3,409	11,621,281
6,000	−2,909	8,462,281
6,782	−2,127	4,524,129
7,400	−1,509	2,277,081
8,304	−605	366,025
8,400	−509	259,081
9,059	150	22,500
13,600	4,691	22,005,481
13,701	4,792	22,963,264
15,585	6,676	44,568,976
21,425	12,516	156,650,256
35,508	26,599	707,506,801
		$1,279,179,832

Total Mean Loss = $8,909.

Variance = Sum of column 3 ÷ (Number of losses −1)

= $1,279,179,832 ÷ 18

= $71,065,546*

$s = \sqrt{\$71,065,546}$

= $8,430.*

*Rounded

Coefficient of variation
A measure of dispersion calculated by dividing a distribution's standard deviation by its mean.

The **coefficient of variation** is a measure of dispersion calculated by dividing a distribution's standard deviation by its mean. For example, the coefficient of variation for the distribution of total points in rolling two dice equals 2.4 points divided by 7.0 points, or 0.34.

For the dollar amount of machinery losses, a coefficient of variation can be calculated from the adjusted dollar amounts of individual losses shown in Exhibit 11-4. Using individual losses generates a mean loss of $8,909 and a standard deviation of $8,430. From these individual loss data, the coefficient of variation is calculated as follows:

$$\text{Coefficient of variation} = \text{standard deviation} \div \text{mean}$$
$$= \$8,430 \div \$8,909$$
$$= 0.95.$$

The coefficient of variation is useful in comparing the variability of distributions that have different shapes, means, or standard deviations. The distribution with the largest coefficient of variation has the greatest relative variability. The higher the variability within a distribution, the more difficult it is to accurately forecast an individual outcome.

Normal Distribution

Normal distribution
A probability distribution that is symmetrical about the mean and that has proven useful in accurately forecasting the variability of many physical phenomena.

The **normal distribution** is a probability distribution that is symmetrical about the mean and that has proven useful in accurately forecasting the variability of many physical phenomena. This special distribution can help to accurately forecast the variability of many physical phenomena that involve chance variations around some central, average, or expected value. The normal distribution therefore applies to many real-world situations.

As an example, suppose that a manufacturing plant uses 600 electrical elements to heat rubber. The useful life of each element is limited, and an element used too long poses a substantial danger of exploding and starting an electrical fire. Suppose that the average life of such an electric heating element is 5,000 hours. Although 5,000 hours is the average, some elements become hazardous at 4,500 hours, some at 5,500 hours, and others, earlier or later. It is reasonable to assume that the life of each heating element will have a normal distribution.

The characteristics of the normal probability distribution provide a way of scheduling maintenance so that the likelihood of an element becoming very dangerous before it is replaced can be kept below any specified margin of safety. To see how this can be done, one must understand a little more about the normal distribution.

Exhibit 11-16 illustrates the typical bell-shaped curve of a normal distribution. Note that the curve never touches the horizontal line at the base of the diagram. In theory, the normal distribution assigns some probability for every outcome regardless of its distance from the mean.

EXHIBIT 11-16

The Normal Distribution—Percentages of Outcomes Within Specified Standard Deviations of the Mean

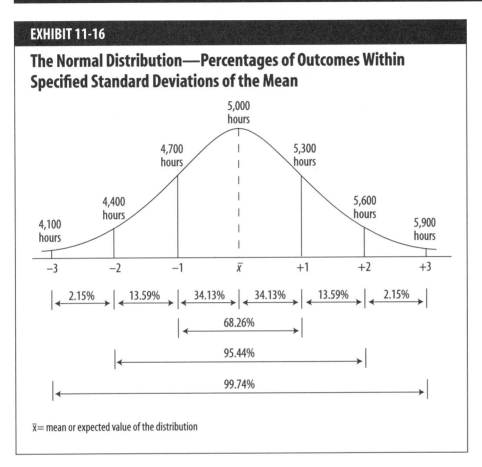

x̄ = mean or expected value of the distribution

In all normal distributions, certain percentages of all outcomes fall within a given number of standard deviations above or below the mean of a distribution. For example, 34.13 percent of all outcomes are within one standard deviation *above* the mean. Similarly, because every normal distribution is symmetrical, another 34.13 percent of all outcomes fall within one standard deviation *below* the mean. By addition, 68.26 percent of all outcomes are within one standard deviation above or below the mean. The portion of a normal distribution that is between one and two standard deviations above the mean contains 13.59 percent of all outcomes, as does the portion between one and two standard deviations below the mean. Hence, the area between the mean and two standard deviations above the mean contains 47.72 percent (34.13 percent + 13.59 percent) of the outcomes, and another 47.72 percent are two standard deviations or less below the mean. Consequently, 95.44 percent of all outcomes are within two standard deviations above or below the mean.

Similarly, 2.15 percent of all outcomes are between two and three standard deviations above the mean, and another 2.15 percent are between two and three standard deviations below the mean. Therefore, 49.87 percent (34.13 percent + 13.59 percent + 2.15 percent) of all outcomes are within three standard deviations above the mean, and an equal percentage are within three standard deviations below the mean. The portion of the distribution between three standard deviations above the mean and three standard deviations below it contains 99.74 percent (49.87 percent × 2) of all outcomes. Only 0.26 percent (100 percent – 99.74 percent) of all outcomes lie *beyond* three standard deviations from the mean, and these are divided equally—0.13 percent above the mean and 0.13 percent below it. Furthermore, because the normal distribution is a symmetrical distribution, the mean, median, and mode are all the same value and the skewness is equal to zero.

The relationships involving standard deviations can be applied to the previous example involving the electrical elements. Suppose that the expected safe life of each element conforms to a normal distribution having a mean of 5,000 hours and a standard deviation of 300 hours. If the maintenance schedule requires replacing each element after it has been in service for 5,000 hours (the mean, or expected, safe life), there is a 50 percent chance that it will become unsafe before being changed because 50 percent of the normal distribution is below this 5,000-hour mean. If each element is changed after having been used only 4,700 hours (one standard deviation below the mean (5,000 – 300)), there is still a 15.87 percent (50 percent – 34.13 percent) chance that an element will become unsafe before being changed. If this probability of the element becoming unsafe is still too high, changing each element after 4,400 hours (two standard deviations below the mean (5,000 – [2 × 300])) reduces the probability of high hazard to only 2.28 percent, the portion of a normal distribution that is more than two standard deviations below the mean. A still more cautious practice would be to change elements routinely after only 4,100 hours (three standard deviations below the mean (5,000 – [3 × 300])), so that the probability of an element becoming highly hazardous before replacement would be only 0.13 percent, slightly more than one chance in 1,000.

Using this analysis, management may select an acceptable probability that an electrical element will become unsafe before being replaced and can therefore schedule maintenance accordingly. Suppose, for example, that management is willing to accept one chance in ten that an element would become dangerous before being replaced. That is, they want 90 percent of the elements to be replaced before they could become dangerous. In terms of Exhibit 11-16, achieving this goal requires finding the point along the bottom of the diagram where 10 percent of the entire distribution is below (to the left of) the time of replacement and the remaining 90 percent is above this point. This point is between one and two standard deviations below the mean—that is, between 15.87 percent of the total distribution and 2.28 percent. Statisticians have shown that a value of 1.28 standard deviations below the mean cuts off the lowest 10 percent of any normal distribution. Therefore, scheduling replacement of each element after 4,616 hours of use (calculated as 5,000 – [1.28 × 300]) would ensure that only 10 percent of the elements became hazardous before replacement. For still greater assurance, say, 95 percent, one must move 1.65 standard deviations below the mean or replace each element after 4,505 hours of use (5,000 – [1.65 × 300]).

One of the problems with using only probability analysis to forecast accidental losses is that the risk management professional may be ignoring some valuable information. If there are other factors (variables) that affect accidental losses of which the risk management professional is aware, they are not used in basic probability analysis. One way to incorporate this additional information is to use trend analysis.

TREND ANALYSIS

Trend analysis identifies patterns in past losses and then projects these patterns into the future. The two most common types of trend analysis are time trends and regression analysis. Trend analysis allows for a dynamic, changing environment and looks for predictable patterns in how the environment is changing. For example, changes in loss frequency or severity might coincide with changes in some other variable, such as production, in such a way that loss frequency or severity can be forecasted more accurately.

Trend analysis
An analysis that identifies patterns in past losses and then projects these patterns into the future.

To improve forecasting future losses, many risk management professionals use trend analysis to adjust loss data for anticipated changes in those factors presumed to affect the frequency or severity of accidental losses. A simple example is the adjustment of forecasted future dollar amounts of losses using an anticipated inflation rate.

Care must be taken when extending projections far beyond the range of any past experience. Automatic use of trend projections can produce unrealistic results. Used with discretion, however, these techniques permit useful analysis.

For example, in estimating the property losses that an organization will finance through retention if it adopts a particular deductible, a risk management professional should recognize that projected inflationary trends will increase the cost of future physical damage. Installing a sprinkler system in a building is likely to increase savings in expected fire losses as the amount or financial value of the property in that building increases. Therefore, inflation and growing property values might increase the deductibles and investments involved in an organization's property loss prevention. Making informed decisions on such matters requires trend analysis.

Some trends in losses, or in other variables such as price levels, may be intuitive and may be estimated by making mental projections or by sketching. A common-sense way of representing this trend uses a ruler to draw a line passing as nearly as possible through the data points. Extending the dotted portion of the trend line into the future provides a basis for forecasting a continued trend. A **trend line** is a line on a graph indicating a pattern. The trend line is the eye's best estimate, drawn to minimize the total distances of all data points from the trend line. However, given the availability and ease of use of computer spreadsheets, there is little justification in using the less accurate method of intuitive trending. Arithmetic trending techniques define more precisely the location of this distance-minimizing straight line.

Trend line
A line on a graph indicating a pattern.

Time Trends

One method of tracking accidental losses through time (that is, trending loss data) is to look for a linear time trend line. Exhibit 11-17 contains a chart of the number of machinery losses per year from Exhibit 11-3. A linear trend line (the blue line) for the number of machinery losses appears to indicate an increasing frequency of losses over time. However, in many situations, a linear trend line is unrealistic because of the additive nature of the trend (a more thorough discussion of this is in the subsequent regression discussion). In Exhibit 11-17, the linear trend line adds 0.7 losses every year for a trend. That is, in Year 5 the organization can expect 6.5 ([0.7 × 5] +3 = 6.5) losses, and in Year 6 it could expect 7.2 losses ([0.7 × 6] + 3 = 7.2).

In many cases, trends are not additive, they are multiplicative; that is, they increase by a certain percentage each year, rather than by a fixed amount. When a trend line is curved, it is called a curvilinear trend line. Because many trend lines are curvilinear, it is common practice to call all trend lines, including straight-line ones, curves. An example of a time trend line is to assume that losses increase by approximately 19 percent each year, starting with a minimum number of losses of three. The equation for this curved trend line is $3 \times (1.19)^x$ where x is the year. The curved trend line would project higher losses than the linear trend line beginning in Year 4. The curved trend line would project 8.5 losses in Year 6 and more than 10 losses in Year 7.

EXHIBIT 11-17

Diagram of Time Trend Lines

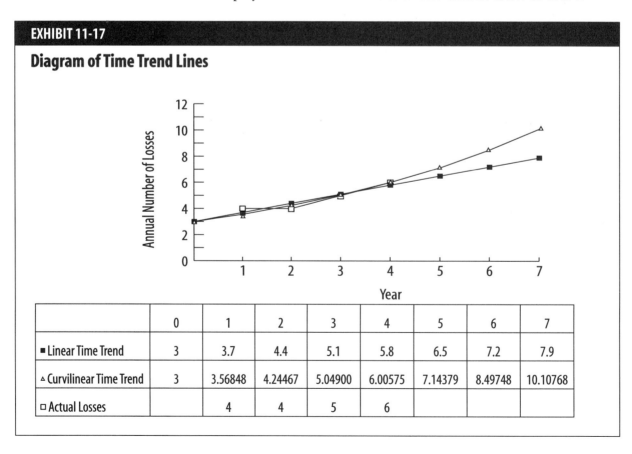

	0	1	2	3	4	5	6	7
■ Linear Time Trend	3	3.7	4.4	5.1	5.8	6.5	7.2	7.9
▲ Curvilinear Time Trend	3	3.56848	4.24467	5.04900	6.00575	7.14379	8.49748	10.10768
□ Actual Losses		4	4	5	6			

Because calculating a curvilinear trend line is complex, most risk management professionals turn to a trained statistician when the need arises. However, arithmetic linear trending, which is more straightforward and has many uses, is a procedure that risk management professionals should be able to apply.

Arithmetic trending techniques provide a procedure for developing a precise equation for the trend line that "best fits" the data. The example of linear trending in Exhibit 11-17 is a linear "time" trend, simply plotting losses through time. The mathematics involved in calculating trend lines is referred to as regression analysis and can be used with many other factors (variables) other than time.

Regression Analysis

Regression analysis is a statistical technique that is used to estimate relationships between variables. Regression analysis, another method of trending loss data, assumes that the variable being forecast varies predictably with some other variable. The variable being forecast is the **dependent variable**. The variable that determines the value of the variable being forecast is the **independent variable**. **Linear regression analysis** is a form of regression analysis that assumes that the change in the dependent variable is constant for each unit of change in the independent variable. For example, if the independent variable is time

Regression analysis
A statistical technique that is used to estimate relationships between variables.

Dependent variable
The variable being forecast.

Independent variable
The variable that determines the value of the variable being forecast.

Linear regression analysis
A form of regression analysis that assumes that the change in the dependent variable is constant for each unit of change in the independent variable.

EXHIBIT 11-18

Diagram of Linear Time Series Analysis Trend Line

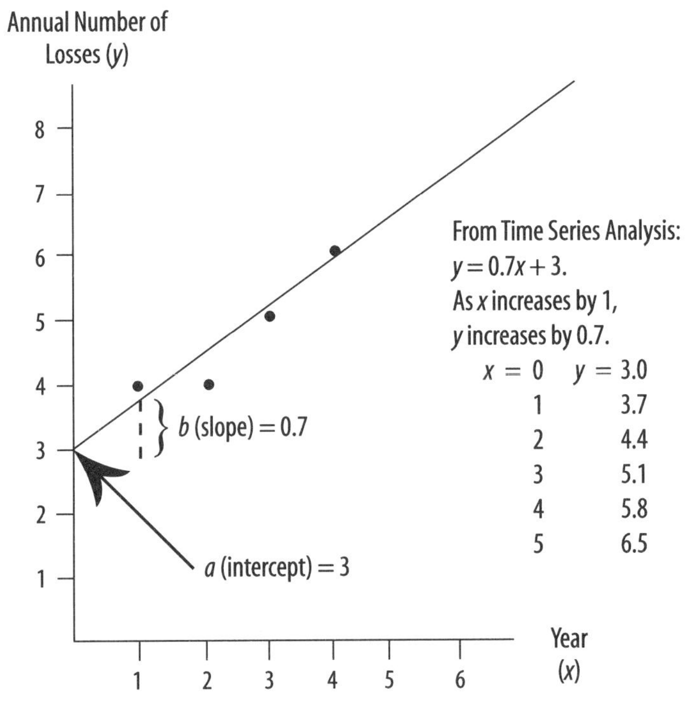

measured in years, then a linear regression analysis assumes that the change in the dependent variable is the same from year to year. In this case, the regression line is straight (or linear), not curved.

Exhibit 11-18 plots annual machinery losses on a graph. The dependent variable (annual number of losses) is charted on the vertical (y) axis; the independent variable (years) is charted on the horizontal (x) axis. The data points show that 4, 4, 5, and 6 losses occurred, respectively, in Year 1 through Year 4. The goal of regression analysis is to find the equation for the line that best fits these four data points and to project this line to forecast the number of future losses.

A logical first step in calculating a linear regression line is to plot the data points and sketch an approximate line. Such a sketch helps to intuitively estimate the two determinants of any linear regression line. The first determinant is the point at which the line crosses the vertical y axis, labeled "a" in the diagram (y-intercept) or the value of y when x equals zero. The second determinant is the slope of the line, the amount by which y increases or decreases with a one-unit increase in x. The length of the dashed line labeled "b" signifies the slope. A line slanting upward from left to right has positive slope; a line slanting downward has negative slope. Therefore, the y-intercept and the slope determine a line. The equation of a line can be written as $y = bx + a$, where y is the dependent variable, x is the independent variable, a is the y-intercept, and b is the slope of the line. In the current example, y is the number of machinery losses, and x is the number of years beyond year zero.

Given data for x and y, the values of a and b that give the best fit of the data are given by the following equations:

$$a = \frac{\left(\sum y\right)\left(\sum x^2\right) - \left(\sum x\right)\left(\sum xy\right)}{n\left(\sum x^2\right) - \left(\sum x\right)^2}.$$

$$b = \frac{n\left(\sum xy\right) - \left(\sum x\right)\left(\sum y\right)}{n\left(\sum x^2\right) - \left(\sum x\right)^2}.$$

In these equations, n indicates the number of data points, or the number of paired x and y values, which is four in this case. For clarity, these formulas also use Σ to mean the sum of the observations of the variable following that symbol.

Exhibit 11-19 shows the calculation of a linear regression line of the annual number of machinery losses, using the above formulas. Columns 1 and 2 simply repeat the data gathered from Exhibit 11-3. Each figure in Column 3 represents the product of multiplying each x value by the y value on the same line. Column 4 squares the figures in Column 1. The totals of these four columns—10, 19, 51, and 30—permit solving for a and b, as shown.

Interpreting these results is, for the most part, straightforward. The value of 3 for a in the equation indicates that, at the y-intercept when x equals zero (Year 0), y would be 3. The value of 0.7 for b means that the number of losses can be expected to increase by seven-tenths of a loss each year. (Had *b* been negative, the number of losses would have been forecast to decrease each year). Furthermore, if this trend or pattern continues, the number of losses in Year 5 could be forecast as 3 + 5(0.7) = 6.5, making it reasonable to forecast either 6 or 7 losses in Year 5. The forecast for Year 6 would be 7.2 (basically 7) losses, calculated as 3 + (6 × 0.7).

Two aspects of interpreting linear regression lines need to be recognized. First, a linear regression line might not be accurate when it gets very far away from the actual data values used. For example, it may be suitable to use this linear trend line to forecast losses in Year 5 or Year 6, but it probably would not be accurate for forecasting losses in Year 25 or Year 26.

EXHIBIT 11-19

Calculation of Linear Time Series Trend Line

[1] Years	[2] Losses	[3]	[4]
x	y	xy	x^2
1	4	4	1
2	4	8	4
3	5	15	9
4	6	24	16
10	19	51	30

$$a = \frac{(\Sigma y)(\Sigma x^2) - (\Sigma x)(\Sigma xy)}{n(\Sigma x^2) - (\Sigma x)^2}$$

$$= \frac{(19)(30) - (10)(51)}{4(30) - (10)^2}$$

$$= \frac{570 - 510}{120 - 100}$$

$$= \frac{60}{20}$$

$$= 3.0.$$

$$b = \frac{n(\Sigma xy) - (\Sigma x)(\Sigma y)}{n(\Sigma x^2) - (\Sigma x)^2}$$

$$= \frac{4(51) - (10)(19)}{4(30) - (10)^2}$$

$$= \frac{204 - 190}{120 - 100}$$

$$= \frac{14}{20}$$

$$= 0.7.$$

Second, for any past year, the dependent variable's value calculated by the linear regression line is not likely to exactly equal the historical value for that past year. Any regression line represents a "best fit" of a straight or smoothly curved line to actual historical data for all past years. For any given year, the projected trend value will probably differ from the actual outcome, both in the past and in the future. The size of this difference between actual and projected values will also vary. For example, in Exhibit 11-19, the historical outcome for Year 1 is farther from the projected regression line than is the outcome for Year 2.

In the previous example, the dependent variable (the annual number of losses) varied only with the passage of time (the independent variable). An alternative possibility is to assume that the annual number of machinery losses is affected by a variable such as the volume of items processed or the number of hours in operation. Therefore, one of these other variables (such as, volume of output) could be substituted for time as the independent variable that projects the number of future machinery losses.

Indeed, any reasonable causative variable that can be measured and projected with more accuracy than accidental losses can be an independent variable. Regardless of the variables used, the procedures for calculating the a and b determinants of the linear regression line remain the same.

For example, a risk management professional may want to use the annual output (in 100,000-ton units) to project the annual number of machinery losses. To illustrate, the data in Exhibit 11-20 are used. These data show the number of machinery losses suffered and the tons of output (in hundreds of thousands) in each year from Year 1 to Year 4. This information, along with regression analysis, will be used to project trends that relate the number of machinery losses to tons of output.

EXHIBIT 11-20

Relationship of Losses to Exposure (Tons of Output)

Year	Annual Number of Losses	Tons of Output (× 100,000)
1	4	35
2	4	60
3	5	72
4	6	95
	19	262

This information can be used to project trends that relate the number of machinery losses to time and to annual tons of rubber output.

Exhibit 11-21 graphs annual tons of output horizontally on the x axis as the independent variable and annual number of machinery losses vertically on the y axis as the dependent variable. The four data points in the exhibit correspond to the pairs of numbers of losses and tons of output shown in Exhibit 11-20, and the solid portion of the linear regression line approximates the trend of the historical data. The dashed extension of the regression line projects annual numbers of machinery losses for levels of output (in units of 100,000) beyond the range of these particular historical data. Developing such a diagram and approximating a regression line help in visualizing and confirming the results obtained by calculating the values of a and b for the actual linear regression line.

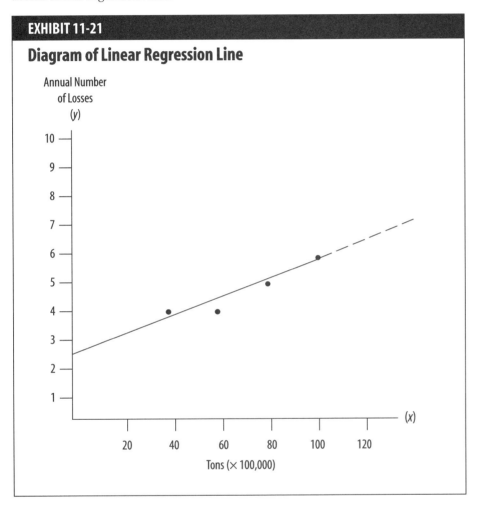

EXHIBIT 11-21

Diagram of Linear Regression Line

The procedure for calculating values for a (y-intercept) and b (slope) of the regression line relating losses to output, as seen in Exhibit 11-22, is the same procedure described previously, when time was the independent variable. As calculated at the bottom of Exhibit 11-22, the indicated value for a is 2.46 machinery losses, and the value for b is 0.035. If the number of losses is linearly related to output for all possible levels of output, the 2.46 value for a means that, even if annual output were zero, it would still suffer 2.46 (actually 2 or 3) machinery losses each year. The 0.035 value for b implies that, with each 100,000-ton increase in output, 0.035 additional machinery losses can be expected. Also, one more machinery loss can be expected with approximately each additional 2,900,000 tons of output (calculated as 100,000 tons × [1 ÷ 0.035]).

Although arithmetically correct, these values may not be valid for very low or very high volumes of output, again indicating that one should not extend a regression line too far beyond the bounds of past experience.

EXHIBIT 11-22

Calculation of Linear Regression Line

	[1] Output (Tons × 100,000) (x)	[2] Losses (y)	[3] (xy)	[4] (x)²
	35	4	140	1,225
	60	4	240	3,600
	72	5	360	5,184
	95	6	570	9,025
	262	19	1,310	19,034

$$a = \frac{(\Sigma y)(\Sigma x^2) - (\Sigma x)(\Sigma xy)}{n(\Sigma x^2) - (\Sigma x)^2}$$

$$= \frac{(19)(19,034) - (262)(1,310)}{4(19,034) - (262)^2}$$

$$= \frac{361,646 - 343,220}{76,136 - 68,644}$$

$$= \frac{18,426}{7,492}$$

$$= 2.46.$$

$$b = \frac{n(\Sigma xy) - (\Sigma x)(\Sigma y)}{n(\Sigma x^2) - (\Sigma x)^2}$$

$$= \frac{4(1,310) - (262)(19)}{4(19,034) - (262)^2}$$

$$= \frac{5,240 - 4,978}{76,136 - 68,644}$$

$$= \frac{262}{7,492}$$

$$= 0.035.$$

To forecast losses from these regression results, assume the organization expects to produce 10 million (or 100 hundred thousand) tons of products next year. The expected number of machinery losses next year then can be calculated as follows:

$$y = 2.46 + (0.035 \times 100)$$
$$= 2.46 + 3.50$$
$$= 5.96 \text{ losses.}$$

Because fractional numbers of machine losses are impossible, a reasonable forecast would be for six machinery losses in a year when production is expected to be 10 million tons.

A risk management professional can also use more sophisticated statistical techniques to develop either curvilinear or linear regression lines, which incorporate many independent variables simultaneously. An example is an equation that would forecast the number of losses in a future year based on combined effects of forecast freight volumes, weather conditions, price levels, and perhaps other independent variables more easily forecast than the losses themselves.

Forecasts should be accepted only if the underlying assumptions are valid. Therefore, knowing these assumptions and recognizing the potential limitations in these forecasting techniques are important.

Probability and trend analyses can be powerful tools for forecasting future losses, but they must be used with care. Their results must be interpreted with reason and not with automatic acceptance just because they are mathematically based. Furthermore, perhaps more for risk management than for some other uses of these forecasting techniques, the seeming scarcity of loss data, when compared with the apparent wealth of data in other management specialties, makes forecasts of accidental losses more difficult.

SUMMARY

Risk management decisions depend on loss forecasts. Forecasting accidental losses, like any other future event, requires detecting past patterns and projecting them into the future. Forecasts are important to organizations because they allow the organization to make more informed decisions about future activities. Forecasts are important to risk management professionals because they help determine the costs and benefits of various risk management techniques, which in turn enables them to make more informed decisions in the later steps of the risk management process. Forecasts are important to the risk management process because they are vital to the accuracy of the analysis of the loss exposures. Without proper forecasts, inaccurate analysis would lead to poor decisions in the remaining steps of the risk management process.

Forecasting future accidental losses begins with deciding which of two basic patterns, "no change" or "change in a predictable way," applies. To find patterns that might be discovered in past losses, a risk management professional should try to find data that are relevant, complete, consistent, and organized. The data need to be relevant to the loss exposure that the risk management professional is trying to project. They need to contain all of the relevant information (complete information) necessary for the forecast. They also need to be reported in consistent dollar figures and organized in a format that is useful to the risk management professional.

The probability of an event is the relative frequency with which the event can be expected to occur in the long run in a stable environment. Probability can be developed either from historical (empirical) data or from theoretical considerations. Empirical probability distributions are particularly effective for forecasting future accidental losses in organizations that have a substantial volume of data on past losses and that have fairly stable operations, with patterns of past losses that presumably will continue in the future. The larger the volume of data on past losses and the more stable the environment that produces those losses, the more reliable the forecasts of future losses will be.

Most probability estimates are compiled from several sources, including the organization's own loss experience, that of similar organizations, and nationwide data from companies in the same industry.

A probability distribution is a presentation (table, chart, or graph) of probability estimates of a particular set of circumstances and the probability of each possible outcome. Probability distributions are described in terms of skewness, central tendency, and dispersion. One of the most common probability distributions is the normal distribution. The normal distribution has well-known characteristics that enable risk management professionals to estimate probabilities based on the number of standard deviations from the expected value.

Trend analysis identifies patterns in past losses and then projects those patterns into the future. For example, trend analysis looks for changes in loss frequency or loss severity that might coincide with changes in some other variable that is easier to forecast accurately. Many risk management professionals use trend analysis to adjust loss data for anticipated changes in variables presumed to affect the frequency or severity of accidental losses.

Some loss trends can be discerned by using intuitive judgment; however, calculation of time trends or regression analysis provides more reliability to the analysis. Regression analysis assumes that the variable to be forecast—the dependent variable—varies predictably with another variable—the independent variable. The independent variable can be any variable that the risk management professional can predict with more certainty than the accidental losses (the dependent variable) he or she is trying to analyze.

CHAPTER NOTES

1. 2001 Commissioners Standard Ordinary Mortality Table, www.actuary.org/pdf/life/cso_dec01.pdf (accessed February 10, 2005), p. A-3.

2. Insurance Information Institute, *The III Insurance Fact Book 2004* (New York: Insurance Information Institute, 2004), p. 106.

Chapter 12

Direct Your Learning

Applying Forecasting

After learning the content of this chapter and completing the corresponding course guide assignment, you should be able to:

■ Calculate the joint probability of the following:

- Two or more independent events
- Two or more dependent events
- Two or more sequential events
- Two or more events not occurring

■ Calculate the alternative probability of the following:

- Two mutually exclusive events
- Two nonmutually exclusive events

■ Calculate trend lines showing the following:

- Combined effects of two or more trends that can properly be added
- Constant percentage rate of change

■ Define or describe each of the Key Words and Phrases for this chapter.

Develop Your Perspective

What are the main topics covered in the chapter?

Building on the forecasting methods explained in the preceding chapter, this chapter describes how probability analysis and trend analysis can be expanded to help analyze more complex situations.

Identify two factors that can lead to an accidental loss.

- What is the probability that either event A or event B will occur in a given period?

- What is the probability that event A will occur, given that event B has already occurred or will occur in a given time period?

Why is it important to learn about these topics?

Risk management professionals need to accurately forecast future losses. Probability analysis can be extended to multiple combinations of events, and trend analysis can be extended to situations in which combining the effects of several independent variables permits more accurate forecasting of a dependent variable.

Consider the sequence of events that led up to an accidental loss that your organization suffered.

- How did these events interact to cause the loss? Were they independent events?

- Are there any trends that will change the accidental losses in the future?

How can you use what you will learn?

Evaluate the workers' compensation losses your organization might face.

- What information would you need to accurately forecast workers' compensation losses for your organization? Why?

- What risk management techniques might you recommend to minimize the financial effects of these workers' compensation losses on your organization?

Chapter 12

Applying Forecasting

Applying probability and trend analysis to loss forecasting often involves making forecasts in situations that are more complex (for example, more factors or variables involved) than those described in the previous chapter. This chapter describes how to recognize and analyze those more complex situations so that forecast accuracy can be improved.

The previous chapter introduced two useful forecasting methods, probability analysis and trend analysis, for situations in which one variable helps forecast another variable. More advanced applications of each of these two methods help in dealing with more complex situations. For example, probability analysis can be extended to multiple combinations of events, and trend analysis can be extended to situations in which combining the effects of several independent variables permits more accurate forecasting of a dependent variable.

The discussion in this chapter describes elementary models and examples of forecasting techniques to illustrate their significance and their mechanics, and it uses examples from a hypothetical firm called Galston Transport (Galston), a common carrier trucking company. While understanding the formulas that the forecasting techniques involve is important, most risk management professionals will likely use computer spreadsheet programs to help develop the forecasts. However, this chapter presents the formulas to give risk management professionals a better understanding of how the spreadsheet programs function.

APPLIED CALCULATIONS INVOLVING PROBABILITIES

The previous chapter defined the nature of probability and explained how to develop probability distributions to estimate the probabilities of specific individual events and how to use probability calculations to help determine the probabilities of various combinations of events. These calculations depend on the estimates of probabilities that make up the probability distributions. Therefore, it is important to understand how to calculate these initial probability estimates.

Basic Notation

Probability calculations are usually expressed through symbols in a standardized notation.

Probability Notation

The symbol p is a generic notation meaning "probability." The symbol $p(\ )$ means probability of the item in parentheses.

The probability that an event, A, will occur in a given period is denoted as follows:

$$p(A)$$

The probability that an event, A, will not occur in a given period is denoted:

$$p(\text{not } A)$$

The probability that both event A and event B will occur in a given period is denoted:

$$p(A \text{ and } B)$$

The probability that either event A or event B will occur in a given period is denoted:

$$p(A \text{ or } B)$$

The probability that event A will occur, given that event B has already occurred or will occur in a given period, is denoted:

$$p(A|B)$$

The symbol "n" also appears frequently in probability calculations to designate the number of exposure units (exposures) or trials from which a probability is developed or to which it is applied. The symbol "m" designates the number of occurrences of the event whose probability is sought. Therefore, the general equation for the empirical probability of an event (A) is expressed as follows:

$$p(A) = m \div n.$$

For example, suppose Galston made 20,000 trips (runs) in Year 1 through Year 4, and that during that time the company suffered nineteen collisions involving its trucks. The empirical probability of a collision on any particular run could be calculated as follows:

$$p(\text{collision}) = m \div n$$
$$= 19 \div 20{,}000$$
$$= .00095.$$

Suppose Galston wanted to estimate the number of collisions that it can expect in Year 5. Using data from Years 1 through 4, the best estimate of the probability of a collision on any one run in Year 5 is .00095. If Galston plans on 7,000 truck runs in Year 5, then the expected number of collisions in Year 5 equals .00095 multiplied by 7,000, or 6.65. Because fractional collisions are impossible, Galston's expected number of collisions in Year 5 is 7.

The expected number of collisions per year is the average number of collisions expected to occur annually in the long run, not necessarily the number that will occur in the next twelve months.

The concept of expected value is so common in working with probabilities that a symbol, $E(\ )$, is used as shorthand for the expected number or value of the event specified in parentheses. If C stands for the annual number of collisions in the year in which Galston makes n runs, then

$$E(C) = n \times p(\text{collision}).$$

This equation can be read as "the expected annual number of collisions equals the number of runs multiplied by the probability of collision on any one run."

Most probability calculations rest on two assumptions that should be made explicit to avoid mistakes when these assumptions are not true. The first assumption is that the probability, p, remains constant and is valid for the future events whose probability is being calculated. This is true whether the value for p is derived from experience (as for collisions) or wholly from logic (like the probabilities involved in rolling dice). In other words, the conditions that have generated any particular value for p are assumed to remain unchanged so that p also applies to the future.

The second assumption is that an event either occurs or does not occur. The "occurs" and "does not occur" possibilities are mutually exclusive (meaning that one or the other, but not both, must occur), and together they exhaust all possibilities (no other possibilities exist). Therefore, the probability of any event occurring, $p(A)$, and the probability of its not occurring, $p(\text{not } A)$, add up to one. For example, if the probability of a collision on any one run is .00095, the probability of no collision on any run is .99905. Therefore, the following are true:

$$p(A) + p(\text{not } A) = 1.$$
$$p(A) = 1 - p(\text{not } A).$$
$$p(\text{not } A) = 1 - p(A).$$

In these equations, A may represent a single event or a set of events. The equations are useful when the probability of A is unknown and might be difficult to calculate directly. Consequently, finding $p(A)$ by calculating $p(\text{not } A)$ and subtracting the result from one may be easier than finding $p(A)$ directly. This basic equation applies to all probability analyses.

Calculations of joint probabilities (the probability that two or more events will occur together in a given period) and of alternative probabilities (the probability that any one of two or more events will occur in a given period) are also useful in risk management.

Joint Probabilities

A **joint probability**, often called a compound probability, is the probability that two or more events will happen together. Examples are the probability

Joint probability
The probability that two or more events will happen together.

that two collisions involving Galston's trucks will occur in a particular month, that eight persons will be injured in an auto accident within one year, or that Galston will suffer a fire loss and a theft loss within one month.

The joint probability of two or more events depends on whether these events are independent. Two events, A and B, are independent if the occurrence or nonoccurrence of one does not affect the probability of the occurrence of the other. In other words, if A and B are independent, the probability of A is unchanged by the occurrence or nonoccurrence of B. Similarly, the probability of B is unchanged by the occurrence or nonoccurrence of A.

For example, consider two of Galston's trucks. The event that Truck One burns and the event that Truck Two burns will be independent of each other if the factors that cause a fire at one truck are unrelated to the factors that cause a fire at the other truck. However, if common factors affect the occurrence of a fire at the two trucks, such as if the two trucks are positioned close enough that fire can spread from one to the other, then the event that Truck One burns and the event that Truck Two burns will not be independent. The fact that one of the trucks is on fire increases the probability that the second truck will catch fire. In terms of probability, each truck alone may have a 2 percent chance of fire in a given year, but if the trucks are close together, then knowing that a fire damaged one of them will raise the probability of fire damage in the other. In other words, the 2 percent chance of a fire may rise to, for example, 10 percent.

Independent Events

If two or more events are independent, the joint probability that all the events will occur is the product (multiplication) of their separate probabilities. To illustrate, suppose that $p(F1)$ is the probability of Truck One having a fire and $p(F2)$ is the probability of Truck Two having a fire. If $F1$ and $F2$ are independent, the probability that they will both burn in one year, $p(F1$ and $F2)$, is equal to the probability of fire in one, $p(F1)$, multiplied by the probability of fire in the other, $p(F2)$, expressed as follows:

$$p(F1 \text{ and } F2) = p(F1) \times p(F2).$$

Using a 2 percent probability of fire to the trucks, the probability that both will burn is calculated as follows:

$$\begin{aligned} p(F1 \text{ and } F2) &= p(F1) \times p(F2) \\ &= .02 \times .02 \\ &= .0004. \end{aligned}$$

Dependent Events

If $F1$ and $F2$ are not independent events, then the joint probability that both trucks will burn is slightly more complicated. The probability of two events happening if one is conditional on the other depends on which is conditional on the other and is calculated as follows:

$$\text{If } F1 \text{ is dependent on } F2: p(F1 \text{ and } F2) = p(F2) \times p(F1|F2).$$
$$\text{If } F2 \text{ is dependent on } F1: p(F2 \text{ and } F1) = p(F1) \times p(F2|F1).$$

These probabilities are known as conditional probabilities because they are conditional on the occurrence of another event—in this case, the existence of fire in the other truck. **Conditional probability** is the likelihood that an event will occur if it is certain that another event has occurred or will occur in a given period.

Assume, for example, that it has been observed over the years (creating an empirical probability) that on 40 percent of the occasions when one truck catches fire, another truck also catches fire. Then, even though the $p(F1) = .02$ and $p(F2) = .02$, the conditional probability of a fire in the second truck given a fire in the first truck is 40 percent ($p(F2 \mid F1) = .4$). Consequently, the probability of a fire in both trucks, $p(F1$ and $F2)$, equals $(.02) \times (.4) = .008$. Notice that this is much higher than the probability calculated above when the events were assumed to be independent.

> **Conditional probability**
> The likelihood that an event will occur if it is certain that another event has occurred or will occur in a given period.

Sequential Events

The previous examples examined the probability of two events occurring in a given period. In these examples, the order of the events was not considered. In addition, the conditional probabilities, such as $p(F1 \mid F2)$, did not consider the ordering of the events. This conditional probability gives the probability that $F1$ occurs during the period given that $F2$ occurs during the period. $F1$ could occur first or $F2$ could occur first. However, when the probability of one event changes depending on whether another event has already occurred, it is critical to specify not only the nature but also the sequence of the events whose joint probability is being calculated.

For example, assume that Truck One is much older than Truck Two and therefore more likely to catch fire. Assume also that the probability of fire in Truck One—denoted as $p(F1)$—is .05, while the corresponding probability for Truck Two—denoted as $p(F2)$—is .01. Furthermore, perhaps because Truck One contains a more flammable cargo than does Truck Two or because Truck One is upwind from Truck Two, the probability of a fire spreading from Truck One to Truck Two is .60, and the probability of fire spreading in the other direction is .10. In other words, $p(F2$ following $F1) = .60$, while $p(F1$ following $F2) = .10$. The probability that Truck Two will catch fire as a result of a fire in Truck One is equal to the probability that Truck One will catch fire multiplied by the probability that this fire will spread to Truck Two, expressed as follows:

$$p(F1 \text{ followed by } F2) = p(F1) \times p(F2 \text{ following } F1)$$
$$= .05 \times .60$$
$$= .03.$$

Conversely, the probability that a fire will begin in Truck Two and spread to Truck One is calculated as follows:

$$p(F2 \text{ followed by } F1) = p(F2) \times p(F1 \text{ following } F2)$$
$$= .01 \times .10$$
$$= .001.$$

Notice that each of these calculations derives the probability of a particular sequence of events and does not allow for any other sequence.

As another illustration, if the probability that one of Galston's warehouses will suffer a fire, $p(F)$, is .005, and if the probability that the contents of the warehouse will be looted if fire occurs, $p(L$ following $F)$, is .60, then the probability that the warehouse will burn and then be looted in the wake of the fire is as follows:

$$p(F \text{ followed by } L) = p(F) \times p(L \text{ following } F)$$
$$= (.005) \times (.60)$$
$$= .003.$$

Notice that this is the probability of fire followed by looting, which is not the same as the probability of looting followed by fire or the probability of looting and fire occurring in two unrelated events. This equation does not calculate the latter two probabilities. Generally, great care should be taken in defining the events whose joint probability is being calculated.

Other Joint Probability Calculations

Joint probabilities can also be used to calculate the likelihood that an organization will *not* suffer a loss. Suppose that the probability that one of Galston's truck drivers will be injured in a job-related traffic accident during the next year is .03. Because $p(\text{not } A) = 1 - p(A)$, the probability of no injury to the driver is .97. Also assume that the probability that one driver is injured is independent of the probability of another driver being injured. Then, the probability that neither will be injured is $(.97) \times (.97)$, or $.97^2$, which is .9409, or roughly 94 percent. The probability of events that are independent of each other occurring multiple times can be expressed as follows:

$$p(A \text{ occurring } x \text{ times}) = p(A)^x.$$

Similarly:

$$p(A \text{ not occurring } x \text{ times}) = p(1-A)^x.$$

In the previous example, as the number of drivers increases, the probability that none will suffer injury decreases until, at seventy-six drivers, the probability of no injuries among these drivers falls to less than 10 percent ($.97^{76} = .0988$) if injuries are independent. However, even though the probability of injury to any one employee is small, any organization with even a moderate number of employees is likely to experience at least one employee injury in any given year. As a result, the risk management professional can determine that the organization is likely to experience at least one workers' compensation claim in a given year.

With extremely small probabilities of some loss (that is, extremely large probabilities of no loss), the number of separate exposure units must become large before some loss is virtually certain. For example, for Galston the .99905 probability that any one truck will reach its destination without a significant collision means that, for any two trucks, a .998101 probability exists that both will reach their destination without a collision—this probability being calculated as $.99905^2$ (assuming that these events are independent). As the number of truck runs increases, the probability of no collisions continues to decrease. However, it is not until Galston has 2,423 separate truck runs that the probability of no significant collisions falls to less than 10 percent. It takes approximately 4,850 runs before the probability of no significant collisions falls below 1 percent, making a significant collision virtually certain.

These examples illustrate the following two basic points:

1. As the number of exposure units increases, some loss becomes virtually certain.
2. The smaller the probability of loss to any one exposure unit, the greater the number of units required to reach a given probability that some loss will occur in a given period.

What is true for the probability of loss with a given number of exposure units in one year is also true for a single exposure unit over a number of years. Some loss is likely to occur. For example, assume that the probability is 1 in 8 (.125 or 12.5 percent) that, during a given winter, heavy snow will force at least one closure of Snowy Hill Road, a crucial mountain road for Galston. Assuming that the weather in one year is independent of the weather in another year, the equation used to calculate the probability that Snowy Hill Road will not be closed by snow during four consecutive years is as follows:

$$p(\text{no snow closure for 4 years}) = p(1 - \text{probability of closure})^4$$
$$= (1 - .125)^4$$
$$= (.875)^4$$
$$= .586.$$

Similarly, the probability that Snowy Hill Road will not be closed by snow in one decade is $(.875)^{10}$, which is approximately 26.3 percent. In other words, an almost 74 percent chance $(1 - .263 = .737)$ exists that, unless special measures are taken to keep it open, Snowy Hill Road will be closed by snow at least once every ten years.

Alternative Probabilities

An **alternative probability** is the probability that any one of two or more events will occur within a given period. Examples are the probability that either a three or a five will come up in one roll of one die (mutually exclusive events), the probability that a card drawn from a deck will be either a five or a club (not mutually exclusive), and the probability that Galston Transport will suffer either a fire loss or a burglary loss within the next year.

Alternative probability
The probability that any one of two or more events will occur within a given period.

The formula for calculating alternative probabilities is determined by whether the events involved are mutually exclusive. Two or more events are mutually exclusive if the occurrence of one makes the other impossible. For example, rolling a three on a die makes it impossible to roll a five (or any other number) on the same roll, so three and five on one roll of one die are mutually exclusive events.

Similarly, the probabilities that Galston will suffer no collision loss in a particular year, that it will suffer only one collision loss, that it will suffer only two collision losses, and that it will suffer more than two collision losses are probabilities of four mutually exclusive events, because in no one year can the number of collision losses fall into any two or more of these categories.

Examples of events that are not mutually exclusive include drawing a five or a club from a deck of cards on one draw (because the five of clubs may be drawn) and Galston suffering both collision and snow closure losses in a particular year (because in one year, Galston could experience both of these causes of loss).

Mutually Exclusive Events

For mutually exclusive events, the probability that any one of them will occur is the sum of their separate probabilities:

$$p(A \text{ or } B) = p(A) + p(B).$$

Therefore, the probability of rolling either a three or a five on one roll of one die is

$$p(3 \text{ or } 5) = \frac{1}{6} + \frac{1}{6} = \frac{2}{6} \text{ (or } \frac{1}{3}).$$

Another set of mutually exclusive events concerns the dollar amounts of individual losses. Because a given loss can be only one particular dollar amount, no individual loss can fall into two loss severity categories. A loss is, for example, either (1) less than \$5,000 or (2) equal to or more than \$5,000. In a probability distribution of losses by size (severity distribution), the probability of a loss equal to or less than a given figure is the sum of the probabilities of losses up to this figure. As mentioned previously, the sum of the probabilities of all possible mutually exclusive events—events that are both mutually exclusive and collectively exhaustive—is one.

Probabilities of mutually exclusive events are also relevant to risk management situations in which loss can be caused by one of two causes of loss but not by more than one. For example, Galston Transport might lose a particular truck by fire or by flood, but not by both causes of loss. In other words, the truck being lost by fire and the truck being lost by flood are mutually exclusive events. Suppose that the probability that a given truck will be destroyed by fire in a given year is .04 and that the probability of this truck being lost to flood in that year is .06. The probability of the truck being lost to either fire or flood during that year is expressed as follows:

$$\begin{aligned} p(\text{flood or fire}) &= p(\text{flood}) + p(\text{fire}) \\ &= .06 + .04 \\ &= .10. \end{aligned}$$

Nonmutually Exclusive Events

When two or more events can occur within a specified time period, they are not mutually exclusive. For such events, the probability that at least one, and possibly both or all of them, will occur is the sum of their separate probabilities minus the joint probability that they will both or all occur. For two nonmutually exclusive events, A and B, this can be expressed as follows:

$$p(A \text{ or } B \text{ or both}) = p(A) + p(B) - p(A \text{ and } B).$$

With more than two events that are not mutually exclusive, the calculations become more complex. Therefore, this discussion of alternative probabilities for nonmutually exclusive events is restricted to cases involving only two events.

For example, the probability of drawing a five from a deck of cards without jokers is $1/13$, the probability of drawing a club is $1/4$, and the probability of drawing the five of clubs is $1/52$. Therefore, the probability of drawing a five or a club is calculated as follows:

$$
\begin{aligned}
p(\text{five or club}) &= p(\text{five}) + p(\text{club}) - p(\text{five and club}) \\
&= 1/13 + 1/4 - 1/52 \\
&= 4/52 + 13/52 - 1/52 \\
&= 16/52 \\
&= 4/13.
\end{aligned}
$$

Subtracting the joint probability of events that are not mutually exclusive is necessary to avoid overstating the probability of the alternative events by double-counting the five of clubs as both a five and a club.

The problem of double-counting becomes more serious with events that have large probabilities. Suppose that the climate in a particular area is such that the probability of rain at noon on any given day is .50 and that the probability that the noon temperature will exceed 70 degrees is .80. On some days, it is both raining and warmer than 70 degrees at noon, so rain and heat above 70 degrees are not mutually exclusive. In this example, rain and heat are assumed to be independent. If the joint probability of rain and heat is not subtracted, the probability of either rain or heat, or both, is mistakenly calculated as p(rain or heat or both) = .50 + .80 = 1.30. This is an impossible result because, by definition, no probability can exceed 1.0. The following is the proper calculation:

$$
\begin{aligned}
p(\text{rain or heat or both}) &= p(\text{rain}) + p(\text{heat}) - p(\text{rain and heat}) \\
&= p(\text{rain}) + p(\text{heat}) - [p(\text{rain}) \times p(\text{heat})] \\
&= .50 + .80 - (.50 \times .80) \\
&= .50 + .80 - .40 \\
&= .90.
\end{aligned}
$$

Therefore, the probability that at noon it will be raining, or the temperature will exceed 70 degrees, or both is .90.

Calculating the alternative probability of two events, but not both, when one does not know the probability of both, involves (1) identifying each of the mutually exclusive ways that the events may occur, (2) calculating the probability of each of these ways, and (3) adding the resulting probabilities. For two nonmutually exclusive events, A and B, this can be expressed as follows:

$$p(A \text{ or } B \text{ but not both}) = [p(A) \times p(\text{not } B)] + [p(B) \times p(\text{not } A)]$$
$$= [p(A) \times (1-p(B))] + [p(B) \times (1-p(A))].$$

For example, the probability of heat or rain but not both at noon on a particular day is equal to the probability of heat and no rain plus the probability of rain plus no heat. Those two combinations of circumstances are the only two ways of having rain or heat but not both. Because the probability of rain is .50 and the probability of heat is .80, the alternative probability of the two events is calculated as follows:

$$p(\text{rain and no heat}) = p(\text{rain}) \times p(\text{no heat})$$
$$= p(\text{rain}) \times [1-p(\text{heat})]$$
$$= .50 \times (1 - .80)$$
$$= .50 \times .20$$
$$= .10.$$

$$p(\text{heat and no rain}) = p(\text{heat}) \times p(\text{no rain})$$
$$= p(\text{heat}) \times [1-p(\text{rain})]$$
$$= .80 \times (1 - .50)$$
$$= .80 \times .50$$
$$= .40.$$

Therefore:

$$p(\text{rain or heat but not both}) = p(\text{rain and no heat}) + p(\text{heat and no rain})$$
$$= .10 + .40$$
$$= .50.$$

In risk management, alternative probabilities of nonmutually exclusive events arise when dealing with two or more causes of loss that can each occur either independently or simultaneously. For example, the cargo inside one of Galston's trucks could be affected by both water damage (by less than total flooding) and theft (of less than an entire truck load). Assume, for example, that the probability of theft loss (pilferage) to a shipment is .09 and that the probability of water damage is .06. The probability of loss by pilferage or water damage or both is calculated as follows:

$$p(\text{pilferage or water damage or both}) = p(\text{pilferage}) + p(\text{water damage})$$
$$- p(\text{pilferage and water damage})$$
$$= .09 + .06 - (.09 \times .06)$$
$$= .15 - .0054$$
$$= .1446.$$

Calculating the probability of theft or water damage but not both requires summing the probabilities of the two mutually exclusive ways that this result can occur. Those are the probabilities of (1) pilferage but no water damage and (2) water damage but no pilferage. These calculations yield the following:

$$p(\text{pilferage but no water damage}) = p(\text{pilferage}) \times [1 - p(\text{water damage})]$$
$$= .09 \times (1 - .06)$$
$$= .09 \times .94$$
$$= .0846.$$

$$p(\text{water damage but no pilferage}) = p(\text{water damage}) \times [1 - p(\text{pilferage})]$$
$$= .06 \times (1 - .09)$$
$$= .06 \times .91$$
$$= .0546.$$

$$p(\text{pilferage or water damage but not both}) = .0846 + .0546$$
$$= .1392.$$

The probability of either kind of damage but not both is smaller than the probability of either kind of damage and possibly both because the former excludes the chance of both happening.

Summary of Probability Calculations

$m =$ the number of occurrences of the event whose probability is sought.

$n =$ the number of opportunities for the event to occur (exposure units or exposures).

The probability that an event, A, will occur in a given period:

$$p(A) = m \div n.$$

The expected number of events in a given period:

$$E(\text{total number of events}) = n \times p \text{ (single event)}.$$

The probability that an event, A, will not occur in a given period:

$$p(\text{not } A) = 1 - p(A).$$

The probability that *both* event A and event B will occur in a given period:

If A and B are independent: $p(A \text{ and } B) = p(A) \times p(B).$

If A is dependent on B: $p(A \text{ and } B) = p(B) \times p(A|B).$

If A is sequentially dependent on B: $p(B \text{ followed by } A) = p(B) \times p(A \text{ following } B).$

The probability of events that are independent of each other occurring multiple times:

$$p(A \text{ occurring } x \text{ times}) = p(A)^x.$$

The probability that either event A or event B will occur in a given period:

If A and B are mutually exclusive:

$$p(A \text{ or } B) = p(A) + p(B).$$

If A and B are not mutually exclusive:

$$p(A \text{ or } B \text{ or both}) = p(A) + p(B) - p(A \text{ and } B).$$

or:

$$p(A \text{ or } B \text{ but not both}) = [p(A) \times p(\text{not } B)] + [p(B) \times p(\text{not } A)].$$

The previous discussion has emphasized the number of ways that two (or more) events or factors can interact when using probability analysis. A risk management professional needs to be aware of whether the events are independent or dependent (or sequentially dependent) as well as whether the events are mutually exclusive. He or she also has to determine whether the analysis should include joint probabilities or alternative probabilities. The interaction of events or factors may often be difficult to model, and great care is needed in ensuring the accuracy of the analysis.

If the underlying probabilities are changing, then the previous discussion of probability analysis is not as useful as trend analysis. Similar to the previous discussion on probability analysis, trend analysis can be expanded to cover more complex situations than were presented in the previous chapter.

APPLIED TREND ANALYSIS

Risk management professionals often may want to use trend analysis to forecast loss frequency, loss severity, or the costs of insurance or retention—any of which could be the joint result of several independent factors (variables). Forecasting in this case requires combining the effects of the independent variables.

For example, the risk management professionals for an organization that retains its automobile physical damage losses may, for forecasting purposes, envision each year's losses as the joint result of three variables: (1) the number of vehicles the organization operates, (2) the frequency of losses per 100 vehicles, and (3) the costs of repairing physical damage losses. Forecasting each of these variables separately and combining the results are likely to generate a more accurate loss forecast than combining results and then trying to forecast.

Similarly, an organization that wants to budget its annual aggregate workers' compensation costs for the next year might find no predictable pattern in its past annual aggregate costs, because several underlying variables determine these costs. However, predictable patterns may emerge when the annual aggregate costs are analyzed as the combined result of separate, more predictable trends in (1) the size of the organization's work force, (2) changes in the wage and salary rates that the organization pays its employees, and (3) the levels of workers' compensation benefits mandated by the states in which the organization's employees work.

To illustrate how multiple variables can be combined to formulate a forecast, suppose Galston wants to forecast its annual losses from collisions. The risk management professional assumes that the losses from collisions depend on two underlying relationships. First, the risk management professional relates Galston's annual losses from collisions (in constant dollars) to output (in ton-miles of freight) using regression analysis. Second, the risk management professional converts constant dollar income losses (obtained in the first step) to current dollars by multiplying by an inflation factor determined from a forecast of common-carrier truck freight rates per ton-mile of freight.

This approach to forecasting the combined effects of two or more variables rests on an important assumption: the two variables are independent. In this case, ton-mileages and freight rates are not related to one another in any defined pattern. If they were, then this additive, sequential combining of trends would not be valid.

Combining Trends—Defining the Model

Business forecasters often develop models (simulations of relationships) that describe, in a simplified way, how the world appears to work. When used for forecasting, a model identifies and describes the effects of specific relevant causes of the dependent variable being forecast.

The elementary model presented here assumes that the two independent variables are ton-miles of freight carried and changes in freight charges, which are useful predictors of the dependent variable, annual dollar totals of Galston's net income losses from collisions on a particular route. Because this is an elementary model, it does not consider important factors such as weather, expenditures for private-truck and public-highway maintenance, experience level of the truck drivers and maintenance personnel, the time interval since the last major collision, and even the passage of time (which might change the conditions that generate these two trends). These are just some of the factors that might reasonably be used as predictors of annual dollar amounts of net income losses from truck collisions, assuming that these predictors could be reasonably forecast. But, for understanding the procedure and for practicing how to apply it, two independent variables (ton-miles and freight rates) are sufficient.

First Independent Variable: Ton-Miles

It is reasonable to assume that the frequency and severity (annual totals of collision losses) that a common-carrier trucking company suffers each year will increase or decrease as the volume of its freight hauling increases or decreases. Exhibit 12-1 shows the calculation of the regression equation that relates Galston's annual collision losses to its annual ton-miles of cargo carried during Years 1 through 4 in order to estimate this relationship. (A ton-mile is one ton carried for one mile.) In Exhibit 12-1, and in the equation it derives, ton-miles is the independent variable (x, expressed in hundreds of thousands), and the annual dollar amount of collision losses is the dependent variable (y, expressed in thousands of constant Year 4 dollars).

EXHIBIT 12-1

Regression of Annual Collision Losses Against Annual Ton-Miles

Year	x: Ton-Miles (00,000s)	y: Losses ($000s)	xy	x^2
1	35	9.8	343.0	1,225
2	60	32.9	1,974.0	3,600
3	72	45.1	3,247.2	5,184
4	95	82.0	7,790.0	9,025
Total	262	169.8	13,354.2	19,034

$$a = \frac{(\Sigma y)(\Sigma x^2) - (\Sigma x)(\Sigma xy)}{n(\Sigma x^2) - (\Sigma x)^2}$$

$$= \frac{(169.8)(19,034) - (262)(13,354.2)}{4(19,034) - (262)^2}$$

$$= \frac{3,231,973.2 - 3,498,800.4}{76,136 - 68,644}$$

$$= \frac{-266,827.2}{7,492}$$

$$= -35.61.$$

$$b = \frac{n(\Sigma xy) - (\Sigma x)(\Sigma y)}{n(\Sigma x^2) - (\Sigma x)^2}$$

$$= \frac{4(13,354.2) - (262)(169.8)}{4(19,034) - (262)^2}$$

$$= \frac{53,416.8 - 44,487.6}{76,136 - 68,644}$$

$$= \frac{8,929.2}{7,492}$$

$$= 1.192.$$

Regression equation: $y = a + bx$.

or: Losses ($\times$ $1,000) = $-35.61 + 1.192$ Ton-Miles ($\times$ 100,000).

Some of the data included in Exhibit 12-1 are taken from the previous chapter. The resulting equation for the regression line indicates that the annual dollar total of losses (y) can be expected to increase by $1,192 for each 100,000 ton-mile increase in cargo carried.

The negative $35,610 value for the intercept ("*a*") in the equation errone-ously suggests that net income losses from collisions would be less than zero if Galston's ceased to operate and if ton-mileages were zero. Because a regression line is only an accurate model in the data range for which it was calculated, this result can be ignored for practical purposes. This regression equation should not be used for making forecasts significantly beyond the range of ton-mileages (3,500,000 through 9,500,000) from which it was calculated. Any use of this regression line significantly beyond the range of data available would almost certainly be erroneous.

It is important not to ascribe false accuracy to the results shown in any exhib-its in the remainder of this chapter. The forecast that expected, annual dollar totals of loss will rise or fall by $1,192 each time that annual ton-mileages rise or fall by 100,000 is only the best estimate, based on the limited available data and the assumptions underlying the model. To the extent that those assump-tions are not true, and to the extent that other causal factors are ignored in the model, the accuracy of this forecast is limited. At best, actual results can be expected only to fall within a range of this single-value forecast. The width of this range depends on many factors, analysis of which requires statistical expertise beyond the scope of this text.

Second Independent Variable: Freight Rates

Changes in the general level of prices often is forecasted using regression analysis with a time trend as the dependent variable. Exhibit 12-2 shows the calculation of a trend line of changes in truck common-carrier freight rates from Year 1 through Year 4. (These freight rates are the dollar amounts that a regulated common carrier, such as Galston's, is permitted to charge for each ton of cargo transported. A state or federal regulator typically publishes a schedule of allowable freight rates. The freight charge for a shipment is the freight rate for a ton of the given cargo multiplied by the number of tons in the shipment.)

The index figures in Column 2 of Exhibit 12-2 are taken from Exhibit 11-2, and the calculation follows the procedure illustrated in Exhibit 11-2. The resulting equations suggest that if the economic conditions of Year 1 through Year 4 do not change and price levels move in a linear fashion, then the price index can be projected to increase by 11.45 index points each year.

Many forecasting models assume that price levels change by a constant percentage rate from year to year rather than by a constant number of index points. The assumption of a constant percentage rate of change yields a curvi-linear (or curving), rather than a linear (or straight), trend line. As years pass, any positive or upward rate of change implies larger annual increases, while a persistent negative or downward rate of change implies an increasingly rapid decrease. Because rates of change can vary, projecting a constant-rate curvi-linear trend over many years can lead to unrealistic results.

EXHIBIT 12-2

Linear Trend of Truck Common-Carrier Freight Rates

[1] x: Year	[2] y: Index	[3] xy	[4] x^2
1	115.2	115.2	1
2	125.9	251.8	4
3	140.2	420.6	9
4	148.6	594.4	16
Total 10	529.9	1,382.0	30

$$a = \frac{(\Sigma y)(\Sigma x^2) - (\Sigma x)(\Sigma xy)}{n(\Sigma x^2) - (\Sigma x)^2}$$

$$= \frac{(529.9)(30) - (10)(1,382.0)}{4(30) - (10)^2}$$

$$= \frac{15,897.0 - 13,820.0}{120 - 100}$$

$$= \frac{2,077}{20}$$

$$= 103.85.$$

$$b = \frac{n(\Sigma xy) - (\Sigma x)(\Sigma y)}{n(\Sigma x^2) - (\Sigma x)^2}$$

$$= \frac{4(1,382.0) - (10)(529.9)}{4(30) - (10)^2}$$

$$= \frac{5,528 - 5,299}{120 - 100}$$

$$= \frac{299}{20}$$

$$= 11.45.$$

Regression equation: $y = a + bx$.

or: Index = 103.85 + 11.45 (Year).

Exhibit 12-3 demonstrates that linear and curvilinear trends can forecast strikingly different results, especially in more distant years. (The freight rates in this exhibit are hypothetical, unrelated to Galston's actual experience.) In the linear projection, each succeeding year's forecast is 11.45 index points greater than the last. The values in Column 3 of Exhibit 12-3 are generated by the regression equation at the bottom of Exhibit 12-2. In the percentage projection, each year's forecast is 8.86 percent greater than the last. The values in Column 4 of Exhibit 12-3 are generated by a curvilinear regression equation not shown. As more years pass, the 8.86 percent growth is much more rapid than the 11.45 index point growth. Because these two trending techniques produce such markedly different results, long-range forecasts can be inaccurate. To improve accuracy, both in the long and the short term, a risk manager or another qualified person should complete the following steps:

- Obtain as much relevant data as possible for calculating trends, especially current data that can be particularly valuable in making short-term forecasts.
- Experiment with both linear and curvilinear trending techniques to see which approach better fits historical data and presumably better projects the future. (A simple way to experiment is to graph both the historical data and the linear or curvilinear trend lines, as shown in a previous chapter, to make an intuitive judgment about the better "fit." Alternatively, a statistician can be consulted, especially if the importance of the forecast justifies the cost.)
- Redraw or recalculate trend lines to incorporate new data, either adding to the total volume of data on which the trends are based or, if conditions are changing and the earliest data no longer reflect existing conditions, deleting any inapplicable loss data.

These steps help to refine the forecasting model by adding to the historical data on which the model is founded and clarifying the patterns of change on which it relies. To illustrate the principles involved, this discussion intentionally focuses on an elementary model, which includes only four years of data and two variables. A large organization with many years of experience may want to use a model with five or six trended variables and perhaps two decades of accumulated data. For risk management professionals in small organizations, however, even a model as simple as the one explained here can sharpen loss forecasts.

An Illustrative Forecast

Exhibit 12-4 illustrates one technique for forecasting Galston's annual collision losses in both constant Year 4 and current dollars, based on the following:

- The regression equation in Exhibit 12-1 that relates collision losses to ton-miles
- A forecast from Galston's senior management that, because of an expected general economic decline in the region that Galston's serves, ton-mileages will be 8 million in Year 5, 5.5 million in Year 6, and 4.3 million in Year 7

EXHIBIT 12-3

Comparison of Linear and Curvilinear (Constant Percentage Change): Projection of Freight Rates

[1]	[2]	[3]	[4]
Year	Actual Index	Linear Projection (11.45 index points per year)	Constant Percentage Projection (8.86% per year)
1	115.2	115.30	115.20
2	125.9	126.75	125.41
3	140.2	138.20	136.52
4	148.6	149.65	148.61
5		161.10	161.78
6		172.55	176.11
7		184.00	191.72
8		195.45	208.70
9		206.90	227.20
10		218.35	247.32
11		229.80	269.24
12		241.25	293.09
13		252.70	319.06
14		264.15	347.33

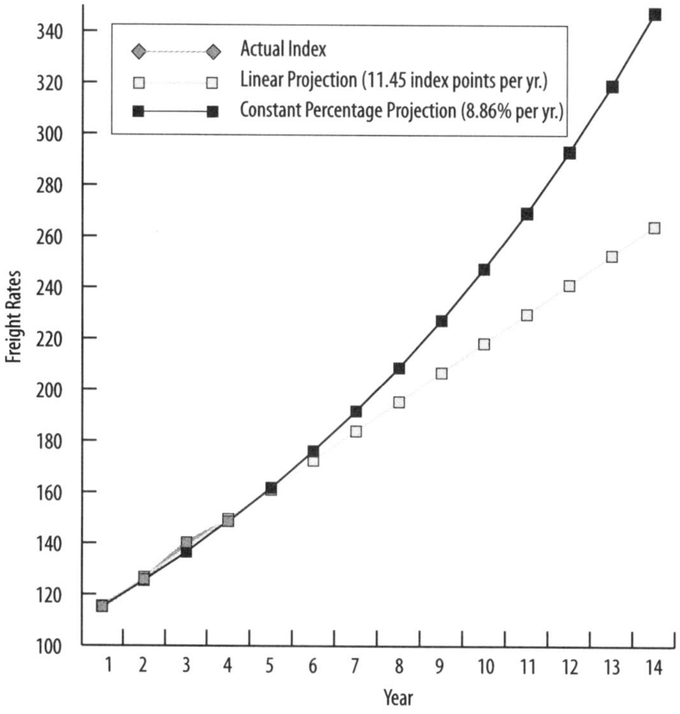

- A forecast from Galston's finance department that the 8.86 percent increase in motor truck common-carrier freight rates will continue for Year 5 but that the rates will increase only 7.00 percent in Year 6 and, in Year 7, the rates will fall 5.00 percent from their Year 6 level

The forecasts from senior management and from the finance department should enhance the accuracy of the overall forecasts that risk management professionals could make. Without this information, these forecasts might have to rely on linear or curvilinear projections of both future ton-mileages and future freight rates.

Exhibit 12-4 recaps these trends and performs the calculations that apply the regression equation for Years 5, 6, and 7. These calculations involve two separate steps. The first is to calculate losses in constant dollars based on projected ton-mileages. This step is similar for all three years, involving only substitution of different ton-mileage figures for each of the three years. The resulting loss projections—$59,750 in Year 5; $29,950 in Year 6; and $15,650 in Year 7—are in constant Year 4 dollars.

The second step in the calculations for each of these three years converts the constant dollar losses to current dollars, reflecting Year 5, 6, and 7 projected freight rates. These rate-adjusting calculations differ between the three years because of different projected price-level changes and because of the differing number of years for which the constant Year 4 dollar losses need to be adjusted.

Therefore, for Year 5, the freight rate change merely involves multiplying $59.75 by $(1 + 0.0886)$, reflecting an expected 8.86 percent increase in freight rates from Year 4 to Year 5. Consequently, Year 5 losses are forecast to be $65,040 in Year 5 dollars. For Year 6, the freight rate adjustment involves multiplying the amount of losses in constant dollars by two factors: $(1 + 0.0886)$ to bring these losses to Year 5 levels and $(1 + 0.0700)$ to reflect the expected 7.00 percent freight rate increase from Year 5 to Year 6. By this procedure, expressed in Year 6 dollars, losses are projected to be $34,890 in Year 6. For Year 7, when freight rates are projected to fall by 5.00 percent, three factors are needed to adjust to the Year 7 rate level: $(1 + 0.0886)$ to reach the Year 5 rate level, $(1 + 0.0700)$ to reach the Year 6 rate level, and $(1 - 0.0500)$ to reflect the Year 7 projected rate decrease. Weighted by these three factors, Year 7 losses in then-current dollars can be forecast as $17,320.

(These rate-adjustment factors are equivalent to 1.0886, 1.0700, and 0.9500, respectively. Had the projected changes in freight rates been a constant 8.86 percent for each of the three years, the respective freight rates adjustment factors could have been expressed as 1.0886, 1.0886^2, and 1.0886^3.)

EXHIBIT 12-4

Forecasts of Annual Collision Losses for Years 5, 6, and 7

Assumptions

For Year 5

1. Ton-miles = 8,000,000 (or 80 × 100,000).
2. Freight rates continue to rise at 8.86% over Year 4 level.

For Year 6

1. Ton-miles = 5,500,000 (or 55 × 100,000).
2. Freight rates rise at 7.00% over Year 5 level.

For Year 7

1. Ton-miles = 4,300,000 (or 43 × 100,000).
2. Freight rates fall 5.00% from Year 6 level.

Calculations

For Year 5

1. Losses (in thousands of constant Year 4 dollars)

$$L = -\$35.61 + (\$1.192 \times 80)$$
$$= -\$35.61 + \$95.36$$
$$= \$59.75.$$

2. Adjusted for freight rate change (8.86% increase for Year 4)

$$\text{Losses} = \$59.75 \times (1 + 0.0886)$$
$$= \$65.04.$$

For Year 6

1. Losses (in thousands of constant Year 4 dollars)

$$L = -\$35.61 + (\$1.192 \times 55)$$
$$= -\$35.61 + \$65.56$$
$$= \$29.95.$$

2. Adjusted for freight rate change (7.00% increase over Year 5)

$$\text{Losses} = \$29.95 \times (1 + 0.0886) \times (1 + 0.07)$$
$$= \$34.89.$$

For Year 7

1. Losses (in thousands of constant Year 4 dollars)

$$L = -\$35.61 + (1.192 \times 43)$$
$$= -\$35.61 + \$51.26$$
$$= \$15.65.$$

2. Adjusted for freight rate change (5.00% decrease from Year 6)

$$\text{Losses} = \$15.65 \times (1 + 0.0886) \times (1 + 0.07) \times (1 - 0.05)$$
$$= \$17.32.$$

SUMMARY

By applying the concepts of probability and trending analysis to loss forecasting, risk management professionals can improve forecasts of potential accidental losses and of the costs of preventing or paying for such losses.

Calculating the probabilities of one or more of several events involves calculating joint probabilities and alternative probabilities. A joint probability is the probability that two as more events will happen together. To calculate a joint probability, one must know the separate probability of each event alone, and then also know (or judge) whether the occurrence of one event changes the probabilities of the other events (making these probabilities dependent).

For alternative probabilities of any one of two or more events occurring within a given period, one must determine whether the events are mutually exclusive—that is, whether the happening of one event does, or does not, make the happening of other events impossible.

These calculations enable risk managers to determine or estimate the likelihood that an organization will experience various combinations of losses in one year or another time period. Arithmetic trending techniques can also improve these loss forecasts.

The trending concepts discussed in the previous chapter help in determining how several separate trends, in this chapter ton-miles and freight rates, can be projected in isolation and then combined to develop loss forecasts that recognize the combined effects of several trends influencing an organization's particular loss experience (annual collision losses).

This chapter uses a two-factor trend model to predict annual losses from collisions for a hypothetical transport company. The two factors, output (in ton-miles of freight) and inflation (freight rates), are each forecast separately and then combined into a single trend. To keep the model simple, it does not consider important factors such as weather, level of experience of the truck drivers and maintenance personnel, or other factors. These are just some of the factors that might reasonably be used as predictors of annual dollar amounts of net income losses from truck collisions, assuming that these predictors could be reasonably forecast. But, for understanding the procedure and for practicing how to apply it, two independent variables (ton miles and freight rates) are sufficient.

Chapter 13

Direct Your Learning

Understanding Cash Flow Analysis

After learning the content of this chapter and completing the corresponding course guide assignment, you should be able to:

- Explain why net cash flows are important to an organization.

- Explain why money has a "time value" and how to determine the present value.

- Calculate the present values of future single payments or streams of future payments using present value tables.

- Explain how to use the net present value and internal rate of return methods to evaluate capital investment proposals.

- Apply the net present value and internal rate of return methods to rank capital investment proposals.

- Calculate the internal rate of return for a capital investment proposal using interpolation.

- Explain how to calculate differential annual after-tax net cash flows for an investment proposal.

- Given a case, evaluate two investment proposals using net cash flow analysis.

- Define or describe each of the Key Words and Phrases for this chapter.

Develop Your Perspective

What are the main topics covered in the chapter?

Investment proposals are opportunities for the organization to spend (invest) capital today with the expectation that this expenditure will increase net cash flows in the future. This chapter describes cash flow analysis as an approach to comparing various investment proposals using two of the most commonly used methods for evaluating net cash flows: the net present value method and the internal rate of return method.

Choose a risk control technique your organization uses and identify the elements necessary for cash flow analysis.

- What cash inflows does this risk control technique generate?
- What cash outflows does this risk control technique generate?

Why is it important to learn about these topics?

Most organizations use the net present value decision criterion to guide business decisions. Understanding cash flow analysis will enable a risk management professional to analyze the net cash flows of any risk management activity at any organization.

Consider the cash flow analysis data you gathered above.

- What are the current costs of the risk control activity?
- What are the possible future benefits of the risk control activity?

How can you use what you will learn?

Based on your analysis, recommend specific risk management techniques.

- What risk control techniques might you choose? Why?
- How did you come to these decisions?

Chapter 13
Understanding Cash Flow Analysis

Risk management professionals, as is true for professionals in other disciplines, must be able to financially justify business decisions they make. For example, risk management professionals must be able to show that the selection of particular risk management techniques is financially sound from a cost/benefit perspective. Cash flow analysis is a financial tool that enables a risk management professional to select one or a combination of risk management techniques that will maximize the net present value (the value today) of the organization's future cash flows. It also enables comparison among alternative investment proposals, by showing which proposal has the greatest net present value over the long term. Most organizations (whether for-profit or not-for-profit) use cash flow analysis to guide business decisions. Doing so allows risk management decisions to be made on the same basis as most other financial decisions within the organization. Specifically, cash flow analysis enables the risk management professional to do the following:

- Explain how any proposal, including a proposed risk management technique, would affect an organization's cash inflows and cash outflows.
- Calculate the present value of the net cash flows of proposals that require an organization to commit resources to risk management.
- Express, evaluate, and rank proposals, including alternative risk management techniques, according to their differential annual after-tax net cash flows and rates of return.

This chapter describes basic concepts of managerial finance used to forecast the cash flow effects of alternative risk management techniques. Fundamental to this discussion are the reasons why money has a time value, what factors determine this value, and how this value is measured. The two most commonly used decision criteria to evaluate and rank alternate proposals are net present value and internal rate of return. Taxes and depreciation must also be considered for their effect on cash flows. For the purposes of this discussion, it is assumed that present and future cash flows are known with certainty. The next chapter examines problems associated with making decisions when future net cash flows are uncertain.

IMPORTANCE OF NET CASH FLOWS

Net cash flow (NCF) is cash receipts minus cash disbursements over a given period. If an organization's receipts exceed its disbursements, net cash flow

Net cash flow (NCF)
Cash receipts minus cash disbursements over a given period.

is positive (meaning the organization has made money). If disbursements exceed receipts, net cash flow is negative. By projecting net cash flows likely to be generated by investment in assets or activities, an organization's managers have a valid financial criterion for choosing those assets or activities that would provide the greatest financial benefit to the organization. Therefore, cash flow analysis is important because cash flow drives the decision making of the organization.

Net cash flows help an organization measure its short-range capabilities and its long-range value to its owners and to those it serves. The greater the value today (present value) of the net cash flows that an organization can command in the long run, the more fully it can realize its organizational goals. Therefore, when selecting assets or activities in which to invest, managers should give high priority to alternatives that promise net cash flows with the greatest present values.

Cash flow analysis typically involves situations in which an asset or activity requires immediate cash expenditures but will generate future cash receipts. **Capital budgeting** is the process of evaluating alternative capital investment proposals (the acquisition of long-term assets) in terms of the cash outlays that the proposals require and the present values of the cash inflows that the proposals are likely to generate. Capital budgeting is used when cash expenditures or receipts are expected to span several accounting periods.

Organizations have two types of expenditures: operating expenditures and capital expenditures. **Operating expenditures** are disbursements for assets that will be consumed in a relatively short period, usually within one year or a single accounting period. **Capital expenditures** are disbursements for assets that will be consumed over a relatively long period, usually over multiple accounting periods. Capital budgeting focuses on capital expenditures that generate cash receipts or require cash disbursements over a long period of time. For example, if a manufacturer builds a new plant (immediate cash disbursement), the cash receipts (inflows) attributable to that investment proposal will be received over the plant's entire useful life (cash receipts over a long period). To make sound decisions about purchasing capital assets, present values of future cash inflows and outflows must be compared with the investment proposal's initial cost. In carrying out this cash flow analysis, it is important to recognize that money has a time value.

TIME VALUE OF MONEY

The **time value of money** is the ability to invest and generate income over time on a dollar available today. A dollar received today is worth more than a dollar to be received in the future because investing money over time in an asset or activity can generate income. In contrast, a dollar to be received in the future cannot be invested to generate income until that future date. Calculating the present value of a sum of money to be received in the future is based on its time value.

Capital budgeting
The process of evaluating alternative capital investment proposals in terms of the cash outlays that the proposals require and the present values of the cash inflows that the proposals are likely to generate.

Operating expenditures
Disbursements for assets that will be consumed in a relatively short period, usually within one year or a single accounting period.

Capital expenditures
Disbursements for assets that will be consumed over a relatively long period, usually over multiple accounting periods.

Time value of money
The ability to invest and generate income over time on a dollar available today.

The following two factors influence the time value of money:

1. The rate of return
2. The length of the time period until the future dollar is received

The **rate of return** is an asset's or activity's annual profit or surplus, expressed as a percentage of its original cost. The greater the rate of return that today's dollar can generate, the greater its value relative to a future dollar. Conversely, the longer the time period until a future dollar is to be received, the lower its present value when compared with the value of today's dollar.

Rate of return
An asset's or activity's annual profit or surplus, expressed as a percentage of its original cost.

Present Value

Present value is the value today of money that will be received in the future. The process by which the present value is calculated is called discounting. The following two factors determine the present value:

Present value
The value today of money that will be received in the future.

1. The appropriate discount rate
2. The length of time before each cash flow occurs

Although discount rate and interest rate are often used interchangeably, they are slightly different. An interest rate is used to calculate future values—that is, to take something from the present value up to a future value. A discount rate is used to calculate present values—that is, to take a future value and bring it back to the present value.

The first factor in determining present value is selecting an appropriate discount rate. The appropriate discount rate is the time value cost associated with the use of money, normally expressed as a percentage for each year that the money is being used. Except in cases in which money has been borrowed from an outside lender, this time value cost does not usually entail any explicit outlay for the use of money. The cost arises because selecting one use for money necessarily prevents that money being used for some other purpose. Expressed as a discount rate, the **opportunity cost** of money that is used for one purpose is the rate of return that money could have earned had it been put to the best alternative use that entails comparable risk.

Opportunity cost
The rate of return that money could have earned had it been put to the best alternative use that entails comparable risk.

In for-profit corporations with publicly traded common stock, the shareholders and other investors bear the opportunity costs of committing funds to various assets or activities. Those opportunity costs equal the returns the investors would expect to achieve on alternative investment proposals with comparable risk. To provide investors with incentives to make risky investments that the organization considers worthwhile, expected rates of return for risky investment proposals must exceed those for other, safer investment proposals. The greater the risk, the greater the return that investors would expect and therefore the greater the opportunity cost of using funds for that particular asset or activity.

Large, for-profit corporations usually make investment proposal decisions using an estimate of the overall opportunity cost of the investors' funds.

Cost of capital
The opportunity cost of funds provided by investors.

The opportunity cost of funds provided by investors is called the organization's **cost of capital**. The organization's overall cost of capital is called the weighted average cost of capital, which weights the estimated capital (opportunity) cost for each source of funding (for example, common stock, preferred stock, and debt) by the amount of funds obtained from each source. Under suitable conditions, this cost of capital becomes the discount rate used to calculate present values of future net cash flows.

Blithe, Inc. and the Weighted Average Cost of Capital

Blithe, Inc. (Blithe) is a publicly traded organization that manufactures and distributes children's toys. Blithe has two main sources of funds from investors: stock sales (equity) and bond sales (debt). Investors in Blithe stocks provided $3 million in investments and expect a 15 percent return on their investment. Investors in Blithe bonds provided $2 million in investments and expect a 10 percent return on their investment. Therefore, Blithe's weighted average cost of capital is calculated as the percentage of funds provided by stock investors ($3/5$, or 60 percent) multiplied by the expected rate of return of stock investors (15 percent) plus the percentage of funds provided by bond investors ($2/5$, or 40 percent) multiplied by the expected rate of return of bond investors (10 percent). This produces the following weighted average cost of capital:

$$\text{Weighted average cost of capital} = [0.6 \times 0.15] + [0.4 \times 0.10]$$
$$= 0.09 + 0.04$$
$$= 0.13 \text{ or } 13 \text{ percent.}$$

Since Blithe's weighted average cost of capital is 13 percent, Blithe could use 13 percent as its discount rate when calculating net present value for capital expenditure decisions.

The second factor that determines the present value of a cash flow or stream of net cash flows is the length of time; that is, the number of years or units of time until the cash flow(s) are received or paid. To illustrate, if today's money can generate a return of 10 percent per year, then an initial sum of $100 (present value) increases to $110 (future value) at the end of one year. Conversely, a future value of $110 to be received one year from now has a present value of $100 at the 10 percent discount rate. If the payment (future value) were to be received in two years, it would have to equal $121 to have a present value of $100 at the 10 percent discount rate, because $100 invested today would grow to $121 in two years at that rate. Note that the future value in two years is *not* $120 ($10 in interest per year for two years). Compounding of interest applies. The $100 invested today is worth $110 at the end of one year. Then, that $110 is reinvested for another year, earning 10 percent to yield $121 ($121 = $110 × 1.10 or $121 = $100 × 1.10 × 1.10).

Generally, capital budgeting decisions involve investment proposals that are expected to extend well into the future. In most cases, the longer the expected life of a proposal, the less accurate are its estimated future net cash flows. Using forecasting methods such as those discussed previously can improve the accuracy of the expected cash flows to some degree. However, these forecasting methods become less accurate the further out the forecasts go.

The risk management professional can apply the two key components of present value—the appropriate discount rate or cost of capital and the length of time—to the forecasted cash flows to calculate the present value of an investment proposal.

Present Value Calculations

Calculating a present value can involve any of the following values:

- Present payment
- Present value of single future payment (PV_p)
- Present value of stream of equal future payments (PV_{ep})
- Present value of stream of unequal future payments (PV_{up})

Present Payment

The present value of a present payment (either a receipt or a disbursement) is simply the value today of that payment. For example, $100 received or disbursed now—in the present accounting period—has a present value of $100. The present payment most frequently encountered in capital budgeting situations is the initial outlay of funds required by investment in a proposed asset or activity, such as purchasing fire extinguishers and training employees in their use.

Single Future Payment

The single future payment (one payment at some future date) most often encountered in capital budgeting situations is the salvage or resale value; for example, the resale value of a purchased building. To assist in calculating the present value of a single future payment, Appendix A gives present values of a single payment of $1 received at the end of various time periods at various discount rates. This appendix shows the present value factors for each pair of variables (discount rate and time period) used to determine the time value of money. A present value factor is a factor by which a single future payment of money can be multiplied to determine that sum's equivalent value in the present, given the applicable time period and discount rate. (In this text, present value factor is abbreviated PVF. Where the present value factor is for a single future payment (from Appendix A), the notation used is PVF_a. Where the present value factor is for a stream of future payments (from Appendix B), the notation used is PVF_b.)

Mathematically, a present value factor for a single future payment (PVF_a) is calculated as follows:

$$PVF_a = \frac{1}{(1+r)^n},$$

where n = number of time periods and r = discount rate.

In addition to using present value tables, such as those contained in Appendixes A and B, present values can be calculated readily with financial or other calculators and with computer spreadsheets.

Present value factors indicate the amount that must be invested today at a given interest rate for a given time period in order to receive $1 as a single payment at the end of that period. The applicable formula is:

$$PVF_a \times (1+r)^n = \$1.$$

Therefore, PVF_a is the amount of money today that would grow to $1 at the end of the time period (year n) if invested at rate r with annual compounding of interest.

For example, using a 10 percent annual discount rate, the present value of $1 received at the end of one year is $0.909, or about 91 cents. This result is obtained by multiplying $1 by the present value factor, 0.909, in the one-time-period row of the 10 percent column of Appendix A. If approximately 91 cents is invested today for one year—earning 10 percent interest per year—the interest is 9 cents, and the amount resulting at the end of that year is $1.

If interest is compounded annually for two years, 82.6 cents must be invested initially to produce an ending amount of $1. Appendix A indicates that the present value factor for this investment proposal is 0.826, indicating that 82.6 cents is needed initially if the ending amount is to be $1 after two years at 10 percent annual interest. At the end of one year, 82.6 cents grows to 90.9 cents, and at the end of the second year, the 90.9 cents grows to $1. Viewed prospectively, the present value of $1 to be received after two years at interest compounded annually at the rate of 10 percent per year is 82.6 cents.

An inverse relationship exists between the present value of $1 and the time period until the single future payment occurs. As the time period increases, the present value decreases. An inverse relationship also exists between the present value of $1 and the discount rate. The higher the discount rate for any given time period, the lower the present value, and vice versa.

Time Period	Present Value of $1 at a 10% Discount Rate
$n = 0$	$1.00
$n = 1$	$0.91
$n = 10$	$0.39
$n = 50$	$0.01

and

Discount Rate	Present Value of $1 Received After One Year
$r = 0.10$	$0.91
$r = 0.12$	$0.89
$r = 0.20$	$0.83
$r = 0.50$	$0.67

These present values are for future payments of $1. If the future payments differ from $1, their present value (PV_p) is calculated by multiplying each future payment by the present value factor for the specified discount rate and time period.

$$PV_p = PVF_a \times \text{Future payment.}$$

For example, to calculate the present value of a single payment of $100 to be received at the end of three years at interest compounded annually at the rate of 10 percent, determine the present value factor for $1 to be received under these conditions. The correct factor from Appendix A is 0.751. Multiplying this factor by $100 indicates that $75.10 is the present value of $100 to be received at the end of three years at interest compounded annually at the rate of 10 percent. Similarly, if the discount rate remains 10 percent, but the single payment to be received at the end of three years is $7,800, the present value of that future payment is $7,800 times the present value factor of 0.751, or $5,857.80.

Stream of Equal Future Payments

Many capital expenditures do not just generate a single future payment, they generate a stream of future payments. For example, the savings on insurance premiums generated by installing a sprinkler system represent a stream of future payments. The present value of a stream of future payments, often called an annuity, is equal to the sum of the present values of each of the separate payments. If that sum were invested at the given interest rate, it would be able to generate the future payment stream exactly.

Exhibit 13-1 shows the present values for a stream of three payments of $100 received at the end of one, two, and three years when the discount rate is 10 percent per year compounded annually. The present value of a single payment of $100 at the end of one year under these conditions is $90.91. Similarly, the present value of $100 received at the end of two years is $82.64, and the present value of $100 received at the end of three years is $75.13. These present values are calculated from the present value factors in Appendix A. If the three present values are added, the total of $248.68 is the present value of $100 received at the end of each year for a period of three years at interest compounded annually at the rate of 10 percent. Stated differently, $248.68 is the amount that must be invested today at 10 percent interest per year compounded annually to receive $100 at the end of each of the next three years.

With streams of equal payments, present value calculations quickly become repetitive. Appendix B can be used to reach the same result without requiring the summing of the separate present values from Appendix A. The present value factors in Appendix B (PVF_b) can be used only with streams of equal payments using the following formula:

$$PV_{ep} = PVF_b \times \text{Future payment value.}$$

For example, Appendix B can be used to determine the present value of $100 received annually for a period of three years at interest compounded annually at the rate of 10 percent using this formula.

EXHIBIT 13-1

Present Value of a Stream of Payments at 10 Percent Interest

Timeline

	Year 1	Year 2	Year 3
		$100	$100	$100

Mathematical Calculation Using Appendix A

	Amount received at end of year	$\times$	$PVF_a\ (1 \div (1+r)^n)$	=	Present value
Year 1	$100	$\times$	0.9091	=	$90.91
Year 2	$100	$\times$	0.8264	=	$82.64
Year 3	$100	$\times$	0.7513	=	$75.13
Total					$248.68

Mathematical Calculation Using Appendix B

Present value = Amount received each time period $\times PVF_b$

= $100 × 0.2487

= **$248.70**.

Pre-Funded Account

	Year 1	Year 2	Year 3
Beginning balance	$248.68	$173.55	$90.91
Plus interest @ 10%	24.87	17.36	9.09
	273.55	190.91	100.00
Less payment	(100.00)	(100.00)	(100.00)
Ending balance	$173.55	$90.91	$0

In the 10 percent column of Appendix B, where the time period, n, equals 3 years, the present value factor (PVF_b) is 2.487. This present value factor, applied to future payments of $100 each, yields a present value of $248.70 ($100 × 2.487). Except for the slight difference resulting from rounding, this amount is the same as the $248.68 calculated by adding the three separate present value factors from Appendix A, as illustrated in Exhibit 13-1. Mathematically, the present value factor for a stream of annual payments for n years beginning one year from the present is:

$$PVF_b = \frac{1}{(1+r)} + \frac{1}{(1+r)^2} + \cdots + \frac{1}{(1+r)^n}$$

The present value factors in Appendix B are derived from those in Appendix A. The top line is the same in both tables because $1 is received at the end of only one time period, therefore, the stream of payments is only one future payment. The values on Line 2 of Appendix B equal the sums of the present values shown on Lines 1 and 2 in Appendix A. For example, at the 10 percent discount rate in Appendix A, the figures for the first and second years are 0.909 and 0.826. The present value at 10 percent on Line 2 in Appendix B is the sum of those two figures, 1.736. Because the present value factors are rounded to three decimal places, comparisons between the two tables may differ by one thousandth or even several thousandths.

Exhibit 13-1 also illustrates how the present value of a stream of equal annual payments is sufficient to generate the stream of payments with nothing left over at the end of the overall period. The present value of a three-year payment stream of $100 annually at a 10 percent discount rate is $248.70. Starting with a fund of $248.68, add 10 percent interest for the first year and subtract $100 at the end of the first year. At the beginning of the second year, start with $173.55. Repeat the process of adding interest and subtracting $100 at the end of each year for the second and third years. When the third $100 amount is subtracted, the amount remaining in the fund is $0. That calculation demonstrates that investing approximately $249 at 10 percent interest enables one to pay $100 at the end of each year over a three-year period with nothing left over. The difference between the sum of the payments and their present value represents the interest earned by the investment, a total of $51.32 ($300 – $248.68 = $51.32). Exhibit 13-1 shows that $90.91 invested for a one-year period at 10 percent earns $9.09 interest. Similarly, $82.64 invested for a two-year period earns $17.36, and $75.13 invested for a three-year period earns $24.87. Those earnings total $51.32.

Although the present value factor from Appendix B can be used to easily calculate the correct result, understanding the underlying calculations is useful.

For example, the present value of three annual payments of $100 can be written as:

$$PVF_b = \frac{1}{(1+r)} + \frac{1}{(1+r)^2} + \frac{1}{(1+r)^3}$$

$$= \frac{1}{1.10} + \frac{1}{1.10^2} + \frac{1}{1.10^3}$$

$$= 2.487$$

$$PV_{ep} = PVF_b \times \text{Future payment}$$

$$= 2.487 \times \$100$$

$$= \$248.70.$$

Stream of Unequal Future Payments

Capital expenditures can also generate a stream of future payments that are not equal to one another. For example, the installation of a sprinkler system may require an increasing amount of maintenance costs every year. Therefore, the annual savings on the insurance premiums are not level payments, when the increasing amount of maintenance is considered.

When different dollar amounts are to be received or paid at the end of different time periods, Appendix B cannot be used. Instead, each time period's payment must be valued separately, using the present values for single payments in Appendix A. The present value of the entire stream of unequal payments is the sum of the present values of the individual payments. Mathematically, the present value of a stream of n unequal annual payments beginning after one year is:

$$PV_{up} = \frac{\text{Payment 1}}{(1+r)} + \frac{\text{Payment 2}}{(1+r)^2} + \cdots + \frac{\text{Payment } n}{(1+r)^n}.$$

For example, Exhibit 13-2 shows the present values of a stream of unequal payments ($200, $300, and $400) at 10 percent interest. The present value of the $200 to be received at the end of the first year is $200 × 0.9091, or $181.82. Similarly, the present value of $300 to be received at the end of the second year is $300 × 0.8264, or $247.92. The present value of $400 to be received at the end of three years is $400 × 0.7513, or $300.52, making the present value of the three years' payments $730.26. For more lengthy calculations, it is better to use financial calculators or computer spreadsheets.

Once a risk management professional has determined the appropriate present value formulas apply to particular net cash flows, he or she must focus on the appropriate methods and evaluate net cash flows.

EXHIBIT 13-2

Present Value of a Stream of Unequal Payments at 10 Percent Interest

Timeline

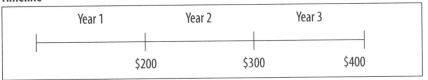

	Year 1	Year 2	Year 3
	$200	$300	$400

Mathematical Calculation Using Appendix A

	Amount received at end of year	$\times$	$PVF_a\,(1 \div (1+r)^n)$	$=$	Present value
Year 1	$200	$\times$	0.9091	$=$	$181.82
Year 2	$300	$\times$	0.8264	$=$	$247.92
Year 3	$400	$\times$	0.7513	$=$	$300.52
Total					$730.26

Formulas for Calculating Present Value and Present Value Factors

Single future payment of $1:

$$PVF_a = \frac{1}{(1+r)^n}, \text{ or } PVF_a + (1+r)^n = \$1,$$

where $n =$ time periods and $r =$ discount rate.

To calculate the present value of a single future payment using the present value factor:

$$PV_p = PVF_a \times \text{Future payment.}$$

Stream of annual payments of $1 for n years beginning one year from the present:

$$PVF_b = \frac{1}{(1+r)} + \frac{1}{(1+r)^2} + \cdots + \frac{1}{(1+r)^n}.$$

To calculate the present value of a stream of equal future payments:

$$PV_{ep} = \text{Future payment} \times PVF_b.$$

Stream of n unequal annual payments beginning after one year:

$$PV_{up} = \frac{\text{Payment 1}}{(1+r)} + \frac{\text{Payment 2}}{(1+r)^2} + \frac{\text{Payment 3}}{(1+r)^3} + \cdots + \frac{\text{Payment } n}{(1+r)^n}.$$

METHODS FOR EVALUATING CAPITAL INVESTMENT PROPOSALS

Capital budgeting decisions use cash flow analysis in two main ways. The first involves determining whether a particular investment proposal is expected to meet a predetermined minimum acceptable level of return. As explained earlier, the rate of return that an organization considers minimally acceptable often represents its average cost of obtaining funds (that is, its cost of capital).

The second way cash flow analysis is used in capital budgeting decisions involves selecting the most appropriate proposal by comparing the results of each proposal's cash flow analysis to the amount of investment it requires. This is often done if the proposals are mutually exclusive (that is, they are alternative methods of achieving the same result) or if constraints on obtaining funds prevent the organization from accepting all proposals that it would prefer.

Two closely related evaluation methods are used to apply cash flow analysis as a decision criterion: the net present value method and the internal rate of return method. The net present value method calculates whether, at a specified rate of interest, the present value of a proposal's net cash flow is positive or negative. If the net cash flow is positive, the proposal generates a rate of return higher than the specified rate. If the net cash flow is negative, the proposal generates a rate of return lower than the specified rate.

The second evaluation method, the internal rate of return method, calculates the discount rate at which the present value of a proposal's net cash flow is zero. If this calculated discount rate is equal to or exceeds the minimally acceptable rate, the proposal is acceptable. Conversely, if the calculated discount rate is below the minimally acceptable rate, the proposal is not acceptable. When used consistently, the methods generally support the same decision on any given proposal. However, as discussed subsequently in this chapter, the methods may rank competing proposals differently.

To evaluate capital investment proposals, the following information is required:

- The amount of initial investment
- The acceptable annual rate of return
- The amount and timing of the differential (incremental) annual after-tax net cash flows associated with the proposal over its estimated useful life
- The salvage value (if any) of the investment

Salvage value
The residual value of an original investment at the end of its useful life.

The **salvage value** is the residual value of the original investment at the end of its useful life. Exhibit 13-3 illustrates the information necessary for the evaluation of a capital investment proposal. The proposal involves acquiring an asset for $30,000 cash. The estimated useful life of the asset is three years, and the asset is expected to generate additional annual after-tax net cash inflows of $12,000, or a total of $36,000 over three years, with no salvage value. The minimum acceptable rate of return is 10 percent annually.

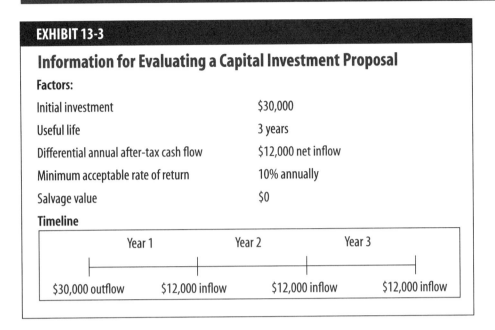

EXHIBIT 13-3

Information for Evaluating a Capital Investment Proposal

Factors:

Initial investment	$30,000
Useful life	3 years
Differential annual after-tax cash flow	$12,000 net inflow
Minimum acceptable rate of return	10% annually
Salvage value	$0

Timeline

	Year 1	Year 2	Year 3
$30,000 outflow	$12,000 inflow	$12,000 inflow	$12,000 inflow

Net Present Value (NPV) Method

An asset or activity's **net present value (NPV)** is the present value of all future net cash flows (including salvage value) discounted at the cost of capital, minus the cost of the initial investment, also discounted at the cost of capital. This can be expressed as follows:

$$NPV = PV \text{ (sum of future net cash flows)} - PV \text{ (initial investment)}.$$

For most proposals, a single investment is initially made—that is, the present value of the required investment will equal the initial required cash outlay and no discounting is needed.

The net present value (NPV) method can be used only when a minimum acceptable rate of return is predetermined. Typically, this minimum acceptable rate of return is the organization's cost of capital and generally will be given to, not established by, a risk management professional.

Any proposal whose projected cash inflows have a present value greater than the present value of the required outflows is acceptable by the NPV method. The net cash flow (NCF) from a proposal in any specified time period equals the cash inflows that the proposal is expected to produce, minus any cash outflows it requires. If inflows exceed outflows, the net cash flow from that proposal is positive. If outflows exceed inflows, net cash flow is negative. The **differential annual after-tax net cash flow** is the change in an organization's aggregate annual net cash flows resulting from implementing a proposal. In Exhibit 13-3, for instance, the additional annual net cash inflows are a constant $12,000 each year, and the only required cash outflow is the $30,000 initial cost of the asset.

Net present value (NPV)
The present value of all future net cash flows (including salvage value) discounted at the cost of capital, minus the cost of the initial investment, also discounted at the cost of capital.

Differential annual after-tax net cash flow
The change in an organization's aggregate annual net cash flows resulting from implementing a proposal.

The first step in using the NPV method is to calculate the present value of the differential annual after-tax net cash flows, as shown in Exhibit 13-4. The effect of taxes on net cash flows is discussed subsequently in this chapter.

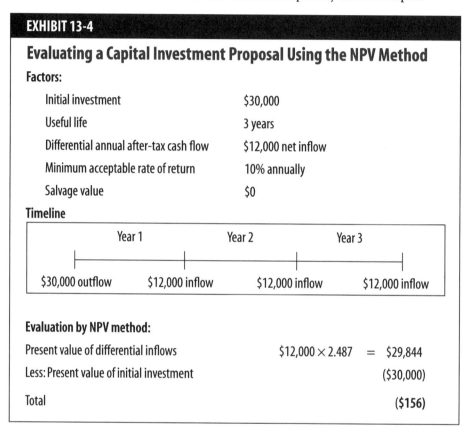

EXHIBIT 13-4

Evaluating a Capital Investment Proposal Using the NPV Method

Factors:

Initial investment	$30,000
Useful life	3 years
Differential annual after-tax cash flow	$12,000 net inflow
Minimum acceptable rate of return	10% annually
Salvage value	$0

Timeline

	Year 1	Year 2	Year 3
$30,000 outflow	$12,000 inflow	$12,000 inflow	$12,000 inflow

Evaluation by NPV method:

Present value of differential inflows	$12,000 × 2.487 = $29,844	
Less: Present value of initial investment		($30,000)
Total		($156)

Appendix B indicates that the present value factor for $1 received annually at the end of each year for three years at 10 percent interest compounded annually is 2.487. Multiplying this present value factor by $12,000 yields the present value of the differential (additional) net cash inflows, $29,844. In other words, $29,844 is the amount that would have to be invested today at 10 percent interest compounded annually to receive $12,000 at the end of each year for a period of three years.

The proposal's NPV is the present value of the additional net cash inflows minus the investment's present value. Therefore, the NPV of this proposal is a negative $156, calculated by subtracting the $30,000 initial investment that the proposal requires from the $29,884 present value of the proposal's future cash inflows. This negative result shows that the proposal will not generate the minimum acceptable rate of return of 10 percent. The present value of the additional net cash flows does not outweigh the investment's initial cost. Therefore, undertaking the proposal would reduce the organization's value. The following worksheet sets out the steps involved in evaluating a capital investment proposal using the NPV method.

Internal Rate of Return (IRR) Method

Another method of evaluating investment proposals is the internal rate of return (IRR) method. The **internal rate of return (IRR)** is the discount rate at which the net present value of all net cash flows equals zero. Notice that Exhibit 13-5 illustrates the same result as the previous example but this time using the IRR method. Because the asset's price in Exhibit 13-5 is $30,000, and acquiring that asset is expected to generate $12,000 per year for three years, the IRR is that discount rate at which the present value of $12,000 received annually for a period of three years equals $30,000. Dividing $30,000 by $12,000 gives an implied present value factor for the three $12,000 payments of 2.500. Therefore, $2.50 is the present value of $1 received annually for a three-year period at the yet-undetermined IRR for this proposal. This rate can be estimated by finding the present value factor that comes closest to 2.500 in the three-year row of Appendix B. The factor of 2.500 lies between 2.577 for an 8 percent return and 2.487 for a 10 percent return over a three-year period. Therefore, the IRR for this proposal is between 8 and 10 percent, compounded annually.

> **Internal rate of return (IRR)**
> The discount rate at which the net present value of all net cash flows equals zero.

A more exact rate of return can be obtained by interpolating—or splitting the differences—between known present value factors and the known rates of return associated with these factors. For example, a present value factor about halfway between the present value factors for an 8 percent IRR and a 10 percent rate would be the present value factor for a 9 percent rate of return. A present value factor closer to, but still less than, the present value factor for a 10 percent rate of return would indicate a rate of return between 9 and 10 percent a year. In practice, precise solutions are usually obtained using a financial calculator or spreadsheet. However, risk management professionals should know how to interpolate so that they can spot-check the reasonableness of the result obtained by other means. The Calculating the IRR Through Interpolation text box shows how the rate of return, r, can be interpolated more precisely.

Had the cost of the asset in Exhibit 13-5 been $27,000 instead of $30,000, and the other three factors had remained unchanged, the net present value of the proposal would have been positive, as shown in Exhibit 13-6. The net present value method shows that the present value of the differential net cash flows ($29,844) exceeds the present value of the initial investment, $27,000, by $2,844.

Work Sheet for Evaluating Capital Investment Proposal Using the NPV Method

1. Identify the initial investment required for the proposal: _____

   (How much is the initial cash outlay?)

2. Identify the useful life of the proposal: _____

   (How long will the proposal generate differential cash flows?)

3. Identify the differential annual after-tax cash flow: _____

   (Consider all cash inflows and outflows generated by the proposal, including salvage value)

4. Identify the minimum acceptable rate of return: _____

5. Determine the appropriate present value factor to use based on the minimum acceptable rate of return and your answers to the following questions regarding the useful life of the capital investment proposal:

   a. Does the differential cash flow extend beyond this year?

      i. Yes – use the present value factors from Appendix A or B; proceed to Question 5b.

      ii. No – the cash flows are generated this year and are the present value; no need to use present value factors; proceed to Step 7 (see present value calculations for a present payment).

   b. Does the differential cash flow occur in more than one year?

      i. Yes – proceed to Question 5c.

      ii. No – use present value factor from Appendix A; proceed to Step 6b (see present value calculations for a single future payment).

   c. Is the differential cash flow consistent (the same every year)?

      i. Yes – use present value factor from Appendix B; proceed to Step 6a (see present value calculations for a stream of equal future payments).

      ii. No – use multiple present value factors from Appendix A; proceed to Step 6b (see present value calculations for a stream of unequal future payments).

6. Calculate the NPV of the future payments:

   a. Multiply the appropriate present value factor from Appendix B by the annual differential cash flow to calculate the present value of the future differential cash flows generated by the proposal. Proceed to Step 7.

   _____

   b. Multiply the appropriate present value factors from Appendix A by the annual differential cash flows to calculate the present value of the future differential cash flows generated by the proposal. Proceed to Step 7.

   _____

7. Calculate the NPV of the cash flows. Subtract the initial investment from the present value of future payments calculations done in Step 6.

   _____

8. If the answer generated by Step 7 is zero or positive, the proposal is acceptable by the NPV method; if it is negative, it is not acceptable.

EXHIBIT 13-5

Evaluating a Capital Investment Proposal Using the IRR Method

Factors:

Initial investment	$30,000
Useful life	3 years
Differential annual after-tax cash flow	$12,000 net inflow
Minimum acceptable rate of return	10% annually
Salvage value	$0

Timeline

	Year 1	Year 2	Year 3
$30,000 outflow	$12,000 inflow	$12,000 inflow	$12,000 inflow

Evaluation by IRR method:

Present value factor (PVF_b) = Initial investment ÷ Differential cash flow

= $30,000 ÷ $12,000

= 2.500.

Interpolation to find the IRR (r):

Rate of Return	PVF_b	PVF_b
8%	2.577	2.577
r		2.500
10%	2.487	

Differences:	2%	0.090	0.077

r = 8% + [(0.077 ÷ 0.090) × 2%]

= 8% + 1.711%

= 9.711%.

Calculating the Internal Rate of Return (IRR) Through Interpolation

Calculating the internal rate of return (IRR) through interpolation gives the risk management professional a more precise estimate of the internal rate of return generated by the cash flows of the capital investment proposal and requires just a few steps to calculate. This example is based on Exhibit 13-5. The first step is to divide the initial investment in the proposal by the annual differential after-tax cash flows ($30,000/$12,000 = 2.5). This yields the estimated present value factor reported in Column 4, Row 3. The risk management professional then needs to refer to the appropriate appendix of present value factors (in this case, Appendix B) and find the two present value factors (in this case, 2.577 and 2.487) that bracket the present value factor just calculated (2.5) on the row related to the useful life of the proposal (in this case, 3 years). The risk management professional then needs to record both the present value factors and discount rates associated with them, as shown in the table below.

	Rate of Return	PVF (appendix)	PVF (calculations)
PVF 1 (appendix)	8.00%	2.577	2.577
PVF (calculated)	*r*		2.5
PVF 2 (appendix)	10.00%	2.487	
Differences:	2.00%	0.090	0.077

Once the differences have been calculated, the interpolation formula is:

$$r = \text{Smaller discount rate} + \left[\left(\frac{PVF\,(\text{calculations differences})}{PVF\,(\text{appendix differences})} \right) \times \text{Discount rate differences} \right].$$

In this example,

$$r = 8\% + [(0.077 \div 0.090) \times 2\%]$$
$$= 8\% + 1.711\%$$
$$= 9.711\%.$$

To use the IRR method, divide $27,000 by $12,000. The result is an implied present value factor of 2.250. Appendix B shows that 2.250 lies between the present value factors for 15 percent and 16 percent on the three year row. Knowing that the rate of return is between 15 percent and 16 percent may be adequate for many purposes. For example, it shows that the rate of return exceeds the 10 percent minimum. The following work sheet sets out the steps involved in evaluating a capital investment proposal using the IRR method:

Work Sheet for Evaluating a Capital Investment Proposal Using the IRR Method

1. Identify the initial investment required for the proposal: _____
   _____
   (How much is the initial cash outlay?)
2. Identify the useful life of the proposal: _____
   (How long will the proposal generate differential cash flows?)
3. Identify the differential annual after-tax cash flow: _____
   (Consider all cash inflows and outflows generated by the proposal)
4. Identify the minimum acceptable rate of return: _____
5. Calculate the present value factor by dividing the initial investment by the differential annual after-tax cash flow: _____
6. Determine which appendix to use to look up PVFs to determine IRR.
   a. Does the differential cash flow extend beyond this year?
      i. Yes – use the present value factors from Appendix A or B; proceed to Question B.
      ii. No – the cash flows are generated this year and are the present value; the IRR is the annual differential cash flow divided by the initial investment minus 1 ((annual differential cash flow/initial investment) – 1).
   b. Does the differential cash flow occur in more than one year?
      i. Yes – proceed to Question C.
      ii. No – use Appendix A to look up present value factors in the row related to the useful life of the proposal; proceed to Step 7.
   c. Is the differential cash flow consistent (the same every year)?
      i. Yes – use Appendix B to look up present value factors in the row related to the useful life of the proposal; proceed to Step 7 (see Exhibit 13-6).
      ii. No – use multiple present value factors from Appendix A in the rows related to the time period for each cash flow; proceed to Step 6 (see Exhibit 13-7). This is the most difficult use of IRR, and often the risk management professional must guess at the first discount rate to use to begin the interpolation. It is often easier to use a financial calculator or computer spreadsheet program.
7. In the appropriate appendix, look up the PVFs on the useful life row that the PVF calculated in Step 5 falls in between. *PVF 1:* _____   *PVF 1 Discount Rate:* _____
   PVF 2: _____   *PVF 2 Discount Rate:* _____
8. Interpolate between the two discount rates obtained in Step 7 (see calculating rate of return through interpolation discussion).

	Rate of Return	PVF (appendix)	PVF (calculations)
PVF 1 (step 7):			
PVF (step 5):	*r*	XXXXXXXXX	
PVF 2: (step 7)			XXXXXXXXX
Differences:			

$$r = \underline{\hspace{1cm}} + [(\underline{\hspace{1cm}} \div \underline{\hspace{1cm}}) \times \underline{\hspace{1cm}}] = \underline{\hspace{1cm}}.$$

9. If the answer generated by Step 8 is equal to or greater than the minimum acceptable rate of return, the proposal is acceptable by the IRR method; if it is less, it is not acceptable.

EXHIBIT 13-6

Evaluating an Alternative Capital Investment Project

Factors:

Initial investment	$27,000
Useful life	3 years
Differential annual after-tax cash flow	$12,000 net inflow
Minimum acceptable rate of return	10% annually
Salvage value	$0

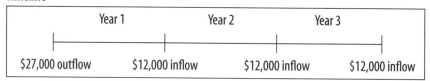

If the cost of the asset is $27,000 instead of $30,000, the present value of the differential net cash flows exceeds the present value of the initial investment: $29,844 exceeds $27,000 by $2,844.

Timeline

	Year 1	Year 2	Year 3
$27,000 outflow	$12,000 inflow	$12,000 inflow	$12,000 inflow

Evaluation by the NPV Method:

Present value of differential inflows ($12,000 × 2.487)	$29,844
Less: Present value of initial investment	($27,000)
Net present value	$2,844

Evaluation by the IRR Method:

$$\text{Present value factor } (PVF_b) = \text{Initial investment} \div \text{Differential cash flow}$$
$$= \$27,000 \div \$12,000$$
$$= 2.250.$$

To use the IRR method, divide $27,000 by $12,000. The result is a present value factor of 2.250. Appendix B shows that 2.250 lies between the present value factors for 15 percent and 16 percent. Knowing that the rate of return is between 15 percent and 16 percent may be adequate for many purposes, and certainly for showing that the rate exceeds 10 percent.

Interpolation to find the IRR (r):

Rate of Return	PVF_b	PVF_b
15%	2.283	2.283
r		2.250
16%	2.246	
Differences: 1%	0.037	0.033

$$r = 15\% + [(0.033 \div 0.037) \times 1\%]$$
$$= 15\% + 0.89\%$$
$$= 15.89\%.$$

In many cases, calculating the more precise rate of return by hand is unnecessary, because many calculators and spreadsheets can perform this calculation. However, risk management professionals should know the procedures, including the interpolation technique, so that they can spot-check the reasonableness of the result obtained by other means.

Exhibit 13-7 illustrates the application of capital budgeting criteria to a proposal with unequal estimated differential annual after-tax net cash flows. The initial investment is $10,000, the estimated useful life is six years, and the differential annual after-tax net cash flows are as shown in the exhibit. The minimum acceptable rate of return is 16 percent. Because the annual net cash flows are not equal, the present value of each year's differential net cash flows must be calculated separately, using the factors from Appendix A.

As shown in Exhibit 13-7, the present value of the proposed investment equals $9,881, which is less than the $10,000 present value of the initial investment. The net present value of the proposal is therefore negative $119. Calculating the IRR for this proposal requires calculating two present values—one each for two different rates of return (16 percent and 15 percent). The present value of the differential net cash flows at a 16 percent rate of return was calculated when evaluating the proposal by the NPV method. As also shown in Exhibit 13-7, at 15 percent, the present value of the net cash inflows is $10,220. By interpolation, the internal rate of return is 15.65 percent compounded annually, less than the specified minimum acceptable rate of 16 percent. The proposal should therefore be rejected.

As noted previously, when used consistently, the NPV method and the IRR method generally support the same decision for a given proposal. Specifically, if the discount rate used to calculate NPV and the minimum acceptable return used for the IRR method are equal, the methods normally support the same decision. If the NPV is positive at the minimum acceptable discount rate, the IRR exceeds the minimum acceptable rate and vice versa.

An exception can arise in some cases in which net cash flows alternate from positive to negative over time. In those cases, solving for the IRR may produce more than one answer. Apart from that exception, many managers prefer the IRR method as a communication device. For some audiences, saying that a proposal has a positive or negative NPV will have little meaning. It is more informative to say that the expected rate of return on the proposal is higher or lower than the minimum accepted rate of return.

The discussion to this point has shown how both the NPV method and the IRR method can be used to distinguish acceptable from unacceptable proposals. When there are several proposals with positive NPVs and IRRs above the minimum acceptable rate, but only some of those proposals can be undertaken, both methods can be used to rank the acceptable proposals.

CAPITAL INVESTMENT PROPOSAL RANKING

Choosing the proposals with the highest NPV or IRR maximizes the organization's value. If all of the proposals require the same initial investment, choosing those with the highest IRR will achieve the same result. However, if the proposals differ substantially in terms of the amount of initial investment, and limitations on capital prevent all acceptable proposals from being implemented,

EXHIBIT 13-7

Evaluation of a Capital Investment Proposal—Unequal Cash Flow

Factors:

Initial investment	$10,000
Useful life	6 years
Minimum acceptable rate of return	16% annually
Salvage value	$0

Timeline

Year 1	Year 2	Year 3	Year 4	Year 5	Year 6
$10,000 outflow	$1,000 inflow	$2,000 inflow	$3,000 inflow	$3,000 inflow	$4,000 inflow	$5,000 inflow

Evaluation by the NPV Method:

Year	Cash Inflows	Present Value Factor (16%)	Present Value
1	$1,000	0.862	$ 862
2	2,000	0.743	1,486
3	3,000	0.641	1,923
4	3,000	0.552	1,656
5	4,000	0.476	1,904
6	$5,000	0.410	2,050
Present value of net cash inflows			$9,881

Present value of differential inflows	$9,881
Less: Present value of initial investment	($10,000)
Net present value	($119)

> Because the annual net cash flows are not uniform, the present value of each year's differential net cash flows must be calculated separately, using the factors from Appendix A.

> The present value equals $9,881, which is less than the $10,000 present value of the initial investment. The net present value of the proposal is negative $119. Therefore, the proposal should be rejected.

Evaluation by the IRR Method:

Year	Cash Inflows	Present Value Factor (15%)	Present Value
1	$1,000	0.870	$ 870
2	2,000	0.756	1,512
3	3,000	0.658	1,974
4	3,000	0.572	1,716
5	4,000	0.497	1,988
6	$5,000	0.432	2,160
Present value of net cash inflows			$10,220

> Using the IRR method for evaluating the proposal requires calculating two present values—one each for two different rates of return (16 percent and 15 percent). The present value of the differential cash flows at a 16 percent rate of return was calculated when evaluating the proposal by the NPV method.

Interpolation to Find the Internal Rate of Return (r):

Rate of Return	Present Values	Present Values
15%	$10,220	$10,220
r		$10,000
16%	$9,881	
Differences: 1%	$339	$ 220

$$r = 15\% + [(\$220 \div \$339) \times 1\%]$$
$$= 15\% + 0.65\%$$
$$= 15.65\%.$$

> At 15 percent, the present value of the net cash inflows is $10,220. By interpolation, the IRR is 15.65 percent compounded annually, which is less than the specified minimum acceptable rate of 16 percent. Therefore, the proposal should be rejected.

NPV Method Versus IRR Method

In some situations, the NPV method and the IRR method may not agree on which proposals to undertake. Two conditions must be met for the two methods to disagree:

1. The amount of initial investment must be substantially different.

2. Limitations must exist on capital that prevents an organization from funding all acceptable proposals.

Consider the following example:

Barnley Manufacturing has exactly $100,000 that it can use to invest in one of two new proposals. Any part of the $100,000 not used in the new proposals will be invested at Barnley's opportunity cost of capital, 15 percent. The two proposals in which Barnley can invest are as follows:

	Proposal 1	**Proposal 2**
Initial cost:	$10,000	$100,000
Useful life:	1 year	1 year
Differential after-tax cash flow:	$15,000 net inflow at end of year 1	$130,000 net inflow at end of year 1
Salvage value	$0	$0

NPV Method:

Proposal 1:	Present value of differential inflows	$15,000 \times 0.870 =$	$13,050
	Less: Present value of initial investment		($10,000)
	Net Present Value		$3,050
Proposal 2:	Present value of differential inflows	$130,000 \times 0.870 =$	$113,100
	Less: Present value of initial investment		($100,000)
	Net Present Value		$13,100

IRR Method:

Proposal 1:	Present Value Factor PVF_a	=	Initial Investment ÷ Differential cash flow
		=	$10,000 ÷ $15,000
		=	0.667. Produces a 50% return.
Proposal 2:	Present Value Factor PVF_a	=	Initial Investment ÷ Differential cash flow
		=	$100,000 ÷ $130,000
		=	0.769. Produces a 30% return.

Based on both methods, both proposals are acceptable.

Proposal Ranking:

- Based on net present value, Proposal 2 is more valuable to the organization.
- Based on internal rate of return, Proposal 1 is better for the organization.

Considering the facts in this case, the two methods generate different rankings. If Proposal 1 is chosen, the remaining $90,000 generates a rate of return of 15 percent, or the total internal rate of return on the potential $100,000 invested under Proposal 1 would be [($10,000 x 0.5) + ($90,000 x 0.15)] ÷ $100,000 = 18.5 percent, compared with the 30 percent IRR on Proposal 2.

In other words, for the IRR method to generate different rankings than the NPV method, some foregone investment would have to generate a substantial return.

selecting proposals with the highest IRRs may not maximize NPV. An example of when rankings based on NPV and IRR do not agree is shown in the NPV Method Versus IRR Method text box.

When all proposals with positive NPV and IRR above the cost of capital cannot be undertaken, proposals can be ranked using both methods and the profitability index. The **profitability index** is the present value of future net cash flows divided by the present value of the initial investment. This can be expressed as follows:

Profitability index = *PV* (net cash flows) ÷ *PV* (initial investment).

Profitability index
The present value of future net cash flows divided by the present value of the initial investment.

If the proposal's NPV is positive, the profitability index is greater than one. If the NPV is negative, the profitability index is less than one. The profitability index of a proposal that just meets the minimum acceptable rate of return is 1.0—the present value of the expected net cash flows equals the present value of the required investment when both are discounted by the present value factor for the minimum acceptable rate of return. All acceptable proposals have a profitability index of at least 1.0. Therefore, any proposal with a profitability index of less than 1.0 is unacceptable. When ranking proposals with positive NPVs (profitability indices above one) that cannot all be undertaken, proposals with higher profitability indices are preferred. However, risk management professionals should compare the results using the profitability index ranking to those obtained by selecting proposals using total NPV and IRR.

CALCULATION OF DIFFERENTIAL ANNUAL AFTER-TAX NET CASH FLOWS

Both the NPV and IRR methods for evaluating cash flows use after-tax net cash flows when evaluating a capital investment proposal. However, the examples presented so far have not explained how these differential after-tax net cash flows are calculated.

In practice, capital budgeting often requires calculating net cash flows from revenue and expense data. When reviewing these revenue and expense data, cash flow analysis involves looking at the *net* cash inflows rather than the *gross* cash inflows. Therefore, buying a piece of equipment, for example, does not just involve looking at the increases this would provide to ongoing revenue and the initial outlay of cost. It involves both looking at the increases in maintenance expenses going forward and offsetting these increases in expenses with the resulting decreases in income taxes. It also involves looking at the benefit in terms of income tax reduction that is provided by depreciation.

In for-profit organizations, income taxes are cash outflows and must be deducted from cash revenues in calculating net cash flows. Taxes are treated like any other cash outlay and do not alter the basic procedure for calculating net cash flows. However, income taxes are calculated as a percentage of taxable income, not as a percentage of net cash flows. Taxable income recognizes some noncash revenues and expenses. In calculating the cash outflow for income taxes, these noncash revenues and expenses must be considered. For organizations not subject to income taxes, these noncash revenues and expenses can be ignored, simplifying cash flow calculations for not-for-profit entities.

In capital budgeting decisions, the main noncash item affecting income taxes is depreciation of long-term assets. **Depreciation** is a noncash expense used to allocate the cost of long-term assets over multiple accounting periods. Depreciation is not a cash outflow in the period in which the expense is recognized. That outflow usually occurs when the asset is purchased. Depreciation merely recognizes the outlay in a way that spreads the cost of the asset over the years that it is expected to produce revenue, matching expenses with revenues period by period.

Depreciation
A noncash expense used to allocate the cost of long-term assets over multiple accounting periods.

Many organizations also have other substantial noncash revenues and expenses that are recognized by their generally accepted accounting principles (GAAP) accounting systems but that have no cash flow effects until they generate actual receipts or disbursements. All such noncash revenues and expenses are ignored in cash flow calculations until they result in an actual receipt or expenditure.

The simplest depreciation method is the straight-line depreciation method, although other methods are recognized by the IRS. The **straight-line depreciation method** is an accounting method of calculating depreciation by taking an equal amount of an asset's cost as an expense for each year of the asset's expected useful life. The following illustrations calculate depreciation expense by the straight-line method. Salvage value, the resale value of used property, is assumed to be zero unless otherwise specified. For example, if the initial investment in an asset with a seven-year useful life is $35,000, the annual depreciation expense is $35,000 ÷ 7 years = $5,000. Although not a cash outflow, depreciation should be added to other expenses when calculating taxable income. For illustrative purposes, marginal income taxes (the amount of tax paid on the next dollar earned) are assumed to be 40 percent of taxable income, unless otherwise specified.

Straight-line depreciation method
An accounting method of calculating depreciation by taking an equal amount of an asset's cost as an expense for each year of the asset's expected useful life.

Exhibit 13-8 illustrates the procedure for calculating the differential annual after-tax net cash flow from a proposal in which depreciation represents a noncash but tax-deductible expense. The exhibit also evaluates the proposal by using both the NPV and the IRR methods. The proposal involves an organization's purchase of a risk management information system (RMIS) that costs $35,000 and that has an expected useful life of seven years. Maintaining this system will add $500 annually to the organization's operating expenses and $100 per year to its property insurance outlay, both of which are cash expenses. Notice that maintenance and insurance expenses are differential expenses—the organization's total cash outlays for all maintenance and all insurance are far more than $500 and $100 per year, respectively. Under this proposal, the differential cash revenues to the organization attributable to use of the risk management information system are $12,000 per year. (Again, this is a differential amount because the organization's total revenues from all operations exceed $12,000.)

EXHIBIT 13-8

Calculation of Differential Annual After-Tax Net Cash Flow

Calculations of Differential Annual NCF

Differential cash revenues		$12,000
Less: Differential cash expenses		
(except income taxes):		
Maintenance expense	$500	
Insurance expense	$100	($600)
Before-tax NCF:		$11,400
Less: Differential income taxes:		
Before-tax NCF	$11,400	
Less differential depreciation		
expense ($35,000 ÷ 7 years)	(5,000)	
Taxable income	$6,400	
Income taxes (40%)		($2,560)
After-Tax NCF:		$8,840

> Under this proposal, the differential cash revenues to the organization attributable to use of the machine are $12,000 per year.

> Use of this machine will add $500 annually to the organization's operating expenses and $100 per year to its property insurance outlay, both of which are cash expenses.

> This calculation involves an organization's proposed purchase of a machine that costs $35,000 and that has an expected useful life of seven years.

> Here, annual depreciation expense is $5,000 ($35,000 ÷ 7 years), making taxable income $6,400 and differential income tax $2,560. After the deduction of the cash outflow for taxes, this machine's annual after-tax net cash flow becomes $8,840.

Evaluations of Differential Annual NCF

Factors:

Initial investment	$35,000
Useful life	7 years
Differential annual after-tax NCF	$8,840
Minimum acceptable rate of return	14% annually

Evaluation by the NPV Method:

Present value of differential NCF ($8,840 × 4.288)	$ 37,905.92
Less: Present value of initial investment	($35,000.00)
Net present value	$ 2,905.92

Evaluation by the IRR Method:

Present value factor = Initial investment ÷ Differential NCF

$$= \$35,00 \div \$8,840$$

$$= 3.959.$$

Interpolation to find the internal rate of return (r):

Rate of Return	Present Value Factor	Present Value Factor
16%	4.039	4.039
r		3.959
18%	3.812	
Differences: 2%	0.227	0.080

$$
\begin{aligned}
r &= 16\% + [(0.080 \div 0.227) \times 2\%] \\
&= 16\% + 0.70\% \\
&= 16.70\%.
\end{aligned}
$$

The procedure for calculating differential annual after-tax net cash flows from this risk management information system starts by subtracting annual differential cash expenditures, other than income taxes, from differential cash revenues. The result is annual differential before-tax net cash flows ("before-tax NCF").

As stated previously, although income taxes are like every other cash outflow in that they must be deducted from cash inflows to determine the net cash flow for any period, income taxes must be calculated separately because they are a percentage of taxable income. Here, annual depreciation expense is $5,000, making taxable income $6,400, after subtracting the depreciation expense from the before-tax NCF ($11,400 − $5,000), and differential income taxes $2,560 ($6,400 × 0.40). After the deduction of the cash outflow for taxes, the system's annual after-tax net cash flow ("after-tax NCF") becomes $8,840 ($11,400 − $2,560).

For organizations not subject to income taxes, after-tax net cash flows are equal to before-tax net cash flows. Therefore, the noncash expense of depreciation (which must be accounted for in calculating income taxes) also has no effect on the net cash flows of not-for-profit organizations. For example, if the RMIS, whose net cash flows are calculated and evaluated in Exhibit 13-8, had been purchased by an organization whose income is not taxable, the annual net cash flows to this organization from this system would have been $11,400 (the result of the first subtraction at the top of Exhibit 13-8) rather than the $8,840 net cash flow to a taxable organization. Therefore, the nontaxable organization would have a higher internal rate of return on this system than would a taxable one.

This $8,840 after-tax NCF for a for-profit organization is equivalent to "differential annual after-tax net cash flow" in previous exhibits in this chapter. Exhibit 13-8 shows how this $8,840 after-tax NCF can be evaluated by either the NPV method or the IRR method. This evaluation reveals that this RMIS proposal surpasses the minimum acceptable rate of return of 14 percent compounded annually. Discounted at 14 percent, the NPV of the system is $2,905.92. The IRR is 16.70 percent per year, which exceeds the 14 percent required rate of return.

The present value of this $11,400 NCF to a nontaxable organization over seven years (assuming that this organization also required a 14 percent minimum annual rate of return) would be $48,883.20 ($11,400 × 4.288). Therefore, for an organization not subject to income taxes the NPV of this investment would be $13,883.20 ($48,883.20 − $35,000). Using the IRR method, the present value factor for this system to a nontaxable organization would be approximately 3.070 ($35,000 ÷ $11,400), in contrast with the 3.959 present value factor for a taxable organization. Therefore, for a nontaxable organization, the interpolated IRR for the risk management information system (calculated by the same procedure illustrated at the bottom of Exhibit 13-8) would be 26.18 percent.

Regardless of whether the organization must consider the effect of income taxes, the procedure for calculating net cash flow and determining the NPV or the IRR provides a basis for evaluating all risk management investments.

SUMMARY

Risk management professionals use cash flow analysis to select risk management techniques. This approach allows risk management professionals to financially justify the business decisions they make. By projecting net cash flows likely to be generated by alternative assets or activities, the risk management professional gives management a valid criterion for choosing those assets or activities that promise the most benefit to the organization. When selecting assets or activities to which to commit an organization's resources, management should give high priority to alternatives that promise net cash flows with the greatest present values.

Capital budgeting is the decision-making process involving the evaluation of multiple capital investment proposals in terms of the cash outflows that they require and the present values of the cash inflows that they are likely to generate. Capital budgeting techniques recognize that money has a time value. The additional amount of money that a given dollar can earn if invested over a given time period is the time value of that dollar over that period. Calculating the present value of a sum of money to be received in the future incorporates its time value.

The two factors that determine the present value of a particular sum (future value) are the appropriate discount rate and the length of time before each cash flow occurs.

There are two common methods for making capital budgeting decisions. The net present value (NPV) method involves determining whether a particular proposal is expected to produce net cash flows with a present value that exceeds the amount of funds invested using a discount rate that reflects the organization's opportunity cost of funds (its cost of capital). The internal rate of return (IRR) method involves selecting proposals with expected rates of return that exceed the minimally acceptable rate of return, most commonly the organization's cost of capital. When used consistently, both methods support the same decision for a given proposal. When all proposals with positive NPV and IRR above the cost of capital cannot be undertaken, proposals can be ranked using both methods and the profitability index (the present value of future net cash flows divided by the present value of the amount of the initial investment).

After-tax net cash flows, positive or negative, determine the NPV and IRR on a proposal that involves investing a specified amount of cash. The net cash flow from a proposal in any specified time period equals the cash inflows it produces minus the cash outflows it requires. If inflows exceed outflows in any specified time period, the net cash flow from that proposal is positive. If outflows exceed inflows, net cash flow is negative. Subject to the possible effects of income taxes, the net cash flow from a proposal in a given time period equals the cash revenues that it generates, minus the cash outlays it requires during that period. For for-profit organizations, income taxes, like other cash outlays, must be deducted from cash revenues, after accounting for depreciation, in calculating net cash flows. Taxes are treated like any other cash outlay and do not alter the basic procedure for calculating net cash flows.

Appendixes
Present Value Tables

These appendixes contain the following present value tables:

- Present value of $1 received at the end of a period
- Present value of $1 at the end of each period for n periods

APPENDIX A

Present Value of $1 Received at the End of a Period

Number of
Time Periods (n)   Discount Rate (r)

	1%	2%	4%	6%	8%	10%	12%	14%	15%	16%
1	0.990	0.980	0.962	0.943	0.926	0.909	0.893	0.877	0.870	0.862
2	0.980	0.961	0.925	0.890	0.857	0.826	0.797	0.769	0.756	0.743
3	0.971	0.942	0.889	0.840	0.794	0.751	0.712	0.675	0.658	0.641
4	0.961	0.924	0.855	0.792	0.735	0.683	0.636	0.592	0.572	0.552
5	0.951	0.906	0.822	0.747	0.681	0.621	0.567	0.519	0.497	0.476
6	0.942	0.888	0.790	0.705	0.630	0.564	0.507	0.456	0.432	0.410
7	0.933	0.871	0.760	0.665	0.583	0.513	0.452	0.400	0.376	0.354
8	0.923	0.853	0.731	0.627	0.540	0.467	0.404	0.351	0.327	0.305
9	0.914	0.837	0.703	0.592	0.500	0.424	0.361	0.308	0.284	0.263
10	0.905	0.820	0.676	0.558	0.463	0.386	0.322	0.270	0.247	0.227
11	0.896	0.804	0.650	0.527	0.429	0.350	0.287	0.237	0.215	0.195
12	0.887	0.788	0.625	0.497	0.397	0.319	0.257	0.208	0.187	0.168
13	0.879	0.773	0.601	0.469	0.368	0.290	0.229	0.182	0.163	0.145
14	0.870	0.758	0.577	0.442	0.340	0.263	0.205	0.160	0.141	0.125
15	0.861	0.743	0.555	0.417	0.315	0.239	0.183	0.140	0.123	0.108
16	0.853	0.728	0.534	0.394	0.292	0.218	0.163	0.123	0.107	0.093
17	0.844	0.714	0.513	0.371	0.270	0.198	0.146	0.108	0.093	0.080
18	0.836	0.700	0.494	0.350	0.250	0.180	0.130	0.095	0.081	0.069
19	0.828	0.686	0.475	0.331	0.232	0.164	0.116	0.083	0.070	0.060
20	0.820	0.673	0.456	0.312	0.215	0.149	0.104	0.073	0.061	0.051
21	0.811	0.660	0.439	0.294	0.199	0.135	0.093	0.064	0.053	0.044
22	0.803	0.647	0.422	0.278	0.184	0.123	0.083	0.056	0.046	0.038
23	0.795	0.634	0.406	0.262	0.170	0.112	0.074	0.049	0.040	0.033
24	0.788	0.622	0.390	0.247	0.158	0.102	0.066	0.043	0.035	0.028
25	0.780	0.610	0.375	0.233	0.146	0.092	0.059	0.038	0.030	0.024
26	0.772	0.598	0.361	0.220	0.135	0.084	0.053	0.033	0.026	0.021
27	0.764	0.586	0.347	0.207	0.125	0.076	0.047	0.029	0.023	0.018
28	0.757	0.574	0.333	0.196	0.116	0.069	0.042	0.026	0.020	0.016
29	0.749	0.563	0.321	0.185	0.107	0.063	0.037	0.022	0.017	0.014
30	0.742	0.552	0.308	0.174	0.099	0.057	0.033	0.020	0.015	0.012
40	0.672	0.453	0.208	0.097	0.046	0.022	0.011	0.005	0.004	0.003
50	0.608	0.372	0.141	0.054	0.021	0.009	0.003	0.001	0.001	0.001

Discount Rate (r)

18%	20%	22%	24%	25%	26%	28%	30%	35%	40%	45%	50%
0.847	0.833	0.820	0.806	0.800	0.794	0.781	0.769	0.741	0.714	0.690	0.667
0.718	0.694	0.672	0.650	0.640	0.630	0.610	0.592	0.549	0.510	0.476	0.444
0.609	0.579	0.551	0.524	0.512	0.500	0.477	0.455	0.406	0.364	0.328	0.296
0.516	0.482	0.451	0.423	0.410	0.397	0.373	0.350	0.301	0.260	0.226	0.198
0.437	0.402	0.370	0.341	0.328	0.315	0.291	0.269	0.223	0.186	0.156	0.132
0.370	0.335	0.303	0.275	0.262	0.250	0.227	0.207	0.165	0.133	0.108	0.088
0.314	0.279	0.249	0.222	0.210	0.198	0.178	0.159	0.122	0.095	0.074	0.059
0.266	0.233	0.204	0.179	0.168	0.157	0.139	0.123	0.091	0.068	0.051	0.039
0.225	0.194	0.167	0.144	0.134	0.125	0.108	0.094	0.067	0.048	0.035	0.026
0.191	0.162	0.137	0.116	0.107	0.099	0.085	0.073	0.050	0.035	0.024	0.017
0.162	0.135	0.112	0.094	0.086	0.079	0.066	0.056	0.037	0.025	0.017	0.012
0.137	0.112	0.092	0.076	0.069	0.062	0.052	0.043	0.027	0.018	0.012	0.008
0.116	0.093	0.075	0.061	0.055	0.050	0.040	0.033	0.020	0.013	0.008	0.005
0.099	0.078	0.062	0.049	0.044	0.039	0.032	0.025	0.015	0.009	0.006	0.003
0.084	0.065	0.051	0.040	0.035	0.031	0.025	0.020	0.011	0.006	0.004	0.002
0.071	0.054	0.042	0.032	0.028	0.025	0.019	0.015	0.008	0.005	0.003	0.002
0.060	0.045	0.034	0.026	0.023	0.020	0.015	0.012	0.006	0.003	0.002	0.001
0.051	0.038	0.028	0.021	0.018	0.016	0.012	0.009	0.005	0.002	0.001	0.001
0.043	0.031	0.023	0.017	0.014	0.012	0.009	0.007	0.003	0.002	0.001	
0.037	0.026	0.019	0.014	0.012	0.010	0.007	0.005	0.002	0.001	0.001	
0.031	0.022	0.015	0.011	0.009	0.008	0.006	0.004	0.002	0.001		
0.026	0.018	0.013	0.009	0.007	0.006	0.004	0.003	0.001	0.001		
0.022	0.015	0.010	0.007	0.006	0.005	0.003	0.002	0.001			
0.019	0.013	0.008	0.006	0.005	0.004	0.003	0.002	0.001			
0.016	0.010	0.007	0.005	0.004	0.003	0.002	0.001	0.001			
0.014	0.009	0.006	0.004	0.003	0.002	0.002	0.001				
0.011	0.007	0.005	0.003	0.002	0.002	0.001	0.001				
0.010	0.006	0.004	0.002	0.002	0.002	0.001	0.001				
0.008	0.005	0.003	0.002	0.002	0.001	0.001	0.001				
0.007	0.004	0.003	0.002	0.001	0.001	0.001					
0.001	0.001										

APPENDIX B

Present Value of $1 Received at the End of Each Period for *n* Periods

Number of
Time Periods (*n*)   Discount Rate (*r*)

	1%	2%	4%	6%	8%	10%	12%	14%	15%	16%
1	0.990	0.980	0.962	0.943	0.926	0.909	0.893	0.877	0.870	0.862
2	1.970	1.942	1.886	1.833	1.783	1.736	1.690	1.647	1.626	1.605
3	2.941	2.884	2.775	2.673	2.577	2.487	2.402	2.322	2.283	2.246
4	3.902	3.808	3.630	3.465	3.312	3.170	3.037	2.914	2.855	2.798
5	4.853	4.713	4.452	4.212	3.993	3.791	3.605	3.433	3.352	3.274
6	5.795	5.601	5.242	4.917	4.623	4.355	4.111	3.889	3.784	3.685
7	6.728	6.472	6.002	5.582	5.206	4.868	4.564	4.288	4.160	4.039
8	7.652	7.325	6.733	6.210	5.747	5.335	4.968	4.639	4.487	4.344
9	8.566	8.162	7.435	6.802	6.247	5.759	5.328	4.946	4.772	4.607
10	9.471	8.983	8.111	7.360	6.710	6.145	5.650	5.216	5.019	4.833
11	10.368	9.787	8.760	7.887	7.139	6.495	5.988	5.453	5.234	5.029
12	11.255	10.575	9.385	8.384	7.536	6.814	6.194	5.660	5.421	5.197
13	12.134	11.343	9.986	8.853	7.904	7.103	6.424	5.842	5.583	5.342
14	13.004	12.106	10.563	9.295	8.244	7.367	6.628	6.002	5.724	5.468
15	13.865	12.849	11.118	9.712	8.559	7.606	6.811	6.142	5.847	5.575
16	14.718	13.578	11.652	10.106	8.851	7.824	6.974	6.265	5.954	5.669
17	15.562	14.292	12.166	10.477	9.122	8.022	7.120	6.373	6.047	5.749
18	16.398	14.992	12.659	10.828	9.372	8.201	7.250	6.467	6.128	5.818
19	17.226	15.678	13.134	11.158	9.604	8.365	7.366	6.550	6.198	5.877
20	18.046	16.351	13.590	11.470	9.818	8.514	7.469	6.623	6.259	5.929
21	18.857	17.011	14.029	11.764	10.017	8.649	7.562	6.687	6.312	5.973
22	19.660	17.658	14.451	12.042	10.201	8.772	7.645	6.743	6.359	6.011
23	20.456	18.292	14.857	12.303	10.371	8.883	7.718	6.792	6.390	6.044
24	21.243	18.914	15.247	12.550	10.529	8.985	7.784	6.835	6.434	6.073
25	22.023	19.523	15.622	12.783	10.675	9.077	7.843	6.873	6.464	6.097
26	22.795	20.121	15.983	13.003	10.810	9.161	7.896	6.906	6.491	6.118
27	23.560	20.707	16.330	13.211	10.935	9.237	7.943	6.935	6.514	6.136
28	24.316	21.281	16.663	13.406	11.051	9.307	7.984	6.961	6.534	6.152
29	25.066	21.844	16.984	13.591	11.158	9.370	8.022	6.983	6.551	6.166
30	25.808	22.396	17.292	13.765	11.258	9.427	8.055	7.003	6.566	6.177
40	32.835	27.355	19.793	15.046	11.925	9.779	8.244	7.105	6.642	6.234
50	39.196	31.424	21.482	15.762	12.234	9.915	8.304	7.133	6.661	6.246

Discount Rate (r)

18%	20%	22%	24%	25%	26%	28%	30%	35%	40%	45%	50%
0.847	0.833	0.820	0.806	0.800	0.794	0.781	0.769	0.741	0.714	0.690	0.667
1.566	1.528	1.492	1.457	1.440	1.424	1.392	1.361	1.289	1.224	1.165	1.111
2.174	2.106	2.042	1.981	1.952	1.923	1.868	1.816	1.696	1.589	1.493	1.407
2.690	2.589	2.494	2.404	2.362	2.320	2.241	2.166	1.997	1.849	1.720	1.605
3.127	2.991	2.864	2.745	2.689	2.635	2.532	2.436	2.220	2.035	1.876	1.737
3.498	3.326	3.167	3.020	2.951	2.885	2.759	2.643	2.385	2.168	1.983	1.824
3.812	3.605	3.416	3.242	3.161	3.083	2.937	2.802	2.508	2.263	2.057	1.883
4.078	3.837	3.619	3.421	3.329	3.241	3.076	2.925	2.598	2.331	2.108	1.922
4.303	4.031	3.786	3.566	3.463	3.366	3.184	3.019	2.665	2.379	2.144	1.948
4.494	4.192	3.923	3.682	3.571	3.465	3.269	3.092	2.715	2.414	2.168	1.965
4.656	4.327	4.035	3.776	3.656	3.544	3.335	3.147	2.752	2.438	2.185	1.977
4.793	4.439	4.127	3.851	3.725	3.606	3.387	3.190	2.779	2.456	2.196	1.985
4.910	4.533	4.203	3.912	3.780	3.656	3.427	3.223	2.799	2.468	2.204	1.990
5.008	4.611	4.265	3.962	3.824	3.695	3.459	3.249	2.814	2.477	2.210	1.993
5.092	4.675	4.315	4.001	3.859	3.726	3.483	3.268	2.825	2.484	2.214	1.995
5.162	4.730	4.357	4.003	3.887	3.751	3.503	3.283	2.834	2.489	2.216	1.997
5.222	4.775	4.391	4.059	3.910	3.771	3.518	3.295	2.840	2.492	2.218	1.998
5.273	4.812	4.419	4.080	3.928	3.786	3.529	3.304	2.844	2.494	2.219	1.999
5.316	4.844	4.442	4.097	3.942	3.799	3.539	3.311	2.848	2.496	2.220	1.999
5.353	4.870	4.460	4.110	3.954	3.808	3.546	3.316	2.850	2.497	2.221	1.999
5.384	4.891	4.476	4.121	3.963	3.816	3.551	3.320	2.852	2.498	2.221	2.000
5.410	4.909	4.488	4.130	3.970	3.822	3.556	3.323	2.853	2.498	2.222	2.000
5.432	4.925	4.499	4.137	3.976	3.827	3.559	3.325	2.854	2.499	2.222	2.000
5.451	4.937	4.507	4.143	3.981	3.831	3.562	3.327	2.855	2.499	2.222	2.000
5.467	4.948	4.514	4.147	3.985	3.834	3.564	3.329	2.856	2.499	2.222	2.000
5.480	4.956	4.520	4.151	3.988	3.837	3.566	3.330	2.856	2.500	2.222	2.000
5.492	4.964	4.524	4.154	3.990	3.839	3.567	3.331	2.856	2.500	2.222	2.000
5.502	4.970	4.528	4.157	3.992	3.840	3.568	3.331	2.857	2.500	2.222	2.000
5.510	4.975	4.531	4.159	3.994	3.841	3.569	3.332	2.857	2.500	2.222	2.000
5.517	4.979	4.534	4.160	3.995	3.842	3.569	3.332	2.857	2.500	2.222	2.000
5.548	4.997	4.544	4.166	3.999	3.846	3.571	3.333	2.857	2.500	2.222	2.000
5.554	4.999	4.545	4.167	4.000	3.846	3.571	3.333	2.857	2.500	2.222	2.000

Chapter 14

Direct Your Learning

Applying Cash Flow Analysis

After learning the content of this chapter and completing the corresponding course guide assignment, you should be able to:

- Explain how the recognition of expected losses alters the cash flows of a capital investment proposal.

- Describe the effect that various risk control techniques have on net cash flows.

- Calculate the net present value and the internal rate of return on a capital investment proposal that uses various risk control techniques.

- Describe the effect that various risk financing techniques have on net cash flows.

- Calculate the net present value and the internal rate of return on a capital investment proposal that uses various risk financing techniques.

- Describe the effect that a combination of risk management techniques has on net cash flows.

- Calculate the net present value and the internal rate of return on a capital investment proposal that uses a combination of risk management techniques.

- Explain how to consider uncertainty in cash flow analysis.

- Select the risk management technique that offers the highest net present value and internal rate of return for a given capital investment proposal.

- Define or describe each of the Key Words and Phrases for this chapter.

Develop Your Perspective

What are the main topics covered in the chapter?

Many organizations choose risk management techniques by financial criteria. This chapter describes cash flow analysis as an approach to comparing various risk management techniques.

Identify the cash flows associated with a particular activity of your organization.

- What cash *outflows* are associated with a particular risk management technique?
- What cash *inflows* are associated with a particular risk management technique?

Why is it important to learn about these topics?

Cash flow analysis can uncover the cost-effectiveness of different risk control and risk financing techniques applied to specific loss exposures. Understanding cash flow analysis helps the risk management professional make decisions about what technique is most appropriate to manage the accidental losses associated with those cash flows.

Calculate the NPV and IRR of the inflows and outflows above.

- What are the current costs of the activity?
- What are the future benefits of the activity?

How can you use what you will learn?

Recommend risk management techniques to apply to accidental losses associated with specific cash flows.

- What technique would you choose for the construction of a new assembly plant? Why?
- What technique would you choose for the acquisition of a new warehouse? Why?

Chapter 14
Applying Cash Flow Analysis

Selecting the best risk management technique or, as is more often the case, the best combination of risk control and risk financing techniques, involves two steps. The first step is forecasting the effects that the available risk management techniques are likely to have on the organization's ability to fulfill its goals. The second step is defining and applying criteria that measure how well and how cost effectively each alternative risk management technique contributes to each organizational goal.

Most private profit-seeking organizations select risk management techniques by financial criteria; that is, they choose techniques with the greatest positive (or least negative) effect on rate of return. Risk management techniques are chosen based on effectiveness and economy. A technique is effective if it enables an organization to achieve desired goals, such as the pre-loss goals of economy of operations, tolerable uncertainty, legality, and social responsibility or the post-loss goals of survival, continuity of operations, profitability, earnings stability, growth, and social responsibility. A technique is economic if it is the least expensive of the possible effective options.

Given a loss exposure and the feasible alternative risk management techniques, cash flow analysis helps an organization determine which techniques should be used to protect the organization from the loss exposure. For example, cash flow analysis indicates whether the loss exposure should be avoided or insured, whether both insurance and loss prevention risk management techniques should be used, or whether the organization should form and use a captive insurer to finance the loss exposure.

This chapter uses simplified cash flow analysis examples to show how cash flow analysis uncovers the cost-effectiveness of different risk control and risk financing techniques that could be applied to specific loss exposures. Although the examples are specific and simplified, they effectively illustrate a decision-making process that has broad applicability.

The major advantage of using cash flow analysis for selecting risk management techniques is that it places risk management decisions on the same footing as other value-maximizing decisions and thereby helps the organization maximize its value. Theoretically, net present value (NPV) and internal rate of return (IRR) methods are appropriate for any organization that seeks this goal. They also are useful for not-for-profit organizations striving to increase their efficiency.

Limitations of cash flow analysis include the weaknesses of the assumptions that often must be made to conduct the analysis and the difficulty of accurately estimating future cash flows. Moreover, cash flow analysis is sometimes criticized for assuming that the organization's only goal is to maximize its economic value. Cash flow analysis does not take into account any of the other organizational goals or selection criteria (other than financial criteria) discussed previously. For example, legality and social responsibility goals are not directly considered in cash flow analysis.

Most of the examples in this chapter focus on the cash flow effects of a single risk management technique. Studying one risk management technique at a time enables the risk management professional to understand the effects that technique has on cash flow while holding all the other variables that may affect cash flows constant. The cash flow analysis tool can also be used to analyze the net cash flow effects of combining several risk financing and risk control techniques, as is described toward the end of the chapter. Unless otherwise noted, the risk control examples assume that any such losses are fully retained and paid as current expenses.

Net Cash Flow Effects of Risk Management Techniques

The examples and discussion that follow demonstrate how the following risk management techniques can be analyzed using cash flow analysis:

1. Recognizing expected losses when evaluating an investment or activity

2. Loss exposure avoidance

3. Prevention or reduction of losses

4. Separation of loss exposures

5. Loss transfer through a captive insurer

6. Loss transfer through an unrelated insurer

7. Loss transfer through a hold-harmless agreement

8. Loss transfer through hedging (business risks)

9. Loss retention with current funding (current expenses)

10. Loss retention with current funding (an unfunded reserve)

11. Loss retention with pre-funding (a funded reserve)

12. Loss retention with post-funding (borrowed funds)

13. Combining risk management techniques

RECOGNIZING CASH FLOWS RELATED TO RISK MANAGEMENT TECHNIQUES

To isolate the effects of each risk management technique on cash flows, this chapter focuses on only two loss exposures: the property loss exposure related to fire damage at a hospital and the business risk to a cookie company from possible changes in the price of flour. Most of the techniques are illustrated for the fire property loss exposure; the bakery example is used to illustrate the cash flow effects of hedging a business risk. However, the cash flow analysis presented can be extended to most loss exposures.

The first example is the possibility of a property loss resulting from a fire at Atwell Hospital (Atwell), which is considering using one of its buildings, previously leased out as office space, to house the Ames Research Center (ARC). ARC would be run by Dr. Ames, an established medical practitioner who is also well known for his medical research. According to the terms of the proposed ten-year contract (ARC proposal), Dr. Ames will conduct his research under Atwell's auspices with the commitment that all revenues generated from the research will go to the hospital. The hospital projects that its association with Dr. Ames will yield an additional $60,000 in annual revenues compared with its prior net revenues from leasing the building. In addition to using the building, Atwell will provide Dr. Ames with a $200,000 grant to help establish the research facility and obtain necessary equipment.

According to the ARC proposal, the hospital's only significant loss exposure attributable to ARC is the risk of physical damage to the building from fire. Because Dr. Ames's research involves a variety of flammable chemicals, the probability of fire damage is expected to increase significantly during his occupancy. Under the terms of the ARC proposal, the hospital is not responsible for any damage to the building's contents, furnishings, and fixtures, which will all be owned by Dr. Ames. The doctor has agreed to hold the hospital harmless for any liability claims that might arise from his use of the building. In addition, the doctor is required to purchase and maintain adequate insurance from an insurer that is highly rated by A.M. Best Company or another financial rating organization to back the hold-harmless agreement.

To adequately consider the financial effects of an investment or activity such as the ARC proposal on an organization, cash flow analysis should incorporate the estimated differential after-tax net cash flows (NCFs) related to all the proposal's costs and benefits, including any risk management techniques that could be implemented. Cash flow analyses should explicitly recognize that the one-time costs of implementing risk management techniques should often be added to a proposal's initial investment, while continuing risk management costs should be deducted from the projected annual NCFs.

Cash Flows When Expected Losses Are Ignored

To highlight the importance of considering risk management in proposal analysis, first consider how the proposal would be evaluated if the cash flow implications of any changes in expected losses were ignored. Exhibit 14-1 shows the expected differential annual after-tax cash flows from the ARC proposal under the assumption that no differential changes exist caused by expected losses. The cash flows using the NPV and IRR methods are evaluated. The $60,000 differential cash inflow (revenue) in this and related

EXHIBIT 14-1

Differential Annual After-Tax Cash Flows—When Expected Losses Are Ignored

NCF Calculations

Differential cash revenues		$60,000
Less: Differential cash expenses (except income taxes)		(0)
Before-tax NCF		$60,000
Less: Differential income taxes		
Before tax NCF	$60,000	
Less: Differential depreciation expense ($200,000 ÷ 10 years)	($20,000)	
Taxable income	$40,000	
Income taxes (40% × $40,000)		($16,000)
After-tax NCF		$44,000

> The $60,000 "differential cash revenues" represents the revenue the hospital expects to collect because of its association with Dr. Ames.

> Depreciation of the $200,000 grant is taken on a straight-line basis.

NCF Evaluation

Factors:

Initial investment	$ 200,000
Life of project	10 years
Differential annual after-tax NCF	$ 44,000
Minimum acceptable rate of return (annual)	10.00%

Evaluation by NPV Method:

Present value of differential NCF ($44,000 × 6.145)	$ 270,380
Less: Present value of initial investment	($200,000)
NPV	$ 70,380

Evaluation by IRR Method:

Present value factor = Initial investment ÷ Differential NCF

$$= \$200,000 \div \$44,000$$
$$= 4.545.$$

Interpolation to find the IRR (r):

Rate of Return	Present Value Factor	Present Value Factor
16.00%	4.833	4.833
r		4.545
18.00%	4.494	
Differences: 2.00%	0.339	0.288

$$r = 16\% + [(0.288 \div 0.339) \times 2\%]$$
$$= 16\% + 1.70\%$$
$$= 17.70\%.$$

> Notice in this and the following exhibits that the hospital must pay taxes (based on a 40 percent marginal tax rate). If the hospital were a public tax-exempt entity, calculations for differential income taxes would be unnecessary. The NCF would be $60,000 and would be substituted throughout the cash flow analysis.

exhibits is the added revenue that the hospital expects because of the ARC proposal. Depreciation of the $200,000 grant is calculated for income tax purposes on a straight-line basis over ten years, the marginal tax rate is 40 percent, and Atwell's minimum acceptable required rate of return is 10 percent per year. Ignoring the possibility that the ARC building could be damaged by fire and other risk management considerations, the net present value of the investment at 10 percent interest is $70,380, and the internal rate of return is 17.7 percent. As Atwell's minimum acceptable required rate of return is 10 percent, this cash flow analysis indicates that the investment is profitable and Atwell should consider accepting the proposal.

Cash Flows Recognizing Expected Losses

Having considered how a proposal is evaluated when expected accidental losses are ignored, compare this with an evaluation in which expected accidental losses are recognized. The recognition of these losses and the choice of risk management techniques affect the NCF. Changes to the NCF can alter the NPV and IRR of an investment proposal and, ultimately, the decision as to which proposal an organization will devote its resources.

Exhibit 14-2 shows the probability distribution of differential annual fire losses to the building resulting from Dr. Ames's occupancy drawn up by Atwell's risk management professional from a variety of data.

EXHIBIT 14-2

Differential Annual Fire Loss Probability Distribution

Probability	Annual Fire Damage	Expected Value
.80	$ 0	$ 0
.10	$ 30,000	$ 3,000
.07	$100,000	$ 7,000
.03	$200,000	$ 6,000
1.00		$16,000 = Annual expected value

The expected value of the differential fire loss is $16,000 per year. This average annual expected accidental loss reduces the proposal's annual expected cash flows. The revised NPV and IRR for the ARC proposal are shown in Exhibit 14-3. If Atwell considers the cost of retaining the expected differential annual fire losses to the ARC building when evaluating the proposal, the resulting net present value is $11,388 and the internal rate of return is 11.34 percent. Therefore, the proposal has a positive NPV and an IRR greater than the required 10 percent, even though the NPV and IRR are

EXHIBIT 14-3

Differential Annual After-Tax Cash Flows—Recognizing Expected Losses

NCF Calculations

Differential cash revenues		$60,000
Less: Differential cash expenses (except income taxes)		
Expected value of fire losses		($16,000)
Before-tax NCF		$44,000
Less: Differential income taxes		
Before-tax NCF	$44,000	
Less: Differential depreciation expense ($200,000 ÷ 10 years)	($20,000)	
Taxable income	$24,000	
Income taxes (40% × $24,000)		($9,600)
After-tax NCF		$34,400

The annual expected value for fire losses reduces the after-tax NCF and the rate of return.

NCF Evaluation

Factors:

Initial investment	$200,000
Life of project	10 years
Differential annual after-tax NCF	$34,400
Minimum acceptable rate of return (annual)	10.00%

Evaluation by NPV Method:

Present value of differential NCF ($34,400 × 6.145)	$ 211,388
Less: Present value of initial investment	($200,000)
NPV:	$ 11,388

The annual expected value for fire losses reduces the after-tax NCF and the rate of return.

Evaluation by IRR Method:

Present value factor = Initial investment ÷ Differential NCF

$$= (\$200,000 \div \$34,400)$$

$$= 5.814.$$

Interpolation to find the IRR (r):

	Rate of Return	Present Value Factor	Present Value Factor
	10.00%	6.145	6.145
	r		5.814
	12.00%	5.650	
Differences	2.00%	0.495	0.331

$$r = 10\% + [(0.311 \div 0.495) \times 2\%]$$

$$= 10\% + 1.34\%$$

$$= 11.34\%.$$

The annual expected value for fire losses reduces the after-tax NCF and the rate of return.

substantially lower than those in Exhibit 14-1. The calculations in Exhibit 14-3 recognize only the expected value of differential fire losses, not the effects that any other risk management technique (other than the assumed retention through current expensing) might have on expected losses and NCF. The remainder of the examples in this chapter using Atwell examine the effect of various risk management techniques on the same set of facts presented here.

The recognition of expected accidental losses in cash flow analysis may have a significant effect on the decision to undertake a proposal. The substantial difference between the rates of return in Exhibits 14-1 and 14-3 arises because of the recognition of the expected value of differential fire losses—$16,000 per year before taxes. The relatively large value of the differential expected losses compared with the $200,000 investment is used to highlight the importance of recognizing expected accidental losses and risk management considerations. However, the same principles in evaluating the ARC proposal would apply even if the amounts and effects were smaller.

The calculations in Exhibit 14-3 assume that fire damage to the ARC building is the only differential loss; that is, that physical damage from causes of loss other than fire will not occur. Perhaps more important, the calculations assume that the before-tax expected value of fire losses represents the only cost of retention. The calculations do not specifically consider the potential adverse effects and costs to Atwell of annual variability in the amount of fire damage. This uncertainty in cash flow analysis is discussed subsequently in this chapter.

This section highlighted the need to recognize expected accidental losses in cash flow analysis of proposals from a risk management perspective. Once the risk management professional recognizes the costs associated with the accidental losses, he or she will be able to analyze the effects of various risk control and risk financing techniques on those expected accidental losses.

RECOGNIZING CASH FLOWS RELATED TO RISK CONTROL TECHNIQUES

A variety of risk control techniques are available to Atwell. Therefore, Atwell needs to understand how cash flow analysis can be used to aid in the proper selection of the appropriate risk control techniques. The risk control techniques available to Atwell include avoidance, loss prevention to reduce loss frequency, loss reduction to reduce loss severity, and separation of loss exposures to better project losses.

Avoidance

When an organization chooses to avoid a loss exposure by refraining from some activity, it forgoes the benefits that the activity would otherwise generate. By choosing avoidance as a risk control technique, the organization implicitly or explicitly concludes that the activity's potential benefits are not worth the loss exposure. More precisely, the NPV or IRR from an activity, using the best risk management techniques (other than avoidance) to deal with the loss exposure, falls below the minimum amount necessary to justify investment in the activity.

For the risk of differential fire damage to the building occupied by ARC, the only way to avoid the increased loss exposure from fire is to deny the grant to Dr. Ames. That would decrease the hospital's value by depriving the hospital of the prestige of, and anticipated revenue from, being associated with Dr. Ames's research. However, if the ARC proposal's NPV is negative even if the best risk management techniques were used, avoiding the loss exposure would increase the hospital's value. The benefits of the ARC proposal would be less than its costs.

Prevention or Reduction of Losses

If a risk management professional can prevent or reduce accidental losses associated with a particular capital investment proposal, it may make the proposal more appealing to senior management. For example, management may reject the ARC proposal if it requires acceptance of a $16,000 increase in expected annual fire losses. In an attempt to make the proposal more appealing, the hospital's risk management professional has developed a probability distribution for differential annual fire losses if a $10,000 sprinkler system is installed when Dr. Ames moves in. The expenditure would be depreciated for tax purposes on a straight-line basis over the ten-year life of the contract. The sprinkler system would have a $400 annual cash maintenance expense and would have no salvage or residual value at the end of the ten years. The risk management professional has estimated that the system will reduce the expected value of the differential fire losses from Dr. Ames's occupancy as shown in the following probability distribution:

Differential Fire Loss Distribution With Sprinkler System

Probability	Annual Fire Damage	Expected Value
.80	$ 0	$ 0
.10	$ 5,000	$ 500
.07	$ 10,000	$ 700
.03	$100,000	$3,000
1.00		$4,200

With the installation of the sprinkler system, a loss reduction measure, the before-tax expected value of annual fire losses decreases to $4,200. The addition of a sprinkler system produces the following changes to the proposal's net cash flows compared with not installing such a system:

- The sprinkler system reduces the expected value of fire losses that Atwell will retain.
- The sprinkler system's initial cost is added to the cost of the proposal's initial investment.
- The depreciation and maintenance expenses for the sprinkler system are considered in calculating after-tax net cash flows each year.

The differential annual after-tax NCF from the ARC proposal with a sprinkler system installed in the building is calculated in the upper portion of Exhibit 14-4. The lower portion shows the evaluation of the ARC proposal's cash flow using the NPV method and the IRR method.

Exhibit 14-4 shows that installing a sprinkler system increases the hospital's initial investment to $210,000. The proposal's NPV is $45,878 and the IRR is 14.88 percent. As the NPV and IRR are higher with the loss reduction measure than without it, the sprinkler system installation makes the ARC proposal more attractive. Without the sprinkler system, the project is not as attractive (see Exhibit 14-3). However, loss prevention or reduction techniques do not necessarily increase an organization's value. Whether risk control increases the NPV and IRR in practice depends on the details of a particular proposal.

Separation of Loss Exposures

As discussed previously, separation and duplication are two closely related loss control techniques. Separation involves dividing one unit into two or more independent units, each normally used in daily operations, whereas duplication creates standby units that are used only when a regular unit has been lost. For example, spreading inventory equally between two warehouses is separation; having duplicate records or spare parts for key machines is duplication. In both cases, the number of loss exposures increases, which often increases the frequency of losses that may occur but reduces the severity of those losses because there is a lower value associated with each loss exposure. The net result generally makes losses more predictable. An example of separation is discussed subsequently in this chapter in tandem with funded loss reserves.

Using cash flow analysis enables a risk management professional to determine which risk control techniques are most economical. Once this has been accomplished, the risk management professional can then use cash flow analysis to determine the appropriate risk financing technique to apply to the organization's loss exposures.

RECOGNIZING CASH FLOWS RELATED TO RISK FINANCING TECHNIQUES

As for risk control techniques, cash flow analysis is also a valuable decision-making tool for many risk financing techniques. Unless otherwise specified, the analysis assumes that the full amount of potential losses is managed with

EXHIBIT 14-4

Differential Annual After-Tax Cash Flows—Loss Reduction or Prevention Device

NCF Calculations

Differential cash revenues		$60,000
Less: Differential cash expenses (except income taxes)		
Expected value of fire losses	$4,200	
Sprinkler maintenance	$ 400	($4,600)
Before-tax NCF		$55,400
Less: Differential income taxes		
Before-tax NCF	$55,400	
Less: Differential depreciation		
expense ($210,000 ÷ 10 years)	($21,000)	
Taxable income	$34,400	
Income taxes (40% × $34,400)		($13,760)
After-tax NCF		$41,640

> The before-tax expected value of annual fire losses decreases to $4,200 (the value of fire losses the hospital will retain).

> The maintenance expenses on the sprinkler system are considered when calculating taxable income.

NCF Evaluation

Factors:	
Initial investment	$210,000
Life of project	10 years
Differential annual after-tax NCF	$41,640
Minimum acceptable rate of return (annual)	10.00%

> The sprinkler's cost is added to the cost of this proposal's initial investment when calculating taxable income.

Evaluation by NPV Method:

Present value of differential NCF ($41,640 × 6.145)	$255,878
Less: Present value of initial investment	($210,000)
NPV	$45,878

> Installing a sprinkler system would raise the initial investment to $210,000 and the internal rate of return on the proposal to 14.88 percent annually, giving it a $45,878 net present value when discounted at 10 percent.

Evaluation by IRR Method:

Present value factor = Initial Investment ÷ Differential NCF

= $210,000 ÷ $41,640

= 5.043.

Interpolation to find the IRR (r):

	Rate of Return	Present Value Factor	Present Value Factor
	14.00%	5.216	5.216
	r		5.043
	15.00%	5.019	
Differences:	1.00%	0.197	0.173

r = 14% + [(0.173 ÷ 0.197) × 1%]

   = 14% + 0.88%

   = 14.88%.

one risk financing technique in each specific example, without considering any risk control techniques. In practice, risk control techniques are usually combined with risk financing techniques.

Loss Transfer Through a Captive Insurer

One risk financing technique is financing losses through a captive insurer. An organization may establish an insurance subsidiary (captive) through which it insures some or all of its loss exposures. The captive can be owned by a single parent organization or by a number of parent organization whose loss exposures the captive insures. The captive might also insure some outside business—loss exposures of organizations that are not the captive's owners.

Largely because of tax and regulatory issues, considerable controversy exists about whether using a captive insurer constitutes retention or insurance for the parent organization. To be considered insurance for tax purposes, risk must be transferred. In other words, the Internal Revenue Service (IRS) wants to ensure that a captive is a legitimate business expense, like insurance, and not just a subsidiary established in an attempt to avoid taxes. Determining whether the risk transfer requirement is satisfied is complex and beyond the scope of this chapter.

If using the captive is legally considered to be retention—that is, the IRS has determined that no risk transfer has taken place—then the premiums paid to the captive are not tax-deductible and the cash flows are similar to those for loss retention with a funded reserve (discussed in a subsequent section of this chapter). Without the IRS recognition of risk transfer, the differences between a captive and a funded reserve include (1) that the captive requires a higher initial investment to establish it and (2) that the captive has administrative expenses associated with running it.

If using the captive is legally considered to be insurance for tax purposes, then the premiums paid to the captive are tax deductible. Consequently, net cash flow analysis for this risk financing technique is the same as in the following discussion of financing losses through an unrelated or a commercial insurer.

Loss Transfer Through an Unrelated Insurer

Rather than using internal funds to finance losses, an organization can transfer the financial consequences of the loss exposure to an outside organization that will pay for losses with no obligation to repay. The most common form of this type of transfer is purchasing insurance from an unrelated insurer (a commercial insurer). The insurer agrees, in exchange for a premium, to pay to the insured or on the insured's behalf any losses that the insurance policy covers. The insurance premium replaces the expected value of losses that the insured would otherwise retain. In some respects (ignoring some of the tax complexities of insured and uninsured losses), calculating NPV and IRR when insurance is used to finance losses parallels those techniques shown in previous examples, just replacing the expected value of losses and other administrative expenses with the insurance premium and any deductibles.

Because of expense loading (the amount insurers charge to cover expenses), the insurance premium required by an insurer normally exceeds the expected value of insured losses. The amount of the expense loading included in the insurance premium—which is designed to provide for the insurer's sales expenses, overhead, and profit—has a major effect on cash flows compared with retention. Exhibit 14-5 provides an example. Atwell purchases $200,000 of fire insurance on the ARC building. Under the existing insurance market conditions, Atwell's fire insurer designed its premiums so that 60 percent of the gross premium was allocated to paying insured losses, which were expected to average $16,000, and 40 percent was devoted to the insurer's overhead. The total additional annual premium for fire insurance on the ARC building, with Dr. Ames's occupancy, P, can be calculated as follows:

$$60\% \text{ of } P = \$16,000$$
$$P = \$16,000 \div 0.60$$
$$P = \$26,667.$$

The differential insurance premium is a tax-deductible expense. Therefore, he differential annual after-tax NCF is calculated using the $26,667 additional annual insurance premium. At a 10 percent annual rate of return, fully insuring the ARC building at this premium gives the proposal an NPV of negative $27,940. The IRR is 6.67 percent per year. The IRR is much lower than with retaining all losses, either with a sprinkler system (14.88 percent, Exhibit 14-4) or without one (11.34 percent, Exhibit 14-3).

As long as the expected value of accidental losses is assumed to be the only cost of retention, and the benefits of risk reduction through insurance are assumed to be ignored, insurance usually produces a lower NPV or IRR than does retention. Again, the reason insurance produces a lower NPV or IRR is that the insurance premium typically is greater than the expected value of the insured losses. The amount of reduction in the NPV and IRR with insurance under those assumptions depends on the following:

- Size of the insurer's premium loading for its expenses and profit (40 percent in this case)
- Any additional costs of retention to an organization, such as the expenses of safety, loss settlement, and other services that the insurer otherwise would provide

Of course, many organizations purchase insurance despite the expense loading in premiums, because the benefits of the risk transfer outweigh the expense loading. The main reasons, and how those benefits might be quantified (the reduction in the cost of uncertainty regarding accidental losses), are described subsequently in this chapter.

EXHIBIT 14-5

Differential Annual After-Tax Cash Flows—Full Insurance

NCF Calculations		
Differential cash revenues		$60,000
Less: Differential cash expenses (except income taxes)		
Insurance Expense		($26,667)
Before-tax NCF		$33,333
Less: Differential income taxes		
Before-tax NCF	$33,333	
Less: Differential depreciation expense ($200,000 ÷ 10 years)	($20,000)	
Taxable income	$13,333	
Income-taxes (40% × $13,333)		($5,333)
After-tax NCF		$28,000

> Atwell purchases $200,000 of fire insurance on the ARC occupied building. The $26,667 premium is a tax-deductible expense.

NCF Evaluation	
Factors:	
Initial investment	$200,000
Life of project	10 years
Differential annual after-tax NCF	$28,000
Minimum acceptable rate of return (annual)	10.00%

Evaluation by NPV Method:

Present value of differential NCF ($28,000 × 6.145)	$172,060
Less: Present value of initial investment	($200,000)
NPV	($27,940)

Evaluation by IRR Method:

Present value factor = Initial investment ÷ differential NCF
= $200,000 ÷ $28,000
= 7.143.

Interpolation to find the IRR (r):

Rate of Return	Present Value Factor	Present Value Facto
6.00%	7.360	7.360
r		7.143
8.00%	6.710	
Differences: 2.00%	0.650	0.217

r = 6% + [(0.217 ÷ 0.650) × 2%]
= 6% + 0.67%
= 6.67%.

Loss Transfer Through a Hold-Harmless Agreement

Another possible risk financing technique is contractual transfer, most commonly through some form of hold-harmless agreement. Effectively using hold-harmless agreements requires that (1) the agreement clearly specify the indemnitee's (transferor's) losses for which the indemnitor (transferee) agrees to be financially responsible and that (2) the indemnitor have adequate financial resources to meet its obligations under the contractual transfer.

From the indemnitee's standpoint, hold-harmless agreements generally have the following characteristics:

- The losses paid by the indemnitor are no longer the indemnitee's expenses.
- The indemnitee may, depending on the transfer agreement's terms, pay some compensation to the indemnitor for entering into the agreement.
- The indemnitee may incur some administrative expenses in enforcing the transfer agreement, such as for collecting indemnity payments from the indemnitor.

Although hold-harmless agreements typically are used for shifting liability loss exposures, such agreements can also shift property loss exposures. An example of a contractual transfer through a hold-harmless agreement for property loss exposures is provided in Exhibit 14-6. To give Dr. Ames an added incentive for fire safety, suppose that Atwell required Dr. Ames to sign a contract to reimburse the hospital for the first $5,000 of each fire loss to the ARC building. From the probability distribution in Exhibit 14-2, Atwell expects one fire every five years from the hazards inherent in the research activity. Also, the hospital has projected a $1,000 annual reimbursement from Dr. Ames for fire losses and $160 in additional administrative costs. The expected $1,000 indemnity payments from Dr. Ames are treated as differential revenue, and the $160 administrative costs are treated as differential expenses. The proposal's NPV using contractual transfer for risk financing is $14,485, and the IRR is 11.68 percent, which makes this type of risk financing technique more appealing than insurance.

Loss Transfer Through Hedging (Business Risks)

Another risk financing technique is hedging business risks. Unforeseen changes in prices that an organization pays for supplies, raw materials, or product components—as well as changes in the prices it receives for the goods or services it sells—are major sources of business risk that can greatly affect the organization's operations and value. Price increases for its inputs and price decreases for its outputs reduce an organization's cash flows and net income. Conversely, decreases in input costs and increases in selling prices increase cash flows and net income. Many organizations' managers know that input and output prices will change during the next accounting period, but they cannot reliably project the direction or size of these price changes.

EXHIBIT 14-6

Differential Annual After-Tax Cash Flows—Hold-Harmless Agreement

NCF Calculations

Differential cash revenues	$60,000	
from Dr. Ames for fire losses	$1,000 ←	
Total cash revenues		$61,000
Less: Differential cash expenses (except income taxes)		
Expected value of fire losses	$16,000	
Administrative expenses	$160	
Total cash expenses (except income taxes)		($16,160)
Before-tax NCF		$44,840
Less: Differential income taxes		
Before-tax NCF	$44,840	
Less: Differential depreciation expense ($200,000 ÷ 10 years)	($20,000)	
Taxable income	$24,840	
Income taxes (40% × $24,840)		($9,936)
After-tax NCF		$34,904

> Dr. Ames has signed a contract to reimburse the hospital for the first $5,000 of each fire loss to the ARC occupied building. Expecting one fire every five years, the hospital has projected a $1,000 annual reimbursement from Dr. Ames and $160 in additional administrative costs. Dr. Ames' $1,000 indemnity payments are treated as a source of incremental revenues, and the $160 administrative costs are incremental expenses.

NCF Evaluation

Factors:
Initial investment	$200,000
Life of project	10 years
Differential annual after-tax NCF	$34,904
Minimum acceptable rate of return (annual)	10.00%

Evaluation by NPV Method:

Present value of differential NCF ($34,904 × 6.145)	$214,485
Less: Present value of initial investment	($200,000)
NPV	$14,485

Evaluation by IRR Method:

Present value factor = Initial Investment ÷ Differential NCF
$$= \$200,000 \div \$34,904$$
$$= 5.730.$$
Interpolation to find the IRR (r):

Rate of Return	Present Value Factor	Present Value Factor
10.00%	6.145	6.145
r		5.730
12.00%	5.650	
Differences: 2.00%	0.495	0.415

$$r = 10\% + [(0.415 \div 0.495) \times 2\%]$$
$$= 10\% + 1.68\%$$
$$= 11.68\%.$$

Organizations unwilling or unable to tolerate such fluctuations in their operating results often use hedging as a financing technique to stabilize their cash flows. However, when hedging with forward, futures, or option contracts, the organization's management must be willing to sacrifice some or all of the potential net revenue gains that could arise from favorable price changes in order to achieve protection against net income losses from adverse price changes. That sacrifice enables the organization to come closer to its projected operating results despite unpredictable price changes.

ARC's activities offer few opportunities for hedging. Millwright Cookie Company (Millwright) provides a better example to illustrate opportunities for managing business risks through hedging. Assume, for example, that Millwright's profitability depends heavily on prices it must pay for its ingredients, especially flour. Millwright needs an average of 10,000 units of wheat flour each month. The price of flour changes over time, roughly corresponding to changes in the price of the wheat from which the flour is made. If Millwright must pay $3.00 per unit of flour, then—as shown in Millwright's simplified typical anticipated monthly income statement presented in Exhibit 14-7—the company's anticipated net profit would be $11,000. This monthly net profit is without any hedging of flour price changes. Exhibit 14-8 provides a comparison of the effects of hedging if the price of flour increases or decreases. Exhibits 14-7 and 14-8 implicitly assume that Millwright cannot pass the changes in input prices on to the end consumer. That is, Millwright would not charge more (less) for the cookies because the price of flour has gone up (down). This is in contrast with airlines and trucking companies, for example, which often add fuel surcharges to their prices to pass the increased cost of fuel (input costs) on to the consumer.

EXHIBIT 14-7

Millwright Cookie Company
Typical Anticipated Monthly Income Statement, No Hedging

Revenues		
Sales	$100,000	
Other Income	$3,000	
Total Revenues		$103,000
Expenses		
Flour (10,000 units @$3.00 each)	$30,000	
Other Expenses	$62,000	
Total Expenses		($92,000)
Net Profit		$11,000

> If Millwright must pay $3.00 per unit of flour, the organization's anticipated profit would be $11,000.

Hedging (Business Risks)

Virtually all organizations are exposed to business losses (reductions in revenues or increases in expenses) because of changes in the economic environment. For example, increases in raw materials costs, foreign exchange rates, interest rates, wage rates, taxes, or other operating expenses can reduce an organization's net income, as can price decreases for output because of a competitor's use of improved technology, new market regulations, or declining customer demand. The resulting net income losses from those business risks created by price changes can be just as devastating to the organization as the net income losses from a major fire or flood that strikes the organization's facilities.

An important difference between many business losses and the financially identical accidental losses that an organization might suffer from a fire or flood is that opposite movements of the economic forces that caused the business losses could, conversely, increase the organization's net income. Decreased production costs, government regulation, and access to newer and more efficient technology can bring gains rather than losses to organizations whose management is willing to take the business risks that can possibly lead to those gains. Fires and floods, in contrast, offer no prospects for potential gain.

For business risks created by price changes, a risk financing technique known as hedging enables an organization (or individual) to transfer those risks to the other party in the hedging transaction. Hedging is a financial transaction in which one asset (typically a contract) is held to offset the risks associated with another asset. Hedging is well suited to business risks created by price changes. Energy, metal and agricultural commodities, common foreign exchange rates/currencies, and interest rates are all frequently hedged. The risk transferred is the exposure to loss from declines (or increases) in the market price of a commodity, which the transferor must hold for an extended period as a normal part of doing business. Hedging of speculative business risks allows an organization to protect itself against possible price-level losses by sacrificing possible price-level gains.

Any asset that has a price or another financial value that is uncertain in the future and can be objectively measured, such as a stock market index, common stock price, bushel of corn, barrel of oil, or consumer or industrial price index, can be the basis for a hedge. Those assets, as well as others, are known as underlying assets. The hedging contracts that are based on those underlying assets are known as derivatives because the value of the contract is derived from the values of the underlying asset.

Derivatives can be created by individuals who can (1) devise an investment others are willing to trade because they think they can forecast changes in the investment's value more accurately than others can and (2) create or obtain access to a market in which their newly created investments can be traded. However, for a derivative contract to be a successful hedging contract, there typically have to be two parties looking to hedge that underlying asset. For example, it would be much more difficult for a trucking company (exposed to loss when fuel prices increase) to hedge fuel prices if there were no oil companies (exposed to loss when fuel prices decrease) willing to enter into a hedging agreement.

Advantages and Disadvantages

As with all risk management techniques, hedging has both strengths and weaknesses. On the positive side, hedging against possible net income losses from price changes can reduce an organization's business risk exposures. Consequently, an organization that implements hedges has a greater capacity to bear both business risks and risks of accidental loss—while lessening its dependence on traditional financial and insurance markets for risk-bearing funds. Furthermore, when an organization's management recognizes that all risks, business and accidental, must be managed as a whole, it becomes better positioned to manage those risks more effectively. Many of the financial instruments now available also open new investment opportunities for risk managers, pooling captive operators, financial executives of traditional insurers, and others who can provide funds to finance accidental loss recovery. Properly selected and managed, these instruments can effectively generate risk financing funds and help reduce an organization's cost of risk.

On the negative side, however, hedging can destabilize not only an organization's general risk financing plans but also its entire financial structure. If an organization's retained earnings or surplus are seriously jeopardized by unwise speculative investments, the earnings or surpluses no longer reliably pay for retained accidental losses. Consequently, the financial security that hedges provide could be greatly impaired.

EXHIBIT 14-8

Millwright Cookie Company

Monthly Income Statement With and Without Hedging Using a Wheat Call

Wheat	
Units	10,000
Normal price	$3.00
Strike price	$3.00
Call fee	$300
Purchase price of call	$5,200
Selling price of call (high)	$15,200
Selling price of call (low)	$0.00

Note: If the market price of wheat is less than the price specified in the call contract ($3), the call contract is not exercised.

Wheat Prices Fall to $2.50

	A—Without Call		B —With $3 Call	
Revenues				
Sales	$100,000		$100,000	
Profit on call	$0		$0	
Other income	$3,000		$3,000	
Total Revenues		$103,000		$103,000
Expenses				
Flour	$25,000		$25,000	
Call fee	$0		$300	
Loss on call	$0		$5,200	
Other expenses	$62,000		$62,000	
Total Expenses		($87,000)		($92,500)
Net Profit		$16,000		$10,500

Wheat Prices Rise to $4.00

	C—Without Call		D—With $3 Call	
Revenues				
Sales	$100,000		$100,000	
Profit on call	$0		$10,000	
Other income	$3,000		$3,000	
Total Revenues		$103,000		$113,000
Expenses				
Flour	$40,000		$40,000	
Call fee	$0		$300	
Loss on call	$0		$0	
Other expenses	$62,000		$62,000	
Total Expenses		($102,000)		($102,300)
Net Profit		$1,000		$10,700

If, without hedging, Millwright had to pay $4.00 for each unit of flour, its monthly net profit would drop to $1,000 (Exhibit 14-8, Example C). But, if flour prices fell to $2.50 per unit, then the company's monthly net income would rise to $16,000 (Exhibit 14-8, Example A).

Assume that Millwright's management is uncomfortable with this potential $15,000 swing (from as low as $1,000 to as high as $16,000) in the company's monthly profits as a result of a change in the price of one unit of flour of $1.50 or less. To smooth these largely unpredictable fluctuations in flour prices and, therefore, in monthly operating results, Millwright could hedge this business risk with forward or futures contract, giving up potential profits from falling flour prices to protect against losses from rising flour prices. This approach would give Millwright greater assurance that its monthly profit would be consistently closer to the normal $11,000 despite any change in the cost of flour.

Instead of a forward or futures contract, Millwright could also purchase a type of option contract called a call. The call would offset losses from any increase in the price of flour, but Millwright would have to pay a premium for the contract analogous to an insurance premium. Consequently, even though option contracts are not insurance contracts, using option contracts to manage risk is sometimes called insurance.

Consider the effects on cash flows if Millwright were to purchase a call option on wheat (wheat call). A wheat call is a contract that gives the holder the right to buy wheat at a given price (strike price) at any time before the contract's expiration date. Therefore, if the market price (called the spot price) of wheat is higher than the strike price, then in theory the owner could use the contract to buy wheat at the strike price and then sell it for a profit at the spot price. This profit-making potential gives the contract a commercial value, and the contract is called "in the money." Because the contract has value, it can be traded in an organized market. Therefore, an alternative to buying and selling wheat is to sell the contract.

Even if the spot price is lower than the strike price (called "out of the money"), the contract still has some value because there is a chance that the spot price will rise before the expiration date. However, the value of the contract will be lower than if it was in the money. Therefore, as the spot price rises the value of the call rises, and as the spot price declines the value of the call declines.

If Millwright buys a call contract and the price of wheat rises, then Millwright could sell the call and use the profits to offset some of the additional costs caused by the price increase in wheat. Alternatively, if the price of wheat declines, Millwright could chose not to sell the contract. Some of the increased profit that results from the lower flour costs is offset by the loss on the call contract.

Exhibits 14-8, Example B and 14-8, Example D illustrate the effects of buying a call option on wheat, which brings Millwright's net profits back to a range near the normal $11,000 level. Exhibit 14-8, Example D gives a simplified general example of rising wheat prices, falling operating profit on cookies, and opportunities for profiting from the rising price of wheat call options. Assume that, in a particular month, Millwright pays $5,200 for a call for enough units of wheat to produce the 10,000 units of flour that the company plans to use during the month. As the wheat price rises during the month (as Exhibit 14-8, Example D assumes), Millwright may be able to sell this wheat call option for $15,200, making a $10,000 ($15,200 – $5,200) profit. The brokerage firm handling Millwright's purchase and sale of its wheat call charges Millwright a $300 commission. The overall result, shown at the bottom of Exhibit 14-8, Example D, is a $10,700 profit, close to the $11,000 normal profit that Millwright would have earned had the price of flour been $3.00. Millwright's only real cost in this example is the $300 brokerage commission. Without it, the company would have made its anticipated $11,000 profit.

Exhibit 14-8, Example B shows what happens if wheat prices fall, causing Millwright to make a greater profit producing cookies but to lose money on its wheat call. Assume that the spot market price of wheat falls below the $3.00 per unit price available under Millwright's call and remains below $3.00 until the option expires. In that case, Millwright loses the $5,200 purchase price if it holds the option until expiration. (It might reduce this loss if it sells the option before expiration.) A $5,200 expense is shown in the lower portion of the exhibit, along with the expense of the $300 brokerage commission for the option's purchase and sale. The loss on the call and the related broker-age commission reduce to $10,500 the $16,000 profit that Millwright would have earned because of falling wheat prices had it purchased no call (see Exhibit 14-8, Example A). Again, however, this $10,500 profit is close to the $11,000 normal monthly profit.

Loss Retention With Current Funding (Current Expenses)

Exhibit 14-3 illustrates the most basic form of retention: treating losses as cur-rent expenses paid out of operating cash flows, in other words, loss retention with current funding. An organization that pays losses as they occur considers them as any other business expense. However, an organization practicing any form of retention must be prepared to pay other loss costs, including various administrative expenses. For example, expenses the insurer incurs to inves-tigate, defend, or settle claims, called **loss adjustment expenses**, should be added to the other loss costs. These additional costs are not recognized in the cash flow analysis conducted in Exhibit 14-3.

Loss adjustment expenses
Expenses the insurer incurs to investigate, defend, or settle claims.

Exhibit 14-9 considers loss adjustment expenses and evaluates Atwell's expected NCF if it treats the expected value of fire damage to the ARC build-ing as a current expense. To allow Dr. Ames to resume his research as quickly as possible after a fire loss, Atwell anticipates paying an average of $2,000 per year to expedite building repairs. Because of these additional cash outlays, the NPV and IRR of the ARC proposal are lower in Exhibit 14-9 than in

Exhibit 14-3. In Exhibit 14-3, Atwell recognized expected losses but did not directly control or finance them.

Because current expensing of losses is the least formal risk financing technique, it tends to be the least expensive method, provided that the following two significant conditions are met:

1. Actual losses do not exceed levels that the organization can comfortably absorb as current expenses.
2. The organization does not need, or can efficiently perform itself, the administrative and risk control tasks typically performed by an insurer or another transferee.

Although current expensing of losses often appears attractive before losses occur, depending on the severity of any losses that do occur, some other risk financing technique (alone or in combination with current-expense retention) could actually be less costly.

Loss Retention With Current Funding (An Unfunded Reserve)

Another risk financing technique that falls into the category of loss retention with current funding is retaining losses with an unfunded reserve. Except for some possible extra administrative costs, the cash flow effects of an unfunded reserve are identical to the cash flow effects of retaining losses as current expenses. The analysis would be analogous to that shown in Exhibit 14-9. An unfunded reserve represents no formal commitment or source of funds. It is merely an accounting recognition of an anticipated expense and is designed to more nearly match the timing of expenses and revenues among accounting periods.

Loss Retention With Pre-Funding (A Funded Reserve)

Using a funded reserve to finance losses is discussed subsequently in this chapter in the context of separating loss exposures. The basic purpose of a funded reserve (pre-funding of losses) is to smooth over time the highly fluctuating demands that retaining unpredictable losses would otherwise place on an organization's cash flows. The funded reserve helps to ensure that the organization will have access to the cash needed to finance recovery from a particularly large loss.

Loss Retention With Post-Funding (Borrowed Funds)

A risk financing technique using retaining losses with post-funding is using borrowed funds. When losses exceed the capacity of current funding, the organization may be able to borrow the difference. Some organizations may choose to borrow even if current funds are adequate to pay losses because those current funds are needed for other uses in the operation of

EXHIBIT 14-9

Differential Annual After-Tax Cash Flows—Retention With Current Funding (Current Expensing of Losses and Administrative Expenses)

NCF Calculations		
Differential cash revenues		$60,000
Less: Differential cash expenses (except income taxes)		
Expected value of fire losses	$16,000	
Administrative expenses	$2,000	
		($18,000)
Before-tax NCF		$42,000
Less: Differential income taxes		
Before-tax NCF	$42,000	
Less: Differential depreciation expense ($200,000 ÷ 10 years)	($20,000)	
Taxable income	$22,000	
Income taxes (40% × $22,000)		($8,800)
After-tax NCF		$33,200

> To allow Dr. Ames to resume his research as quickly as possible after a fire loss, Atwell anticipates paying an average of $2,000 per year to expedite building repairs.

NCF Evaluation	
Factors:	
Initial investment	$200,000
Life of project	10 years
Differential annual after-tax NCF	$33,200
Minimum acceptable rate of return (annual)	10.00%

Evaluation by NPV Method:

Present value of differential NCF ($33,200 × 6.145)	$204,014
Less: Present value of initial investment	($200,000)
NPV:	$4,014

> Because of the additional cash outlays for expediting expenses, the rate of return and net present value of the ARC proposal are lower than in Exhibit 14-3. Atwell recognized losses without directly controlling or financing them.

Evaluation by IRR Method:

Present value factor = Initial investment ÷ Differential NCF
= $200,000 ÷ $33,200
= 6.024.

Interpolation to find the IRR (r):

Rate of Return	Present Value Factor	Present Value Factor
10.00%	6.145	6.145
r		6.024
12.00%	5.650	
Differences: 2.00%	0.495	0.121

$r = 10\% + [(0.121 ÷ 0.495) × 2\%]$
$= 10\% + 0.49\%$
$= 10.49\%.$

the organization. In fact, the key reason for borrowing funds to finance recovery from accidental losses is that it may involve a lower cost than using the organization's own funds, which could otherwise be invested in other activities. If an organization can earn more by investing funds in its operations than it costs to borrow funds (whether to pay for losses or for any other purpose), borrowing will improve cash flows. In this type of scenario, retaining losses with borrowed funds may be a viable risk financing alternative.

Using borrowed funds further complicates the capital investment decision because there are many variables to consider, such as the interest rate, term, or repayment provisions. An organization's risk management professional should work closely with the organization's financial officers, analyzing the types and terms of short-term and long-term borrowing, the effects of borrowing on the organization's taxes, and the possible effects on the organization's capacity to borrow for other purposes. Exhibit 14-10 shows the NPV and IRR calculations when $16,000 is borrowed and used to pay the expected $16,000 loss.

Note that borrowing funds to finance losses is a form of loss retention rather than transfer because the organization is responsible for repaying any borrowed funds. Except for uncertainty about the borrower's ability or willingness to repay, the lender assumes no additional loss exposures. With borrowing, the loss exposure remains with the borrower.

Internal Versus External Capital

When an organization is presented with a capital investment proposal that requires an upfront investment (negative cash flow), one decision that the organization's management must make is where it will obtain the needed capital. The first source of capital for most organizations is internal to the organization—obtaining the needed money from cash flows, retained earnings, liquidation of other assets, or some other internal means. The other source of capital for an organization is external to the organization. External sources of capital could be borrowing from a bank, issuing debt securities (bonds), issuing equity shares (stock), or other capital market solutions.

For most organizations, as well as individuals, it is cheaper to use internal capital to fund capital investment proposals than external capital. For example, consider an individual purchasing a home. It is typically cheaper for that individual to use his/her own funds to finance the purchase (if available) than it is to acquire a mortgage. The same can be said for organizations. The risk financing technique of paying for accidental losses with borrowed funds is not a common practice. It is rare that an organization finds that it is cheaper to borrow funds to pay for accidental losses than it is to pay for accidental losses from internal sources. In general, if organizations can borrow funds at one rate and generate a higher rate of return using those funds in operation (the premise presented above), they do so without waiting for accidental losses to occur. The borrowing decision is part of their capital structure plan, not necessarily a risk management decision.

EXHIBIT 14-10

Differential Annual After-Tax Cash Flows—Retention With Post-Funding (Borrowed Funds)

NCF Calculations

Differential cash revenues		$60,000
Borrow ($16,000)		$16,000
Use of $16,000 in operations ($16,000 × 0.10)		$1,600
Total revenues		$77,600
Less: Differential cash expenses (except income taxes)		
Expected value of fire losses	$16,000	
Repayment of loan ($16,000 × 1.08)	$17,280	($33,280)
Before-tax NCF		$44,320
Less: Differential income taxes		
Before-tax NCF	$44,320	
Less: Differential depreciation expense ($200,000 ÷ 10 years)	($20,000)	
Taxable income	$24,320	
Income taxes (40% × $24,320)		($9,728)
After-tax NCF		$34,592

> Borrowing $16,000 to pay for the expected $16,000 loss releases $16,000 of internal capital for use in operations. This release of capital will generate a 10 percent rate of return (the organization's cost of capital).

> Atwell borrows $16,000 on January 1 for one year at an annual effective interest rate of 8 percent. On December 31, Atwell owes $17,280 ($16,000 principal + $1,280 interest) on the loan.

> Depreciation is still $20,000 because borrowing does not change the amount of the overall investment.

NCF Evaluation

Factors:

Initial investment	$200,000
Life of project	10 years
Differential annual after-tax NCF	$34,592
Minimum acceptable rate of return (annual)	10.00%

Evaluation by NPV Method:

Present value of differential NCF ($34,592 × 6.145)	$212,568
Less: Present value of initial investment	($200,000)
NPV	$12,568

Evaluation by IRR Method:

Present value factor = Initial investment ÷ Differential NCF

$$= \$200,000 \div \$34,592$$

$$= 5.782.$$

Interpolation to find the IRR (r):

Rate of Return	Present Value Factor	Present Value Factor
10.00%	6.145	6.145
r		5.782
12.00%	5.650	
Differences: 2.00%	0.495	0.363

$$
\begin{aligned}
r &= 10\% + [(0.363 \div 0.495) \times 2\%] \\
&= 10\% + 1.47\% \\
&= 11.47\%.
\end{aligned}
$$

RECOGNIZING CASH FLOWS RELATED TO COMBINED RISK MANAGEMENT TECHNIQUES

Each of the preceding examples of the effects of risk management techniques on an organization's net cash flows has focused on a single risk control or risk financing technique. In practice, however, organizations usually apply several risk management techniques to each significant loss exposure. Using several risk management techniques usually reduces an organization's cost of risk from accidental losses more than does using any single risk management technique.

The possibilities for combining techniques to manage a single loss exposure, and for using a technique to a greater or lesser degree (such as a large, complex firefighting sprinkler system rather than a small, basic one), are virtually infinite. Each possibility has its own projected levels of initial investment and annual net cash flows. As an example, Atwell might consider both installing sprinklers to reduce the severity of fire losses as well as buying insurance against fire losses that occur.

According to the law of large numbers, the more independent loss exposures an organization has, the more accurately it can project its average loss per exposure. To illustrate one possible benefit of accurate loss projection, consider the case in which an accurate projection reduces the size of a funded reserve (a pre-funded contingency fund) that an organization might need to fund retained losses. Any funds the organization does not use for the contingency fund can be used for other investment opportunities. To see how separation can reduce the amount of funded reserve needed to absorb retained losses, compare Exhibits 14-11 and 14-12.

Establishing a funded reserve to pay losses increases the initial investment in the asset or activity. The reserve's amount must be added to the cost of the asset or activity as part of the initial investment. Beyond that large initial investment, however, using a funded reserve does not change the cash outflows that would otherwise arise from paying losses as current expenses. A funded reserve does create one significant cash inflow not characteristic of other forms of retention—earnings on the fund held in the reserve. The reserve funds are normally invested in highly liquid securities—that is, securities that can be quickly sold. The risk management professional must be aware, however, of the increase in business risk that is associated with a funded reserve. Because funded reserves are typically invested in some type of speculative vehicle (such as stocks or bonds), there is a possibility that the fund value will decrease during the investment period.

To illustrate combining risk management techniques, the cash flows to Atwell from a funded reserve earning 8 percent, and used to pay the $16,000 expected value of fire losses to the ARC building, would be as calculated and evaluated in Exhibit 14-11. As described previously, because establishing a funded reserve requires a higher initial investment (compared with paying losses out of cash

EXHIBIT 14-11

Differential Annual After-Tax Cash Flows—$100,000 Funded Reserve

NCF Calculations

Differential cash revenues	$60,000	
from funded reserve ($100,000 × 8%)	$8,000	
Total cash revenues		$68,000
Less: Differential cash expenses (except income taxes)		
Expected value of fire losses	$16,000	
Total cash expenses (except income taxes)		($16,000)
Before-tax NCF:		$52,000
Less: Differential income taxes		
Before-tax NCF	$52,000	
Less: Differential depreciation expense ($200,000 ÷ 10 years)	($20,000)	
Taxable income	$32,000	
Income taxes (40% × $32,000)		($12,800)
After-tax NCF		$39,200

> Atwell established a funded fire loss reserve that would pay for 97 percent of all fire losses that may possibly occur.
>
> If the funded reserve can earn an 8 percent annual rate of return, then the resulting cash flows equal $8,000 of revenue each year (pre-tax).

> Annual depreciation is unchanged because the funded reserve is not depreciated

NCF Evaluation

Factors:	
Initial investment	$300,000
Life of project	10 years
Differential annual after-tax NCF	$39,200
Minimum acceptable rate of return (annual)	10.00%

> $200,000 initial investment + $100,000 funded reserve

Evaluation by NPV Method:

Present value of differential NCF ($39,200 × 6.145)	$240,884
Less: Present value of initial investment	($300,000)
NPV	($59,116)

> Using the funded reserve yields an annual after-tax NCF of $39,200. However, because establishing a funded reserve increases the initial investment by $100,000, the resulting annual after-tax NCF yields a negative NPV and falls well below the 10 percent required IRR.

Evaluation by IRR Method:

Present value factor = Initial investment ÷ Differential NCF
$$= \$300,000 \div \$39,200$$
$$= 7.653.$$
Interpolation to find the IRR (r):

Rate of Return	Present Value Factor	Present Value Factor
4.00%	8.111	8.111
r		7.653
6.00%	7.360	
Differences: 2.00%	0.751	0.458

r = 4% + [(0.458 ÷ 0.751) × 2%]
  = 4% + 1.22%
  = 5.22%.

EXHIBIT 14-12

Differential Annual After-Tax Cash Flows—Separation and $25,000 Funded Reserve

NCF Calculations

Differential cash revenues	$60,000	
from funded reserve ($25,000 × 8%)	$2,000	
Total cash revenues		$62,000
Less: Differential cash expenses (except income taxes)		
Expected value of fire losses	$15,000	
Total cash expenses (except income taxes)		($15,000)
Before-tax NCF		$47,000
Less: Differential income taxes		
Before-tax NCF	$47,000	
Less: Differential depreciation		
expense ($200,000 ÷ 10 years)	($20,000)	
Taxable income	$27,000	
Income taxes (40% × $27,000)		($10,800)
After-tax NCF:		$36,200

> Atwell established a funded fire loss reserve that would pay for 97 percent of all fire losses that may possibly occur.
>
> The funded reserve is reduced because the separation of the research areas has reduced the amount needed to fund 97 percent of all fire losses that may possibly occur.

NCF Evaluation

Factors:	
Initial investment	$225,000
Life of project	10 years
Differential annual after-tax NCF	$36,200
Minimum acceptable rate of return (annual)	10.00%

> The separation of the research areas has also lowered the expected value of the fire losses.

> $200,000 initial investment + $25,000 funded reserve

Evaluation by NPV Method:

Present value of differential NCF ($36,200 × 6.145)	$222,449
Less: Present value of initial investment	($225,000)
NPV	($2,551)

> Using the smaller funded reserve yields an annual after-tax NCF of $36,200. Although the NPV and IRR are more attractive than the larger funded reserve alone, they are still below minimum requirements.

Evaluation by IRR Method:

Present value factor = Initial investment ÷ Differential NCF

= $225,000 ÷ $36,200

= 6.215.

Interpolation to find the IRR (r):

Rate of Return	Present Value Factor	Present Value Factor
8.00%	6.710	6.710
r		6.215
10.00%	6.145	
Differences:	2.00%	0.565	0.495

r = 8% + [(0.495 ÷ 0.565) × 2%]

= 8% + 1.75%

= 9.75%.

flows), retaining losses through a funded reserve reduces the NPV and IRR (compared with other forms of retention) whenever the funds placed in the reserve earn less than the funds that the organization uses for normal productive activities. To be attractive, the benefits of reduced uncertainty from using the funded reserve must outweigh that disadvantage of higher initial investment.

Assume that Atwell believes that without separation it must establish a funded reserve for differential fire losses equal to an amount that will cover the fire losses 97 percent of the time. Based on the probability distribution of fire losses without a sprinkler system in Exhibit 14-2, Atwell will need to establish a contingency fund in the amount of $100,000 (and replenish the fund as needed at the beginning of each year). If this fund can earn an 8 percent annual before-tax rate of return, the resulting cash flows are shown in Exhibit 14-11 (ignoring the possibility that the funded reserve may not be exhausted at the end of ten years). The fund is expected to generate $8,000 of revenue each year before taxes, yielding an annual after-tax NCF of $39,200. However, because establishing a funded reserve of $100,000 increases the required initial investment to $300,000, the resulting annual after-tax NCF yields a negative NPV and produces an IRR below the 10 percent that the hospital requires. That result partly reflects the assumption that the fund is exhausted at the end of the ten years. But the basic problem is that the after-tax return on the investment earnings from the funded reserve is much less than 10 percent. Therefore, if the hospital believed that it had to commit the $100,000 to the funded reserve, it should not undertake the proposal.

An implicit assumption of the analysis is that the hospital's opportunity cost of investing in the funded reserve is 10 percent. That assumption would be true if investing in the funded reserve caused the hospital to not accept other proposals with that expected return and comparable risk. Generally, holding funded reserves in safe and liquid securities will produce lower returns than expected on an organization's main activities.

Now consider what would happen if, hypothetically, Atwell could invest $20,000 in each of ten separate proposals disbursed throughout its complex ($200,000 in total, as before). This investment strategy would greatly change the differential loss distribution of fire losses presented in Exhibit 14-2. (The new distribution would be far more complicated and is beyond the scope of this text.) The result is that the ability to project any resulting fire losses would improve, and the expected loss may not change much or even increase. However, the volatility in fire losses would decrease and their maximum likely size would decrease. Specifically, assume that separation would reduce the expected differential fire losses to $15,000 per year. Also, assume that management believes that only a 3 percent chance exists of having losses greater than $25,000 (compared with the 3 percent chance of losses being greater than $100,000 without separation). Assuming that Atwell has the same goal of maintaining funding at a level that would cover 97 percent of fire losses, it needs a funded reserve of only $25,000.

The resulting cash flows under these assumptions are shown in Exhibit 14-12. Although the amount of the annual after-tax NCF is smaller with separation

($36,200, compared with the $39,200 shown in Exhibit 14-11), reducing the required investment from $300,000 to $225,000 increases the NPV of the research facilities to a negative $2,551 (in contrast to the negative $59,116 in Exhibit 14-11) and produces a 9.75 percent IRR. Separation makes the proposal more attractive in this example, but it is still unacceptable because the NPV is negative and the IRR is below 10 percent.

Allowing for additional cash flows, such as possible recovery of some money from the funded reserve at the end of ten years, would not alter the basic point of this example. Separation of loss exposures reduces the amount of resources that an organization might need to commit to ensure that losses can be paid from available funds.

Using cash flow analysis with the risk financing techniques discussed in this chapter gives the risk management professional financial information that can be used to help choose the appropriate risk financing techniques that will make capital investment proposals most attractive to senior management.

CONSIDERING UNCERTAINTY IN CASH FLOW ANALYSIS

The preceding examples of using cash flow analysis to make risk management decisions did not formally consider many of the effects of uncertainty about the severity of future losses. The risk of net cash flows should be reflected in the choice of the discount rate (the cost of capital) used to calculate the present values of expected NCF or as the minimum acceptable return for the IRR method. The greater the risk of future net cash flows, the greater the minimum required rate of return.

For large corporations with widely held common stock, the risk that matters to shareholders is the risk that cannot be substantially eliminated by investing in a diversified portfolio of securities. Many of the possible losses that are the focus of risk management may not increase risk for diversified investors, or may present no greater risk than that associated with an organization's other cash flows. If accidental losses present no greater risk than the organization's net cash flows, an organization's normal cost of capital should be used to discount risk-management-related net cash flows. For organizations without widely held stocks, owners may increase the required rate of return used in the NPV and IRR methods to reflect their subjective assessments given the perceived risk of proposals.

Another approach when considering risk-management-related net cash flows is to identify and quantify the possible effects of retaining the risk of relatively large losses. Examples of such effects include:

- Increased risk to managers, employees, customers, and suppliers, which could adversely affect the organization's net cash flows by, for example, requiring higher salaries and wages, or reducing the prices the organization can charge for products and services. It is often difficult for higher-risk organizations to attract and retain quality employees, suppliers, and customers without compensating them for the additional risk they are taking.

- The expected value of legal and related costs that may be incurred if large losses prevent the organization from meeting contractual obligations.

- Possible increases in the organization's cost of raising funds and the associated possible loss of valuable investment opportunities after large uninsured losses.

- Possible increases in the organization's expected income taxes because large uninsured losses may be only partially deductible for tax purposes.

In each case, reducing the risk of large losses through insurance, hedging, or other risk management techniques reduces the expected loss of net cash flows from these sources. Ideally, managers should attempt to quantify the effects on the organization's expected net cash flows and incorporate the costs into NPV and IRR calculations. However, many of these costs cannot be measured with much precision.

When the expected costs of uncertainty are difficult to measure, an approach that is sometimes used is to subjectively assign a "price tag" or cost to the uncertainty. This implicit after-tax cost can then be treated like any other cost, or cash outflow, in a cash flow analysis of a risk management technique. The cost so assigned is called the cost of uncertainty.

The first step in this approach is to assign a subjective estimate of the cost of uncertainty to each alternative risk management technique. The greater the risk of large losses that could disrupt operations and investment and thereby adversely affect parties such as employees, customers, or suppliers, the greater should be the cost assigned. The more insurance that is purchased, or the more risk that is hedged, the lower should be the cost assigned.

The second step is to deduct the assigned cost of uncertainty from the after-tax cash inflow (or add it to the after-tax net cash outflow) for each period in which the particular technique would be used for a given loss exposure.

The third step is to calculate the NPV and IRR for each technique using the net cash flows adjusted for the assigned costs of uncertainty.

To illustrate the approach, reconsider Exhibit 14-4, which calculates and analyzes the annual after-tax NCF of the ARC proposal when Atwell retains fire losses and installs a sprinkler system as a loss reduction technique. The after-tax net cash flow (calculated without reference to the cost of uncertainty) is $41,640. Given the other facts in that example, the NPV, discounted at 10 percent, is $45,878 and the IRR is 14.88 percent.

Now assume that the hospital's senior administrators are disturbed by the uncertainties associated with retaining the losses on the ARC building and subjectively assign a cost of $5,000 per year to that uncertainty. As shown in Exhibit 14-13, deducting this $5,000 cost from the previously calculated annual after-tax NCF of $41,640 gives an NCF of $36,640. The present value

EXHIBIT 14-13

Differential Annual After-Tax Cash Flows—Recognition of the Cost of Uncertainty

NCF Calculations

Differential cash revenues		$60,000
Less: Differential cash expenses (except income taxes)		
Expected value of fire losses	$4,200	
Sprinkler maintenance	$400	
		($4,600)
Before-tax NCF		$55,400
Less: Differential income taxes		
Before-tax NCF	$55,400	
Less: Differential depreciation expense ($210,000 ÷ 10 years)	($21,000)	
Taxable income	$34,400	
Income taxes (40% × $34,400)		($13,760)
After-tax NCF		$41,640
Less: Cost of uncertainty		($5,000)
After NCF uncertainty adjustment		$36,640

Deducting the $5,000 cost of uncertainty from the previously calculated annual after-tax NCF of $41,640 gives an NCF of $36,640.

NCF Evaluation

Factors:	
Initial investment	$210,000
Life of project	10 years
Differential annual after-tax NCF	$36,640
Minimum acceptable rate of return (annual)	10.00%

Evaluation by NPV Method:

Present value of differential NCF ($36,640 × 6.145)	$225,153
Less: Present value of initial investment	($210,000)
NPV	$15,153

The cost of uncertainty has reduced the NPV and IRR; however, the proposal does remain above the acceptable threshold.

Evaluation by IRR Method:

Present value factor = Initial investment ÷ Differential NCF
= $210,000 ÷ $36,640
= 5.731.

Interpolation to find the IRR (r):

Rate of Return	Present Value Factor	Present Value Factor
10.00%	6.145	6.145
r		5.731
12.00%	5.650	
Differences: 2.00%	0.495	0.414

$r = 10\% + [(0.414 ÷ 0.495) × 2\%]$
$= 10\% + 1.67\%$
$= 11.67\%.$

of this adjusted NCF, discounted at 10 percent, is $225,153, giving an NPV of $15,153. The IRR is 11.67 percent. Therefore, incorporating the adjustment for the cost of uncertainty makes the proposal less attractive.

To go one step further, recall that the IRR if the building is fully insured is 6.67 percent (Exhibit 14-5). If no cost of uncertainty exists in that situation, that IRR can be compared with the 11.67 percent return in Exhibit 14-13. The proposal in Exhibit 14-5 of insurance without sprinklers is unattractive because the IRR is below 10 percent. However, if the assigned cost of uncertainty for retention with sprinklers (as shown in Exhibit 14-14) were $15,000 rather than $5,000 (as shown in Exhibit 14-13), the full insurance alternative (Exhibit 14-5) would have a higher NPV and IRR (although the ARC proposal would still be unattractive).

Adjusting cash flow analysis for estimates of the cost of uncertainty provides a relatively straightforward and understandable method for reflecting the uncertain environment in which many risk management decisions must be made. This approach makes the cost of uncertainty explicit and adjustable to reflect estimates of the effects of large losses on net cash flows, senior management's attitudes, and so on. Although necessarily somewhat subjective, this approach is sufficiently straightforward to appeal to many organizations. In organizations in which more complex methods of adjusting for the lack of certainty are used, the risk management professional should use those methods.

USING CASH FLOW ANALYSIS TO SELECT RISK MANAGEMENT TECHNIQUES

Previous sections of this chapter have demonstrated how a proposal's NPV and IRR are affected by the costs of possible accidental losses and by the costs of risk management techniques implemented to handle these losses. To maximize an organization's value, NPV and IRR should be used to select risk management techniques. For this purpose, the NPV criteria can be restated as follows: an organization should prefer the risk management technique that promises the highest positive NPV for the proposal to which that technique is applied. Similarly, the IRR criteria is the following: an organization should select the risk management technique that promises the highest IRR above the minimum rate of return on the proposal to which that technique is applied.

The risk management professional still needs to remain aware of the organization's goals regarding risk management decisions. The NPV and IRR decision rules are purely financial decision rules and have no bearing on decision making regarding other organizational goals such as social responsibility or meeting externally imposed obligations (legality).

Exhibit 14-15 contains the risk management techniques presented in this chapter, ranked by the NPV decision criteria. In this case, the ranking by IRR is the same as the ranking by NPV. The first four risk management techniques in Exhibit 14-15—prevention or reduction of losses, loss transfer

EXHIBIT 14-14

Differential Annual After-Tax Cash Flows—Increased Cost of Uncertainty

NCF Calculations

Differential cash revenues		$60,000
Less: Differential cash expenses (except income taxes)		
Expected value of fire losses	$4,200	
Sprinkler maintenance	$400	($4,600)
Before-tax NCF		$55,400
Less: Differential income taxes		
Before-tax NCF	$55,400	
Less: Differential depreciation expense ($210,000 ÷ 10 years)	($21,000)	
Taxable income	$34,400	
Income taxes (40% × $34,400)		($13,760)
After-tax NCF		$41,640
Less: Cost of uncertainty		($15,000)
After NCF uncertainty adjustment		$26,640

> Deducting the $15,000 cost of uncertainty from the previously calculated annual after-tax NCF of $41,640 gives an NCF of $26,640.

NCF Evaluation

Factors:

Initial investment	$210,000
Life of project	10 years
Differential annual after-tax NCF	$26,640
Minimum acceptable rate of return (annual)	10.00%

Evaluation by NPV Method:

Present value of differential NCF ($26,640 × 6.145)	$163,703
Less: Present value of initial investment	($210,000)
NPV	($46,297)

> The increased cost of uncertainty has reduced the NPV and IRR below the acceptable threshold.

Evaluation by IRR Method:

Present value factor = Initial investment ÷ Differential NCF
= $210,000 ÷ $26,640
= 7.883.

Interpolation to find the IRR (r):

	Rate of Return	Present Value Factor	Present Value Factor
	4.00%	8.111	8.111
	r		7.883
	6.00%	7.360	
Differences:	2.00%	0.751	0.228

r = 4% + [(0.228 ÷ 0.751) × 2%]
= 4% + 0.61%
= 4.61%.

through a hold-harmless agreement, loss retention through borrowed funds, and loss retention with current expenses—all meet both the NPV and IRR decision criteria as acceptable risk management techniques based on financial criteria, with prevention or reduction being the most attractive technique based on cash flow analysis. The remaining three techniques—separation of exposure units and loss retention with a funded reserve, loss transfer through full insurance with an unrelated insurer, and loss retention with a funded reserve—are all unacceptable based on the NPV and IRR decision criteria. They do not generate a positive NPV, nor do they meet the 10 percent required rate of return in the IRR method.

These rankings are based only on the financial decision criteria (cash flow analysis) for the selection of the appropriate risk management technique. If an organization is using any other decision criteria to meet its organizational goals, these rankings could change drastically. For example, an organization may have a requirement as part of a debt arrangement that it has property insurance with a highly rated unrelated insurer. As part of this externally imposed obligation, the organization would be required to have a loss transfer contract with an unrelated insurer even though that risk financing option was unacceptable based on the NPV and IRR decision criteria.

To select the technique giving the highest NPV or the highest IRR, a risk management professional must consider all relevant possibilities. This can be done by evaluating each proposal (such as the ARC proposal in the previous examples) not as a stand-alone proposal but as a proposal coupled with a risk management technique. Such a list of possibilities might resemble those in the following box.

ARC Proposal With:

Risk Control

Through loss prevention/reduction

Through separation of loss exposure

Through avoidance

Risk Financing

By retaining losses as current expenses

With a funded reserve

With borrowed funds

Through a captive insurer

Through an unrelated insurer

Through contractual transfer

Through hedging

Ignoring the possibility of using two or more risk management techniques simultaneously, the listing in the text box is reasonably complete because it (1) allows for "doing nothing" about risk management (a phrase that usually signifies planned or unplanned retention), (2) includes the major types of risk management techniques, risk control and risk financing, and (3) allows the ARC proposal to be compared with all other proposals.

EXHIBIT 14-15

Risk Management Techniques Ranked by NPV and IRR

Risk Management Technique	NPV and IRR	Ranking by NPV and IRR
Loss reduction or prevention device	NPV – $45,878 IRR – 14.88%	1
Loss transfer through a hold-harmless agreement	NPV – $14,485 IRR – 11.68%	2
Loss retention through borrowed funds	NPV – $12,568 IRR – 11.47%	3
Loss retention with current expenses funding	NPV – $4,014 IRR – 10.49%	4
Separation with a funded reserve	NPV – ($2,551) IRR – 9.75%	5
Loss transfer through full insurance with an unrelated insurer	NPV – ($27,940) IRR – 6.67%	6
Loss retention with funded reserve	NPV – ($59,116) IRR – 5.22%	7

If the organization has limited funds and another proposal yields a higher NPV or IRR than the ARC proposal, the loss exposures associated with the ARC proposal should be avoided by investing in that other proposal.

In all organizations, effective risk management deals with business risks as well as risks of accidental losses (hazard risks). In many organizations, risk management equally considers both these types of risk to (1) increase an organization's net cash flows, (2) speed its cash inflows and slow its cash outflows, and (3) smooth its cash flow fluctuations, regardless of whether those risks arise from accidents or from adverse business developments. This enterprise risk management can increase an organization's operating efficiency/profitability; its value to the organization's owners; and its appeal to risk-averse creditors, customers, employees, and other stakeholders.

SUMMARY

The selection of risk management techniques often involves using the NPV and IRR methods. Those methods help with selecting the risk management techniques that promise to most cost effectively counter the adverse effects of accidental losses forecast by the statistical techniques discussed in previous chapters. Cash flow analysis provides decision criteria for dealing with these adverse effects in ways that enhance the present value of an organization's NCF and IRR.

Using these methods requires, first, identifying and analyzing the effects that exposures to accidental losses can be expected to have on an organization's NCF if these loss exposures are not managed. Second, it requires estimating the cash flow effects of each of the separate risk control and risk financing techniques that could be applied to each loss exposure. Third, it requires selecting the technique with the highest NPV or IRR.

Using the Atwell Hospital and Millwright Cookies examples, this chapter explained how to account for the various risk control and risk financing expenditures in cash flow analysis. While most examples use only one risk management technique, this chapter does present an example in which two risk management techniques are used. The methodology for incorporating multiple risk management technique expenditures into cash flow analysis is the same as that for one risk management technique.

After determining the NPV and IRR for each technique, this chapter ranks each of the alternative risk management proposals based on NPV and IRR. Most of the examples in this chapter assume that the cash flows were known with certainty. The chapter concludes by discussing how to incorporate the cost of uncertainty into cash flow analysis. Incorporating the cost of uncertainty into the analysis allows risk management professionals to account for the variability in future cash flows using different risk management techniques.

Index

Page numbers in boldface refer to definitions of Key Words and Phrases.

V

W